Persia, Politics & Prison

A Life in Three Parts

DISCLAIMER

The following memoir is a work of non-fiction, based on the author's recollections and personal experiences. While every effort has been made to ensure the accuracy and authenticity of the events and individuals depicted in this book, the nature of memory and the passage of time may result in occasional inaccuracies or variations in details. The views, opinions, and emotions expressed within this work are those of the author and do not necessarily reflect the views of others mentioned in the book. Additionally, the author's interpretation of events may differ from the perspectives of other individuals involved.

Persia, Politics & Prison

A Life in Three Parts

HASSAN NEMAZEE

Marmont Lane
BOOKS

PERSIA, POLITICS & PRISON: A LIFE IN THREE PARTS

Copyright © 2024 Pasha Publishing LLC. All rights reserved. No part of this book may be used or reproduced in any matter whatsoever without written permission except in the case of brief quotations embodied in critical articles and reviews.

For information address:
Marmont Lane Books
260 South Beverly Drive Suite 302
Beverly Hills, CA USA 90212

Visit marmontlane.com

FIRST EDITION

Publisher: Bobby Woods/Marmont Lane Books

Design: ♡×☕=⚡

Cover Photograph: Joshua Lott/New York Times/Redux

Photo Editor: Andrew Golomb/OMIH NYC

Printed in China

ISBN: 978-1-7345904-4-9
Library of Congress Control Number: 2023947682

Dedicated to:

MALEKEH NAZIE

For:

YASMINE, KAMYAR, AND LAYLA

SORAYA, DARYA, PASHA, THEO, MAYA
AND ALL THE OTHER GRANDCHILDREN
STILL TO COME

Contents

Prologue: *Self-Surrender* 9

Part I: Persia

1: Everybody Knows Nemazee......................20
2: Mosaddegh On The Farm......................26
3: As The World Turned..........................33
4: A Persian Education..........................40
5: Nonsense....................................47
6: Transfusion..................................59
7: A Visit To Niavaran..........................65
8: My Father's Shoes............................70
9: Prospects....................................78
10: The Shah's Last Dance.......................86
11: Revolution..................................97

Part II: Politics

12: Starting Over...............................112
13: Angel Falls.................................117
14: Trumped....................................128
15: Achilles' Heel..............................137
16: No Harm, No Foul...........................147
17: Argentina..................................152
18: Recount...................................166
19: The Bubble Bursts..........................172

20: THE NEXT PRESIDENT OF THE UNITED STATES...179
21: LESSONS..185
22: AUDACITY, HOPE, AND OBAMA..................193
23: THE END..213

PART III: PRISON

24: NIGHTMARE..230
25: THE GAUNTLET...238
26: THE LOST YEAR..245
27: TEXARKANA...262
28: TIME..270
29: DETOUR..288
30: OTISVILLE...299
31: CUMBERLAND..315
32: FIRST STEPS..327
33: NOWRUZ...337
34: HOME..346

EPILOGUE: *Lily of the Valley* 358

ACKNOWLEDGEMENTS......................................368
ABOUT THE AUTHOR..370
INDEX..372
ILLUSTRATIONS..I-XXIV

PROLOGUE

SELF-SURRENDER

TWICE IN MY LIFE I've been forced to leave a home I'd never see again, taking only what I could carry. Both times I lost nearly everything.

The first time was in the early days of the Iranian Revolution, December of 1978, when my then-wife, Sheila, and I boarded an Air France flight to Paris. Carrying two suitcases each, we slipped out of the country with hardly a moment to spare, leaving behind a beautiful house in a small village on the outskirts of Tehran, along with friends and family, horses and dogs, and dozens of priceless family heirlooms. I was certain that we would soon return to Iran and our home. I was wrong.

The second time was in August of 2010, when I walked out of our 17-room duplex on Park Avenue in New York to surrender myself to federal custody in Texas. This time, I knew there would be no going back.

Strangely, I remember more about the first departure than the second. As our plane took off from Tehran and rose over the city, I was angry, deeply disturbed by the situation on the ground below, and concerned for friends and family we left behind. But I was also young and naïve enough to believe that only good things awaited me. Furthermore, I had done nothing to bring about the events in Iran. Later, I'd come to realize that I did share a kind of collective responsibility for the revolution, but at the moment I considered myself, like millions of Iranians, an innocent victim of history.

The second departure was a calmer and more personal event. I was not angry, nor was I naïve. I was resigned, numb, and despondent. I was also sixty, not twenty-nine. And I was unmistakably, personally, to blame: my forced exile was of my own making.

My memories of that summer morning in 2010 are murky. I moved through the apartment in a kind of daze. Morning sun streamed into the apartment from across Park Avenue. The kitchen was in shambles. Sheila had undertaken a major renovation shortly before my arrest, and when our funds were frozen by the government, the renovation was halted in its tracks. Countertops were missing, appliances hooked up to nothing, wires dangled from empty fixtures. The toaster still worked, though: my last breakfast was a slice of toasted Persian bread layered with soft Persian cheese. Sheila sat across from me. We ate silently. On the street below, people walked their dogs, doormen stepped from under awnings to whistle for cabs, deliverymen bicycled by at high speed, heading the wrong way on East 73rd Street. Had I been in a poetic frame of mind, instead of a catatonic state, I might have recalled that famous poem by W.H. Auden, the one about a painting of Icarus falling from the sky and no one noticing—*how it takes place while someone else is eating or opening a window or just walking dully along*. No poetry came to my mind that morning, though. Not much of anything did.

After breakfast, I took a final pass through the downstairs rooms. For nineteen of the years we'd lived in this duplex, it had been a warm and mostly happy home where we'd raised our three remarkable children and enjoyed all the pleasures and comforts a man could desire. Then, for one year, one final terrible year, it had been kind of purgatory. You might think that I took special care to notice everything now that I was leaving. I did not. The federal government had moved to take possession of not only the apartment, but most of its contents—furniture, art, Persian rugs. Many of these objects had once been very important to me, but they were no longer mine and they meant nothing to me now.

The photographs were another matter. Some of these I cared about very deeply. They were in my study, the handsome little sanctum overlooking Park Avenue where I'd retired at night to read, smoke cigars, and make calls. The most important of the photographs, propped on the bookshelves in silver frames, were of my family. There were also a few black-and-white images I'd managed to take out of Iran when we fled: my father as a young man in Hong Kong with his family, my father with the Shah of Iran, Nemazee Hospital on its inauguration day in 1955.

And then all the rest: the mementos of my friendships, if they ever really were that, with senators, presidents, and would-be presidents. Most of these had been snapped inside the apartment, at one of our many dinners or cocktail parties. Me with Hillary Clinton. Me with Bill. With Obama. With Kerry and Gore and Biden. Virtually every major Democratic politician of the previous decade had passed through our doors. They'd come to eat and drink with us, but mainly to raise the money they needed to fuel their ambitions. A lot of that money I raised for them, on the phone in my study, at parties in the dining room and living room of our apartment, in offices and conference rooms and ballrooms around the country. There were a lot of memories there, most of them good, some not so good.

Upstairs, I entered the small dressing room off the master suite. From the top drawer of the dresser I pulled out a leather jewelry box. Inside were my cufflinks, watches from my father, and a strand of lapis lazuli rosary beads. The beads had been given to me by a Greek friend, years earlier, on the eve of a presentation I was to make at the Clinton White House. I'd asked my friend what he did to calm his nerves; he'd handed me the beads and told me to keep them in my pocket and run them through my fingers. It worked like a charm.

I carried the box to my son's childhood bedroom and knocked on the door. He opened it. He was no longer a child but he'd come home to see me off.

"I want you to have this."

He took the box. A serious and handsome young man, wise beyond his years, Kamyar reminded me of old photographs of my father in his younger days. Both my father and I had been dropped into positions of responsibility at a young age and forced to grow up fast. Now the same had happened to Kamyar, but under far more difficult circumstances.

"I'll give it back to you when you come out," he said.

"No, it's yours. Keep it."

We hugged. Then I went to see each of my daughters in their rooms and hugged them, too. My eldest, Yasmine, was now a doctor and had recently married, but she'd come home to see me off. My youngest, Layla, was a recent graduate of Brown University and working in finance in New York. They were both smart and strong young women, but I knew the last year had taken every ounce of their courage and resilience to endure, and infinite grace to forgive. There was nothing to say now, and nearly anything I did say would only provoke tears. There had been enough of those already.

It was almost 10:00 a.m. now, time for me to go. We collected in the front hall, at the bottom of the stairs. In my hand I had the small gym bag of clothes I'd packed the previous night. Inside was everything I'd need to get me through the next 24 hours. A few items of clean clothing. My Blackberry and my cell phone. A book to read on the flight. The five of us entered the elevator and descended to the lobby in silence. As we passed through the lobby, the doormen, John and Wayne, came out from behind the desk and each shook my hand. "Good luck, Mr. Nemazee." "Take care yourself, Mr. Nemazee."

Park Avenue was quiet. Everyone had left the city to enjoy the last glorious days of summer, just as I would have done were I not on my way to prison—just as I had been doing, in fact, the August day everything changed a year earlier. The sun was bright but the air cool for August. I'd worried the press might show up, tipped off by someone at the U.S. Attorneys office, so I was relieved to see no reporters or cameras. Instead, standing at the curb next to a town car, were Edgar, John, and Kim. Knowing that this journey would be too much for my family to bear, my friends had generously volunteered to deliver me to Texas. A fourth friend, Fouad, would join us at LaGuardia Airport.

John took my bag and opened the passenger door for me. I looked back at my family. The four of them stood together on the sidewalk, side by side, arms locked around each other. I ducked into the car.

■ ■ ■

Hassan Nezamee?

Nemazee. Hassan Nemazee. Who are you?

Special Agent Barker, FBI, sir. We'd like to ask you some questions.

I'm on my way to Rome. What's this about?

Just a few questions, Mr. Nemazee.

I'd not been on an airplane since FBI agents approached me at Newark Liberty International Airport almost exactly a year earlier. Now, as I waited to check in at LaGuardia, the memory of that evening at Newark started to rattle around in my head. My friends knew their job was to keep me distracted from such thoughts, and they bantered and told stories and kept me laughing. We boarded the flight to Dallas and took our seats. No more first class for me—in fact, my friends had purchased my coach seat for me, as I had no money to purchase it myself. They could have afforded the front, but they joined me in back.

I recall nothing of the flight. I suppose I read and tried to sleep. As we deplaned in Dallas, we came upon a small airport barber shop, right outside the gate, empty but for the barber who stood behind the chair as if expecting me. I stepped into the barber shop and took a seat.

"How much you want off?" asked the barber.

"All of it," I said. "I'm going to prison tomorrow."

I could see his eyes widen a little in the mirror. But that was it for conversation. He brought out the clippers, and ten minutes later I emerged with a shaved head.

■ ■ ■

That evening we went to a strip-mall steak house in Texarkana. Knowing my fondness for steak, Edgar had thoughtfully found the best steak house in Texarkana and reserved a table for us. My last dinner in freedom: a ribeye, a baked potato with sour cream and bacon bits, a salad. I ordered a vodka on the rocks with lemon. Over the previous year, I'd developed a fairly serious drinking problem, so my tolerance was high. Also, I knew

I would not taste alcohol for another decade, so why not enjoy it while I could? That first vodka went down fast, and so did the second. Then I turned to red wine.

Later that night, we commandeered some chairs from the lobby of the Hampton Inn and dragged them outside. I'd brought a few of my finest cigars and we sat under the portico, directly across the state highway from a Hooters, smoking in the hot Texas night. My friends kept the conversation lively and funny. The alcohol, the banter, the cigars, the warm breeze on my newly shaved head, the cars coming and going at Hooters—all of it kept my mind cheerfully distracted and kept the inexorable math at bay: a 60-year-old man + a 12-year sentence.

I slept surprisingly well that night, better than I'd slept in months, and woke up feeling refreshed and impatient to get moving. A few months earlier, I'd hired a prison consultant to prepare myself for what was coming. He turned out to be mostly a waste of money, but he did tell me two things that proved useful. First, he told me that when I arrived, I should look up a man named J.P., a prisoner who more or less ran the place from the inside. (More on him later.) Second, he told me to arrive early. The later in the day you self-surrender, the longer you wait. I'd never been one for lines, and I did not want to wait in one now. Not even a line into prison.

The heat was already brutal before 9:00 a.m. Edgar drove. John, Kim, and Fouad sat in back. I rode shotgun, bathing in the last air conditioning I'd feel for a while. The prison was twenty minutes down a two-lane highway. From the road, it looked like any bland public utility building or third-tier industrial park. A wide lawn of fresh cut grass glimmering under a blistering sun. A chain link fence. An American flag high on the pole, limp in the windless air. Only the narrow towers rising from the flatness gave it away as either a municipal airport or a prison. The sign on the state highway made clear that it was no airport: *U.S. DEPARTMENT OF JUSTICE - FEDERAL BUREAU OF PRISONS.* As we turned into the main entrance, I could see bales of concertina wire stacked in rank and file around some of the buildings.

It took us a while to find the correct gate. Edgar parked and we all got out into the blistering heat. I found a button next to the gate and pressed it. As I waited, I handed over my gym bag with all my earthly possessions to Edgar. My Blackberry, my cell phone, my wallet. I kept only my driver's license, which I'd been told to bring. Then I hugged each of my friends. Five grown men trying not to get teary-eyed. "Thank you, guys."

"Good luck, Hassan. Stay strong."

The gate opened to reveal a guard with a clipboard.

"Name?"

"Nemazee," I said. "Hassan Nemazee."

He glanced down at this clipboard. "This way, Nemazee."

■ ■ ■

If you know anything about my case, I can guess what you are thinking: *good riddance*. I still find my name in articles and other people's books, generally preceded by words like "disgraced" and "fraudster," sometimes uttered in the same breath as Bernie Madoff and the names of other criminal masterminds. You think I had it coming, and I don't disagree.

This is not to say that what happened to me was entirely fair. I did wrong, but I was not in fact running a Madoff-like Ponzi scheme. My crime was declaring false assets to banks in order to obtain loans, large loans, nearly $300 million worth by the time of my arrest. Because I had a high profile, and because it suited the needs of some high-powered officials to make an example of me, I was punished harshly. Of course, no punishment compared to the one I inflicted on myself and, far worse, on those I loved. They had to deal with the shame of my deceit. My immediate family. My cousins and my in-laws. The larger Iranian-American community who looked up to me and had revered my father and our name. I let them all down.

This is a story about many things, but at its center is hubris. I use the Greek word because the Greeks were obsessed with it. The arrogant confidence that comes with success or power, hubris is the notorious psychological response to triumph. Centuries of stories have been written about people who ride their hubris straight to their doom. "The greater a man's success," mused Hannibal, "the less it must be trusted to endure."

But if what follows is a story of hubris, it is also a story of reckoning and resilience, of transformation and hope. Every life suffers setbacks and even disasters, some deserved, some not. Resilience begins with accepting your fate and confronting your flaws honestly. Hope begins with seeing the possibilities that come of that acceptance.

Over the course of life, success and failure will mean different things at different times. When young, we tend to define success in response to our parents, either by emulating them or by rebelling against them. The ancients believed that success meant doing your duty to your best ability, fulfilling your purpose in life. The Romans called this *pietas*. Finding such a purpose in life is the journey. The fear of failure becomes less overwhelming, the yearning for success less consuming.

■ ■ ■

For a year I'd fought tooth and nail to avoid or delay my prison sentence. I'd been living under house arrest during that last year at home, paying $25 million in bail for the privilege. If I had to do it all over again, I'd insist on starting to serve my time immediately. I'd wasted a year of my life, and not a day of it counted toward my sentence.

I'd been warned that the surrendering process would be humiliating, and it was. But the guard who greeted me at the gate and then ushered me into the system, a middle-aged African American man, treated me respectfully and made it no worse than it had to be. I was fingerprinted, photographed, and strip-searched, then handed a new set of clothes—khakis, a t-shirt, slip-on sneakers. Then I was sent to a small room to await my escort to the unit where I would live.

It was in that room that a kind of light went off in my head. I remember it vividly. The room was small and square, with pale blue walls that needed a fresh coat of paint. There was a thin horizontal window that ran the length of the room, but most of the light was provided by several fluorescent rods on the ceiling. As I sat there on the hard bench in my prison-issued clothes, I came as close to a religious awakening as I'd ever been. With sudden clarity, I saw that I had a choice to make. I'd gotten myself into this situation by *avoiding* responsibility for my actions—by ignoring things, letting them happen as if I were a passive participant in my own misdeeds, ignoring the jeopardy into which I was putting myself and my family. To make matters worse, I'd been living in an ineffectual stupor for the last year, ever since my arrest. My brain had been frozen in low gear, as if bathed in slush. I'd gained weight. I'd drunk heavily. I'd fallen into profound despair. But I was done with that now. I had a dozen years to get through, and it was up to me how I spent them.

In every prison there's a guy who can get you what you need, for a price, whether it's a bottle of Jack Daniels or a tube of Crest or a socket wrench. In Texarkana, that guy was J.P. The otherwise worthless prison consultant had recommended J.P. to me, but I probably would have made his acquaintance without the recommendation. In any case, I met him not long after I arrived in Texarkana. I told him I wanted a desk and reading lamp, along with pens, and paper—lots of paper. Also, if possible, someone who could read my handwriting and translate it into typed copy. He set me up with everything I needed to begin this book.

What follows is not meant to be an explanation or an excuse. It is not an apology, either—I've made my apologies to those who most deserved them, and most have forgiven me. This is the story, rather, of my life—of where I come from and where I am going. My origins and my destination. My successes and my failures. My hubris and, I hope, my *pietas*. It's a story of life's twists and turns. From the sun-drenched heights of Park Avenue to the dismal depths of a Brooklyn prison known as "the dungeon," from political friendships with U.S. presidents to prison friendships with convicted murderers—and many other places and people along the way. It hasn't all been wonderful, but it's certainly been a hell of a ride.

■ ■ ■

But where to begin? My birth in Washington, D.C.? My years in Iran? My successes, my glories? My arrest and downfall?

No, we begin in Shiraz, the home of my ancestors, in the Persian year 1249. Or, as we know it by our calendars in the West, 1870.

HASSAN NEMAZEE

Part I

Persia

1

EVERYBODY KNOWS NEMAZEE

MY SHIRAZI ANCESTORS were merchants. Mid-rank in Persian society, between the aristocracy of the Qajar dynasty and the vast majority of the population that lived there—the tribesmen, the peasantry, the farmers—merchants were inheritors of a 2000-year tradition of trade going back to the Silk Road. Most Persian merchants were based in Tehran or Tabriz, in northern Persia, but a smaller group of Shirazi merchants traded along southern sea lanes, through the port of Bushehr on the Persian Gulf, some 115 miles to the southeast. They traded with Arab nations of the Gulf, and with British India (including modern-day Afghanistan and Pakistan) and China.

Unfortunately, that trade had shrunk to a trickle. By 1870, the prospects of a Shirazi merchant, never good, were nearly hopeless. Shiraz remained a beautiful, even enchanted place, but for a young and ambitious man, it was a city of dead ends.

One day in the early 1870's, my grandfather, Mohammed Hassan Nemazee, 21 or 22 and recently wed in an arranged marriage, decided that the only way to love Shiraz was to leave it. He bid his family farewell, promising his young wife to send for her when he was settled, and headed out into the world.

I imagine my grandfather departing from his home by foot, or in a camel caravan, passing through the gates in the foothills at the western end of Shiraz. Perhaps he looked back over his shoulder at the city he might never see again. He was risking everything he had for the fortune he hoped to find. That predilection for risk is a theme that would play out often in years to come. His son— my father—would inherit it and go on to take great risks of his own in pursuit of good fortune. So, eventually, would I.

My grandfather traveled overland to Bushehr. There he boarded a ship and sailed east along the old maritime trade route. He sailed across the Persian Gulf, through the Indian Ocean and into the Arabian Sea, and arrived in Bombay.

PERSIA, POLITICS & PRISON

■ ■ ■

Bombay is where my grandfather took the name Nemazee. Last names would not become common among Iranians until the 1930's, during the reign of Reza Shah Pahlavi, but my grandfather decided he needed one in India. The word *nemaz* means prayer in Persian. Supposedly my grandfather borrowed it from a village outside of Shiraz where our family originated. Another piece of family lore has it that my grandfather was inspired by an extremely religious ancestor. This man was praying in his home when a robber entered. Rather than interrupt his devotions, the ancestor continued to pray as the robber relieved him of every one of his earthly possessions.

However he obtained it, my grandfather made good use of his new name. Bombay was teeming with life and business and opportunities. He established a trading business, M.H. Nemazee & Company, to carry goods between Bombay and Shiraz. As soon as he had the means, he brought his wife to join him and began a family. Several children died in infancy, but three sons and four daughters survived. My father, Mohammed Nemazee, born in Bombay in 1896, was the eldest son.

In little over a decade, my grandfather built a solid and prosperous business in India. But he saw that even greater opportunity lay further east, in China. So again he took a calculated risk. Leaving the Bombay office in the hands of trusted aides, he moved his family to Hong Kong. He built a home on the Peak, the steep verdant hill rising from western part of the city, where wealthy Europeans and Chinese enjoyed sweeping views of Kowloon Bay and cool breezes that brought refuge from the oppressive heat below.

Nemazee & Company continued to grow, trading in cotton, silk, and tea, including a brand packaged under the family name, Chai Nemazee.[1] Because a major cost of the import/export business was shipping, my grandfather decided to buy his own ships and transport goods himself. This turned out to be a wise move, not only saving him a great deal of money but providing him with a new revenue stream as he used his ships to transport goods for others.

---

[1] In the 1970's, in Iran, I was given a very old box of Chai Nemazee by a family friend; after boiling water and dipping in the leaves, I found the tea still quite drinkable.

By the start of the 20th Century, the company had new offices in Singapore, Indonesia, and the Philippines, along with its offices in India and China. This is when my grandfather turned to philanthropy. At the time, Americans like Andrew Carnegie and John D. Rockefeller were giving away millions of dollars. The same was true of several Jewish families that had achieved great wealth as merchants in the India and China, such as the Sassoons and the Kadoories. But philanthropy was not inculcated into Persian culture. Generally, wealthy Persians waited until they were near the end of life, then endowed religious shrines to secure themselves a contented afterlife. My grandfather began to change that mindset. He funded a scholarship for school children in Hong Kong. He opened an orphanage in Bombay. He shipped food to Persia to stave off a famine that gripped the country.

Then, in 1922, after a lifetime abroad, my grandfather sailed back home to Shiraz to give something back to the city of his birth. He founded a hospital called the Behbudistan Nemazee—the Nemazee Clinic.

The reason my grandfather could leave Hong Kong and focus on philanthropy was that he now had a son who showed great aptitude for the trade and shipping business. That son was Mohammed Nemazee, my father. At the age of 26, he became the chief executive of Nemazee & Company.

■ ■ ■

I used to have a photo of my father as a young man. Somehow it got lost in the shuffle after my arrest. I remember it well, though. Taken in a photographer's studio in Hong Kong, among potted ferns and other props, it was a formal portrait of my father with his brothers and sisters. My father was still in his late teens, but he had the grave look people assumed in photos before smiling became fashionable. Later in life he would grow heavy and bald, but in the photo he was trim and his hair was dark and full.

My father never graduated from university, but by the time he took over the shipping business he was fluent in English and Persian and had a working knowledge of Cantonese, German, and Spanish. While managing the business, he taught himself to read and write French in six months, taking lessons every day and studying every night. He also read a great deal and had a broad knowledge of world affairs. I have known many brilliant men and women in my life, from professors at Harvard to CEOs of companies and world leaders, but few matched my father's range of curiosity and knowledge.

That said, he was never one to flaunt his erudition. He was humble in a way that is unusual in people who achieve so much. I never met another man who could dominate a room so forcefully by saying so little.

Even as a young man, my father had the two most valuable attributes an entrepreneur can possess: a high tolerance for risk—evidently inherited from his father—and a preternatural gift for timing. Under my father, Nemazee & Company shifted its core business from trade to shipping. My father's ships still carried Nemazee products—tea, sugar—but generally transported any cargo that paid, including cotton, silk, spices, and lumber. A typical voyage might take a Nemazee ship across the Pacific from Asia to Oregon, then down the Pacific coast, through the Panama Canal, then north again to New York, then back again to Asia. Nemazee ships carried Chinese men to the West Indies to work as laborers, and they carried Muslim pilgrims to Jeddah to attend the Hajj in Mecca.

Shipping was lucrative but mercurial, lurching between economic swells and troughs. As my father took control in the post-war 1920's, the business was in one of its periodic contractions. But rather than shrink the business, as caution might have dictated, he took the opportunity to buy ships at low prices and expand the fleet. In 1923, the Nemazee fleet was 17 tramp steamers; by 1924, the number had risen to 30 ships. That year, a newspaper article called my father the richest 30 year old in Hong Kong. In fact, he was still in his 20's.

■ ■ ■

Like his father before him, my father lived on the Peak, near the main artery of May Road. His house was large and surrounded by a garden lush with flowers and populated by numerous statues and fountains. He was there in early December of 1941, when

Japan invaded Hong Kong. There was not much fighting on the Peak, but errant shells sometimes landed near my father's house as the Japanese tried to destroy the tramway that transported residents to and from the city below.

Because he was Persian and therefore not considered a belligerent, my father was relatively safe from the Japanese, at least for a time. He threw open the doors of his home to anyone who needed a roof and a meal. For a time, the house became a kind of refuge for dispossessed Westerners. The *New Yorker* writer and memoirist Emily Hahn was one of those who came to my father for help in these early days of the occupation. Hahn needed to travel through the occupied city to get a pass from Japanese authorities, a dangerous prospect, especially for a woman, in those early days of the occupation. "It's quite simple," announced a friend, "we'll go down and ask Nemazee to help us."

"Who's Nemazee?" asked Hahn.

"Haven't you heard of *Nemazee*? Everybody knows Nemazee."

When Hahn arrived with her friend at my father's house, she found it occupied by a huge group of blond men, women, and children sitting around a table in a large dining room with two tables. As Hahn later wrote in her famous memoir, *China to Me*, the blonds were Norwegians my father had taken in after their own home was destroyed by bombing. Like everyone else, my father was cash starved—the Japanese had closed all the banks—but he had stores of rice and flour, and he managed to get what he needed to keep everyone fed if not entirely full. Mainly, he gave his guests the gift of his calm. "Nemazee was serene," wrote Hahn. "He was an immense comfort."

My father also attempted to purchase the freedom of some members of the international Hong Kong community, including that of several British friends confined to the internment camp in Stanley, where conditions were overcrowded and terrible. At the same time, he tried to maneuver his fleet out of the hands of the Japanese, sailing his ships under Liberian or Panamanian flags.

While luckier than most, he realized that staying in Hong Kong was not viable. The Japanese military had already commandeered his office building in Shanghai as staff headquarters; how long before they did the same in Hong Kong? How long before they got their hands on his ships and turned them into vessels not of trade but war? How long before they helped themselves to his home? The time had come to leave, and my father knew exactly where he wanted to go: America.

He cabled his sister, Safieh Firouz, in Tehran. As it happened, Safieh was married to Mohammed Hossein Firouz, a prince of the fallen Qajar dynasty and a senior military officer in Iran. (He would later serve as Minister of War under the Shah.) My father explained his desire to go to America. But how? He had no visa, and the United States was not welcoming foreigners to its shores during World War II. They came up with the plan to secure diplomatic credentials for my father. With help from his brother-in-law, my father was appointed Commercial Attaché to the Iranian Embassy in Washington, D.C. This was a good solution for several reasons. It allowed my father to leave occupied Hong Kong and travel under Persian diplomatic cover. Equally important, it would allow him to live in the United States, a safe harbor where he could continue to run his business.

First, though, he had to get there. That was no easy matter in the summer of 1942. Leaving behind a skeleton staff and vowing to arrange for their transfer to America as soon as possible—a vow he kept—my father steamed north from Hong Kong, through the East China Sea and the Sea of Japan, to Vladivostok, in far eastern Russia, where Nemazee & Company had a small office. He boarded the Trans-Siberian Railroad and passed through the vast expanses of tundra, the steppes of central Russia, and the pine forests of the taiga, finally disembarking after some 4,000 miles, most likely at Omsk. From there he somehow made his way overland through present-day Kazakhstan, to the top of the Caspian Sea, and boarded a commercial barge that happened to be going south to Persia.

When he finally made it to Shiraz, my father visited his father's grave. Then he made his way to the small hospital that my grandfather had endowed. He was disheartened to find the hospital poorly run and physically neglected. He decided to make the restoration of the Behbudistan Nemazee one of the missions of his life. And then he resumed his long journey to America.

2

MOSADDEGH ON THE FARM

IT'S DIFFICULT TO SAY how old my mother was when my parents met. Her age was always a treated as a state secret. It changed so often that in her later years I'm not sure she even knew the truth. Her passport showed 1923 as the date of birth, but that was at least a few years off. More certain is the place of her birth: Isfahan, in central Iran, where her father—my maternal grandfather—was one of Iran's earliest industrialists.

At a very young age, my mother was given to a much older man in an arranged marriage. She soon had two children—Manucher, a son, born in 1935, and Shahla, a daughter, born in 1942. By the time Shahla was born, my mother knew she could no longer remain married to a man she did not love. She went to her father and asked him to arrange a divorce. This was a remarkable thing for a woman to do at the time. But my mother was an uncommonly strong and willful person. First, she intended to get divorced, she informed her parents, and then she intended to go to America. Her parents opposed both of these plans, but my mother deployed her full arsenal of charm and tears, and they finally relented. Her father arranged her divorce, then arranged her passage to America.

Much to her disappointment, my mother got bumped from the flight she was scheduled to take from Cairo to the United States. Like my father, though, she had a gift for timing. That plane crashed, killing all on board.

Shortly after her safe arrival in Washington, my parents were introduced to each other by Hossein Ala, the Iranian Ambassador to United States at the time. It did not take long for my father to become enchanted. He bought her jewels from Harry Winston and Van Cleef. He bought her a fire-engine red Packard, though she did not drive, and he offered to buy her an apartment at the Shoreham Hotel, though she had no use for it. But he did not propose marriage, not until my mother—as deft a negotiator as my father in her subtle way—began to talk about leaving Washington and moving on to Los Angeles. My father understood this as the ultimatum it was. He proposed, she accepted, and they were married in March, 1949.

Ten months later, on the bright but bitterly cold afternoon of January 27, 1950, I was born in Georgetown University Hospital in Washington. My parents decided to name me after my grandfather. "Hassan be Donya amad," my father announced as he lifted me over his head. *Hassan has been born.*

■ ■ ■

My father was a very wealthy man by the time I came along. Along with the Greek shippers Aristotle Onassis and Stavros Niarchos, he'd purchased a number of so-called called "liberty ships" after the war, at a great discount, adding to his already considerable fleet. His timing was perfect. The shipping business was flourishing as the world came back together after the war, so the new ships immediately turned a profit.

Even while running his shipping business from Washington, my father devoted much of his time to diplomatic service for Iran. His official title at the embassy was Commercial Attaché to the United States but his responsibilities extended well beyond the usual attaché portfolio. He had lived abroad all his life, was fluent in English and several other languages, and had run a large international business since early adulthood, giving him a singular grasp of international laws and trade practices. He also had a naturally even-handed disposition, ideal for a diplomat.

At first, the most pressing issue before the Iranian embassy was containing the Soviet Union. Iran had been divided into three different zones during the war, occupied by the British, Americans, and Russians respectively. The Allies had agreed that occupying forces would be removed at the conclusion of the war. However, now that the war was over, Stalin was unwilling to cede the territory he occupied in northern Iran. My father's task was to convince President Truman and his aides that the United States could not afford to capitulate to Stalin. In the end, with some credit due to my father, the Truman administration played hardball. Stalin reluctantly withdrew from Iran.

Once the issue of Soviet occupation was resolved, the diplomatic focus for my father became oil. Since 1908, when oil was first discovered in Iran by a wealthy Englishman named William D'Arcy, the Iranians had been hampered by a lopsided agreement that gave the British nearly all of the oil profits. The unfairness of the deal was obvious to most reasonable people, but the British opposed any revision. Their view was that they had discovered the oil and developed the technology to drill for it, so it was theirs. My father considered the British position untenable. He pressed the United States to back Iran's demand for a more equitable deal.

Convincing the Americans to accept a compromise turned out to be the easy part. More difficult was convincing the Iranian government, now run by Prime Minister Mosaddegh.

A Persian aristocrat educated in Paris and London, Mohammad Mosaddegh had been leader of the opposition National Front party for years. For years, Mosaddegh—or Mossy, as the British press called him—had condemned the oil agreement as a form of colonial exploitation, loudly venting not only to the British but to the entire international press corps. A highly-strung man of eccentric habits, he often conducted press conferences in his pajamas, in bed, resorting to tears to punctuate his grievances.

Mosaddegh may have been histrionic, but his arguments became harder to refute after other oil-rich countries like Saudi Arabia and Venezuela signed more equitable deals with American oil companies. Should he ever become prime minister, vowed Mosaddegh, he would nationalize the oil wells or seal them with mud. Then, in the spring of 1951, much to the horror of the British, he did become prime minister.

My father saw the train wreck that would come if Mosaddegh followed through on his threat to nationalize the oil. He drafted a memo that laid out a sensible deal. The memo argued for a structure that ensured Iran's profits from oil, while also expanding ownership to a consortium of American, Dutch, and British interests. Iran would obtain a 60/40 profit sharing arrangement, and Britain would lose control of the ownership structure. My father circulated this memo among his colleagues at the Iranian embassy in Washington and to the Mosaddegh government in Tehran. It was ignored by Mosaddegh.

In the autumn of 1951, when I was a toddler uttering my first words of English (no Persian, much to my later regret), Mohammad Mosaddegh arrived in Washington, D.C., for a state visit. On a drizzly Sunday, my father invited the prime minister out to a farm he'd recently purchased in Germantown, Maryland. The name of the property, so-christened in honor of my birth and painted in large white letters on the roof of the barn, was HASSAN'S FARM.[2]

Regrettably, I never discussed the Mosaddegh visit with my father, so I don't know for certain what they talked about as they sipped tea in the drawing room of the old farmhouse and toured the barns to look at the chickens and cows. That was my father's style—to put his interlocutor at ease with hospitality, then apply the gentle but persistent force of reason.

I am quite sure my father encouraged Mosaddegh to reach for an alliance of mutual benefit with western nations, one that gave the Iranians a fair portion of oil proceeds but also left the western powers with a sizable stake. This would ultimately serve the nation's interest, promoting goodwill, generosity, and possible protection against encroachments from the Soviet Union.

Alas, whatever my father said that day on the farm, Mosaddegh did not listen. Rather, in a miscalculated bluff, he went back home to Iran and played right into British hands. Much as Fidel Castro would do more successfully in Cuba a decade later, Mosaddegh sought leverage against western powers by raising the specter of an Iranian alliance with the Soviet Union, on the assumption that this would protect him. It did the opposite. It convinced the United States that the British had been right to fear Mosaddegh—he was a puppet of the Soviets and had to go.

In March 1953, CIA director Allen Dulles gave Frank Wisner, head of covert operations, a green light to proceed with Operation Ajax, a collaboration between British and U.S. intelligence agencies to overthrow Mosaddegh in a coup. The

---

[2] The 550-acre farm had formerly belonged to Walter Johnson, aka "The Big Train," famed pitcher of Washington's American League baseball team, the Senators. Johnson called the farm Mountain View and hunted raccoon and foxes on its property. My father turned it into a working dairy farm.

operation commenced in August of 1953. CIA-sponsored mobs, posing as members of the communist Tudeh party, took to the street, attacking mullahs and mosques, to the outrage of most Iranians. Other mobs, also in the pay of the agency, denounced Mosaddegh and hailed the Shah. An attempt by Shah's Imperial Guard (at the direction of the C.I.A.) to arrest Mosaddegh failed and sent the young Shah into flight from Iran, first to Baghdad, then to Rome (where he accidentally, awkwardly, bumped into Allen Dulles in the lobby of the Excelsior Hotel). Meanwhile, in Tehran, support for the Shah came from the clergy and the bazaar, producing a nationalist reaction, which unexpectedly won the day for the Shah.

A second attempt to capture Mosaddegh was more successful. It led to the prime minister's surrender and resignation. The young Shah returned to Tehran to take full control of the government, and Mosaddegh spent the rest of his days under house arrest.

Today it is generally accepted by historians that America's involvement in the removal of Mosaddegh was the root cause of the animosity that resulted in both the Iranian Revolution of 1978-1979 and the subsequent years of hostility between Iran and the West. But the Americans are given far too much historical credit for Mosaddegh's overthrow. In reality, it was Britain that created the crisis that led to the nationalization of the Anglo-Iranian Oil Company, and it was Britain that pressed Washington repeatedly to undermine Mosaddegh. Britain deserves more credit—or blame—than the United States.

Finally, Mosaddegh himself deserves more blame than history usually accords him. He was both too stubborn, and too weak, to compromise. He might have saved himself, and Iran, a lot of grief had he listened to my father on that rainy autumn afternoon at the farm.

■ ■ ■

Even as he devoted himself to finding a diplomatic solution to the oil crisis, my father undertook a third post-war responsibility during those years in Washington, one that would soon overshadow all others and end up consuming much of his life. This was his philanthropic work. The wealthier he grew, the more determined he was to give away his wealth. He remembered his vow to refurbish the Behbudistan Nemazee—the Nemazee Clinic—in Shiraz, which had fallen into disrepair and was being administered by the Iranian Red Cross. Although my father had never lived in Shiraz, he thought of the city as his home, and he decided to focus his efforts there.

His original objective was merely to renovate the modest 50-bed clinic founded by his father. But when he began to examine the pressing need for public health in Iran, he came to contemplate something far more ambitious. Soon he had a plan to turn the clinic into the first truly modern hospital in Iran: a state-of-the-art 250-bed medical center conjoined with a nursing school and staffed by western-educated doctors. He established an organization called the Iran Foundation, to be headquartered in the Empire State Building in New York. The Iran Foundation would be responsible for the planning of the hospital, from the first architectural and engineering studies to the eventual recruitment of doctors, nurses, and other staff. A sister foundation, Bonyad Iran, would handle construction and operations from Shiraz.

The challenges were staggering. To begin, it was impossible to build a modern hospital without a clean and dependable water supply. But no city in Iran in the 1940's had piped running water, not Tehran and certainly not Shiraz. Before there could be a hospital, there had to be water.

The other great problem was revenue. My father wanted the hospital to serve the generally poor population of Shiraz. Oil income was a small fraction in the 1940's of what it would become by the 1970's, and Iran remained almost entirely underdeveloped. It was clear that the hospital could not be sustained on revenues from the local population—it would need to be subsidized.

My father found a solution he believed would answer both problems. Before undertaking the hospital, he would build a water system in Shiraz, the first modern waterworks in Iran. The water would come from deep wells and be pumped into a network of pipes, which would distribute it to the hospital and throughout the city. Like any utility, the waterworks would charge usage fees. The profit generated by these fees would be channeled to the hospital to provide revenue for its operation.

It was an elegant solution, but it was not going to be easy to achieve. Indeed, my father had talked himself into building, and largely funding out of his own pocket, one of the largest infrastructure projects in Iran's history.

3

AS THE WORLD TURNED

WHEN HE FIRST CAME TO WASHINGTON, my father had lived in the Kalorama section of the city, but after my birth he moved us to a five-acre estate on Glenbrook Road in Bethesda, Maryland. This would be my home for much of my life. Formerly known as Dunrobbin, the property had been built by Charles Spittal Robb, grandfather of future Governor of Virginia and U.S. Senator Chuck Robb. It included a large Tudor-style mansion, a smaller guest house, and—very rare for Washington at the time—a large swimming pool. The lawn was a wide sweep of Kentucky bluegrass, shaded by towering elms and spruce trees and bordered by English boxwoods. In the spring an assortment of magnolias, azaleas, and rhododendrons exploded with color and fragrance. My father moved his offices into the guest house, where he spent his days working with his two secretaries, Mr. Touty and Mrs. Jex. My mother oversaw the main house, assisted by a small staff. The lawn fell under the dominion of our Hungarian gardener, Mr. Vilges.

I recall my childhood as idyllic. My days were spent at Norwood Elementary School, afternoons cruising the neighborhood on a bicycle or playing in the yard with my sister and our friends. We were always in the company of a veritable zoo of pets—a cocker spaniel for me, a miniature bulldog for Susie, plus assorted rabbits, hamsters, and guinea pigs. In the summer, we swam with friends in our pool, and in the winter—this is back when winters were cold even in Washington—we built snowmen, sledded down any hill we could find, and threw snowballs at passing cars.

In the fall of 1953, my father reluctantly said goodbye to us and flew to Tehran to join the Shah's cabinet as a minister without portfolio. My father's main responsibility would be to negotiate a new oil agreement on behalf of the Iranian government and NIOC (the National Iranian Oil Company) with the British and Americans. While he did not especially want the appointment, he decided to take it as a matter of duty to his country. He refused a salary and committed to staying only until the agreement was complete. The memo he'd written a year earlier—the memo ignored by Mosaddegh—became the blueprint for the deal he helped negotiate for Iran.

During the years that my father served in the Iranian government, my mother and I remained in Washington, along with my sister, Susie, who was born in December of 1952. We commuted to Europe at least once a year, aboard the Queen Mary, to visit my father. We would stay at the Georges V Hotel in Paris, then fly to Nice, where we stayed at the Negresco, and then to Geneva and the Hotel Du Rhone. My father would join us for extended visits of several weeks.

On one trip to Switzerland, in the winter of 1955, my parents took us to Crans-Montana, in the Swiss Alps, about a three-hour drive from Geneva. We went to visit my mother's sister, Aghdass, and her husband, Gerard Spinedi. They were an unusual and glamorous couple. Gerard was a dashing Swiss race car driver famous for his gold Ferrari. Aghdass was an attractive blond Iranian who often joined her husband as his co-driver on long and treacherous cross-country races. (In 1961, driving together, they'd win the Rallye de Genève.) I remember nothing of that first visit to Crans—I was only five at the time—but it was apparently there that I inadvertently caused a religious conversion in my mother.

According to the story, I became very ill. My temperature spiked to 105. The doctors were perplexed, and my mother was terrified. Until this moment, neither of my parents was religious. Both had been raised as Muslims but neither practiced any faith, and my father was an agnostic. One night, when my fever was particularly high, my mother left me with our nurse and raced out into the dark mountain town. She entered the first church she found with open doors, which happened to be Roman Catholic. The church was empty and silent. She lit candles in the gloom, knelt near the altar, and prayed, promising God that if I were to recover, she would devote herself to Him ever after. Needless to say, I lived and the crisis was averted. But my mother kept her word. She became a devout Catholic and remained one the rest of her life.

■ ■ ■

A benefit to my father that came from living in Iran during these years was his proximity to the Nemazee Hospital in Shiraz. The hospital had been completed in 1952 and was officially inaugurated in 1955 by the Shah and Queen Soraya. Characteristically, my father never intended to have the hospital named after himself, but my mother insisted. She predicted that if his name were not attached, someone else would end up taking credit for his work. I have no doubt she was right.

Together, the Nemazee Hospital and Nursing School, also funded by my father, comprised the most modern medical center in the Middle East. The hospital launched the modern transformation of medicine and public health not only in Iran, but in the entire region. Emirs and Sheiks from all over the Gulf came to Shiraz for treatment. But the hospital was never meant to be for the rich and prominent. My father had envisioned it as a need-based medical center for the local population, which was predominately poor and unable to afford treatment. He remained determined to treat such patients, but this meant frequent budget shortfalls at the hospital.

Fortunately, my father had money to make up the shortfalls at the time. With the end of the Korean War in 1953, shipping prices had risen to historic highs. The many liberty ships that my father had purchased from the U.S. government for pennies on the dollar were now worth a fortune. My father decided to liquidate his entire fleet, liberty ships and all. Given that he'd spent nearly his entire life in shipping, this was a dramatic move, but his timing turned out to be perfect. Just months later, a glut in capacity precipitated a dramatic fall in prices and led to the bankruptcy of many shippers.

Much of my father's windfall went to the hospital, but some of it he invested in a business venture of my mother's. She'd set her sights on opening a modern textile factory in Iran. That she could have such ambition—that such an ambition was even conceivable in Iran—says something about how far the country had come culturally under the Shah. It also says something about my mother. Forced into a marriage against her choice at an early age, she'd had the strength to insist on divorce. She'd then had courage to leave Iran and make a new life for herself in America. She could have spent her days now luxuriating as the wife of a rich man, but she wanted more. She began to lay plans for a state-of-the-art textile factory in Tehran. The first factory in Iran ever built and run by a woman, it would be named, appropriately, after her: *Fakhr Iran*.

By the end of 1955, the consortium oil agreement, largely conceived and negotiated by my father, had been completed and signed by all parties. His task accomplished, my father planned to return to Washington. But it was not to be. The Shah's new prime minister, Hossein Ala—former ambassador to Washington and my father's good friend—insisted my father remain in the cabinet.

Despite endemic problems of corruption and poor administration, Iran was entering a Golden Age in the mid-1950's. The Shah's so-called White Revolution would not be officially introduced until 1962, but already he was modernizing Iranian society with various reforms, extending rights and opportunities to broad sectors of the population. At the same time, the revised consortium agreement was bringing in oil revenue and American aid. My father played a significant role in negotiating both the acquisition and distribution of these funds, acting as a sort of honest broker between the U.S. and Iran. He argued for Iran's interests but was not afraid to stand up to Shah and steer him away from misallocating or wasting the foreign aid.

The Shah often listened to my father's advice, but he had other voices whispering in ear, too, and was easily swayed by appeals to his vanity and insecurities. My father became more and more frustrated with the palace intrigues and scheming, the sycophantic bowing and scraping before His Majesty. Furthermore, it had become clear to him that the important decisions about Iran's future were being made not in Tehran, but in Washington. No move, large or small, was made without input from the Eisenhower administration.

My father began to press Prime Minister Ala to permit him to resign. Matters resolved themselves when the Shah removed Ala from office and made him Minister of Court. My father returned to Washington in late 1956.

PERSIA, POLITICS & PRISON

■ ■ ■

As I entered third grade, my parents enrolled me at the Landon School for Boys, a private school close our house in Bethesda. They did so on the recommendation of their good friend, Richard Helms, whose son attended Landon. Not until many years later, when I picked up a copy of *Time* magazine to read an article about the Director of the CIA and saw a photo of "Uncle Dick," did I learn that my parents' friend had been in charge of covert operations for the CIA. The *Time* article reminded me of a curious conversation I'd overheard as a boy in our living room between Helms and a visiting Iranian. The Iranian asked Helms what he did for work. "Oh, this and that," responded Helms. The Iranian then asked Helms where he worked. "Oh, here and there," responded Helms.

As I grew older, I began to appreciate how rare and privileged my life was, even compared to my relatively well-off private school friends. For one thing, while my friends arrived on the school bus or in a mother's station wagon, I came and went in a limousine driven by a chauffeur.

But it was not just the wealth—the land, the pool, the staff—that made my life so different. What was truly rare about our home was the way the world seemed to orbit around it. In his guest house office, my father received and entertained an endless stream of visiting guests, men whose faces I'd later see in newspapers and magazines. Any Iranian of stature who came to Washington stayed at the house, and virtually any Iranian living in Washington came sooner or later, too, driving up to our home on Glenbrook to attend the open houses that my parents hosted on Sunday mornings. The house became especially crowded at Nowruz, the traditional Persian New Year's celebration that fell around the vernal equinox. Along with a great spread of Persian food overseen by my mother, every female guest received, courtesy of my father, a lavish gift—the newest style of purse, perhaps, or an elegant scarf.

My father was the consummate host, but he had his own way of doing things. Often in the middle of his own parties he would simply vanish, drifting off to his study, where could be found reading a book. He relished good company and conversation, but he was never happier than when alone with his books.

One frequent guest from those years was David Suratgar. My father and David's father—Lotfali Suratgar, a scholar and poet laureate of Iran—had been close friends since youth. In the 1950's, when David was a young man attending Columbia Law School, he often took the train down from New York to visit us on Glenbrook Road. Many decades later, he still recalled how my father would develop intense curiosities about arcane subjects—the relationship between ancient Persia and China, for example, and how certain textile patterns and dye colors that originated in China later showed up in Persian motifs. When David was back in New York at Columbia, my father would often call to dispatch him on urgent fact-finding missions. Once, he asked David to hurry down to the Museum of Natural History on 79th Street with a tape measure to determine the length of the Tyrannosaurus rex skeleton in the main hall. (Forty feet, as it turned out.) On another occasion, he asked David to consult with one of his Columbia Law professors, a specialist on Koranic law, to settle once and for all where the Koran came down on indulgence in alcoholic spirits. (The answer to that one, David recalls, was complicated.)

No matter what my father was doing, he always made room in this schedule for two rituals. Every afternoon, all activity stopped as he settled into his armchair to watch *As the World Turns*, a television soap opera. And on Sunday evenings, he sat down in his robe, often with his dinner on a tray before him, and tuned into *Alfred Hitchcock Presents*. It was amusing to watch my father watch Hitchcock, who seemed to look right back at him from the black-and-white TV. By this point in his life, the two men—both portly, bald, and brilliant—could have been each other's long-lost twin.

Those were good years for my father, but they did not last. Several problems required his attention in Iran. First, in Shiraz, there were financial difficulties at the hospital. My father had paid for the construction of the entire medical center and waterworks out of his personal fortune. The cost had been close to $15 million, a sum that in today's dollars would be close to $200 million. As for the annual cost of running the hospital, the waterworks was supposed to subsidize this, but because the waterworks was the first ever to operate in Iran—prior even to

Tehran's waterworks—there was no template to guide the pricing of water. Water rates had to be negotiated with the Ministry of Water and Power and the local municipality, both of which had their reasons to keep the rates artificially low. When it came to making up budget shortfalls, there was only one man who could do it: my father.

Another financial problem in Iran concerned Fakhr Iran. The textile factory founded by my mother was losing money. My mother had been bold in her planning, but she had not hired experienced professionals to run the factory, relying instead on her brothers and other relatives. It's surprising that my father had allowed this to occur, as he was very skilled and experienced himself in running a large business, but love and good judgment do not always go in tandem. In any event, the net result was mounting operational losses at the factory. Again, it fell to my father to make up the shortfall.

Although he never wore stress on his sleeve, I am sure the bad financial news from Iran affected his health, which was already compromised by a two-pack-a-day cigarette habit and passion for good food. Still, it was a shock to come home from school one afternoon to an eerily quiet house. My mother was away at the time, in Iran. My father was nowhere to be seen. I found Mrs. Jex sitting in the kitchen, where's she'd apparently been waiting for me. She had tears in her eyes. "What's wrong?" I asked.

"Your father's in the hospital, Hassan. He's had a heart attack."

4

A PERSIAN EDUCATION

MY FATHER'S HEART ATTACK was severe enough to require hospitalization in Washington, but not so severe as to impede a full recovery. He came home from the hospital after a few days, looking gray and tired but otherwise no worse for wear. My mother attempted to put my father on a strict diet and get him to stop smoking, per doctor's orders. Both of these attempts failed miserably.

In 1962, my father departed for Iran to address problems at both the factory and the hospital. He expected to return home to Washington in short order.

When he arrived in Tehran, he turned his attention first to Fakhr Iran. My mother's company was losing money at an alarming rate. He found the solution when a friend introduced him to a brilliant young Iranian entrepreneur named Hushang Ansary. In future years, Ansary would rise to great heights in Iranian politics, then become a legendary businessman and philanthropist in the United States. My father made Ansary the CEO of Fakhr Iran. Almost immediately, Ansary began to turn the company around.

After putting the textile company in good hands, my father turned his attention to the more vexing problems at the medical center. At the time Nemazee Hospital and Nursing School were developed, Shiraz had a small university with an understaffed medical school. Once the hospital opened and proved successful, the Shah decided to expand Shiraz University and to rename it—after himself, of course. Because he wanted Pahlavi University to have a first-rate medical school, and because every medical school needed a teaching hospital associated with it, the Shah decided that Pahlavi University would merge with Nemazee Hospital. In practice, this meant that my father would have to cede control of the hospital to the university. This was hardly what he had intended or wanted, but he had little choice but to accept the merger.

Fortunately, at the very moment the merger became inevitable, the Shah installed his former prime minister—and my father's longtime friend—Asadollah Alam as chancellor of the university. Alam and my father recognized the opportunity for a mutually beneficial relationship. The university would get the advantage of an association with first-rate hospital; in return, it would make up the shortfall in the hospital's budget. While the chancellor retained the right to appoint and remove the director of the hospital, the trustee of the foundation—my father, then later myself—would reserve negative veto rights if we disapproved of an appointment.

If not exactly what my father wanted for the hospital, it was a solution he could live with. More importantly, it was one that would keep the hospital solvent.

We'd been expecting my father to return to Washington once his business was completed in Iran, just as he had done previously. But something changed in his attitude toward Iran during his stay there. He discovered that for all his objections to how the government was run and to certain cultural practices—not to mention the fact that he had been born and raised abroad—Iran was his true home and where he wanted to spend the rest of his days. And it was where he hoped his family would join him.

According to my father's new plan, my mother and Susie would move at once from Washington to Tehran. I would complete my secondary education at a British boarding school—Harrow, my father had decided—then I would move to Tehran as well. All this came as a shock to Susie and me. While we were both Iranian citizens, our entire lives had been in America. Our friends were in America, our cultural tastes and our lifestyles were American—our home was America.

■ ■ ■

Today, Tehran has a population of nearly 9,000,000 inhabitants, making it one of the world's largest cities. When Americans think of Tehran, they are likely to imagine faceless women in hijab and angry mullahs issuing fatwahs—a dour place of religious zealots and harsh justice. I've not been to Tehran in forty years, so I can't speak authoritatively about the city today, but I can say that the place we flew into in 1964 was nothing like that. With a population of just over a million, few cars and few modern conveniences, it was in many ways a less modern city, but it was also more secular, more open-minded, and far more welcoming.

Later, we would usually fly into Tehran at night, which is when most international flights arrived. That first time, however, we came in at daylight. From the plane window, I could see the city spreading out to the folded dirt hills that hugged the northern part of the city. As we taxied down the runway, I saw my father through the plane window. He was waiting for us on the sun-baked tarmac, standing beside a large black Buick, a cigarette in his fingers. He'd had his chauffeur drive right up to the plane to meet us, as if we were foreign dignitaries arriving on a state visit.

Descending the stairs from the plane, I saw a crowd of people waving and cheering from the roof of the main arrivals building. "Who are all those people on the roof waving at us?" I asked my father when we got to him. He laughed. "Those are all your cousins who have come to greet you."

It turned out that many of them were in fact cousins who had come to the airport to meet the new Nemazees from America. We stumbled through introductions in their broken English and my bad Persian. And then we piled into the Buick and sped off through streets of Tehran. I'd traveled fairly extensively for a teenager, but I'd never seen anything like Tehran. Other than a few mosques and a handful of modern high-rises, it was a city of low buildings and high mud walls lining nearly every street and boulevard. I could see rooftops peeking over the walls but not much else.

Between the walls and the mountains in the distance—a few capped by snow even as the city blazed under August heat—Tehran seemed at first glance a shuttered and austere place. That impression was false. Behind those walls, as I'd soon discover, was a city as vibrant with human life and warmth as it was vivid with the flowers and fruits that flourished in the gardens of nearly every home, no matter how modest.

My father had not yet purchased a house in Tehran—he was living at the time with his cousin Mehdi Nemazee—so he'd arranged for us to lease a floor in the new Hilton Hotel. This was in the northern precincts of Tehran, where higher elevations brought cooler temperatures and wealthier residents. The hotel had just opened, so we had most of it to ourselves.

From my American point of view, perhaps the most striking thing about Iran was the gap between rich and poor. In Washington, I knew we were wealthy. We lived in a large house, had a staff, a pool, and generally enjoyed a more luxurious life than any of my friends. I also recognized the respect accorded to my father by the Iranians and Americans he interacted with in Washington. What I saw that summer in Tehran was something very different. I noticed it at once in the way my father was treated by people at the airport, then later at the hotel: a comportment that amounted not merely to respect but to submission. Other men would reach for my father's hand to kiss it, a common sign of deference in Iran. (My father always withdrew his hand before anyone's lips could touch it; such gestures made him uncomfortable.) The country was still extremely hierarchical, and rank was always explicit. My family, I came to discover, occupied a place very near the top.

Learning this changed me in many ways large and small, good and bad. Iran broadened me by making me realize that the world was a more complicated place than I had been exposed to in Washington. But it also brought forth, in my susceptible 14-year-old self, certain characteristics—arrogance, entitlement—that had been held in check in Washington by a general American regard for egalitarianism. Am I blaming Iran for my flaws? No. I am simply suggesting that my summers there were like fertilizer to certain seeds in my personality.

To my surprise, I enjoyed that first summer in Iran enormously. Life revolved around pool parties and tennis matches and festive dinners. There were endless visits to cousins and friends, including members of the royal family, who were part of our social circle. Nearly everybody Susie and I met was new to us, but they welcomed us as if we'd known them forever.

As much as I liked Iran, I still very much considered myself American and had no interest in moving to Iran or starting a new school in England. Both Susie and I were determined to convince our father to allow us to stay in the United States to finish our education. To our surprise, we found a willing co-conspirator in my mother, who turned out to be no more eager to spend the rest of her life in Iran than we were. The three of us now mobilized. My father was subjected to a daily barrage of pleas, tears, and tantrums in an attempt to convince him that it would be best for us to remain in America at least through high school, returning every summer to Iran for visits. My poor father. Serene in the face of a Japanese invasion and other calamities, he was totally unprepared for this type of concerted assault. At last, he capitulated.

In retrospect, our determination to remain in Washington was selfish and unfair to my father. He was in his sixties at the time, and for him to live alone in Tehran, with his wife and children in Washington, was a significant sacrifice. He was not one to complain, but I'm sure he was disappointed.

■ ■ ■

Over the next several years, we shuttled between the United States and Iran. I was in many ways a normal American adolescent boy during the school year, doing homework, playing sports, hanging out with friends, experiencing a burgeoning preoccupation with girls. Every summer, usually on Pan Am flight #1, with a layover in Rome, we flew back to Tehran to be with my father. The preoccupation with girls traveled with me, but otherwise my winter life and summer life were separate and distinct.

While Susie and I made slow progress in our Farsi lessons, we were fortunate that our cousins and friends in Tehran, many of whom attended British or American boarding schools, generally spoke English, so communication was not a problem. Occasionally we left the city to visit other parts of Iran and meet other relatives. We always traveled to Shiraz and stayed for a few weeks in one of the villas my father had built on the grounds of Nemazee Hospital, near an Olympic-sized swimming pool and clay tennis courts. We traveled to Isfahan to visit my mother's family and see one of the most beautiful cities in Iran. We also drove for annual visits to the city of Ramsar on the Caspian Sea, five hours north of Tehran, over the Alborz Mountains.

It was in Ramsar, at 15, that I had my first love affair, though frankly love had little to do with it. Much to my surprise and delight, a beautiful girl, only a few years older but already married and divorced, decided to have a fling with me. During the time we were in the Caspian, and then again on our return to Tehran, we conducted a clandestine but torrid romance. I suppose for her it was an attempt to capture some of the youth that had been stolen from her. For my part, I was just grateful to be the object of her attention and the beneficiary of her experience.

■ ■ ■

I was always happy to return to my American life each fall, but as the years progressed, I was becoming seduced by Iran. I began to think about the future and where I might want to live. The certainty of America was slowly being infiltrated by the possibility of Iran.

As I began to think more seriously about my future, I also took stock of my life. I had enjoyed a happy and fairly carefree youth, but what had I achieved? What did I *want* to achieve? I'd been an indifferent student up until this point. Susie was definitely the academic of the family. While she brought home report cards of straight A's, I was a solid B student, with the occasional A. I did what was required but seldom more. "Hassan is very bright, and when he applies himself is capable of the highest level of achievement," went a typical comment on my report cards. "However, he rarely chooses to put in the necessary work."

The spring of my junior year—Fifth Form, we called it at Landon—the school arranged a week-long college tour for our class. We visited more than a dozen schools, mostly in the northeast. By the end of the tour, I knew where I wanted to go: Harvard. It came to me somewhat belatedly that there was a direct correlation between getting accepted to the college of my choice and my grade point average. To say that Harvard was a stretch would be an understatement.

I worked hard, and with considerable success, in my last year at Landon. When college responses came in the spring, Georgetown and Tufts accepted me. Harvard did not. I was disappointed, but I knew I had only myself to blame for waiting too long to apply myself to my academics. In any case, the schools I'd been accepted to were both great consolation prizes.

I made two decisions that spring of my senior year at Landon. The first was to accept Tufts and decline Georgetown; I wanted to leave Washington and have a college experience away from home. The second was to never again make the mistake of academic laziness. I would work very hard at Tufts, I promised myself. And then I would transfer to Harvard.

That is exactly what happened. I had a great freshman year at Tufts. I made good friends, enjoyed my classes, worked hard, and got straight A's. But I did not give up on my desire to attend Harvard. In the spring, I applied to transfer, this time with a more realistic understanding of my chances.

I returned to Tehran that summer, happy to have enjoyed a great freshman year. I'd not been there long when my father came home for lunch one June afternoon and handed me a telegram. "Well, my respect for American higher education has just gone down a notch," said my father. He broke into a grin. "Congratulations, Hassan. You've been accepted to Harvard."

5

NONSENSE

MAYBE IT WAS GETTING INTO HARVARD, or maybe it was simply that I had matured a little, but my father began to treat me differently. He'd always found me smart and amusing but not quite serious—a boy, not yet a man. That summer in Tehran, though, he clearly began to see me more plausibly as his heir and successor.

To prepare me for my new role, he decided to familiarize me with the operations of the waterworks and hospital. He sent me, first, to meet the head of the waterworks, an elderly gentleman named Mr. Houshmand, then to the director of the hospital, Dr. Ali Farpour. Both Mr. Houshmand and Dr. Farpour spent hours educating me about their respective institutions, escorting me into the bowels of their buildings and bringing me into their offices for tutorials on operations and management.

Before I returned to America, my father asked me to join him for a talk, and to bring a pad of paper and pen. We sat in armchairs in the main reception hall of the house he now owned in northern Tehran. The hall was a large and airy atrium with a view of the garden out back. This was where he often huddled for serious conversations with visiting business associates and friends. The fact we were having our conversation here signaled that we were talking not just as father to son, but man-to-man.

"Hassan, you're now at a stage where you need to become responsible for your financial affairs." I nodded hesitantly, wondering if I was about to be reprimanded for my spending habits or some other failing. "With that in mind, let's review your budget for the coming year. Tuition, room, board, pocket money, airline tickets, all of it. I'll give you the *entire* sum when you leave, and from that sum you will pay *all* of your expenses. I will not expect you to ask for money until you return here next summer. Do you understand?"

I did understand, and I was pleased. I'd been living on a monthly allowance from my parents up until that point. I was proud to take responsibility for my finances and eager to show my father than I could to live within a budget. In any case, it was a very generous sum that my father agreed to give me for the school year.

Carrying the money in U.S. cash and traveler's checks, I departed Iran in early September, bound for Washington, with a stop in Geneva to change planes. As luck would have it, the second leg of my flight was cancelled due to mechanical problems, so I had to spend the night in Geneva. We had often stayed at the Richmond Hotel near the lake. Since it was the only hotel I knew in the city, I asked the taxi driver to take me there.

Later in the afternoon, with nothing else to do, I took a walk along Lake Geneva. After that, still too restless to retire to my room, I loitered in the hotel lobby. My eyes fell upon a sign near the concierge desk. It was for the Casino Divonne, just across the border in France, where gambling was legal. The sign informed me that a free limo departed from the front of the Richmond Hotel every hour on the hour. The next one, I realized as I checked my watch, would be leaving in fifteen minutes. What did I have to lose? I hurriedly took the elevator up to my room and changed into coat and tie, then went back down to the lobby to for the limo. In my pocket, I had all the money my father had given me to last the entire school year at Harvard. It seemed foolish to leave in my hotel room.

The Casino Divonne was every bit as swanky as I'd imagined it. After strolling in under the Art Deco glass awning and under the glimmering chandeliers, and after passing a long wooden bar where I ordered a scotch on the rocks—stopping off at the cashier's window to purchase a modest pile of chips—I found my way to a blackjack table. I'd played some 21 in the past and thought I had a good handle on it. I figured this was a good place to start my night.

It turned out that I was very good at 21. Exceptionally good, in fact. Within minutes—or so it seemed; time warps inside a casino—I won a few hundred dollars. Incredibly, I then doubled this, and doubled it again. I possessed an almost unerring ability to know when to take another card and when to hold.

And then something happened. It's the thing that happens sooner or later to anyone who has ever spent time in a casino: what I confused for skill turned out to be luck—and my luck turned sour. Now every card I drew was wrong, every call I made put me too high or too low. My pile of chips dwindled down to nothing. I returned to the window to buy more chips, first with cash, then traveler's checks. I was a down a few hundred dollars, then, moments later, a few thousand. I knew that if I could only get one decent hand, just one, I could start to recoup and work my way back to even. Now and then I *did* get a good hand and I *did* start to recoup, which emboldened me to raise my stake. Then my luck turned again, and my losses escalated with head-spinning velocity. Before I finally gave up, I had lost nearly half of the money my father had given me for the entire year.

I took a bus back to my hotel; no limo was offered this time. It was a long and sickening ride. I was devastated and mortified. If my father learned of my stupidity, he might forgive me but he would never trust me again. It would be terrible not only for me, but for him.

I determined then and there, on that bus ride back to Switzerland, that I would *never* breathe a word about what had happened at the casino to him or anyone else. In retrospect, it would have been better if I'd come clean and suffered the consequences. A reckoning with myself then might have saved me (and others) a lot of grief later. But at the time, total silence seemed like the only plausible option.

The clammy feeling that followed me out of the casino stayed with me through the long night in my hotel, then the long flight to Washington and the cab ride home to Bethesda. Stepping out of the cab, though, my gloom was immediately lifted by the sight of a car in the driveway. A Porsche 911 T, brand new, all white. "It's for you," said my mother when she met me at the door. "Congratulations on getting into Harvard, Hassan."

■ ■ ■

In the late summer of 1969, after packing my new Porsche to the gills, leaving just enough room for myself behind the wheel, I drove up to Cambridge, Massachusetts, switching from Motown to Creedence Clearwater Revival to the Rolling Stones on the eight-track player, speeding most of the way north. From the moment I pulled up to Harvard Square, it was clear the journey had been worth the effort. From the handsome campus on the Charles River to the extraordinary array of classes and professors, to the remarkable fellow students I soon met—many of whom became lifelong friends—I appreciated everything Harvard had to offer.

I had arranged to room in Winthrop House, one of the dorms along the Charles River, with a friend from Landon named John Peacock. Our suite included a living room with a working fireplace and floor-to-ceiling bookshelves. The shelves were already filled when I got there, mostly with Greek and Latin classics. I soon discovered that the books belonged to the previous occupant of the room, J.C. von Helms. Wearing a tweed jacket with leather patches at the elbows and brown penny loafers, he introduced himself to me. He told me he was a resident tutor at Winthrop House and asked if I'd mind keeping his books on the shelves in our living room for a while, as he did not have shelves in his room yet. I was delighted to have them. They created precisely the atmosphere of avid scholarship and intellectual achievement that had drawn me to Harvard in the first place.

In many ways, I enjoyed a traditional college experience at Harvard, despite the fact that the late 1960's were a turbulent time. Robert F. Kennedy and Martin Luther King had been assassinated the previous year. The Vietnam War was at its height, and American college campuses were at the center of demonstrations against the war. University Hall, the central administration building at Harvard, had recently been taken over and occupied by students, until local police were called in to forcibly remove them.

My father wrote me a letter that fall that captures not only his concerns about the war and protests, but his general approach to political and intellectual matters:

> *Reports of various events in the United States, which indicate a general state of insecurity, have made me very anxious about your safety. So I would like you to associate only with persons of good character and avoid wild parties and involvement in matters which do*

not concern your studies. Remember that you are at Harvard to learn and not express opinions.

The time for expressing opinions will come when you have learnt much more and matured sufficiently to know that nothing is absolutely true or absolutely false, but there are two sides to every question...

My father need not have worried. Between occasional spells of youthful revelry, I was a fairly serious young man now. I was also fairly apolitical. Unlike many of my classmates, I never grew my hair or experimented with drugs. Many years later, when being interviewed by the FBI and Diplomatic Security agents for an ambassadorial appointment, I truthfully answered the question of drug use by responding, "Well, I'm like Bill Clinton – I tried it once, but didn't inhale." Regarding the war in Vietnam, I was fortunate to be an Iranian citizen and therefore exempt from the draft. Not having that threat over my head freed me of anxieties that many other young men of my generation had to carry with them.

With the Porsche at my disposal, I took advantage of everything Cambridge and Boston had to offer, including the bounty of neighboring women's colleges, where the girls I met were not only beautiful, but interesting and smart. My funds had been fully and generously restored by my father by this point, so money was not a problem. In one of his letters, my father admonished me to never flaunt my wealth—"avoid showing that you have money to spend," he'd written, "rather try to show that you have little and have to be careful about spending"—but I found his advice easier to agree to than follow.

One extracurricular activity I pursued while at Harvard was learning to fly. On free afternoons and weekends, I drove out to a small airport in Lincoln, Massachusetts, and took lessons in a Cessna 172. After 40 hours of training, followed by a test that required me to take off and land at three local airports, I got my pilot's license. I enjoyed flying alone over the suburbs of Boston on New England autumn afternoons. It was a quiet reprieve from academic pressures and social life, not to mention the protests that were shutting down the campus.

■ ■ ■

I returned to Tehran as usual the summer after my sophomore year of college. My father had spoken to Hushang Ansary about arranging a job for me. Since taking over Fakhr Iran some years earlier, Ansary had experienced a meteoritic career in both business and government. He had recently returned to Iran as Minister of Economy, after serving as Iranian Ambassador to Washington.

In answer to my father's request, he arranged not one but *two* jobs for me. Part of my summer was spent in the Tehran headquarters of Fakhr Iran, where Hushang's brother, Bahram, now served as Chief Executive Officer. The other part went to a job in the Research Department of the Ministry of Economy. There I reported to one of Hushang's talented young deputies, Hassan Ali Mehran (who went on to become Minister of Finance and Governor of the Central Bank). It was an extraordinary opportunity to work directly under two highly accomplished managers in two very different fields.

Before I returned to Harvard for my junior year, our family made its annual end-of-summer trip to Shiraz. My father had built a number of villas on the grounds of Nemazee Hospital for doctors and administrators. One of these, Villa #1, he'd converted into his personal residence, reserving it for his frequent visits to Shiraz. He'd decorated it in traditional Persian style, with stained glass windows in the reception rooms and a Persian Hamam—a kind of Turkish bath—with rooms for a sauna and hot and cold pools. The hospital compound included a beautiful old Persian garden with villas for the doctors, an Olympic pool, and tennis courts.

The tennis courts were the envy of Shiraz, as they were not only the finest clay courts in the city, but the only ones with lighting at night. They were frequented by Shirazi VIPs, who were not affiliated with the hospital, but believed they had a claim to them by right of their status. Among those who occupied them that summer was General Minbashian, one of the Shah's senior military officers and leader of the Imperial Army in Shiraz. General Minbashian played doubles every afternoon with his oldest son and a cousin of mine, Ahmad Khalili, a local tennis champion.

One afternoon, I went to the courts to play with another cousin, my good friend Reza. We waited for the general's match to end. He was a man of notorious temper, and since he was playing poorly, his temper flared. The object of his wrath was Khalili, who had the misfortune to be his doubles partner. Before I could think about what I was doing, I strode onto the court and took Khalili's arm. "Come on," I said. "You don't need this crap." The general's son, who shared his father's bad temper, charged me with his tennis racquet raised, as if to strike me. I wheeled around and shoved him to the ground.

The next thing I knew, Reza and I were being forcibly dragged from the court by two broad-shouldered and well-armed military police. The general was apoplectic. "Arrest them and take them to the brig!" he screamed. The guards dragged us toward the military jeeps at the front of the hospital compound.

Before we reached the jeeps, someone informed General Minbashian that he had just arrested Mr. Nemazee's son. The general commanded his guards to bring us back to the tennis court. He proceeded to scream at us in Persian. I stood in front of him with my elbow akimbo. "I don't understand a word you are saying," I said when he paused for breath. "My Persian's not good, and you're screaming so much it's impossible to understand you."

He slapped my hands off my hips. "Don't stand like that. Don't you know I'm General of His Majesty's Third Army, and if you disrespect me, you disrespect the Shah."

"I'm certain the Shah would be appalled to see the manner in which his general behaves in public."

"We will see what your father has to say about this!" he yelled, nearly sputtering with rage.

He ordered the MP's to take us to Villa #1 to see my father. Awakened from his daily afternoon nap by the commotion on the tennis courts, my father received us in his Japanese kimono. As my father calmly lit a cigarette, the general began explaining that I had been rude to him and had thrown his son to the ground. Had it not been for the respect he had for my father, the general intimated, I would now be sitting in a military prison. My father listened quietly, took a long drag of his cigarette, then said, "Well, if you think that's what should be done, take him away to prison."

This reduced the general to silence as he contemplated what it would mean to imprison the son of Mohammed Nemazee for an insult on a tennis court. His bluff had been called. After a few more moments of fuming, the general gave up on the idea of arresting Reza and me.

Instead, he drove us in his jeep to his headquarters, where he ended up giving us a tour of the Third Army facilities and showing us a set of newly acquired American tanks. We were all still holding our racquets, inspecting the most modern military equipment in the Middle East. The whole scene felt ridiculous and surreal. I think the general meant to show us what an important personage he was, to be in command of such a powerful arsenal, but it was hard to take him seriously in his tennis whites, especially since we'd just seen him throw a temper tantrum worthy of a toddler.

■ ■ ■

In the summer of 1971, at the end of my junior year of college, I invited two of my closest friends from Landon, David Kixmiller and Howard Burris—both now at Princeton—to join me in Iran for a visit. We met in London, where we were met by several Iranians I'd befriended during my summers in Tehran. Our first night together we went to a wine bar and got rip-roaring drunk. I recall standing on a street corner when a Mercedes convertible pulled up to the curb. In the front seat were two brawny young men, and in the back were two very pretty girls. Somehow I managed to launch myself into the back, landing, with a giant grin, right between the girls. Before their boyfriends could react, Kixmiller and Burris got their hands on me and dragged me out of the convertible. They keeled over with laughter, but my Iranian friends were shocked. My hijinks were something no Iranian, no matter how intoxicated, would ever contemplate. They thought I'd lost my mind.

From London, my American friends and I traveled to Paris, to the South of France, and to Rome, finally arriving in Tehran in mid-August. Immediately after greeting us, my mother told me that we were expected to attend a dinner the following evening at the palace of Princess Shams, older sister of the Shah. My mother and Princess Shams were close friends, and they had been conspiring for some time to encourage a relationship between Princess Shams's daughter and me. The daughter, Shahrazad, was a sweet and pretty girl, but I had no interest in her romantically. Knowing my mother's designs, I objected to the dinner. My mother was adamant we attend.

The next evening, we all drove to Princess Shams's palace, about an hour outside of Tehran. Along the way, I tried to prepare my American friends. For starters, I told them, the palace would be the strangest house they had ever seen. Princess Shams had commissioned the Frank Lloyd Wright Foundation to design a palace of the future. It resembled a flying saucer. Inside was wall-to-wall white carpeting, ultra-modern and very uncomfortable furniture, a wall of birdcages—maybe thirty in total—and no fewer than half a dozen dogs. The noise of the birds and dogs made conversation nearly impossible.

Despite my misgivings, the evening went well. Princess Shams was her most charming if eccentric self, and we had a good time watching a movie with her daughter and two sons. So did they, apparently, because the next day they invited us back to the palace for another dinner and movie. Again, thinking that Princess Shams was trying to tighten the noose around my neck, I declined. My mother told me not to worry. She'd spoken to the Princess that morning and there had been a change of plan. I was not to be Shahrazad's husband after all. Instead, the princess had set her sights on a new match for her daughter: Howard. This news nearly put me on the floor. "I've got good news and bad news," I told Howard when I finally stopped laughing. "Which do you want first?"

The next two weeks were a whirlwind of dinners, water skiing parties, and excursions to the Caspian, all in the company of an entourage of friends, cousins, and minor royalty. By the time we were invited to celebrate the final night of our trip at the Palace of the Queen Mother, it was clear that I was entirely off the hook and that Howard's future with Shahrazad was decided.

Because Shahrazad was the Queen Mother's favorite grandchild, she knew all about Howard and wanted to inspect him herself. She'd decided to host a dinner for us, with her son, the Shah, in attendance.

Off we went to the Queen Mother's palace for drinks and dinner. Howard, David, and I arrived at 7:00 p.m., as instructed, only to find ourselves alone with the Queen Mother in her living room. She wanted to spend some time getting to know Howard. The fact that I, with my still-rudimentary Persian, was meant to translate this interview was amusing enough. Not half as amusing as what followed, though.

The Queen Mother was an elegant but small woman. As she sat on her huge couch, her feet did not quite touch the floor. She was fond of scotch and had the tolerance of a seasoned sailor. As she downed drinks, summoning her servant for a new round for all of us each time she polished one off, I did my best to translate her questions and Howard's answers. She asked about his family, his education, and his ambitions. Finally, via my translation, she asked, "When are you leaving?" To which Howard responded, "Tomorrow."

When I reported Howard's response back to the Queen Mother, she shook her head vigorously. "*Bee khod!*"

"What?" Howard looked over at me. "What did she say?"

"I believe the exact translation is *nonsense*."

"What does that mean, nonsense?"

"It means you aren't going anywhere."

Before Howard could react, a servant entered the room and announced that His Majesty's helicopter was about to land. The Queen Mother drained the last of her scotch and stood, ramrod straight. We followed her lead. We'd been matching her drink for drink, and the moment we were up, it was clear that we were drunk. All of us, that is, except the Queen Mother, who appeared as a sober as when we'd entered forty-five minutes earlier. Fortunately, I'd had some experience with scotch in my life—my father had served it to me since I'd turned 18—so I felt pretty good. Howard, despite the shock of the Queen Mother's pronouncement, also seemed steady, if a bit ashen. But David was clearly plastered. As the Queen Mother charged ahead and we followed, I noticed him swerve a little and put his hand on the back of a chair to regain his equilibrium.

We entered the main hall of the palace. I could hear a helicopter engine somewhere overhead. A few dozen guests, including military officers, members of the royal family, and various other self-important people, had already gathered around the edge of room to await the Shah's entrance. The helicopter engine cut off. The Shah had landed somewhere on the lawn.

At the Queen Mother's direction, we arranged ourselves next to her in the center of the hall to make a reviewing line. David was wobbly, so Howard got on one side and I on another to keep him upright. Shahrazad, looking poised and enviably sober, appeared from a side of the room and joined us, slipping between Howard and the Queen Mother. We all turned to face the large glass front door through which His Majesty would enter at any second. "I don't feel well," David said under his breath. "I'm dizzy."

"Don't worry," I murmured back. "You'll be fine. Try to stand up straight."

"I can't. I think I'm gonna puke."

I looked over at David. He was a curious shade of gray-green. "Keep it together, Kixmiller," I whispered. "Take some deep breaths."

"Seriously, I'm gonna puke. Where's the bathroom?"

Howard and Shahrazad were nervously glancing over at David and me. I gave them a meaningful look that somehow managed to convey that, a) Kixmiller was about to puke, and b) we needed to get him to a bathroom *now*. Shahrazad grasped the situation at once. Gesturing for us to follow, she started across the room. With Howard grabbing one arm and me grabbing the other, we half-dragged, half-carried David after her, passing right through the center of the hall under the astonished glares of the guests.

It was exactly at this moment that the front door opened and the Shah of Iran entered with his entourage. The Shah paused to watch us rush by in front of him. To his credit, he did not flinch but simply waited for us to pass. A second later, we were in a bathroom and Kixmiller was kneeling over a toilet, puking his guts out. Then he cleaned himself up, tightened his tie, and back we all went to formally greet the Shah.

The story did not end that summer. Shahrazad followed Howard back to America, and they eventually married. Howard returned to live in the palace with Princess Shams until the time of the revolution, when they all escaped to California. They survived the revolution, but their marriage did not. They divorced a few years later.

Some years after that, at a dinner at our apartment in New York, Howard turned to my mother with a smile and said, "Mrs. Nemazee, thank you for introducing me to the royal family. You ruined my life."

"Maybe," I said to Howard. "But you saved mine."

6

TRANSFUSION

WHEN MY MOTHER CALLED, I was on a ski trip with friends in Crans, the resort in the Swiss Alps where I had gotten sick as a young child. It was Christmas holiday, 1971. I was a senior at Harvard, still enjoying college life, not yet prepared for what was coming. My mother was in tears and semi-hysterical. Between her sobs, I was finally able to piece together what she was telling me. My father was in the hospital in Tehran. He was in a coma.

By the time I arrived in Tehran the following day, my father had been transferred to Pars Hospital, the newest medical facility in the city. The hospital was so new that my father was one of its first patients. Upon arriving, I discovered that none of the attending doctors had any idea what was wrong with him. More problematically, they were reluctant to take any steps to help him, on the chance that their ministrations might result in his death. Better to let him die than get blamed for killing him.

Over the next several days, as my father remained in a coma, I slept in a reclining chair in his room, showering and shaving in the attached bathroom. When it became clear that nothing at all was going to be done for my father, I realized I needed help. I called Hushang Ansary and explained the situation to him. He immediately set to work to find the best neurologists in New York and London. Within 24 hours, Dr. Fred Plum, from New York Presbyterian Hospital, and Dr. Dennis Wilson, of Harley Street in London, were on airplanes to Tehran.

Dr. Plum was the first to arrive. He insisted on coming directly to the hospital from the airport and never mentioned money. (Dr. Wilson went directly to the Hilton to sleep and billed for every minute.) The Chair of the Department of Neurology at Cornell Medical School, and one of the world's leading experts on brain trauma, Dr. Plum quickly diagnosed a subdural hematoma—a bump on the head, in layman's terms.

My father must have somehow fallen and hit his head, causing a blood clot to develop between his brain and his skull. This in turn had caused the coma. The diagnosis called for an immediate operation to open a small hole in the skull to relieve the pressure brought on by the internal bleeding.

Dr. Plum was not a neurosurgeon and there was no time to bring a surgeon from abroad, so the operation was performed by an Iranian neurosurgeon at Pars Hospital. Within a day, my father had regained consciousness. When informed of the events that resulted in his operation, he became uncharacteristically agitated. He was upset with me for calling in foreign doctors, concerned that this would be interpreted as a criticism of Iranian medicine.

Forty-eight hours after his brain operation, his head bandaged such that he resembled a mullah in a white turban, my father held a press conference in his hospital room. "I would never have allowed my son to call on foreign doctors to come to Iran," he told the press as I stood off to the side. "I would have insisted on being treated by our excellent Iranian doctors." I was not thrilled to be made the scapegoat of this speech, but I understood my father's concern and I stood without objection at his side. And there I remained until he was brought home.

■ ■ ■

I was back at Harvard that March when my father traveled to Shiraz for the Nowruz holidays. My father usually had a house full of guests at the holiday, but this year, still recovering from his operation, he invited just one, the highly esteemed banker and economist Abol Hassan Ebtehaj, one of his oldest and closest friends. Ebtehaj saw that my father was unwell. He insisted that the doctors at Nemazee Hospital come to the villa to examine him. When they did so, they discovered that he had hepatitis. Apparently, during the operation in Tehran, my father had been given a blood transfusion as a precaution. The blood was tainted and my father had contracted hepatitis. Pure bad luck.

On an early spring evening the black rotary phone on my Harvard-issued desk startled me from my studying. It was my mother again, crying. Susie and I must return to Iran at once, she told me. There was no time to waste.

It took me several flights and two full days to get from Boston to Shiraz. I went directly to my father at the villa. He was in bed, my mother and a nurse at his side. It was a shock to see him. He was yellow from jaundice, and quite weak, having lost weight very quickly. He'd also developed bleeding ulcers, possibly from the medication for the jaundice. I called Dr. Plum in New York to tell him what had happened. "Oh, no," he said. When a doctor says, "oh, no," you know the prognosis isn't good.

Having become ill from a blood transfusion he did not need, my father now desperately needed a transfusion he could not get. He had a rare blood type, AB, and Nemazee Hospital did not have an adequate supply of this. An appeal was made on Iranian radio. No name was mentioned, but somehow word spread around Shiraz that the appeal was for my father. By that same afternoon, hundreds, then thousands, of people were lined up outside the hospital to give blood. The line snaked from the door of the main entrance all the way down the long drive of the hospital to a traffic circle called Nemazee Square. It was an astonishing sight, and a testament to the esteem in which my father was held by the citizens of Shiraz.

Despite the blood transfusion, my father continued to decline. My half-sister Shahla came from Venezuela, then Hushang Ansary flew in from abroad. I was outside the room but I could hear my father's last words to Ansary. "*Hushang, man Hassan be dasteh shoma miseparam,*" he said softly. "*Movazebish basheed.*"—Hushang, I put Hassan in your hands, take care of him. Ansary left my father's bedside with tears streaming down his face.

My father insisted on remaining in Villa #1, but after a week, it became necessary to move him into Nemazee Hospital. It was there, in the hospital he built, surrounded by family and friends, that he died on April 9, 1972.

■ ■ ■

I had no time to grieve. No time to think about what my father meant to me, or how his death would change my life. I had dozens of decisions to make immediately. In Iran, funerals are held within 24 hours of death. The memorial service, the burial ceremony, the reception to follow the burial—all of this had to be arranged. My mother was in no condition to handle any decisions. My sister, Susie, and my half-sister, Shahla, were both helpful, but ultimately, as the eldest son and now de facto head of the family, I was expected to assume responsibility.

Long before my father died, he told me that he wanted to be buried on the grounds of the Nemazee Hospital. In Iran, by law, you could only be buried in an official cemetery. These were generally dreary places, as grassless and treeless as parking lots. That was not where my father wanted to be for all of eternity, and not where we wanted him. To inter him on hospital grounds, though, we needed special permission from the government. Within hours of my father's death, I called the Minister of the Royal Court, Asadollah Alam, an old friend of my father's, and asked him if he could obtain the permission. The only one who could grant this, it turned out, was the Shah. An hour later, Alam called back. Not only had the Shah authorized my father's burial, he'd decreed a state funeral with full honors. No matter what else the Shah did or did not do in future years, I would be grateful to him for this kindness.

We buried my father on April 10, 1972. It was one of those spectacular mornings that come to Shiraz in the spring, when the gardens of the city are in bloom, the air fragrant with flowers and spices, the sky cloudless. Inside the Masjed Vakil, hundreds of mourners squeezed together under the mosque's vaulting tiled arches and stained-glass windows. I sat in the middle of a row of chairs, alongside cabinet ministers and high-ranking military officers sent by the Shah to pay their last respects. Jamshid Amouzegar, the Minister of Finance, was there, as was Mr. Alam, Minister of Court. General Minbashian, my foul-tempered nemesis from the tennis court, came in full dress uniform as representative of the Imperial Iranian Army.

The chief ayatollah of Shiraz was there, too, in his flowing robe and long beard. He stood on a raised platform, talking into a microphone. My limited Persian made it difficult for me to follow everything he was saying, but as he spoke, it was clear that he was becoming increasingly strident and agitated. I could feel bodies around me stirring uncomfortably. Listening closely, I realized that the ayatollah was complimenting my father—his benevolence, his generosity—but at the same time harshly criticizing the very men sitting by my side. My father had made his fortune outside of the country, declared the ayatollah, but had been far more generous to Shiraz than many who lived closer to home. Peering down on the wealthy men sitting near me, the ayatollah scolded them, and, by extension, the Shah himself, for their greed and lack of charity.

Even with my poor Persian and still-limited knowledge of Iranian politics, I recognized this as shocking. Until very recently, it would have been unthinkable for a mullah, even an ayatollah, to cast aspersions on the Shah. Only later would I come to understand what I witnessed on that April morning in 1972. These were the first tremors of the religious groundswell that would overtake Iran within a few years.

For the moment, before anyone could take too much offense, the ayatollah himself inadvertently broke the tension. He turned to me and gestured. "And here is Haj Nemazee's son, Hassan," he said. "Hassan has returned to us from America, where he is studying at America's most prestigious university, the University of Hollywood." A chuckle rippled through the mosque. The university I attended was Harvard, not Hollywood. Clearly something had gotten lost in translation.

I led the mourners out of the mosque after the ceremony. My father's body had been wrapped in white cloth and placed in a simple wooden casket to carry him to his final resting place. Our plan for the funeral procession was simple: from the mosque, we would carry my father's body to a hearse, then drive in a cortege to the hospital compound for the internment. But as we filed out into the courtyard, it became apparent that our plan would have to be scrapped. Before us stood a vast sea of people. They and tens of thousands of other Shirazis had listened to the funeral as it was broadcast from speakers around the mosque. Now they had come to claim my father. They surged forward and took hold of the casket.

Before we could object, we found ourselves at the front of an extraordinary procession, walking in the direction of the hospital. The crowd transported the casket with my father's shrouded body, raising it overhead, surfing it along a wave of hands and shoulders. Many in the crowd were weeping, others wailing. The distance to Nemazee Hospital was no fewer than five miles, and as we advanced the crowd continued to gather people from the streets and alleys of Shiraz. Together, these many thousands made a mob, but it was an orderly and benevolent mob. I would often recall it later, when mobs in Iran began to behave very differently.

A large crowd was already gathered around Nemazee Hospital when we arrived. Somehow it parted to let us through to the gravesite. My father's shrouded body was lifted from the casket and lowered into the hole that had been dug by permission of the Shah. The mullah read from the Koran. The crowd of thousands wept quietly. Altogether, it was an extraordinary farewell to my father from the city he loved.

7

A VISIT TO NIAVARAN

It was mid-April. I'd been absent from Harvard for a month. Some of this time had overlapped with my spring break, but I'd still missed several weeks of class. I needed to return so I could graduate in June. But before I could return to Boston, I had to deal with a few matters regarding my father's business and charitable interests. It was clear that some of these could not be put off. If our family wanted to preserve and maintain control of my father's legacy, it was up to us—and specifically me—to do it.

It turned out that my mother had already put considerable time and thought into what needed to be done. Before my father's death, she'd taken steps to ensure that I'd be in a strong position to take over and lead his several philanthropic organizations, which operated under the umbrella of Bonyad Iran. There was an Iranian trust instrument, called a *vaqf*, that had named my father as the original trustee with the sole authority to name a successor. After my father's recovery from his brain surgery, my mother had convinced him to name me *Motevalli*—Trustee, that is—of the *vaqf*. Some members of the board had opposed this, on the grounds that I was too young and inexperienced to be given such authority, but my mother insisted. As a result, upon my father's death, I was suddenly in control of Bonyad Iran. This was control in name only, though. For it to mean anything, I had to use it. And that is what I intended to do.

I requested an audience with the Shah. Primarily, I wanted to thank him for allowing my father to be buried on the hospital grounds, among several other kindnesses he had extended to our family. I had an ulterior motive, too.

On a bright day in April, I went to Niavaran, the Shah's new palace in the northern foothills of Tehran. My father's cousin, Mehdi Nemazee—a senator in the Iranian parliament at the time—accompanied me. We drove to the palace in Mehdi's large sedan, chauffeured by his tiny driver, a man so small his feet barely touched the pedals and his eyes barely cleared the top of the steering wheel.

Arriving at the palace, a stark white two-story building surrounded by acres of grass and trees, we were ushered into a vast room with the largest and the most exquisite Persian carpet I'd ever seen. The room was warm; the Shah considered air conditioning unhealthy and never used it. Thankfully, the summer heat was still a month or two away. The Shah was behind his large desk, a French antique. He stood and came to us. This was clearly meant to be a brief meeting. He did not ask us to sit, despite the fact that Mehdi was a frail 75-year-old.

I'd met the Shah at various functions since the awkward party at the Queen Mother's house. He was unfailingly polite and always seemed genuinely curious about student life in America; he'd ask me questions, and I'd do my best to answer. Now the Shah told me how saddened he was by my father's death. He spoke about the many contributions my father had made to Iran, both his philanthropic gifts and his long public service. He then turned to Mehdi and asked him who had been older, my father or he? Mehdi was flustered and the question seemed to throw him. "I was ten years younger," he declared. The Shah looked puzzled. "*Ajab*," he said. Incredible. I knew enough Persian to realize that my cousin had misspoken. I explained to the Shah, in English, that there'd been just one year's difference in age between Mehdi and my father.

I then continued to speak English, in which the Shah was fluent. Prior to my audience, it had occurred to me that I should take the opportunity to discuss the hospital and waterworks. I launched into the speech I'd prepared in my head on the drive out to Niavaran. The hospital was in need of significant capital improvements and expansion beyond its existing 250 beds, I explained. The waterworks' profitability was being artificially restrained by the municipality's efforts to keep water rates artificially low. If we could raise the water rates, we could produce enough revenue to support the hospital's financial needs and allow the hospital to pay for itself, independent of the university, as originally intended by my father.

My speech went on for several minutes. As I spoke, the Shah considered me with his usual opaque expression, but he was patient and allowed me to finish. He then gave me a very slight smile, either of encouragement or bemusement. "I'll have the Minister of Water and Power look into your suggestions." With that, he turned back to his desk. Our audience was over.

Needless to say, the Minister never contacted me. Mehdi was astonished and a little abashed by my temerity in addressing the Shah. But I felt that I had done my duty to my father. I had tried anyway.

■ ■ ■

I found it difficult to resume my life as an undergraduate that spring. I was no longer the happy-go-lucky college student I'd been when I arrived at Harvard. In addition to mourning my father, I had to think through what his death meant for my future. I was pointedly aware that my role as his heir gave me great opportunities, but also great responsibilities. Suddenly, every decision I made mattered tremendously.

Upon my return to Boston, I learned that I'd been accepted at the Harvard Business School for the Masters Degree Program beginning in September. When I'd applied in the fall, going to business school had been the obvious move. Nothing was obvious now. Should I attend business school, or should I return to Iran? Was I to continue my life as an American with ties to Iran, or was it time to embrace my Iranian citizenship and heritage? Where, for the sake of my father's legacy and my own future, did I belong?

I was working hard to catch up on school after my long absence when Hushang Ansary called to see how I was doing. I shared some of the issues I'd been mulling over since my father's death. After a few minutes, he interrupted. "Look, I'm going to be in the Bahamas this weekend with Maryam and the children. Why don't you come down and we'll talk it through. I'll arrange a ticket for you." Despite the tower of books looming at the corner of my desk, I took him up on the invitation. I understood instinctively that a few days with Hushang would be as valuable as any academic work.

As we strolled the white sand beach, Hushang walked me through my alternatives. He made a strong case for returning to Iran. Not only would I be doing a service for my father's legacy, Hushang insisted, but my experience in Iran would be an education worth several business school degrees. The country was embarking on a massive program of industrialization, a once-in-a-generation opportunity for a young man. Indeed, if he were to give away every dime of his already considerable wealth, he contended, he could make it back, and then some, in the next five years in Iran—that's how explosive growth was going to be.

Hushang was very convincing. He was also absolutely correct, at least regarding the next few years. Indeed, his prediction would turn out to be more prophetic than even he could have known. By the end of that weekend with the Ansarys, I'd decided my future would be in Iran.

I finished my academic career on a high note, graduating with honors. I felt enormously proud and satisfied that I'd taken full advantage of everything that both Tufts and Harvard had to offer. I'd done exactly what I'd planned to do, and had achieved more that I'd ever hoped.

I contacted the Business School and informed them of my decision to return to Iran to attend to my father's affairs and business. The school agreed to grant me a deferral. This meant I could return to Iran and still attend the MBA program the following year without having to reapply. As events turned out, I never did make it back to Harvard.

■ ■ ■

Before returning to Tehran after graduation, I met my friend Cyrus Ardalan for a brief holiday in Spain, a final lark before accepting the responsibilities of my new role as my father's heir in Iran. I was still in Madrid when a message at the hotel reception desk advised me to call my mother immediately. These sorts of phone calls had brought ill-tidings in the past so I dialed my mother with trepidation.

Fortunately, her news was good this time. I'd received a proposal concerning Hassan's Farm, the 520-acre dairy farm in Germantown, Maryland, 30 miles outside of Washington, that my father had purchased when I was born—where he'd hosted Mosaddegh in 1951, and where we spent many happy weekends during my childhood. The farm was not only named after me; it was mine in name. My father had put it in trust for me, so that it would be a kind of birthright when I came of age. By the 1970's, it had become very valuable real estate.

As much as I would have liked to hold onto the farm for sentimental reasons, it would have been financially foolhardy to do so. For one thing, this land was the primary inheritance I'd received from my father. Though he had been a wealthy man, he'd made a point of giving away the great majority of his wealth, as much as 90% of it, to his philanthropies. Furthermore, Germantown had become an area of booming development. Office complexes and residential subdivisions were rising all around it now. Any last remnants of rural charm had been stripped from the farm when the Atomic Energy Agency built its headquarters immediately adjacent to it.

Over the previous few years, I'd been approached by various local developers anxious to get their hands on the property. To field these offers, I'd hired Henry Fox, the senior partner of one of Washington's leading law firms, Arent Fox. Additionally, I called on Cy Ansary, Hushang's brother—a prominent Washington attorney—for his advice. Now, according to my mother, Fox had received a credible proposal that deserved my serious and immediate consideration.

I flew at once to Washington. It turned out that a new real estate development firm, Stanley Martin Communities, had made a strong joint venture proposal. Stanley Martin would put up all the cash to finalize the zoning application, file all necessary papers, and guide one of suburban Washington's largest development projects. I would retain a minimum 50% interest in the project while handing off both the costs and logistical challenges.

Altogether, it was a great deal for me. After a few weeks of negotiations, we signed a joint venture agreement, and I left Washington to begin my new life in Tehran.

8

MY FATHER'S SHOES

For all the time I'd spent in Iran over summers, the truth is that I'd always experienced the country as a visitor. That changed now. No longer was I working at a low-stakes summer job and enjoying myself with friends. I was in Iran to make my way in the world—and to make my home.

I lived at first in my father's house in northern Tehran, which now belonged, per my father's wishes, to Susie. The house was large but not at all ostentatious. The rooms were furnished simply but elegantly, and the garden out back, enclosed by a ring of plain trees and a row of cedars, was an oasis of cool shade on even the most blistering days.

Before turning to my own future, I wanted to put my father's past in order. This required organizing the business papers and correspondence my father had left behind in his office downtown. Included in this great cache of documents was an enormous typed manuscript, several feet high when the pages were stacked. My father had spent much of the last ten years of his life writing a history of civilization, in Persian. He wrote in hand, then his secretary turned his work into a typescript. In many of my memories of him in these latter years, he is sitting at his desk with pen and paper, a cigarette between his lips, or he is in his rocking chair reading a book, a cigarette slowly burning between his fingers. I had often asked him when he expected to finish his tome. He'd invariably smile and say, "I'm still working on it." In truth, I think he would have continued working on it until the day he died, no matter when that day came. I decided that one of my first projects would be to publish what he'd written.

Beyond that, my first serious task as his heir was to have myself installed as Trustee of Bonyad Iran, the organization my father had founded 25 years earlier to oversee the hospital. I needed to be legally confirmed by a vote of the Board of Trustees. This was pro forma but significant, as it would be my public debut as my father's successor. My father had structured the board to ensure that the Iranian government had a stake in the hospital, so the board consisted of numerous senior members of the government presiding *ex officio*—the Prime Minister, the Minister of the Royal Court, the Minister of Health, the Minister of Water and Power, the Minister of Justice, the Director of the Plan Organization, to name a few. In addition, there were a number of senior Iranian businessmen and former government officials. I would be under the scrutiny of some of the most powerful men in Iran.

A general assembly of the board was scheduled. Not only would this be my first appearance before the board, it would be my first attempt to speak publicly in Persian. I was taking Persian language classes with a private tutor, but I was by no means fluent.

I discussed what I intended to say with the foundation's counsel, a lawyer named Sadrezadeh. He offered to write the speech for me, based on my thoughts. He would have the Persian transliterated, he said, so that I could deliver it phonetically. I agreed to this proposal. This turned out to be a mistake. Unbeknownst to me, Sadrezadeh had wanted to be named as the Trustee himself and still harbored that ambition. What he handed back to me was filled with so many formal Persian and Arabic words that it would have been difficult to deliver for someone as eloquent as my father. It was an effective work of sabotage.

Per tradition, the meeting was held at my father's—now Susie's—house in northern Tehran. The day was sunny and warm. The board members sat on the patio in a circle, a table with a bowl of fruit and drinks in front of each. When it came time for me to deliver my speech, I stood.

I knew it was going badly from the moment I began talking. I could feel the eyes of the trustees on me as I sputtered through tortured Persian. If the speech was a struggle to deliver, I'm sure it was even harder to sit through. Imagine a modern American audience hearing a bloated oration delivered in Elizabethan English—by a non-English speaker, no less—and you can appreciate how my audience must have suffered.

One benefit of having so many politicians on the board was that they were well-practiced at sitting through lousy and boring speeches, so their faces betrayed none of the stupefaction I'm sure they felt as I droned on and on. Of far greater benefit—to me—was the fact that many of them had been good friends of my father's and wanted me to succeed on his behalf. They applauded charitably when I was finally done. A vote was taken to make my position official. By unanimous consent, I was now the Trustee, Chairman of the Nemazee Hospital, and Chairman of the Shiraz Water Company. My first act as Trustee was to remove my saboteur, Sadrezadeh, from Bonyad Iran.

■ ■ ■

Almost immediately, I faced a more significant test of my ability to fill my father's shoes. Under the agreement between Pahlavi University and my father, the chancellor of the university could fire the director of Nemazee Hospital at any time without the consent of the Trustee. In order to appoint a new director, though, he needed joint consent of the Trustee, meaning that I had veto power.

Shortly after I joined the board, the chancellor decided to remove the hospital director, Dr. Khalil Alavi, a man who had been close and loyal to my father. I was unhappy with this decision, but legally there was nothing I could do about it. The chancellor nominated a replacement for Dr. Alavi. After consulting with several doctors who had worked with my father, I came to believe that the replacement was a poor choice. I indicated my opposition. The chancellor was shocked that I would presume to interfere in his decision and pressured me to withdraw my opposition. But I stood firm. I believed that if I gave in, he'd take it as license to run roughshod over the hospital now that my father was gone.

I went to see Abol Hassan Ebtehaj, the chairman of Iranians' Bank at the time. Having been one of my father's closest friends, Ebtehaj was now the mentor on whom I most relied. After some discussion, he suggested that I ask to be made a member of the Board of Trustees of Pahlavi University. A seat on the university board might not give me much actual power, but it would give me something even more important: *proximity*. "In Iran, everything is based on the illusion of power, which is based on how close you are to the court and the Shah," Ebtehaj told me. "It's unfortunate, but it's true." He suggested that I approach Asadollah Alam, the Minister of Court, and see what could be done.

I took Ebtehaj's advice. I requested and was granted an appointment by Alam. Meeting him in his large, opulent office, I explained my desire to be named to the board of the university. Alam crossed his hands and smiled. "Very wise," he said. "I will ask his Imperial Majesty if it can be done." Within weeks, a *farman*—an Imperial Order—was issued placing me on the board of Pahlavi University. It sent an immediate message to the chancellor and others in Shiraz that I had the support of the Imperial Court.

■ ■ ■

Now I focused on what I wanted to do for employment. A job at Fakhr Iran was an option but not a terribly attractive one. After my summer at the textile factory, I'd come to realize that I was not temperamentally suited to management in a large enterprise with thousands of employees. My experience of selling the farm in Maryland had given me a taste for real estate development; I'd found it exciting and thought I might have a talent for it. I also thought that Iran was the perfect place to cut my teeth. The country was growing rapidly, and both housing and commercial development were bound to expand.

Just as I was mulling all of this over, the world underwent one of those periodic seismic jolts that suddenly, in a matter of weeks, shift the ground entirely. In this case, the precipitating cause was the so-called "oil crisis" of 1973.

Prior to 1973, world oil prices had been steady and predictable, at about $2 per barrel. At best, half of that, or $1 per barrel, went to the oil-producing countries such as Iran. A five-nation trade alliance of oil-producing countries—four from the Middle East, plus Venezuela—known as the Organization of Petroleum Exporting Countries, or OPEC, had been formed in 1960 but to little practical effect on setting world oil prices.

Then came 1973. That October, Egypt launched an invasion of Israel, setting off the Yom Kippur War. Anwar Sadat, Egypt's president, had planned the invasion to coincide with the Jewish holiday, expecting to gain an element of surprise. He succeeded beyond his wildest expectations. Had the Nixon administration not acted with great speed, resupplying and fortifying the Israelis, the Arabs might have triumphed. As it was, Egypt's invasion focused the world's attention on long festering Arab-Israeli issues and highlighted the extreme significance of the region to U.S. interests.

One immediate by-product of the war was that OPEC, once innocuous but now emboldened, imposed an international oil embargo to punish the U.S. and other countries for aiding the Israelis. This caused a dramatic increase in world oil prices, mainly to the benefit of OPEC nations. In the west and Japan—that is, nations dependent on OPEC oil—inflation raged, economies contracted, and stock markets fell. Meanwhile, treasuries in the Middle East overflowed with newfound wealth.

The Shah hesitated to join the embargo at first. But as oil prices doubled, and then quadrupled, he came around. In these higher revenues he could envision the possibility of restoring Iran to its former imperial glory. Plans for massive capital spending on infrastructure went from fantasy to reality almost overnight. Tehran became the destination of choice for Western bankers, businessmen, builders, and manufacturers who hoped to cash in, bringing with them an influx of expertise and more capital.

In retrospect, all this was not in Iran's long-term benefit. It was too disruptive, both financially and culturally. Ultimately, it would cost the Shah his throne. For the moment, though, Iran was thriving, and I was eager to thrive with it.

My background, my youth, and my drive made me perfectly positioned to do so. I was Iranian but American-educated and western-oriented. I was young but had a family name that opened doors in Iran and elsewhere. The only thing I lacked was cash. Owning valuable land in Washington and manufacturing assets in Iran made for a good balance sheet on paper, but without liquidity there was not much I could do to take advantage of new financial opportunities. Just then, as if summoned by the mercurial spirits of capitalism, some cash appeared.

The Shah was indirectly responsible for my windfall. A man who couched his imperial vanities in idealistic aspirations, he was at this time attempting to institute a number of political, economic, and social reforms in Iran. One of his reforms was meant to broaden the ownership of Iran's manufacturing sector while curtailing corruption by his government officials. The Shah decreed that employees of industrial businesses were to become shareholders in those businesses. Furthermore, no member of the government could own an industrial business.

Hushang Ansary, my father's old friend and now another important mentor to me, was Minister of Economy at this time. He also remained a large shareholder in Fakhr Iran, the textile company founded by my mother that he had turned around from near bankruptcy to a soaring success. Under the Shah's new order, he was required to divest himself of the company. One day Ansary called me to ask if I would be interested in selling my shares, and my family's shares, in Fakhr Iran—that is, to sell the company entirely. The prospective buyer, said Ansary, was the Iranian military, which intended to use the factory to make uniforms. Their offer price was generous. The sale would provide me with liquidity and would provide Susie and my mother with capital that would give them a lifetime of security and independence.

I gave Ansary the go-ahead. Within a matter of months, I had all the cash I needed to move forward.

■ ■ ■

Meanwhile, I'd settled on a business plan that was ambitious, perhaps even audacious, but also, I believed, quite practical. I intended to focus on three sectors of investment: real estate, banking, and insurance. As I saw it, each of these would complement the others.

Real estate development was the leading edge of my plan. I agreed with Hushang Ansary that Iran, with its newfound oil wealth, was poised for massive expansion, which would compel residential and commercial development. The money to fund this development would have to be supplied by both equity and debt. If I were able to control a bank and an insurance company—a combination prohibited in America for regulatory reasons but perfectly legal in Iran at the time—I would be in a unique position to capitalize on Iran's growth.

I incorporated my first company, the Development Corporation of Iran (DCI), in 1974, when I was 24. At the time, both commercial and residential development were undertaken quite haphazardly in Iran. Buildings were often constructed without the benefit of architects or engineers. Most were built by contractors who relied on boilerplate plans. The system was referred to in Iran as *Besaz, Befroosh*. Build and Sell. Little attention was given to design or structural innovation, much less to structural integrity. Only major government buildings, or significant private sector buildings, such as Iranians' Bank Building—where I had my office—were professionally developed. My plan was for DCI to fill this vacuum. We would be professional developers of commercial, residential, and retail projects.

I'd remained in contact with J.C. von Helms, the tutor whose collection of leather-bound classics once adorned my bookshelves at Harvard. J.C. was no longer the tweedy graduate student I'd met in the hall of Winthrop House. He'd gone from Harvard to the Nixon White House to be Vice President Spiro Agnew's speechwriter, where his main claim to fame—according to J.C.[3]— was dreaming up Agnew's famous alliterative description of left-wingers as "nattering nabobs of negativism." J.C. had left the White House after Agnew was forced to resign for ethical lapses. He'd moved to Houston, Texas, where he now worked for Gerald Hines, one of the most successful real estate developers in America. The American economy was functionally in the tank, though, so no development opportunities existed in Texas. I suggested to J.C. that he move to Iran for a while and work with me as a partner in DCI. In turn, J.C. suggested that I travel to Texas to meet with potential partners for Iranian ventures.

I arrived in Houston in sizzling August, not an ideal time to visit southern Texas. Even compared to Tehran, summertime Houston was hard to endure. (Years later, under very different circumstances, I would suffer through an un-air-conditioned Lone Star August and come to know first-hand just how brutal it was.) Von Helms met me at the airport, then had us flown by helicopter to downtown Houston, giving us a bird's eye view of the city. He also arranged for me to be presented with a certificate signed by the Governor of Texas recognizing me as an "Honorary Citizen of Texas."

More to the point of my visit, he'd scheduled back-to-back meetings with potential partners. Our meeting with Leo Linbeck

---

[3] Credit for this line usually goes to Nixon speechwriter William Safire, but von Helms swore it was his.

Jr. clearly stood out. Linbeck was the second-generation owner/manager of his family's construction business. He and his father had turned Linbeck Construction into Houston's largest construction firm, and one of the largest in Texas and the southeast. He was quick to agree to a joint venture. We would call it Linbeck Iran.

By this time, I'd identified several major projects for DCI to develop. The first of these was in Tehran, where the Shah had designated a former military compound to be master planned for residential and retail space. The Shah named the project "Shahestan Pahlavi." I intended to build a complex of office buildings there. Secondly, I wanted to create my own master plan for a large tract of land in Shiraz. Controlled by Bonyad Iran, the land was close to the hospital compound on a hill overlooking the city, directly across from an old Qajar Palace now used by the Shah on his official visits to Shiraz. Finally, I wanted to develop a tract of land I'd recently purchased at a ski resort called Gajereh, in the Alborz mountains. Just an hour's drive from Tehran, Gajereh had good ski conditions from November thru March. The Chalet Gajereh, as I intended to call it, was located on an orchard at the foot of mountains, with a river running through the property. It was a lovely site.

Looking back all these years later, I am amazed by that young man I was. Still in my mid-20's, just a few years out of college, I was bursting with big plans and confident I could pull them off. I was so sure of success, so unacquainted with failure.

9

PROSPECTS

Iran continued to offer a bounty of possibilities through the 1970's. By mid-decade, my company employed about twenty full-time staff. We worked in a suite of offices in the Iranian's Bank Building, the first modern office building in Tehran. Days went to putting together deals. Nights and weekends went to a busy social life.

Much of my socializing in these years was done in the company of the royal family. Princess Shams—whose daughter had now married my friend Howard Burris—insisted that I come to her Friday night movie parties, where we watched first-run releases directly from America. There was always a dazzling crowd in attendance. I remember one night seeing a gorgeous young blond woman sitting by herself. As I moved to approach her, Prince Mahmoud Reza, the Shah's younger brother, swooped in and took the seat next to her. I asked Ardeshir Zahedi—Iran's Ambassador to Washington at the time—who she was. "I invited her to come to Iran," Zahedi told me. "Her name is Candice Bergen." (Years later, I had another occasion to meet Candice Bergen, when her daughter, Chloe Malle, turned out to be one of my daughter's roommates at Brown University.)

Occasionally, I was invited to the palace of the Shah for social gatherings. I always found it amusing to watch the interaction between the Shah and members of Iranian society. Conversation came to a halt whenever His Majesty began to speak to someone, as everyone else eavesdropped for morsels to gossip about later. For his part, the Shah always appeared to be on stage, performing a role he did not particularly enjoy. He was a complete contrast to some of the natural politicians I came to know later, such as Bill Clinton. While Clinton had the good fortune to achieve the job for which he had been born, the Shah had the misfortune to be born into a job for which he was poorly suited.

One paradox of the Shah's doomed reign is that, for all of his flaws as a leader, he did in fact change the country for the better in some ways. In addition to his attempts to improve the economy for Iranians of all classes, he undertook social reforms such as expanding women's rights. Women were starting to come into their own in Iran in the 1970's, with new liberties and opportunities. It was a good time to be a young woman and, consequently, a good time to be a young man. I dated a number of beautiful and free-spirited young women in these years. If we did not socialize with quite the abandon of young Americans or Western Europeans at the time, we lived with a blitheness that would be unimaginable to Iranians in later years.

One day, out of the blue, I received a letter from a young Iranian woman named Sheila whom I had not seen for a few years. Sheila had been living in the United States, attending the University of Southern California. She'd graduated from college and was now finishing a master's degree. She wrote me a multi-page, single-spaced letter on yellow legal paper. Her letter began with belated condolences for my father's death and ended by informing me that she might be soon returning to Iran to live and work. She hoped that I was well and that she looked forward to seeing me. "Sheila," she signed her letter, "if you've forgotten."

I'd met Sheila years earlier, when she was a teenager and had just returned from a two-week holiday on the Caspian Sea, looking tanned and beautiful. Later, we'd engaged in some flirting and dancing. All that had happened years ago, but I remembered her very well.

Sheila called me when she returned to Tehran. We agreed to go to dinner. She was more mature, of course, but still beautiful. Following a series of dinners, tennis and water-skiing parties, and horseback-rides in the country, I asked her to join me on a ski holiday to Switzerland. We skied, lunched on the mountain, and relaxed in the hotel in the evenings. By the time I returned to Tehran, I'd decided to ask Sheila to marry me.

■ ■ ■

Just as the pieces of my personal and professional life were coming together in Iran, I received a call from Henry Fox in Washington. He informed me that I had a problem with my joint venture to develop the farm in Maryland. It turned out that Montgomery County, where my land was located, had experienced such rapid growth and development that the county's Board of Supervisors had decided to institute a freeze. While zoning in Montgomery County was "as of right," meaning that the county could not legally stop or impede the conversion of open land to a developable project, the supervisors had gotten creative and imposed a sewer moratorium. No connections would be permitted to the existing sewer system. The county claimed that there was no capacity. In fact, this was an excuse to stop development in its tracks.

I flew to Washington to meet with my partners at Stanley Martin. The company's founder, Marty Alloy, was in a bind. He'd expended significant funds on the zoning, permits, and architectural plans, but the sewer moratorium prevented him from proceeding. Under our contract, he had to meet certain deadlines to maintain his interest in the project. Clearly, he was not going to meet these. I agreed to renegotiate his deadlines and extend his time.

I met a better result when I shuttled from Washington to New York. In pursuit of my plan to start an insurance company in Iran, I'd managed to set up meetings with top executives at three of the largest insurance companies in America—Met Life, New York Life, and Mass Mutual. None were interested in investing in Iran, it turned out, but several of the executives I met advised me to talk to AIG, a company that was already heavily invested abroad. AIG (American International Group) had been established in Hong Kong and Shanghai in the early 1900's, around the same time my grandfather had moved to China. Now run by the remarkable Hank Greenberg, AIG operated in America but remained focused on insurance operations in countries outside the United States.

When I returned to Tehran, I mentioned AIG to Ebtehaj at one of our weekly lunches. He became quite animated. An executive from Citibank had just called him to suggest that *he* meet with Hank Greenberg. Ebtehaj suggested that we work as partners and approach AIG together to establish a joint venture insurance company. I loved this idea.

At the time, Hank Greenberg was not yet a household name, but he was already a legend in the insurance industry. A former

Marine, he was a tiny but fierce man with ramrod posture and a no-nonsense manner. One of the benefits of putting together a deal with AIG was the chance it gave me to visit Greenberg regularly at his offices on Maiden Lane in Manhattan.

In those days, the AIG staff was still largely Chinese, many having come to New York from Hong Kong. The office atmosphere was formal and cool, but Greenberg was a gracious host, sending his personal car to bring me to private lunches in his office, where we worked through the details of our possible deal. He ate the same plain meal everyday—scrod and vegetables—but lunches with Greenberg were never dull. As he ate, he peppered me with probing questions about the people and economy of Iran. We discussed the fact that very few insurance companies operated in Iran. For some reason, there persisted a belief that insurance products would not appeal to the Muslim world, on the theory that Muslims were fatalistic and therefore would be less likely to buy insurance. We had a tremendous opportunity, I told Greenberg, to prove the conventional wisdom wrong.

Every conversation with Greenberg felt like a test. Apparently, I passed, because we soon had an agreement for a joint venture. The venture would be divided in ownership, 49% by AIG and 51% by the Iranian partners. We named our collaboration the Iran America International Insurance Company.

As we were finalizing the joint venture terms, Greenberg informed us that he had the perfect candidate for the position of Managing Director of the company. His name was Shahbani, and he was an Iranian-American insurance executive who happened to work in the San Francisco office of AIG Not only would Shahbani serve as Managing Director, Greenberg informed us, he would purchase 5% of the company's stock.

By this point, I knew that Greenberg, though always civil in our encounters, was extremely shrewd and competitive. It was clear to me what he intended. He wanted his own man in management and he wanted to effectively control the company. Combining AIG's 49% share and Shahbani's 5% share would give him a controlling interest of 54%. This was a tricky situation. Accepting Greenberg's proposal would take the company out of our hands and hurt our profits. But turning him down might risk igniting his famous temper and, worse, his withdrawal from the deal.

I sought a third solution, one that would prevent Greenberg's ploy but also avoid a confrontation. As I so often did when faced with a quandary in those days, I called Hushang Ansary. Once again, Ansary came to my aid.

As Minister of Finance, Ansary was responsible for regulating the financial industry, a purview which included issuing licenses to insurance companies. The ministry also was responsible for implementing the laws that controlled the percentage that foreign entities could own in financial institutions. The maximum at the time was 49%. I told Ansary of Greenberg's evident scheme. It was likely that the intent of the law would be undermined if Shahbani, an employee of AIG, were to assume an additional 5% and effectively give AIG majority control.

Ansary listened intently. This was a timely discussion, he told me, as the ministry was at that very moment reviewing the current status of foreign ownership in financial institutions. Sure enough, two months later, the ministry announced that foreign ownership would henceforth be limited to 35%. Problem solved. Greenberg was furious, but he had no idea that I'd had anything to do with this, and he had no choice but to accept it.

■ ■ ■

Iran America International Insurance Company grew very quickly. The property casualty business was immediately profitable, largely due to our association with AIG. We also established a life insurance business. We'd begun with the expectation that it would take five years to break even. We were profitable in eighteen months. Iranians turned out to be as interested in protecting themselves against risks as anyone.

To balance Greenberg and AIG, we'd brought a couple of Iranian investors into the insurance company. One of these was a man named Iravani. Known in Iran as a *bazzari*—an insult for someone who made his money in the bazaars and lacked polish—he was in fact an astute businessman. Iravani realized that his investment in the company was very valuable, and could be significantly *more* valuable if he could gain majority control of the company. He called on me and asked if I would sell my position to him for a significant premium. I politely declined and advised Ebtehaj to do the same. Then Iravani came up with another ploy.

Hank Greenberg flew to Tehran every year to attend our annual board meeting. In deference to Greenberg, the meetings were usually conducted in English. Iravani demanded that the next one be in Persian. Ebtehaj was hesitant but agreed; he arranged for a translator. On the day of the meeting, which was always held in a conference room at the Iranians' Bank Building, I told Ebtehaj that I had a feeling we were in for a show, if not a showdown.

Sure enough, five minutes into the meeting, Iravani asked Ebtehaj for permission to speak. He addressed himself first to the translator. "Please translate exactly what I say to Mr. Greenberg." Then he turned to Greenberg. "Mr. Greenberg, you are a thief," he said in measured Persian. "You are taking advantage of our small insurance company." He waited for the translator to say the words in English, then continued. "Your company reinsures all of our company's lines of insurance thru AIG RE." (AIG RE was AIG's reinsurance company, which provided reinsurance of all of Iran American's insurance needs). "I have priced what AIG charges us, and compared that with what we would be charged by all of the other reinsurance companies. You are stealing from your partners."

As Greenberg listened to the translator, he turned beet red. He'd probably never been addressed like this in his life, certainly not in front of his employees and members of the board. Somehow hearing the words through a translator made them even more noxious.

I had yet to see one of Greenberg's legendary outbursts in person, but I'd read about them, and now I had a front row seat. "You ungrateful son of a bitch!" Greenberg suddenly exploded. "You have no idea about how to run an insurance company! If it wasn't for AIG being a partner in this business, no reinsurance company in the world would quote you a price. Everything we've accomplished is because of AIG! You accuse me of taking advantage? Well, if that's how you feel, I'll sell our stock, and then you can see what it's like to operate a penny ante business."

"Fine, I'll buy your stock," said Iravani with a smile. "Name your price."

Greenberg shot to his feet. "I am going to airport!" He strode out of the room.

Greenberg had reacted exactly as Iravani hoped he would. I leaned over to Ebtehaj. "You have to stop him," I whispered. "If you don't, you and I will be minority partners of Iravani's."

Ebtehaj understood at once. He rushed off to the airport, where he managed to catch Greenberg before he boarded his plane. He soothed Greenberg's feelings and put an end to the threat to sell A.I.G's stock. The episode had provided a unique lesson in boardroom management, though. Iravani, a self-taught Iranian businessman, one generation removed from the bazaar, had nearly out-maneuvered Hank Greenberg, one of America's leading financial geniuses. He'd found Greenberg's Achilles Heel—his thin skin—and attacked it.

■ ■ ■

Hiccups notwithstanding, both my development company and insurance company were operating with early success and good prospects. To bring my full plan to fruition, I hoped to add one more endeavor—the third leg of my stool, as it were. This was to be a commercial bank.

American and European securities laws had legislatively split up insurance, banking, and corporate ownership. You could not control a bank and an insurance company and also be the owner of an industrial or other business. In Iran, there were no such limitations, which presented a huge opportunity. The premium income from insurance operations, coupled with the resources of a bank, would provide all the capital I needed for my cash hungry real estate development business.

I had a relationship with the British merchant bank, Morgan Grenfell. David Suratgar, the former Columbia Law student who had visited us on Glenbrook Road as a young man, was now a managing director of Morgan Grenfell, as was another friend, David Douglas Hume. When I visited England, Hume—son of Sir Alec Douglas Hume, the former Prime Minister—invited Suratgar and me to a weekend of shooting at his country estate in Scotland. We sat by the fire in his immense 16th-century manor house and talked about the bank project and my desire to find the right international partner. Because Morgan Grenfell was a merchant bank, not a commercial bank, they could not help me directly. But Hume and Suratgar suggested that I talk to Morgan Guaranty Trust of New York, the U.S. commercial bank with which Morgan Grenfell had historic ties. Even better, they arranged for me to meet with the head of the international division of Morgan, Lewis Preston.

Preston was a somber old-school banker, cut from a stiff cloth. As I tried to convince him of the value of investing in a bank in Iran and of partnering with me, a 26-year-old with no real banking experience, I could see that he was skeptical. Significantly, though, he did not dismiss me. More significantly, our meeting led to a subsequent series of meetings with other senior managers at Morgan who were more receptive to my proposal.

My pitch to them was that Iran, with its large population and fast growth, was the most likely country in the Middle East to productively recycle the huge influx of petrodollars now flooding into the region. Every major corporation, American or international, was in Iran pursuing economic opportunities. All of these companies were clients of Morgan Guaranty. Why would Morgan *not* be in Iran? As far as partnering with a 26-year-old, I argued that they were in fact partnering with the Nemazee name, which had the same credibility and currency in Iran as Morgan had in England and America.

Before I left, I had a deal with the most prestigious bank in the world.

10

THE SHAH'S LAST DANCE

Iran's economy, fueled by oil, grew at an extraordinary rate in the 1970's. The nation's oil income doubled to $4.6 billion in 1973-1974, then skyrocketed to nearly $18 billion the next year. This influx of money produced all sorts of remarkable statistics, including an economic growth rate of 33% in 1973, which rose to 40% in 1974. The Shah had every reason to believe, as he claimed, that the standard of living in Iran would be equal to Europe's within a decade, and would surpass the United States' within two decades.

What the Shah did not anticipate were the downsides of this growth. It produced high inflation and put excessive pressure on the country's underdeveloped infrastructure of roads, ports, railways, and highways. The result was a dramatic rise in prices—of food, imports, and land—all of which contributed to social, cultural, and religious tensions.

The Shah's own behavior did not help. Since the overthrow of Mosaddegh in 1953, the Shah had accumulated more and more power. He was no longer either a figurehead or even a constitutional monarch; he was an authoritarian monarch. He viewed himself as the State incarnate. No government decision, no matter how large or small, was made without his approval. His power was unchecked and unbalanced.

In many ways, the Shah had built a trap for himself. When things were going well, he got all the credit and was heralded as a benevolent patriarch. But when government decisions started to cause economic hardship, he would get all the blame and find himself condemned as a tyrant.

One afternoon I visited an old friend of my father's. A man in his 70's, he was one of Iran's wealthiest businessmen. He had a huge smile on his face as he put down the afternoon paper. "I've been waiting 30 years for today. They finally got the son of a bitch!" He held up the newspaper so I could read the headline:

Habib Sabet Arrested for Profiteering. Sabet was another of my father's contemporaries. He was one of the most visible businessmen in Iran, owner of the Pepsi franchise, the RCA franchise, a television station, and several other large businesses. I was less astonished by Sabet's arrest than by the reaction of my father's friend. "Why are you happy?" I asked him. "If they arrest Sabet, what's to stop them from arresting you? Or me, for that matter?"

"Don't be foolish," he responded. "We are not like Sabet."

Perhaps not. But I had an epiphany that day. Iran was a true autocracy. This was obvious and I had always known it abstractly, but for the first time it hit me what this meant for me personally. The Shah could decide, at any time, for any reason, to condemn anyone. There was no real rule of law, nowhere an accused man could go to appeal for justice. Nor could the accused expect his peers in the business community to come to his defense—they would be too busy gloating over his demise. We were all enjoying our liberty and property at the mercy of the Shah, and that was a dangerous situation to be in. I began to think about ways to control the risks.

My first solution was to move some of our family's assets. Since unloading my family's stake in Fakhr Iran, I had kept our proceeds, including Susie's and my mother's, in Iran, where we earned a very good return as the economy expanded. I now decided to send the bulk of the cash abroad. This was not an easy decision to make, and it was less easy to explain to my mother. Why, she demanded to know, would I give up an excellent return in Iran for a mediocre return in the West? I insisted it was necessary to offset our risks. She questioned me relentlessly, but I prevailed.

It was one thing to decide to move money out of Iran. It was another to get it done. Due to the huge inflow of petrodollars into Iran, there were no currency controls. Anyone could legally sell the Iranian currency of rials and buy dollars, and transfer money anywhere in the world. Nonetheless, out of an abundance of caution, I decided to send the money out via the Havaleh system of money transfer. This was the traditional way of exchanging money through merchants in the bazaar. Havaleh was simple, secure, and—an added bonus—left no paper trail. Employing it turned out to be smart for reasons I could not yet anticipate.

■ ■ ■

Despite occasional and mostly easy-to-ignore signs of trouble, I remained content with my life in Iran. I'd settled in nicely in my position of Chairman of Bonyad Iran. My dealings with the hospital, the waterworks, and Pahlavi University were mostly smooth. I'd commissioned a local architect, Mohandess Agah, to design a gravesite memorial to my father, and he'd come up with an understated yet elegant landscape on the hospital compound where visitors could pray and reflect in a beautiful setting of trees and flowers. I also asked Iran's leading sculptor, Parviz Tanavoli, to create a statue of my father, to be placed in front of the entrance to the hospital. Lastly, I'd moved forward on the publication of "History of Civilization," the manuscript my father had worked on for the last ten years of his life. His good friend, Ehsan Yarshater, Professor of Iranian Studies at Columbia University in New York, had agreed to edit the book.

I was fortunate to have my sister, Susie, nearby. After graduating from Harvard with a degree in Chinese History, Susie had come to Tehran. She'd opened a modern bookstore, Byblos, in the northern suburbs of Tehran, an instant success. I remained in my father's former house—now Susie's—where I felt very much at home. But I knew I wanted my own home, especially as my relationship with Sheila seemed to be moving toward marriage.

One of my greatest pleasures in these years was horseback riding. I'd purchased a stallion named Noor Jahan, a thoroughbred show jumper on whom I learned to ride and jump fairly well. According to an old a Persian saying, a man could not claim to be an accomplished equestrian until he'd fallen seven times. I'd fallen three times while jumping, so was almost halfway there.

On weekends, I often rode Noor Jahan into the countryside around Tehran, accompanied by my dog, Taipan, an Irish Setter who trotted alongside us. Within a few miles of downtown Tehran, we would be transported back to rustic villages untouched by the 20th century. It was on one of these rides that I discovered Poonak, on the western edge of Tehran, just outside the city limits.

Poonak was a pretty village of dirt roads, low houses, and mud walls surrounding beautiful orchards of cherry, peach, and apple trees. The orchards and gardens were irrigated by an ancient aqueduct system, called Qanat, that brought water from the foot of the Alborz mountains in the north. To the west, as far as the eye could see, was open land. To the east, a deep ravine separated Poonak from the borders of Tehran's most modern development, Sharak Gharb, and to the south was Mehrabad airport. Altogether, it was a magnificent setting, a beautiful remnant of old Iran just minutes away from the downtown business center and airport. It occurred to me that this would be an ideal place for a home.

One afternoon while trotting through Poonak, I passed a tall mud wall with impressively large double wooden doors. I pulled in Noor Jahan and eased him up to the wall. From the vantage of my saddle, I found myself looking into an extraordinary estate of several lush acres. To one side was an orchard of mature cherry trees, mixed with walnut and old Persian plane trees. Everywhere flowers and plants grew in abundance, watered by a large irrigation pool. In the middle of this was a very handsome one-story house with a tile roof and several attached structures, including a car garage and a horse stable.

After making some inquiries, I learned that the property belonged to Prince Patrick Ali, a nephew of the Shah. He was the son of Prince Ali Reza, the Shah's younger brother, who had died in a plane crash in the 1950's. The royal family was famous for its eccentricities, but even by their standards Prince Patrick stood out. Long before the advent of the Islamic movement that would eventually lead to the revolution in Iran, Patrick had become a fervent believer in Islam. He was so devout that he insisted that his Swiss wife cover herself in a black chador, a full-length wraparound garment worn by strictly religious women.

I sent a message to Patrick asking if he might be interested in selling his property. His chief of staff replied to me that, for the right price, His Highness would indeed sell. I made a generous offer, and the prince immediately accepted. There was just one condition. As an Islamist, Prince Patrick would not work with banks; they charged interest, against the teachings of Mohammed. Full payment must therefore be made in cash. Furthermore, the payment and transfer of title could not be done in a notary's office, where such transactions usually happened, but must be done at the house in Poonak.

This presented me with at least two major problems. The first was that I needed to obtain a great deal of cash, in rials. The Iranian banking system was not accustomed to handing out large sums of rials and did not keep these on hand. I contacted my father's old friend Abol Hassan Ebtehaj at Iranian's Bank, where I had my account. After laughing at the absurdity of the prince's request, Ebtehaj said he would handle it. "But you know that's a large amount of cash to be carrying around Tehran," he said. "We don't have a Brinks Security system here. You'll have to be very careful about how you protect your money."

He'd identified my second problem—how to get the money to Poonak safely. I arranged for several of my office employees to accompany me on the appointed morning to ensure my safety.

The night before the transaction was to take place, I had the cash ready. It was packed in two Samsonite suitcases, which I'd hidden under my bed. I was getting ready to go to sleep when the phone rang. On the other end was a man who identified himself as General Hasheminejad, commander of the Shah's elite Imperial Guard. "Mr. Nemazee, I understand you are to transact some business with Prince Patrick tomorrow."

"Yes?"

"The Prince will be unable to meet you. Please cancel your arrangements until further notice."

With this, the phone went dead. I was completely taken aback. How did the Royal Palace know of my agreement with Patrick? And why call me at midnight to wave me off?

The headlines in the next afternoon's newspapers gave me a partial answer. There had been a gunfight in a cave in Ghazvin, several miles outside of Tehran, between the Shah's security forces and the Islamic Fedayeen. Several Fedayeen (Islamic Marxists) were killed. A link to the Royal Family had been discovered, and a nephew of the Shah's had been taken into "protective custody." The nephew, of course, was Prince Patrick.

Later, I learned more. The Imperial Guard strongly suspected that Patrick was complicit with the Fedayeen. He had been arrested and transported to Gorgan, in the north of Iran. How General Hasheminejad had learned of my intent to purchase the land I don't know, but he'd done me a favor by calling to cancel my meeting with the prince. I reflected on what would have happened if I'd shown up at the prince's house with a ton of cash packed into two suitcases at the very moment the prince was conspiring with Islamists. How would I have explained that I merely wanted to buy a house?

The arrest of the prince was another foreshadowing of turmoil to come. But for most of us, that turmoil was still unimaginable. Patrick was soon free again, and some months later, after things had settled down, he called to ask if I was still interested in the house. I told him I was, and we agreed to conclude our deal on the same terms we'd discussed before his arrest. Ebtehaj again arranged the cash.

There was no late night call this time, but Patrick did introduce one final complication before we closed. As part of the deal, he wanted me to buy the 1939 Rolls-Royce that had been owned by his grandfather, Reza Shah. The automobile was parked in the center of the living room, which had apparently been built around it, and Patrick had no way to remove it without knocking down a wall. We could not come to terms on a price, nor did I want a car, not even a 1939 Rolls, in the middle of my living room. Patrick ultimately agreed to sell me the house anyway. Rather than knock down any walls, he had the Rolls dismantled and carried out, piece by piece, through the front door.

■ ■ ■

With my business plans in place and a beautiful new home in Tehran, I now did what I'd been planning to do for some time: I proposed to Sheila. She accepted. We were both extremely happy and excited by our future.

We married in Paris, where Sheila's parents lived at the time. The wedding reception and the dinner were at the beautiful Art Deco restaurant Maxim's. At dinner I sat beside Princess Soraya, formerly know as Queen Soraya, the Shah's second wife until he'd divorced her in 1958, due to her failure to produce a male heir. The former queen was elegant and shimmering in her sequined evening gown, but after years of living in Paris she was nervous to be in a gathering that included so many Iranians. By the time the reception ended, though, even she was relaxed and enjoying herself. Dancing lasted until five the next morning. The next day, Sheila and I took off for a round-the-world honeymoon.

On returning to Iran, we moved to Poonak. It had been an excellent house when I bought it from Prince Patrick, and workers had made it even more attractive. The exterior roof was now covered in original Persian tiles brought from the Caspian Sea area. A new wing, including a modern kitchen and billiard room, had been added to one side of the house. The irrigation pool had been converted into a swimming pool, and a clay tennis court with lights had been installed in a corner of the orchard. The horse stable, too, had been renovated. Noor Jahan looked quite content in his new home, and so were we.

■ ■ ■

But clouds were gathering on the horizon. Some were visible, such as the events that led to my transferring assets outside Iran, but others less apparent. The Shah was becoming increasingly isolated, and often behaving in incoherent and contradictory ways. His desire to modernize and democratize had long been in conflict with his compulsion to control everything himself, and over the years the latter impulse had won out. He'd marginalized the role of the Iranian Parliament, the Majles, as well as the Senate, rendering these bodies little more than rubber stamps to imperial decisions.

In 1975, he decided to do away with any pretense of democracy by decreeing that henceforth Iran would have only one political party, the Rastakiz, with two wings; all others would be abolished. He placed Jamshid Amouzegar as the head of one wing of the party, and Hushang Ansary as the head of the other. He was signaling that he would choose one or the other to be the next prime minister. This did not sit well with the vast majority of Iranians, including some of the men he considered his allies. To make matters worse, Iran's rapid growth had brought not just economic disruptions but increasing graft and corruption. Despite the Shah's hopes of raising living standards for every Iranian, the gulf between rich and poor had widened.

Meanwhile, in the United States, a relatively unknown southern governor named Jimmy Carter had come into the

White House, proclaiming America's support for universal human rights. Carter's words were heard on the streets of Iran as an endorsement of the political dissent already taking root.

That dissent took on an increasingly aggressive tone. In October of 1977, for example, fundamentalist students at Tehran University set several of the school's buses on fire, then stormed the school cafeteria, forcibly separating male and female students who were dining together. Many students were horrified and protested, but most conceded to the fundamentalists' demands.

Meanwhile, some of my projects began to meet roadblocks. Iran's rapid development had led to significant shortages in building materials. Rebar and cement were hard to obtain, for example, and those materials that could be obtained ran into transportation bottlenecks. The country did not have a sufficient infrastructure, or even enough truck drivers, to get goods where they needed to be in a timely manner. To make matters worse, building permits and other allowances were slow in coming. In Tehran, where we had bid upon and won two prime development sites, the government had yet to release the land to us, due either to royal caprice or, more likely, malfeasance and corruption down the line. The Chalet Gajereh ski resort project was delayed too, by local opposition, meaning that someone in power probably stood to gain by blocking it. I was becoming frustrated by the situation, as were my partners.

J.C. von Helms, my old Harvard tutor who had come to Tehran at my request, suggested that he return to Texas to look for potential development projects there. The city was showing signs of economic recovery. I agreed. Late in 1977, J.C. flew to Houston.

I could not know it at the time, but the delays in Iran would turn out to a great piece of luck for me. So would our return to Houston.

■ ■ ■

New Year's Eve of 1977 brought President and Mrs. Carter to Iran for a state dinner at Niavaran Palace, accompanied by the usual presidential entourage of aides and press. At the dinner, Carter reassured the Shah of American support, saying "Your

Majesty, Iran is an island of stability in one of the most troubled areas of the world."

Almost immediately, Carter's words were contradicted by events. A week after the dinner, for reasons that are still unclear, a leading Iranian newspaper, *Ettelaat*, published a letter to the editor that had clearly been ordered, if not written, by the Shah. The letter was filled with scathing insults to Ayatollah Khomeini, the long-time opponent of the Shah who had been living in exile in Iraq since 1964. Khomeini had continued to preach in opposition to the Shah, but neither the Shah nor the U.S. embassy believed him to have significant domestic support. The reaction to the letter in *Ettelaat* proved otherwise. Enraged demonstrators took to the streets to condemn the Shah for his insult of the Ayatollah. For the first time since the 1960's, the Shah was forced to call in police and military to control riots.

In the early months of 1978, a dangerous and powerful alliance began to form between Islamic extremists and other anti-Shah groups, including socialists, left-leaning intellectuals, and anarchists. As the secular protestors would eventually discover, they were merely temporary allies—*useful idiots*—to the fundamentalists. While they wanted to overthrow the Shah, or at least making his regime more democratic, the fundamentalists had a more rigid demand: bring Khomeini back from exile. As for what was to happen after that, I don't think anyone, not even Khomeini himself, had any idea.

Protest and riots continued sporadically through the spring and summer of 1978. In the city of Tabriz, riots erupted and were repeated every 40 days. In Shiraz, armed rioters engaged in gun battles with police. In Isfahan, rioters set fire to the luxurious Shah Abbas Hotel, sending tourists fleeing into the streets.

We got an unsettling taste of where things were headed that summer when we took a trip to the south of Iran with our good friend Farhad Diba and his daughter. We flew to Yazd and arranged for a car and driver to leisurely drive us to Tehran by way of Kashan and Qom, two beautiful and historically rich cities we'd never visited. As we approached Qom, the religious capital of Iran, we saw that the city was surrounded on all sides by tanks of the Imperial Iranian Army. We came to a military checkpoint. We told the officer who halted us that we were returning to Tehran and wanted to stop in Qom for lunch. He advised us to avoid the city and drive directly to Tehran, but when we persisted, he gave us permission to enter.

No one was on the streets of Qom; the ancient city appeared deserted. Eventually, we found a restaurant that was open. We asked if we could get some food, as it was well into the afternoon. "Yes, no problem," the manager said. "We serve lunch until three." I looked at my watch. "It's three o'clock now." He laughed. "No, here in Qom we don't use the Shah's time. It's still two." Daylight savings was not observed in Qom because Ayatollah Khomeini had forbidden it.

■ ■ ■

Shortly after our visit to Qom, we were invited to the Caspian as weekend guests of Prince Abdul Reza and Princess Pari Sima. They had an annual summer weekend party at their estate in Gorgan, always attended by the finest of Iranian society and royalty, including the Shah. This year's party was bound to be especially interesting, given all the unrest. There was also a rumor that the Shah had been shot by a member of the royal family—would he come?

He did come. The rumor of his shooting had been false. Along with his wife, Empress Farah, the Shah brought King Hussein of Jordan and the king's new wife, Queen Noor, a young American. Her maiden name was Lisa Halaby. She'd been a student at Princeton, one of the first women admitted. As it happened, I'd met her once before, some years earlier, at the Cottage Club, one of Princeton's eating clubs. I introduced myself to her now, mentioning our earlier meeting. She quickly turned away; apparently, she did not like being reminded of her American past.

I'd already had a number of surreal experiences over the years in Iran, but this one beat them all. Iran was melting down in the summer heat, yet here we were in a royal palace on the Caspian, partying with the Shah as if none of that mattered. To make things even stranger, the year was 1978, the height of the disco era. I recall standing at the edge of the dance floor watching a guy in a white suit do his best impression of John Travolta as a DJ played one Bee Gees song after another. Then the DJ slowed it down a little, and the Shah himself took to the floor. The last time I saw him in person, he was wearing a madras jacket, dancing stiffly with Queen Noor under a glittering disco ball.

11

REVOLUTION

It could not have been more than a week after that party on the Caspian that the Rex Cinema burned down. The Rex was a large theater in the southwestern city of Abadan. On August 19, 1978, while hundreds of residents took refuge from the heat in the air-conditioned theater to watch a movie called *The Deer*, several men lit the Rex on fire, using airplane fuel as an accelerant. By the time the flames were doused, over 400 people were dead. Khomeini's supporters blamed the Shah for the arson. In fact, it was they who set the fire, an act of terror meant to sow panic and chaos. It worked. Before that August day, the revolution had been like cotton smoldering below decks. The Rex ignited a conflagration.

Eleven days later, Sheila and I left Iran for a long-planned trip to Europe and America. I had numerous business meetings to attend, and we planned to visit family and friends along the way. Although Iran was in turmoil, it still seemed possible, even likely, that order would be fully restored.

I was not alone in believing this. In fact, few Iranians in the early fall of 1978 accepted that the Peacock Throne was about to topple. The Shah presided over the largest military and security apparatus in the Middle East, including a standing army of 400,000 men and an impressive air force and navy equipped with the latest weapons from America. His dreaded security service, SAVAK, organized and trained by the CIA, was considered the equal of Israel's Mossad. How could a mere street mob overthrow such a powerful government?

In London, I met the Israeli industrialist Shaul Eisenberg. Along with building oil refineries and a variety of industrial plants, Eisenberg happened to be Israel's largest arms dealer. He was keen to enter the Iranian industrial market and had chosen me to partner on a bid to construct an aluminum plant for the Iranian government. Eisenberg was better informed about Iran than most Iranians. He told me he was skeptical of the military's ability to control the growing demonstrations. Restrictions the U.S. government had placed on the Shah were likely to backfire, he predicted. This included a refusal to allow the sale of rubber bullets, water cannons, and other non-lethal weapons that had been requested by the Iranian military and police. Having no access to non-lethal weapons, Iran's military would resort to lethal force to control demonstrators, resulting in even more violent and deadly riots. Eisenberg would turn out to be exactly right.

As I traveled, I tracked the situation in Tehran via newspapers and frequent phone calls. We were still in London on September 8, a day that would come to be known in Iran as Black Friday. This was the day from which there would be no turning back.

The morning began with a large anti-Shah protest in Tehran's Jaleh Square. Somebody aimed a gun on the crowd—it is not clear who—and mayhem ensued. Before it was done, government troops had opened fire, killing dozens of demonstrators, wounding many more, and causing mass panic and rioting. A ludicrous rumor circulated that the Shah himself—"the Butcher of Jaleh Square," as many now called him—had flown over Tehran in his helicopter, taking shots at the crowd. Such was the power of mob lore, even before social media came into the picture.

From London, we flew to New York, where I met with Alexander "Alec" Vagliano and others at Morgan Guaranty. We agreed to closely monitor events in Iran before committing to formally establishing the bank. I then proceeded to Washington, where I met Dick Helms. Having served as Director of the C.I.A. and U.S. ambassador to Iran, Helms was profoundly disturbed by events in the country he loved. He believed that the Shah was receiving bad and conflicting advice from President Carter's White House. Carter's national security advisor, Zbigniew Brzezinski, favored giving the Shah the green light to do whatever was necessary to put down the disturbances. Secretary of State Cyrus Vance pushed the Shah to accommodate the opposition and avoid loss of life. The Shah himself was paralyzed with indecision.

Ironically, the Shah was one of the few Iranians who now genuinely understood the threat he and the nation faced. Having underestimated Khomeini earlier, he recognized, too late, what the ayatollah represented: nothing short of a return to 7th century Islamic fundamentalist rule. Still, the Shah was confident that if he presented his Western allies and the Iranian people with a stark choice between his monarchy and an Islamic State led by Khomeini, he would be the clear favorite of his countrymen.

One problem with the Shah's assumption was that Khomeini never showed his true face to the world. The Western media, along with the political and intellectual elites in the West and Iran, were happy to believe that the ayatollah was the saintly clergyman he pretended to be. None had bothered to read his book, *Velayat-e-Fagih*. The book described an Islamic State run by a Supreme Leader, who, according to Khomeini, could only be a senior member of the Shiite clergy.

We were scheduled to return to Tehran at the end of October. After a few weeks in America, we flew from New York to Paris. I was in constant contact with my office, getting daily, sometimes hourly, updates on developments in Tehran. Colleagues and friends informed me that the situation on the ground was worse even than the press reported. The night before we were scheduled to depart for Tehran, my chief of staff called me. He advised me not to return. Our office building had been attacked and set ablaze, targeted because of its association with an American bank. This was the first of many attacks on American-owned or affiliated businesses.

We waited a few more days, but I was anxious to return to my office and staff. We finally flew back in early November.

The Tehran we came back to barely resembled the city we'd left two months earlier. Buildings that had been attacked bore the marks of revolutionary fervor. There was broken glass, burnt buildings, and graffiti everywhere. At night shouts of "Allah Akbar"—God is Great—echoed from the rooftops of buildings, along with more harrowing calls of "Death to the Shah!" This was true not just in the poorer and more radical sections of southern Tehran, but also in the wealthier northern suburbs, even those adjacent to the Royal Palace. The military was out in force, but demonstrators continued to take to the streets, inflamed rather than intimidated by the soldiers.

The morning after we returned, I attempted to go to my office. My driver insisted that we take the Iranian-made Paykan, rather than my American Cadillac, which might make us a target of demonstrators. He also wisely suggested that I sit in front. From the west of the city, we crossed east to central Tehran, passing through the war zone that the city had become. As we neared my office, we came upon a crowd of students from Tehran University, blocking traffic and shouting anti-Shah epithets. My driver refused to go further. He did a quick U-turn and we sped back home to Poonak.

I did finally get to my office a few days later. Many of my staff were absent. The support staff, especially, was frightened. Most lived in radicalized areas of the city, where a rumor that they worked for a company with American interests might get them killed. I told all present that they should not come to the office if they were afraid. There was work to be done, but not at the expense of anyone's life.

■ ■ ■

Incredibly, even as Iran was collapsing, a promising real estate development deal was coming together for us in Houston. This was a welcome distraction from the disturbances in Iran. It would also prove to be one of the most fortuitous deals of my career.

Earlier in 1978, with project delays mounting in Iran, I'd sent J.C. von Helms to Houston to scout for opportunities. The Texas oil industry was profiting from significantly higher oil prices, and Houston, as a result, was in the midst of a development boom. Houston had no zoning laws, so a developer could build anything, and anywhere. The only restriction was financial, meaning that if you could obtain financing for a project, you could build it.

J.C. had found a piece of undeveloped land in a great location. Across from the famous Galleria Shopping Center, on the corner of Westheimer Road and Loop 610, the plot was ideal for a commercial office development. During my trip to the United States in September, I'd flown to Houston to negotiate an agreement with the owners to purchase three acres for an initial project, plus an option to buy the adjacent eight acres in the future. Based on our research of the market, we decided to build a 300,000-square-foot office building.

The formula for developing real estate projects in the U.S. in the late 1970's was fairly straightforward. You needed a minimum equity of 5% of the cost of the total project, with the remainder being debt. The debt was typically a construction loan provided by a commercial bank, which would be replaced on completion of construction with a "permanent" loan provided by an insurance company or a pension fund. As this was to be our first project, I assumed that we'd need to put up more than the minimum 5%. I also knew I needed to assemble a world-class team in order to get the necessary bank and permanent financing.

To begin, I launched a development company, HN Properties. I then set up two separate companies to buy the three acres and to hold an option on the raw land. Over the objections of J.C., who thought the cost would be prohibitive, I asked the architect I.M. Pei to take on the assignment. Pei had not yet built an office building in Houston, and he welcomed the opportunity. I knew his fee would be greater than that of a local architect, and that his design would cost more to build, but I believed an association with I.M. Pei would enhance our credibility and help us convince a local bank to lend us the $20 million the project required.

The remarkable thing about doing business in Texas in those days was how quickly decisions were made. By the time I returned to Tehran that November, I.M. Pei had produced a detailed design, the Linbeck construction firm had given me a fixed price contract for the construction, and J.C. had obtained a loan from a local lender, Allied Bank, for $20 million.

The only rub was the loan. It was conditioned on my providing $5 million of liquidity to the project. My assessment of the potential risks and rewards of putting up this money were complicated, to say the least. On one hand, given events in Iran, a real estate project in America would be a prudent reallocation of my assets. On the other hand, the $5 million required by the bank would consume all of my liquidity. Economic conditions in the United States, including rapid inflation, were potential threats to the project.

Such complicated circumstances called for calm reflection. How much longer would the Shah remain in power? What would happen to my assets in Iran if and when he fell? Was it wise to put virtually all my cash into a single project in Houston?

Unfortunately, there was no time to mull such questions. Every decision had to be made yesterday.

The pressure to move fast increased when Leo Linbeck called me in Tehran to inform me that, due to inflation, his construction costs would increase by 10% if I did not sign the contract authorizing commencement of construction by January 1, 1979. A 10% increase in costs would add an additional $2 million to the price tag for the project—and $2 million of equity that I did not have and did not know where to find.

But inflation, I realized, was a double-edged sword. It was a problem for me if construction prices rose. At the same time, though, the price of land in Houston was rising, and quite dramatically. The land I'd agreed to purchase for $12 per square foot was now valued at $25. Here was my solution. I negotiated with Allied Bank, and they agreed to allow the land to be contributed to the project at a value of $25 per square foot. Almost by magic, I had created $2 million of new equity.

■ ■ ■

While my attention was focused on Houston, the political turmoil in Tehran continued to escalate. And then, all at once, it enveloped me. Before this, I'd been watching the revolution the way one watches a weather report of a hurricane gathering strength in the Caribbean—with keen but somewhat impersonal concern. Now it became personal and dangerous.

The revolutionaries were targeting American companies and interests in Tehran, as well as anyone in league with the Pahlavi family. I was American-born and American-educated, in partnerships with major American and Western companies, and considered close to the royals—all factors once helpful to me and now potentially detrimental. Still, like most Iranians, I'd failed to grasp the jeopardy I was in. I was 28 years old and heir to the Nemazee name and all the good will that name generated among all classes and political parties in Iran. Even when I worried that my livelihood might be damaged by the revolution, it never occurred to me that my life might be in danger.

One morning in mid-November of 1978, a list of one hundred names was published in newspapers around the country. Ostensibly released by the Central Bank of Iran, the list purported to identify wealthy Iranians who had transferred funds abroad. Next to each name was the supposed amount the person had transferred. The list was a veritable who's who of Iran, but this was not a who's who list you wanted any part of. When I saw my name on it, I was furious.

According to the document, I'd transferred 700,000,000 rials—about $10 million—out of Iran. That was false. In any case, it was not illegal to transfer money out of the county. Still, I understood that inclusion on this list implied that I had done something wrong. I called every friend I had in the government to demand that the list be refuted immediately. The problem was that most of my friends in government were also on the list and felt powerless to do anything until their own names were cleared. There would be an investigation, I was assured; we must all be patient and wait for the outcome. Until then, I'd remain publicly accused of a crime—that was not in fact a crime—at a time when such an accusation made me a marked man.

I needed to return to the United States in early December to sign the Houston construction contracts with Linbeck. Sheila had planned to stay at home in Poonak, but I insisted that she accompany me at least to New York. It was now clear to anyone with eyes and ears that the Shah was losing control of Iran. As is often the case in fast-moving revolutionary situations, actions that might have calmed the protests a few months earlier were no longer sufficient. The Shah's efforts to placate the mob were fruitless and only undercut his support from the establishment. In one desperate measure, he authorized the detention of numerous government officials, including his long-serving former prime minister Amir Abbas Hoveyda. Another official, Nematollah Nassiri, the hated chief of the notorious SAVAK, was also arrested and jailed. None of these sacrificial lambs appeased the revolutionaries, but they certainly frightened the men in the Shah's government.

In an attempt to restore order, the Shah summoned Fereydoun Djam, former Chief of Staff of the Imperial Iranian Army, from London, where Fereydoun was living at the time. The Shah asked Fereydoun to become his Minister of Defense. I knew Fereydoun well, and we met at Susie's house shortly after his audience with the Shah. He told me the Shah had asked him to take over the military, but when Fereydoun asked for *direct* authority over the military, the Shah had been unwilling to cede it. Fereydoun also told me a little known fact regarding how the Shah managed the military and its leadership. It was the Shah's policy that no meeting be held by heads of the various forces—Army, Navy, Air Force—without His Majesty in attendance. This was to prevent close relationships between leaders of the military that could lead to a potential coup. The policy may indeed have prevented a coup, but it also barred the formation of any personal relationships between senior military officials that could have facilitated a more coordinated response to the mounting unrest.

Fereydoun did something that would have been unthinkable only a year earlier: he turned the Shah down. When he told me he was going back to London, I understood precisely what this meant: the ship was sinking. There was nothing to do now but get off.

■ ■ ■

Sheila and I were booked on the Air France flight to Paris on the morning of December 4. Our plan was to fly to Paris, then onward to the U.S. and ultimately to Houston. I'd arranged to be met at the airport by Mr. Taghavi, a man I employed to facilitate my departures and arrivals from Mehrabad Airport. The convoluted protocol for leaving Iran required passengers to give their passports to the airline 48 hours prior to departure. The airline would process exit documents with the police, then return the passports to passengers after they had checked their bags at the airport. Taghavi always made sure things went smoothly.

Nothing was smooth on this day, however. We arrived to a scene of absolute chaos at the airport. Mehrabad was overwhelmed with Iranians and foreigners trying to depart on any flight they could book, no matter where it was going. Enormous lines had formed at ticket counters. Clusters of panicked foreigners paced nervously near the gates. Others were camped out on the floor, prepared to wait as long as it took. It all brought to mind scenes from the evacuation of Saigon in the hectic days before the departure of American forces in 1975.

Amidst of all this pandemonium, Taghavi somehow managed to get our bags checked. We then proceeded to the kiosk, where we normally retrieved our passports from the police officials. I traveled so frequently that the man at the kiosk recognized me on sight. He lowered his eyes when he saw me now, embarrassed. "*Agha Nemazee, mazarat mekham, vali shoma mamnoo ol khouroj hastid.*"— I'm sorry Mr. Nemazee, but you are forbidden to leave.

Given my imperfect Farsi, I had never heard the expression "*mamnoo ol khouroj,*" so I did not realize what he'd said. I smiled and replied, "*Merci.*" Sheila and Taghavi immediately understood, though, and they pulled me aside to explain. My passport was being held by the airport police.

Anxious not to miss our flight, certain that there must be some mistake, we hurried to the main office of the airport police. Taghavi spoke to the chief of the airport police in Persian, then turned to me to explain. There had not been a mistake after all. The government had decided to stop anyone on the "Central Bank List" from leaving the country until an investigation into the allegations was completed.

Concern about our personal safety would come later. For the moment, I felt only anger. I fumed at the chief in my poor Persian. He shrugged back. "The decision has been made," he replied in Persian. "It was not my decision." My passport would be sent to the central headquarters of the police department pending the investigation. I'd just have to wait. There was nothing else to do.

I turned to Sheila and told her to hurry and catch the flight. "Wait for me in Paris. This won't take long." She refused. She would not leave until my situation was resolved.

We were back at the house in Poonak less than two hours after leaving for the airport that morning. Within minutes of our return, the telephone rang. Sheila picked it up. The color drained from her face as she listened. "It was a man," she said when she put down the phone. "He told me, 'We know you tried to leave the country.' He said, 'If you try again, we'll kill you.'" Our number was unlisted, and we had just moments ago returned from the airport. Clearly the call had come from someone inside the security apparatus—someone who was tracking our moves.

I called Syed Jalal eddin Tehrany. He was an old friend of the family. He was also close to the Shah—in fact, the Shah had recently named him head of the Regency Council. Unlike most of the other men I knew who were close to the Shah, Tehrany was not on the list. I told him what had happened to me at the airport and of the threatening phone call we'd received. He promised to make some inquires. That afternoon, he called back. While he could not determine who called us, Tehrany told me, he'd learned that the Minister of Justice intended to commence an investigation into the bank list in a few days. Until then, I should sit tight and await his call.

And so we waited. The next two afternoons the phone rang, both times an anonymous man threatening me with death. Finally, Tehrany called back. He told me to present myself at the offices of the Central Bank the following afternoon.

■ ■ ■

I arrived at the Central Bank at the appointed time, my attorney by my side. The bank was an impressive white stone building fronted by four columns. I knew it well, having visited often while applying for my banking license. Inside, we climbed the marble stairs to the second floor and arrived at a large waiting room. A secretary handed me a form to fill out. My lawyer offered to do this on my behalf, but I demurred. I knew my poor Persian handwriting would make me look like an idiot, but I figured it was not a bad time to look like an idiot.

After a short wait, the secretary told me to proceed to the office of the Deputy Chairman of the Central Bank. My attorney stood to follow but I stopped him. I wanted to go in alone.

The man inside the office of the Deputy Chairman was not the Deputy Chairman, whom I knew, but someone I'd never seen before. Stocky, mustached, and friendly, he stood and introduced himself as Mr. Nourbaksh. He was the Deputy Minister of Justice, he told me, and had been assigned to investigate the Central Bank allegations. I looked around the enormous room. Along every wall were cardboard boxes stacked floor to ceiling. These were the receipts, the Deputy Minister informed me, of every foreign exchange transaction undertaken by every commercial bank in

Iran for the last year. Sisyphean does not begin to describe the task he had before him.

He then picked up my form. Seeing my name, he asked me which Nemazee I was. I informed him that I was Hassan, the son of Mohammed. "The founder of the hospital?" I nodded. Not for the first time I realized that I was fortunate to be my father's son.

The Deputy Minister told me that I was the first person that they had called in for the investigation and apologized for the inconvenience. Looking back down at my form, he smiled and said, "*Jenab Agha Nemazee, mesle inke shoma kharej az Iran tahsil kardid.*" Your excellency, it appears that you have been educated abroad. This was his polite way of recognizing my semi-literacy in Persian. I responded that, yes, in fact I'd been born and raised in America and had only lived in Iran for the last six years, since my father's death. He took another few moments to scan the form, then put it down.

"Thank you for coming today. You are free to go."

"Am I free to leave Iran? My passport was confiscated at the airport by the police."

"Yes. You should go to the police department and collect your passport."

He spoke with authority, but I was not fully confident. I asked him for a signed note, addressed to the police, instructing them to release my passport to me. He quickly scribbled this down and told me to take it a Col. Shahbazi at police headquarters.

■ ■ ■

From the bank I went directly to police headquarters. It was now 4:00 p.m. on a Thursday, effectively the start of the Iranian weekend.[4] The police building was an ugly brick structure occupying a full city block and surrounded by a high wall. To enter I first had to be admitted through a heavy green metal door in the wall; I pressed a button several times then waited. An officer

---

[4] Iranian workweeks run Saturday through Thursday. Government offices usually close Thursday after lunch.

eventually opened it. "Closed," he said gruffly in Persian. "Come back Saturday." I showed him my note from the Deputy Minister. Reluctantly, he allowed me to pass through the courtyard to the building. "We're closed," said the officer at the front desk when I entered. Again, I showed my note and explained the urgency of my visit. "Col. Shahbazi," he said. "Third floor."

Upstairs, another officer escorted me to the colonel. I found him at a desk in a large open room. The weekend had clearly already started for him. His shirt collar was open, his feet were on the desk, and he was smoking a cigar, laughing it up with several officers. I walked right up to him and presented my paper. He took one look at it then handed it back. "Come back Saturday."

"I can't come back Saturday. I'm flying out on Saturday."

"Too late today. You have to come Saturday."

"Colonel, that letter is from the Deputy Minister of Justice. I am here on his direct orders. And his orders are for you to give me my passport."

The colonel looked again at the letter. He took a puff of cigar. "Okay. Somebody fetch this man his passport."

Somebody eventually did. Slipping the passport into my pocket, I hurried out of police headquarters before somebody else snatched it back.

Only later would I come to learn how lucky I was that afternoon. The following day, the police announced a general strike. Headquarters would close that day, then remain shuttered until the following year. Had I not gotten my passport that afternoon, in other words, I would never have gotten it at all, and very likely I never would have gotten out of Iran. I would have ended up in the same place that many of my friends did: in jail or dead.

■ ■ ■

As soon as I returned home, I called Air France. The president of the airline's Iranian office happened to be a friend. He was the most valuable friend anyone could have in Iran in December of 1978. Not only did he somehow find two available seats for us on the Saturday flight to Paris, he came to our house in Poonak that evening and personally took our passports with him to process them.

The threatening phone calls stopped that day. Some years after the revolution, it became clear what had happened—where that bank list came from and who threatened me with death. SAVAK, the security agency, had split into two factions by December of 1978. One of these supported the Shah, the other supported the revolutionaries. The deputy head of SAVAK, Hossein Fardoust, a childhood friend of the Shah's, had turned against the Shah and joined the forces allied to Khomeini. Not only was the Central Bank list created by the opposition within the government, in other words, it was created by the Shah's own security apparatus. Clearly, it was Fardoust's men in SAVAK who had harassed me.

On Saturday morning, December 11, a week after being stopped from leaving Iran, Sheila and I departed our home in Poonak. Leaving behind directions for the staff and checking in one last time on Noor Jahan—the finest horse I'd ever ridden or ever would—we drove to the airport. As we were not sure when we would return, we'd packed heavy, two large suitcases each. Again, we met Mr. Taghavi at the airport. Mehrabad was even more crowded than it had been the previous Saturday. Desperate to get out, some people were carrying all their earthly possessions, as if they'd never return to Iran. It says something about my naiveté that even after all I'd been through, it did not seem possible to me that they were right.

Again we checked our bags and proceeded to the police kiosk. The same officer was on duty. He looked surprised to see me. "Mr. Nemazee what are you doing here?" I told him I'd resolved my issues and was free to leave. He looked perplexed, and said, "But your passport is not here."

"That's not possible," I responded.

"See for yourself."

The passports were in long file boxes, sorted by initial of last names. Sheila's passport was under the letter N, but mine was nowhere to be seen. I flipped through all the passports. It took a while but at last I found mine. It was in a pile of foreign passports, mixed in, somehow, with those of the Czechoslovakian national soccer team. Clearly somebody had placed it there as a final ploy to delay me. I handed it to the officer.

"It's your passport, Mr. Nemazee, but there is still a problem. The exit visa is not for today. It's for Monday."

Back we went to consult with the police chief we'd spoke to a week earlier. He was in a small windowless office, smoking a cigarette. Keeping my anger in check, I explained the issue, reminding him that I had been detained but had now been cleared to leave. "You can call Col. Shahbazi of the Tehran police. Or Mr. Nourbaksh of the Ministry of Justice. But we must be allowed to board." He looked at me, then at Sheila, who was near tears. He scribbled his signature on the exit visa. We were free to go.

As we sat in the boarding area, Sheila began to cry. I asked her why; she should be happy, I told her. We were finally leaving. "I'm crying because I know we are never coming back," she said.

"Don't be foolish. Of course we'll come back." Half an hour later, we were in the air, rising over Tehran, flying away from the country we'd never see again.

Part II

Politics

12

STARTING OVER

On our flight from Tehran, I spent some time reflecting on everything I'd experienced in the six years since my father's death. My life in Iran had been generally positive and productive. I'd adjusted to a new culture. I'd established the foundations of successful businesses in banking, insurance, and real estate development. I'd made good friends, married, and settled into a beautiful home. But even as I counted the blessings that had come my way, I had to acknowledge my complicity in the ills that had befallen the country. I, and other privileged Iranians, had tacitly signed on to an unspoken pact: in return for the economic and social benefits we enjoyed, we'd ceded total political authority to the Shah. We'd passively supported the system because it served our short-term interests. That was a mistake, both morally and politically.

My father had a saying: "Judgment comes from experience; good judgment comes from bad experience." I was determined that I would gain something from my experience, and put what I learned into practice. I would never again abdicate my political responsibility. I would find a way to be involved in decisions that would affect me and others. I would be a participant, not a spectator.

We landed in New York in the middle of the Christmas season. The city was decked out in holiday splendor. The festive mood was a bizarre contrast to the ominous scenes we'd just fled. U.S. newspapers carried daily bulletins from Iran, but the violence and turmoil there could have been happening in another solar system for all it seemed to matter to the shoppers bustling along Fifth Avenue or the revelers pouring out of bars on Madison.

We'd planned on staying at my mother's apartment on Park Avenue.[5] As it turned out, we could not stay there because she'd already loaned it to Hushang Ansary and his family. I could hardly object. I was pleased to know that Hushang was safe and comfortable in New York; his head would have been one of the first to roll, almost literally, if he were still in Iran. More selfishly, as a frequent beneficiary of Hushang's wisdom and friendship, I was pleased to have him nearby in America.

Instead of going to my mother's, Sheila and I took a suite in the Pierre Hotel on Fifth Avenue. Almost immediately, I returned to the airport and boarded a plane to Texas, where I was due to sign papers before the end of the year. Upon signing, I became 90% owner of the project we planned to develop in Houston.

We celebrated the dawn of 1979 on a yacht in Caribbean with my Iranian friend, Farhad Diba, and his wife. Despite the fact that Sheila spent much of the week throwing up over the side of yacht, the voyage was lovely and tranquil, and a mostly successful attempt to take our minds off events in Iran.

Not until we returned to New York did we learn that Sheila had not been seasick. She was pregnant.

■ ■ ■

We had not yet decided to live in New York permanently. Among other considerations, we still had our home in Poonak. With every passing day, returning to Tehran seemed increasingly far-fetched, but we still held out hope of this possibility. In the meanwhile, we needed a place of our own. After a good deal of searching, we settled on an apartment on Fifth Avenue, across the street from the Metropolitan Museum of Art. It was a perfect pied-à-terre from which we could look over the beauty of Central Park, even as we continued to watch, from a safe distance, the dissolution of the Shah's regime in Iran.

---

[5] My mother had purchased the apartment for a song in the mid-1970's, during the depths of New York's financial crisis, when real estate was practically being given away. Her only mistake was refusing the large modern painting hanging in the dining room. The seller offered to throw it in for an extra $25,000. My mother had no interest in modern art so turned him down. That painting was by Frank Stella. It would soon be worth considerably more than the apartment.

It turned out we were not as far from the turmoil and violence as we'd lulled ourselves into believing. On a few occasions that winter the revolution reached its claws into America. One episode that stands out in my memory occurred in Los Angeles, where Princess Shams, my mother's old friend and the sister of the Shah, had fled in December. Under the protection of a team from the U.S. Diplomatic Security office, Princess Shams took up residence in a mansion in Beverly Hills. In early January, Iranian students stormed her house, chanting violent threats, turning over a car or two, smashing windows, and lighting fires in the underbrush, apparently intending to burn down the house and everything in it.

The incident was covered widely in the press, but some of the more interesting details I learned directly from Howard Burris, my old Landon friend who was now Princess Shams' son-in-law. As Howard told it, Shams had brought her entire menagerie of dogs and parakeets from Iran. When the house came under attack, she refused to leave without them. The head the Diplomatic Security team told her they had no time to collect all the animals—"Forget the goddamned parakeets," were his exact words, according to Howard, "we're not getting killed for some goddamned parakeets"—but Princess Shams was adamant. Long story short, they managed to escape. But not before they packed every last goddamned parakeet into the car.

On the afternoon of January 16, 1979—a month after our departure from Iran, and 37 years after he became the nation's monarch—the Shah, accompanied by Empress Farah and a small entourage of aides, and piloting the plane himself as he always did, flew out of the country for the last time. The Shah promised to return soon, but he never would. Later, it would come out that he was already a very sick man by the time he fled, suffering from lymphoma that had been diagnosed five years earlier. He would die in a Cairo hospital in the summer of 1980.

With the departure of the Shah, the military withdrew to its bases and ceded full control of the country to the revolutionaries. Two weeks later, Ayatollah Khomeini arrived in Tehran in triumph. Crowds in the millions greeted his motorcade, though most Iranians had little concept of what they were welcoming. By mid-February, the new Islamic regime was in full control and Sharia law had been imposed over the country.

Then commenced Iran's version of the Reign of Terror. Within weeks of his return, Khomeini authorized the arrest and execution by firing squad of hundreds of members of the Shah's regime: military officers; former chiefs of the Shah's intelligence agency, SAVAK; former prime ministers; mayors and other government officials; and thousands more who disappeared in the months that followed.

Countless friends and acquaintances of ours were among the victims. A number of my father's old friends and associates were executed—Hoveyda, the former Prime Minister; Habib Elganian, the leading Jewish businessman in Iran; General Khosrodad and General Jahanbani, both of whom I'd often gone horseback riding with in Tehran. Many others were imprisoned and threatened, including my cousin Eskandar Firouz, the Deputy Prime Minister and head of the Environmental Protection Agency. Anyone associated with the former government, the Shah, or American interests was at risk.

I was in regular phone contact with my office through much of this. One call came right before a so-called "revolutionary committee" arrived at our office building to search for anything incriminating. "I want you to know we've taken care of it," my chief of staff told me cryptically over the phone.

"Taken care of what?"

"The object," he said.

"What object?"

"The *thing*. In your office."

Only then did I realize what he was meant. On a shelf behind my desk chair had been a small and inexpensive ceramic bust of the Shah, placed there years earlier and never given another thought. These little figures had been pretty much de rigueur under the Shah, signaling loyalty to the regime even as they gathered dust.

"What did you do with it?"

"We destroyed it."

I figured best to leave it there, on the chance that someone was listening in on our call.

In the spring of 1979, I received word that all of my personal holdings in Iran had been nationalized. Khomeini had identified 51 families and decreed that all assets of these families were now the property of the newly created Islamic Republic of Iran. What was the crime that we were accused and convicted of in the ayatollah's proclamation? *"Vabastegi ba America, vaba khanevadeh Pahlavi."*—Collaboration and association with America and the Pahlavi regime and family. Overnight, everything we owned in Iran—bank accounts, companies, stocks, bonds, land, homes, and personal effects—went into the possession of the Khomeini regime.

Our house in Poonak was taken over by the local revolutionary committee. Men arrived in two large trucks and filled these with everything of real or sentimental value. Persian carpets, furniture, my father's old books, other personal possessions and papers—they took all of it. I was livid, not so much for our own sake as for the members of our staff, some half dozen, who still lived there and were unceremoniously thrown out onto the streets.

The revolutionary committee also claimed our three horses, including my beloved Noor Jahan. I later learned from my groom what occurred. Two men came to the house on a summer morning and announced that the horses had been nationalized. The horses were to be ridden to Qazvin, nearly a hundred miles to the northwest. The men demanded that my groom accompany them to care for the horses along the way, as they knew nothing about horses themselves. The journey had to be made fast, they told him, with a single stop in the town of Karaj. My groom warned them that a journey of such length and speed would be dangerous to the horses in summer heat, but the men insisted. And so off they went, galloping to Qazvin through the hot and arid landscape. Numerous times the groom warned the men that they were riding the horses too hard, but they ignored him, and onward they rode.

Halfway between Karaj and Qazvin, Noor Jahan collapsed and died.

13

ANGEL FALLS

ALL THINGS CONSIDERED, we were fortunate. Yes, I'd lost a great deal of money, nearly 90% of my wealth, which was now in the hands of the Iranian Revolutionary government. Gone were our home, our horses, and most of our assets, along with many friends we'd never see again. But we had our lives and we had our freedom. Moreover, we had the money that I'd sent abroad a few years earlier, after the sale of the textile factory, and a potentially lucrative real estate project underway in Houston.

To make matters easier for me, I was culturally far more comfortable in America than were many of my fellow Iranians of the post-revolution diaspora. Iranians are an adaptable people— we've had millennia of war, regime change, and famine to practice survival skills—and the younger generation of Iranian expatriates would soon acclimate and thrive in the U.S. or wherever they settled. But that was not the case for older Iranians, who found life in the West to be financially draining and culturally sterile. It was difficult to watch some of these men and women, so prominent and comfortable in their former lives, reduced to poverty and ignominy in a foreign land. I would do what I could to help old friends of my father's, sending them money regularly to keep them afloat, but nothing could restore the lives they'd had in Iran.

Even as I counted my own blessings, I knew that I needed my luck to hold. I'd rolled the dice on the development project in Houston. The capital I'd invested had been a significant portion of my net worth when I undertook the project, and now, following the confiscation of my Iranian assets, it comprised nearly everything I had. There was no margin for error, especially not with Sheila's stomach growing larger by the day. I needed this to work.

I began traveling every week to Houston to oversee the construction and financing of the office building. The terms of the loan from Allied Bank called for it to be repaid upon completion of construction. We'd undertaken One West Loop Plaza—as we christened the project—with no major anchor tenant in place, but already we were beginning to pre-lease office space. Houston was just then experiencing a mini-economic boom. Ironically, the boom was largely due to events in Iran. The revolution had caused world oil prices to escalate dramatically, which was economically beneficial for Houston, the energy capital of America. And for a while, that was beneficial to me.

■ ■ ■

On November 4, 1979, Iranian militants stormed the American embassy in Tehran and captured 52 American hostages, setting off a crisis that would last through 1980 and the remainder of the Carter administration. The hostage crisis was a final sign that the lunatics had taken over the asylum. Khomeini would never become the holy savior that many Iranians and Western journalists had mistaken him for; he was just another ruthless tyrant who used guile and treachery to gain power. There would be no return to civil society in Iran, no restitution of property, no restoration of basic civility.

On December 4, 1979—a month after the embassy attack and a year after our escape from Iran—our daughter Yasmine was born. She was absolutely beautiful. She had huge chipmunk cheeks, green-brown eyes, and soft wisps of blond hair. It was stunning to consider how close we had to come to drowning in the nightmare that was now Iran only to be delivered such happiness.

But Yasmine's birth put a fine point on my financial situation. I had a wife and a daughter I needed to provide for, not to mention a mother, a brother, sisters, and an extended circle of family and friends, many still in Iran, that I wanted to help as I could. Given all this, I decided it would be prudent to hedge my bets in Houston.

One West Loop Plaza was proceeding nicely. As I'd predicted, the I.M. Pei mystique had created a buzz about the building that allowed us to lease space at higher than projected rental rates.

Months before the building was complete, we were almost fully rented. Still, I was anxious to lower my exposure. If the project went south, I could be left penniless.

With that in mind, I told my partner J.C. Helms (he'd dropped the *von* by this point) that I wanted to bring in another partner to purchase a 50% interest in the project. J.C. did not greet my proposal warmly. In fact, he adamantly opposed selling any part of the project. I tried to explain my reasoning, but he would not budge. In the end, though, the decision was mine to make, not his. I owned 90% of the building and he owned just 10%.

I began meeting with prospective partners. Alec Vagliano of Morgan Guaranty brought a number of interesting possibilities to me. One meeting I remember particularly well. The setting was La Côte Basque, one of New York's premier restaurants. Our dinner companion was an Italian investor who was aggressively targeting acquisitions in America. The Italian was charming and highly animated. During the course of the dinner, he told us that he had been a singer in his youth, and then, as if to prove it, began to serenade us at full volume in La Côte Basque. Patrons looked over, smiling nervously. Vagliano was mortified. I was amused. As for Silvio Berlusconi, he never became my partner, but he did go on to become the prime minister of Italy.

■ ■ ■

Just as I was giving up on the idea of finding an appropriate partner for the Houston project, I received a phone call from someone at the First National Bank of Chicago. The caller was in charge of the bank's real estate division and represented a buyer who wanted to purchase One West Loop Plaza. I countered that I was only interested in selling 50% of the property. He responded that his client, a large British pension fund called Legal & General, wanted *all* and was prepared to make a very attractive offer to purchase it. When he floated a number, I was astonished. The sum, more than $35 million, was far above the value we had placed on the building in our own projections. It was equal to what we predicted the building would be worth in ten years' time, after significant rent increases.

To sweeten the deal, Legal & General was prepared to lend me cash to purchase eight acres of land, adjacent to our building, that I had retained through an option agreement. The purchase price I'd locked in with the option was $15 per square foot. Due to inflation and the booming real estate market in Houston, the land was now valued at the absurdly high price of $110 per square foot. Even with my option payments, my cost basis would be under $20. And the pension fund was offering to lend me not only the $8 million purchase price, but a significant amount above this as an interest reserve. Altogether, it was an extraordinary deal—a deal no reasonable person, in my opinion, could refuse.

As I say, I had the right and power to decide to take the deal on my own, but I wanted J.C.'s consent, not only out of respect for his partial ownership of the building but also to honor a relationship that took us back to Winthrop House at Harvard. J.C. agreed that the price was far greater than the property was worth, but he insisted that we sell only a partial interest. Again, I explained to him that the deal we were being offered was all or nothing, take it or leave it. And again, the decision was ultimately mine to make, not his.

J.C.'s objections notwithstanding, I decided to take the deal. I knew J.C. would be angry. I did not imagine how far his anger would take him.

■ ■ ■

The closing for the sale of the building was scheduled for late in 1981. We met in the Houston offices of my attorneys, Fulbright & Jaworski. Four sets of attorneys were present—one representing me, another the building partnership, and two others for the buyer and the bank. The lawyers swarmed the conference rooms to deliberate and hammer out last-minute details.

As the lawyers did their work, I waited in a plush seating area with several representatives of the bank. We were sitting there, talking informally, when in walked a man who appeared to have stepped off the set of a Hollywood western. He wore shiny boots on his feet, a ten-gallon hat on his head, a badge on his vest, and a revolver on his hip. "Is there a Mr. Nemazee here?" he asked with a Texas twang.

"How can I help you?" I asked.

He swaggered over to me and handed me a document. "Sir, you've just been served." He turned and strode back out.

A quick glance at the paper told me that I'd been sued by J.C. Helms. It was clearly a frivolous lawsuit—he had no legal ground to stand on—but I understood what he was up to. He assumed that by suing me, Legal & General, reluctant to embroil itself in a messy partnership litigation, would drop out of the deal.

What I very much wanted to do, quite frankly, was crumple up the subpoena and shove it down Helms' throat, but I knew that was exactly what he wanted me to do—the more drama, the better the chances Legal & General would walk. Instead, I spent the next 24 hours, with the help of various intermediaries, trying to get Helms to drop the suit. No amount of reasoning worked on Helms—he'd dug in his heels—but I did manage to keep my cool, and both First National Bank of Chicago and Legal & General remained committed to the property.

In the end, it all worked out for me, but I will always regret that Helms and I were unable to come to an amicable resolution. It was a bad end to what had been a good friendship.

■ ■ ■

For all the trouble Helms stirred up, the Houston deal turned out to be a big winner for me, capping a long run of narrow scrapes and lucky breaks. I made a great deal of money. And my timing could not have been better. Six months later, the Houston market cratered. Had I not sold when I did, I would have been left with a building suddenly severely devalued and largely empty.

Right on the heels of Houston came another remarkable windfall. Marty Alloy, my former partner in Washington, made an unsolicited offer to buy my property in Montgomery County. After years of lying dormant under the sewer moratorium, my 500 acres remained undeveloped. Now the county had decided to concede to development and lift the moratorium, and the land was in great demand. Marty proposed a very attractive price. I'd always intended to participate in the development of the land and retain an ongoing interest, but after my rift with J.C. Helms in Houston, selling the land was an attractive alternative to developing it myself.

Following the sale of the Houston office building, the refinancing of the undeveloped land in Houston, and the sale of the land in Montgomery County, I found myself in possession of a great deal of wealth, somewhere in the neighborhood of $20 million in liquid assets. Today, when billionaires are a dime a dozen, that may not sound like a fortune. But in 1981, it made me one of the wealthiest young men in Manhattan.

■ ■ ■

I was too busy in those years to concern myself with the long-term implications of the debt I'd assumed in the deal with Legal & General. Nor did it ever occur to me, especially after my run of good luck, that I'd ever have reason to regret it. Life with a small child—soon to be joined by another—kept us in a state of constant motion, with little time left over for reflection.

Our social life revolved around children. We developed close friendships with other young couples, many, like us, recently displaced from Iran and adapting to America while starting families. A large percentage of diaspora Iranians had gone to Texas or California, where the climate and terrain were similar to Iran's, but a fair number ended up in New York City, often within a few blocks of us.

Sheila was pregnant again by the fall of 1981. In anticipation of our expanding household, we purchased the apartment adjacent to ours, nearly doubling the size of our home. We added a room for a live-in nanny named Carol and a cook named Ali Agha, who had worked for us in Iran and whom I flew to New York to resume his old role.

Our son Kamyar announced his imminent arrival into our lives late one stormy night in October. "Hassan," Sheila called to me with a voice that managed to be calm yet urgent, "we need to go to the hospital right now." Her water had broken.

A frantic race to get her to the hospital ensued. While Sheila waited in the lobby of our building, I ran into the middle of Madison Avenue, in the slashing rain, and commandeered a passing cab, despite the fact that the cab was already occupied. "It's an emergency," I explained to the well-dressed black man in back as I jumped in. "Thank you for understanding."

"My wife isn't gonna believe this," the man muttered back in shock. "She sure isn't going to believe this."

He would repeat that phrase several more times after we got Sheila stuffed into the back of the cab, alongside him and me, and sped north to Mt. Sinai Hospital, all of us praying we'd make it before she delivered right there in the taxi.

Somehow, we made it. Kamyar was born later that night in Mt. Sinai. For our first child, I'd truly not cared whether we had a girl or a boy. I'd be lying if I said I did not secretly want a son for our second.

■ ■ ■

One late September afternoon, at the end of a long day of touring rental properties in the countryside north of the city, a real estate agent drove us to a 22-acre estate known as Old Apple Farm. Located near the town of Katonah, New York, the property included a lovely turn-of-century farm house, stables, and a guest house and cottage. As we walked across the lawn under the setting sun, we could see horses grazing in the paddocks and deer nibbling at the edge of a woods. We were thousands of miles and worlds away from the dusty orchards of Poonak, but the farm brought back memories of our home there. The sight of horses made me want to ride again, too, something I had not done since my last time on Noor Jahan. Thoroughly enchanted, we made an offer on the spot.

Old Apple Farm became our weekend retreat, a place to ride and pick apples and let the kids run on the lawn and play outside until night, as I had done as a boy. Meanwhile, life in the city had its own rhythms and rewards, including the kind of serendipitous encounters you only get in a place like Manhattan.

Sheila and I were pushing our children in a stroller up Madison Avenue one Sunday afternoon when we ran into Alan Quasha and his wife, who were strolling their own children in the opposite direction. Alan had been at Harvard with me, and had then gone on to earn joint Harvard MBA and law degrees. We'd been scheduled to be in the same MBA section at the business school in the fall of 1972, before I abruptly withdrew due to my father's death.

I'd not seen Alan since then, but now he greeted me warmly. He told me that after graduating with his dual degrees he had established a law firm. He still practiced law but spent most of his time acquiring and restructuring companies.

I began investing with Alan. I particularly remember two companies he brought to my attention in those days. One was Paul Wilmot Enterprises, a perfume and fragrance supplier. Wilmot had the exclusive rights to Sonia Rykiel perfumes, a brand that had a limited following at that time. You might ask what business we had investing in a notoriously difficult industry that neither of us knew anything about, but perfumes have a way of clouding good judgment.

Alan brought another opportunity to me, this one far more lucrative. He had taken control of an oil and gas business, Harken Energy[6], a small publicly traded company that he intended to use as a vehicle to acquire other small oil companies. The energy industry was going through one of its periodic cycles of boom and bust, and we were in a bust phase. Alan correctly perceived an opportunity to pick up failed companies on the cheap and bring in outside investors to capitalize them. He was able to convince the Harvard endowment and George Soros, among others, to participate. Harken was a company that I would remain involved with over the course of many years. Some of those years would be good, others bad, but the gains usually outweighed the losses.

■ ■ ■

Meanwhile, I still had my eye on owning a bank, something I'd wanted since my early days in Iran. I gave Morgan Guaranty a mandate to find me a small U.S. bank to purchase. My intention was to acquire a commercial bank, but after some months of analysis Morgan recommended that I purchase a savings and loan bank instead.

---

[6] Harken Energy later came to play a role in a scandal involving George W. Bush. In 1986, Harken purchased the future president's foundering oil company and put him on its Board of Directors, with compensation that included stock. Four years later, Bush sold nearly a million dollars worth of Harken stock just prior to a bad earnings report. The SEC investigated possible insider trading by Bush but ultimately found no wrongdoing.

S&Ls were a sleepy corner of the banking industry, originally created to provide financing for real estate lending. As a consequence of the downturn in the real estate industry, as well as high interest rates put in place by Fed chairman Paul Volker, many of the thrifts—as these S&Ls were called—had fallen into dire financial shape. To keep them solvent, U.S. bank regulators had decided to allow them to invest in assets that were a lot riskier than bread-and-butter mortgages, including direct investments in equities and real estate development. This made S&Ls extremely attractive opportunities for growth. The industry grew by more than 50% between 1982 and 1985. As Morgan pointed out, the thrifts had a lot to recommend them to me, including cheap access to capital. Their logic made sense, but I still had my heart set on a commercial bank. Alas, none of the commercial banks that Morgan suggested to me were open to being sold.

Whatever regret I suffered on that end was relieved by my decision to avoid purchasing a savings and loan bank. In the late 1980's, as a result of deregulation, the universe of S&Ls crashed and burned. The federal government stepped in to take control of hundreds of failed thrifts. Many owners of thrifts were sentenced to prison for bank fraud. Staying out the thrifts turned out to be a smart move. I knew I'd gotten lucky, but I gave myself some credit. My instincts had been good.

■ ■ ■

After the attack on the American embassy, diplomatic relations between Iran and United States had deteriorated to the point of total collapse. This resulted in all sorts of unforeseen problems for both countries, and it created a fairly immediate problem for me. Although I had been born in Washington, my father had been an accredited Iranian diplomat at the time. This made me an Iranian citizen, with an Iranian passport. Now my Iranian passport was due to expire and needed to be renewed. I had every intention of applying for permanent residence and citizenship in the United States, but that would take time. In the meantime, I needed a valid passport.

When I went to apply for a new passport at the Iranian interest section in Washington—located inside the Pakistani embassy—I was informed that my passport could not be renewed in America.

I would have to return to Iran to obtain a new passport. That was out of the question, of course. I'd probably be arrested the moment I entered Iran.

Fortunately, I had a solution that would buy me time until I could obtain a U.S. passport. My half-sister, Shahla, and her husband, Carlos Cisneros, were now living in Caracas, Venezuela, with their three children. Carlos's family was politically, financially, and socially among the most powerful in Venezuela. Carlos was a good and generous man, and when he learned of my predicament he called to tell me that he would be happy to arrange for me to obtain a Venezuelan passport. Once I had this, I would be able to apply for my permanent residency in the United States while continuing to travel aboard.

First, though, I had to get to Venezuela. There was a man in Washington at the time who knew how turn an expired passport into a valid passport, and I hired him to work his magic on mine. A week later, with an apparently valid Iranian passport in hand, I flew to Venezuela.

I stayed in Caracas about a month. My mother came with me, as she too required a new passport. While I missed my own family, I enjoyed spending this time with my half-sister's family and especially with Carlos, a true gentleman. Carlos had made a difficult decision to branch out on his own from his family's business, which had gone into the hands of his younger brother, Gustavo. As a result, he was not as rich as his brothers, two of whom would later become billionaires. But he was happy with his independence from the Cisneros clan and was devoted to his own successful businesses and, above all, to his family. True to his word, Carlos was able, in record time, to set us up with Venezuelan passports and citizenship. With gratitude, we said goodbye to Carlos and Shahla and their children and flew back home to New York. I then immediately set out to take the necessary steps to become a naturalized American citizen. (I ultimately accomplished this in the early 1990's.)

The following July, I was with my family in a beach house in South Hampton when I received a phone call from Gustavo Cisneros, Carlos's brother.

"Hassan, I have very bad news."

Over the weekend, Shahla and her family had gone to Angel Falls, the highest waterfall in the world, in the interior of Venezuela. Their 13-year-old son had gone swimming in the lake below the falls with a friend. The lake looked placid enough on the surface, but the power of the falling water created tricky currents and whirlpools. When the boy seemed to have difficulty in the water, Carlos jumped in and swam out to help. Before he could reach his son, Carlos found himself caught in a powerful whirlpool. He was a fair swimmer, but he could not break free, and he was dragged under the surface. He never came back up.

Like her son, my sister had watched this tragedy unfold from the beach, unable to do anything. She and her son were still at Angel Falls, Gustavo told me. Rescue workers had yet to recover the body. "I think you must come and be with your sister," said Gustavo. "This is very hard."

Shahla and her children were back in Caracas by the time I landed. The entire Cisneros family was shell shocked and could barely think straight, much less plan a funeral and deal with a hundred other decisions that had to be made. I did what I could to help. My mother came, too, and tried to comfort her inconsolable daughter.

The church service was heartbreaking. For some inexplicable reason, a decision had been made to have an open casket. Carlos's body had been submerged under the falls for 24 hours, and no amount of cosmetics could disguise the toll this had taken on his face. Seeing him like this must have been especially difficult for his son, Carlos Enrique, who had watched his father drown before his eyes. One moment, they had been enjoying life to the fullest, blessed with happiness and good fortune; the next moment, by a stroke of bad luck—a freak whirlpool on a beautiful day—all of it was gone.

14

TRUMPED

In August of 1985, our third child, Layla, burst into our lives, smiling and laughing from the start. She immediately became the object of adoring teasing from Kamyar and gentle affection from Yasmine. From infancy to grammar school, though subsequent years in boarding school and college and beyond, the three children would be devoted to each other. That strength and closeness would be an enormous asset to them—to all of us—later.

After Layla's birth, we began looking for a larger home. For a short while, we considered moving to our country house in Katonah, but we ultimately got cold feet at the thought of living full time in the country. Instead, Sheila turned to finding a more permanent home in the city—and not just any home, but that most elusive object of desire, the perfect New York apartment. The rule of thumb is that if you ever do manage to find your perfect New York apartment, it will be instantly snatched away from you by the fickle gods of real estate.

One day Yasmine came home from a play date with one of her school friends. She announced to Sheila that she had found "the perfect apartment for Mommy." She had been to the home of our friends the Cullmans, who lived in a duplex on the corner of 73rd Street and Park Avenue. There were only a few dozen apartments in the building, and one, just across the hall from the Cullmans, happened to be for sale. It was a pre-war co-op built in an age of New York grandeur. High ceilings, five bedrooms, library, large living room with a fireplace, spacious dining room, and several maids' rooms. The moment we saw it, we knew that Yasmine's assessment had been absolutely correct: it was perfect. And then, all too predictably, we were *gazumped*—screwed, in the argot of New York real estate, by another buyer who swooped in with a higher bid.

Before we had a chance to get too upset, another duplex, on higher floors, became available. This apartment was even better, with more light and better views. We pounced. We paid top dollar but considered ourselves fortunate.

Not long after closing on the apartment, I was walking up Park Avenue with Sheila when we ran into my good friend Kim Fennebresque, whose son, Quincy, was a classmate of Kamyar's. Kim was a very successful investment banker at Lazard, but he was best known for his sharp wit. By his own admission, he'd paid top dollar for his apartment. "I'm so happy to hear about your recent purchase," said Kim. "I was beginning to think I'd go down in history as the idiot who bought the most overpriced apartment in New York. Now you get that prize."

■ ■ ■

If I'd bought at the top of market in New York, I'd also sold at the top in Houston in the early 1980's. More than five years later, Legal & General's purchase of my building, One West Loop Plaza, remained the highest price ever paid per square foot for an office property in Houston. I'd gotten very lucky.

But what Houston gave with one hand, it took with the other. As part of our deal, Legal & General had lent me $20 million to buy the land next to building they purchased from me. The land cost $8 million, which gave me $12 million to play with. This would have been a terrific loan had I been able to quickly develop or turn around the land and sell it. But the same market slump in Houston that I'd beaten with the timely sale of the building now made it difficult, if not impossible, to do anything productive with the land. No one wanted to purchase it, and there was no market for new development. Land once appraised at over $30 million was almost valueless. To make matters worse, interest rates were at historic highs. I'd been servicing my debt throughout the 80's with huge payments, bleeding cash all the way. When the Legal & General loan came due in 1987, I decided to let the fund take possession of it. The loan was non-recourse, meaning that I was not personally liable for it. Walking away was my best option.

As it turned out, Legal & General had no interest in getting encumbered with raw land in a depressed market. They came back to me with a very attractive deal. They offered to "sell" the property back to me for $6 million, or $2 million less than I had originally paid for it. This was for land, mind you, that had once been appraised at $35 million. Given the depressed Houston market, I had every reason to believe that, sooner or later, prices would rebound. I could then sell and not only make back what I'd paid to the bank in interest but accrue additional profit. When Great West Life Insurance Company of Canada agreed to loan me the entire sum to buy back the land, I decided to do it.

So far, all my decisions were sound. The part that was not sound was my acceptance of Great West's condition that I take the loan on with a personal guarantee, rather than the non-recourse clause in my previous loan contract. In doing so, I broke a cardinal rule of real estate, one that I had both practiced and preached, to never provide personal loan guarantees. I was hardly the first or last person to do this—Donald Trump, for example, would make a practice of personal guarantees—but it was a bad idea. It meant that I was now liable for payments of a million dollars a year.

■ ■ ■

For the moment, despite the stiff quarterly payments, the loan gave me nothing to worry about. I still had tremendous liquidity from the sale of One West Loop Plaza and the farm, as well as a number of investments. And potentially lucrative new business opportunities continued to present themselves to me.

The most significant of these was a company called First Capital Asset Management that I founded with a smart young Princeton undergraduate and Harvard MBA named Gerry Angulo. Gerry had worked briefly for the infamous Ivan Boesky, before Boesky was found guilty of insider trading. Gerry was a good stock picker, and even better at publicizing his results, both useful qualities for attracting other investors. First Capital represented clients interested in high yield investments.

Along with investing in publicly traded equities, we purchased companies outright. We turned Diagnostic Sciences, a small publicly traded medical company, into a holding company that bought a number of other companies in diverse industries. We purchased Norton Drilling, a Texas-based oil and gas service company. We also purchased one of the nation's largest flower nurseries in Homestead, Florida—unfortunately, just before

Hurricane Andrew destroyed the entire nursery business in Homestead. There were losses, but there were gains, too, and the risks were generally offset by the rewards. Our largest client was CALPERS, the agency that managed the pensions and health benefits of all public employees of California.

A few opportunities got away from me, some of these regrettable, others that turned out to be lucky escapes. One of the former came when I tried to buy the building where I rented my offices. Known as the Crown Building, 730 Fifth Avenue was owned by infamous Marcos family from the Philippines. It fully deserved its name—it was one of the crown jewels of Manhattan commercial real estate. After Marcos's downfall, litigation had been instigated by the government of the Philippines, alleging that the funds used to buy the Crown Building were government monies. As a result of the litigation, the building was being put up for auction in a bankruptcy proceeding. I saw this as an opportunity to purchase a unique asset at a discount.

I asked Abe Wallach, our real estate expert at First Capital, to put a valuation on the building. I then went to Hushang Ansary, who was still living in New York at the time, and showed him the numbers. He agreed it was a good opportunity and offered to partner with me. He also suggested that we bring in an institutional partner to assist us. Salomon Brothers, run by his friend John Gutfruend, was a good place to start.

With Hushang on board, I was quickly invited to make a lunchtime presentation in the private dining room at Salomon. I made the case for buying the building to John Gutfruend, the legendary and famously gruff "King of Wall Street," and half a dozen of his executives. As they ate—I was too nervous to touch my plate—I went through the numbers. There was no way to read Gutfruend's poker face, but he clearly liked what he heard. A few days later, one of his people called to tell us the Salomon wanted to participate as a 50% partner. We agreed on a bid ceiling of $90 million.

The auction was held in the chamber of the bankruptcy court. Abe Wallach was there to represent us and handle the bidding, running out when he could to report to me by pay phone. The price opened at $75 million. As the price rose, Abe stayed in.

He seemed to have a lock on a $90 million bid when another last-second bid swooped in—for $95 million. It came, we later learned, from a partnership that included the real estate magnate Bernard Spitzer, father of future New York governor Eliot Spitzer.

We were bitterly disappointed. But as luck would have it, the New York real estate market suddenly went into a four-year tailspin, causing Spitzer and his co-investors to put in far more capital than they originally projected. Later, when the market recovered, the Crown reclaimed its title as one of New York's trophy properties, but for the moment, it was another albatross, one I was happy not to have around my neck.

A coda to this story: Abe Wallach liked to talk to the press. I told him to take care to say nothing that could be detrimental to me or to First Capital. Apparently forgetting that directive, he was quoted one morning in the *New York Post* as stating that the Plaza Hotel, then owned by Donald Trump, was functionally bankrupt, and that Trump would soon lose the property. Abe was right—Trump did lose the Plaza—but it was not helpful for him to say it out loud, certainly not about a man as famously litigious as Trump. Sure enough, First Capital was soon served legal papers by the Trump Organization, demanding $100 million in damages for false statements made by a representative of our company. I called Wallach into my office and read him the riot act.

Fortunately, Trump's attorney was Jerry Schrager, a friend and fellow board member of the first co-op building I lived in in New York. I called Jerry and said I want to get rid of the suit immediately—just tell me what we needed to do to placate Trump. After checking with Trump, Schrager called back and said we needed to do two things. First of all, First Capital must issue a retraction of the comments. Secondly, Abe Wallach had to personally apologize.

The next day I sent Wallach across the street to Trump's office to apologize. The apology worked a little too well. Trump not only dropped the suit, but he hired Abe Wallach on the spot. A week later, Wallach left First Capital and went to work for the Trump Organization.

■ ■ ■

In January of 1990, I travelled to Egypt to celebrate my 40th birthday, on a trip organized by our friends Tom and Clem Pulling. It was a great itinerary and an interesting group accompanying the Pullings, including Beverly Sills, the opera singer, and John and Joan McEnroe, parents of John McEnroe, the tennis player.

We arrived in Cairo, having flown directly from New York. It was 10 p.m. We went straight to the hotel, intending to go to bed. But as we checked in at the front desk, we were handed a note by the receptionist. It was from Tom Pulling, advising us to be ready to go out later that night. I called Tom and tried to beg off. We were exhausted, I told him, and needed sleep. Tom would not hear of it. His good friend and college classmate, Frank Wisner, son of the legendary former CIA director of operations (who had greenlighted the agency's attempt to overthrow Mossadegh) and himself the American Ambassador to Egypt, was coming to the hotel momentarily to collect us and take us to a religious ceremony.

"I've survived the Iranian Revolution," I told Tom sleepily. "I think I've had enough of religious ceremonies to last me a lifetime."

"See you in the lobby," said Tom. "You won't be sorry."

Wisner soon arrived at the hotel in an SUV, accompanied by a small entourage of Egyptian security guards. Wisner carried himself with authority and impeccable manners but not a shred of pretension. He was dressed casually in a loose-fitting olive green military style jacket, scruffy boots, and jeans—hardly the picture of your typical supercilious American ambassador. Greeting us warmly, he informed us that we would be going to a religious festival in the City of the Dead. We piled into a couple of SUVs and sped off into the Egyptian night.

The City of the Dead is an ancient cemetery populated by common graves and elaborate and towering mausoleums, including some built centuries earlier for Egyptian royalty. It remains an active and surprisingly vibrant public setting, even at night. As we arrived, a funeral was in progress. Having attended

Islamic funerals in Iran, I expected a lugubrious procession of black-clad mourners. To the contrary, this funeral had a carnival-like atmosphere—quite literally. There were carnival rides, Ferris wheels, cotton candy, roasted corn, and ice cream carts.

We followed Wisner into the crowd. As much as he encouraged us to blend in, that was impossible. For one thing, Tom Pulling was six and a half feet tall, with a handsome patrician face and full head of white hair—he blended in nowhere, and definitely not in Egypt. The armed security detail also made us pretty conspicuous. Soon everyone at the festival knew that the American Ambassador was present. Wisner was totally at ease, greeting all comers with graciousness and enthusiasm. After strolling around the City of the Dead for a while, we entered the mausoleum of an Egyptian Islamic saint. It was truly an awesome place, with a vaulted tiled ceiling and dazzling wall mosaics glimmering in the dim light. We stood in solemn quiet for a few minutes, then followed Wisner back out.

Wisner's curiosity, his interest in learning firsthand about what was happening in Egypt—not just from contacts with upper-class Egyptians but with the poor—was eye-opening for me. Down to earth, extremely knowledgeable about the culture, and, most importantly, totally at ease with all levels of Egyptian society, he was the epitome of what an American Ambassador should be.

Altogether, it was a great and energizing night. It did not end until about three in the morning, after a bountiful dinner in an Egyptian hole-in-the-wall owned by the brother of Wisner's driver. When I finally got into bed, I was more awake than I'd been many hours earlier.

■ ■ ■

Over the years, First Capital had done well in managing funds for various public pension funds and high net worth individuals, but we'd suffered recent losses in our portfolio management business. To add to our difficulties, we were sued by a disgruntled broker, Robert Shea, for purported breach of contract. His lawsuit was eventually thrown out on summary judgment, meaning that the court essentially determined that there was no merit to the suit. But Shea succeeded in harassing most of our clients, by forcing depositions during the discovery phase of his litigation. This made the clients unhappy and uneasy.

As we were contemplating our options, I received an unsolicited offer from an acquaintance in the Iranian-American community, Sohrab Vahabzadeh, to invest in First Capital. We had not been looking to raise capital, but we were certainly not opposed to considering an offer, especially under the circumstances.

Sohrab Vahabzadeh came from a prominent merchant family that had made most of its fortune by owning the Caterpillar mining, engineering and construction equipment franchise in Iran. Prior to the revolution, the Vahabzadehs had done two things that few others in Iran had had the foresight to do. First, they'd sent considerable money aboard prior to the revolution. Secondly, they'd held their Caterpillar dealership in a Swiss-based company, so it could not be nationalized by the Islamic government after the revolution. As a result, they'd held onto most of their money. Sohrab's uncle, the principal in the business, was very shrewd. Sohrab was not, though he did turn out to be conniving.

Sohrab told me that his family wanted to purchase a large minority interest in First Capital. We eventually negotiated an agreement for the Vahabzadehs to purchase a 30% interest. We then contacted all of our clients to advise them of a transaction, as we were required to do by law. Just before closing, Sohrab called me from Geneva. He was practically in tears. He told me that his uncle had backed out of the deal. It's too late for that, I responded. We had already contacted our clients to advise them of the sale. Sohrab swore that it was not his decision; there was nothing he could do to reverse it.

I should never have done business with Vahabzadeh. He was unreliable and not particularly bright, as evidenced by that fact that he'd been willing to overpay significantly for his share of First Capital. Because we needed the cash investment, though, I'd overlooked this and taken advantage of his poor judgment. The real problem, as it turned out, was *my* poor judgment. There is an old saying that you should never make important decisions in anger. Well, I ignored that advice. I instructed our in-house counsel to initiate legal proceedings against Vahabzadeh and his uncle.

The litigation would go on for several years and ultimately result in a total vindication of our position. The court granted us the full amount of the intended investment, and agreed that there had been a breach of contract. Vahabzadeh was personally liable for $5 million. He proceeded to file for personal bankruptcy to avoid payment. The bankruptcy court again found in our favor, determining that Vahabzadeh was fraudulently trying to dismiss his debt. The debt was reinstated, with interest.

That debt, now in excess of $45 million, remains unpaid to this day.

■ ■ ■

My partnership with Gerry Angulo terminated after the lawsuit. We liquidated and sold off First Capital's assets, including all of our operating companies. I moved my office into a suite in a townhouse that Alan Quasha had recently purchased on 73rd Street, just half a block from my home at 770 Park. I found myself, for the first time since graduating from Harvard, underemployed and unsure what I wanted to do next. My Houston real estate project remained stalled, due to market conditions. Other projects and investments were either dormant or self-sustaining. I was restless and eager for a new challenge.

As I'd learned years earlier in a hotel lobby in Geneva, idleness is the devil's plaything. Back then, it had carried me to a blackjack table at the Casino Divonne. Now it took me somewhere even more treacherous: to the inner sanctums of American politics.

15

ACHILLES' HEEL

Before the 1990's, my politics leaned right. I was a so-called Rockefeller Republican—fiscally conservative but socially liberal. Like many Iranian Americans, I'd been turned off from the Democrats by Jimmy Carter's wobbly response to the Iranian Revolution. And I'd not had much regard for Walter Mondale or Michael Dukakis, both of whom struck me as lackluster candidates.

By the 90's, though, the political parties in the United States were changing, and so was I. The Republican Party began to engage more freely in the rhetoric of nativism and xenophobia. As a man of Iranian descent, I took this personally. As an American, I found it offensive and contrary to the values of the United States. The 1994 midterm elections crystallized my concerns. Newt Gingrich's "Contract with America" had become the manifesto of the Republican Party—a party I felt less in tune with every passing day. Meanwhile, a new standard bearer had risen from the Democrats. Bill Clinton was the epitome of what I thought an American president should be. He was fiscally prudent and socially responsible, and he had a big vision and an ambitious agenda, both at home and abroad. He made my decision to change parties easy.

As for why I decided to enter the arena personally, as a fundraiser, I suppose the answer is more complicated. In part, I saw a chance to represent the aspirations of many Iranian Americans, at a time when Iranian Americans had no voice in government. Indeed, ever since the revolution, some Americans seemed to think that Iranian heritage precluded citizens from being fully American, as if anyone who fled Iran in 1978-1979 would be sympathetic to the Ayatollah's regime. That odious impression needed to be addressed and erased. I turned to political fundraising for Democrats to support a view of America as a growth-oriented democracy that was inclusive and enlightened.

It occurs to me that there were other, less laudable, reasons I ended up getting so deeply consumed by my fundraising work. While I can honestly profess that I did not do it for personal gain in any monetary sense, I cannot deny that vanity contributed to my motives. Fundraising at the level I did it was an automatic fast-track to the highest ranks of political power in this country. It was gratifying and heady in a way that, say, a real estate deal never could be. It was also thrilling to take part in the high stakes effort to get a candidate elected to the presidency of the United States.

As my personal financial woes mounted, my fundraising work consumed me, bringing me accolades and a sense of purpose. It would have been wiser, in retrospect, to put more of my attention into my business, which needed it, and less into politics. Then again, one of the attractions of politics was that it kept my mind off my financial problems.

■ ■ ■

My entrance into political work happened fast. This was true partly because I arrived at a time when the Democratic Party, having just suffered huge losses in Congress in the 1994 midterms, was in desperate need of help. For the first time in decades, the Democrats had lost control of Congress. It looked as though they might very well lose the White House in 1996, too.

Never one to ignore political reality, President Clinton set to work to put in place a reelection strategy to re-energize the party. Key to his plan was raising the necessary funds to redefine himself and the Democratic message. He hoped to deploy the Democratic National Committee (DNC) far more aggressively than ever before. This was before the McCain-Feingold bill came along, so campaign contributions from individuals and corporations were unlimited, and Clinton wanted to tap every resource possible. He tapped Christopher Dodd, the senior senator from Connecticut, to be general chairman of the Democratic National Committee. Marvin Rosen, a lawyer from Miami and New York, was finance chair.

As it happened, I knew Marvin. He was a managing partner of Greenberg Traurig, a law firm in New York that occupied offices adjacent to my own in the Citibank building on Park Avenue.

One day in the fall of 1994, Marvin called to tell me that he was hosting a dinner at his home in Miami the following week for Al Gore, to support the Clinton-Gore reelection effort. He invited me to attend. A week later, I found myself sitting next to the vice president.

That dinner was not a propitious introduction to politics in general or to Al Gore in particular. I'd looked forward to meeting Gore and was sure we'd have lots to discuss, from matters of current politics to shared personal history. Though I had no recollection of meeting him in college, Gore and I had overlapped at Harvard. We'd also both grown up in Washington around the same time. He'd attended St. Albans during the period I attended Landon; the two schools were rivals in football, basketball, and baseball, and there was a decent chance we'd played against each other as boys.

I pride myself at being able to talk to just about anyone about pretty much anything, but my efforts to engage the vice president on these or any other topics were futile. He responded with short, blunt answers, and asked not a single question in return. The fact that he'd recently torn his Achilles tendon in a pick-up basketball game and was hobbling around on crutches, probably still in pain, might have contributed to his detachment. But he was also, as I would come to learn, a naturally shy and reserved person. He wasn't arrogant. He wasn't bored. He was just socially awkward. As a politician, this was an Achilles' heel a lot harder to overcome than a torn tendon, but Gore had done pretty well for himself despite it.

I returned to my hotel room that evening feeling disappointed. I'd not been impressed with Gore, and he'd clearly not been interested in me. Or so I thought. I was still in Florida the next day when I received a call from Don Fowler, the chair of the Democratic National Committee. Fowler informed me that the vice president had very much enjoyed meeting me and wanted to invite me to visit him in Washington at my earliest convenience. I was surprised, to say the least. But I made arrangements to fly to Washington the following week and give Gore another try.

I met with the vice president and his chief aide, Peter Knight, in Gore's office in the Old Executive Office Building, adjacent to the White House. This time, Gore could not have been more gracious. As I came to discover, he was more at ease in small groups, and could be even warm and charming. He was also clearly smart, decent, and reasonable. If not a natural politician, he was by all measures a qualified statesman.

As we sipped coffee, Gore explained that he'd been asked by the president to take on an expanded fundraising role for the reelection campaign. He wanted to reach out to a core group of supporters who could help shoulder the effort. He wondered if I'd be interested in participating. "Mr. Vice President," I said, "I'd be honored."

■ ■ ■

A few weeks later, I threw a dinner in New York for the Democratic National Committee, featuring Gore as our "special guest." This was the first of many fundraising events we'd host over the next dozen years, and it was trial by fire. The role of the "host" is not only to serve the dinner but to raise whatever the Finance Committee expects to collect. The expectation for our dinner was $100,000. Soon after I began to make calls, I raised $250,000—more than twice the campaign's goal.

The meal itself was a near disaster. We had a live-in Chinese chef named Mr. Yeung, but Sheila decided to serve Persian food. This was prepared by a wonderful Armenian caterer we often hired, Mr. Reuben. On the afternoon of the dinner, Mr. Reuben dropped off the food, with instructions to Mr. Yeung on how to heat it and serve it. Mr. Yeung was a man of great pride and did not like being told how to run his kitchen, nor did he appreciate having another chef's food served on the night of the vice president's visit. It seems Mr. Yeung got his revenge by intentionally sabotaging Mr. Reuben's Persian food, overheating it to the point that it became practically inedible. Sheila was mortified and I was angry. But the vice president seemed to be in seventh heaven. Declaring the dinner the best Persian food he'd ever eaten—which suggests he'd never eaten Persian food before—he vacuumed every morsel off his plate, then asked for more. Altogether, Gore and his staff were thrilled with the success of the dinner.

It was clear from the start that I was good at raising money. In part this owed to the simple fact that I knew a lot of people. I had a network of friends and associates, including many who were not part of the Wall Street and Upper East Side donor class usually tapped by the Democrats. But the more complete explanation for my success is that whomever I called, I did not just ask for money. I listened. I took the time to hear what a potential donor cared about, and to consider how his or her donation might move the needle on a pertinent issue.

I took my cues from Harvard. For some years, I'd been involved with the university's fundraising efforts. I'd endowed a scholarship at Harvard to bring Iranian students and Iranian professors to Harvard and was a member of the Visiting Committee for the Weatherhead Center for International Affairs. These experiences and others gave me a firsthand view of how Harvard accrued the largest private endowment in the country. It was very simple. Recognizing that the school's alumni were generally smart and successful in their areas of expertise, Harvard not only solicited a donation, but sought to bring the donor into an ongoing involvement with the university in his or her area of interest. When you ask donors to contribute something beyond money—intelligence, knowledge, passion— you enhance their commitment.

Obviously, a political campaign operates differently than a university, but the lesson was the same: no one wants to be an ATM machine in a suit, not for a university and not for a politician. Donors want to engage with campaigns in a meaningful fashion, whether that means an opportunity to talk about their convictions for a few minutes on the phone or to have a one-on-one exchange with a candidate, or simply to join in common cause to elect a qualified man or woman to office.

■ ■ ■

Of course, the same applied to me. I believed that I had something unique to contribute to the political process, and especially to the Democrats. In my very person, I represented an opportunity for the party to broaden its political base and its fundraising potential.

I got a chance to make my case a few weeks after the dinner for Gore when, much to my surprise, I was invited to the White

House for a meeting with President Clinton. I flew to Washington the night before and checked into the Hay-Adams, across from the White House. The next morning, I walked across 16th Street to the gate, showed my identification, and strolled up the drive to the White House.

The meeting was held in one of the White House reception rooms. I was one of half a dozen guests, along with the two Democratic National Committee chairs, Senator Chris Dodd and Don Fowler, and the president's chief of staff, Erskine Bowles. Waiting for the president, we took our seats at a long rectangular table with place cards and coffee servings. There was a palpable tension in the room as we waited, but the moment Clinton entered everyone brightened and relaxed. A great deal has been written about Clinton's extraordinary personal and intellectual gifts. I can only affirm that the man lives up to the hype. He is warm, funny, and instantly likeable. The entire room buzzes with his energy.

After a few minutes of small talk, Clinton sat and we got down to serious conversation. Clinton wanted to know how the Democratic Party could expand its reach, both electorally with votes and, just as importantly, with financial engagement by donors. Up until this point, Republicans had historically outraised Democrats by virtue of their deeper ties to the business community. That needed to change if the Democrats hoped to compete successfully.

Clinton went around the table, soliciting opinions. When he came to me, I made the point, first, that Democrats were more popular in the New York business community than the president believed. Like me, the community tended to be fiscally conservative but socially liberal.

Then I turned to my larger point. I told the president that the Democrats were ignoring an untapped source of votes and funding: the Iranian-American community. Nearly a million strong now, Iranian Americans were highly educated and well assimilated into American life. They were also more financially successful than most immigrant communities. Heretofore, they'd mostly avoided American politics, but they tended to lean right, thanks to Jimmy Carter's muddled response to the Iranian Revolution. But unlike, say, Cuban emigrants who fled Castro's

Cuba in the late 1950's and early 1960's, Iranian Americans were not committed right-wingers. Many of them were as turned off by Newt Gingrich and the rightward drift of the Republican Party as I was. This provided an opportunity to establish a connection between Iranian Americans and the Democratic Party.

It was clear to me that I was telling Clinton something he'd never heard before. He nodded thoughtfully when I finished talking. Then he turned to Chris Dodd and Don Fowler and directed them to follow up immediately on my suggestions. It was a heady feeling to know that I had just given one of the master politicians of his age a piece of useful political advice.

■ ■ ■

The dinner for Gore was the first of many fundraisers I hosted to raise money for Clinton and Gore through the mid-1990's. By the summer of 1996, I had established myself as one the leading fundraisers in the party.

Even as I began raising large sums for politicians, though, my own financial situation was becoming more dire. The Houston real estate market had yet to recover, and I remained saddled with a heavy annual debt service, to the tune of $1 million a year. I was also carrying the costs of three homes—the duplex at 770 Park Avenue, Old Apple Farm in Katonah, and a ski chalet in Telluride, Colorado. For first time, I began to worry about liquidity.

The obvious response to this should have been to tighten my belt and cut expenses. But I had a remarkable ability to convince myself that my financial problems were merely temporary, that I was just a step away from salvation. A number of investments did in fact seem promising, including a newspaper I'd purchased in Puerto Rico. I also knew that Houston real estate would rebound at some point, as real estate nearly always does. I just did not realize that the city was nowhere near the end of the longest slump in its history.

Meanwhile, Yasmine, now 14, had decided to look at boarding schools. It was ironic to me that she would want to go away to school—I had fought very hard to stay out of boarding school as a boy. But she was adamant. When she announced her decision to attend Deerfield Academy in Massachusetts, I was heartbroken.

Again, the wise course would have been to focus on my immediate concerns—my business, my family—and not go looking for new problems to solve. But my response to most difficulties in life was action rather than reflection or introspection. At times, action is the most productive response to a challenge. At other times, it's just a mask for distraction and carelessness.

■ ■ ■

Bill Clinton won a second term. Almost immediately, the Democrats turned their attention to the next round of midterm congressional campaigns, in which the party hoped to make up some of the losses it had incurred under Gingrich. I worked hard to raise money, usually with success. Fundraising took up increasing amounts of my focus. Someone once asked me at a party what percentage of my time I gave to political work. I responded that it was about "15-20%." That gave Sheila a good laugh.

Bill Clinton, for all his gifts, was never more than a few weeks from one crisis or another, and soon enough a new one hit his administration and the Democratic Party. It began when the *Washington Post* reported that illegal campaign contributions had been made by Chinese nationals to the Clinton-Gore campaign. Purportedly, the contributions were given as part of a coordinated effort by the Chinese government to gain influence in the U.S. government. The press and Republicans smelled blood, and almost daily there were new accusations and revelations.

All other business ground to a halt as the White House sought to address the charges. The Democratic National Committee went into full retreat, and the party's finance committee, headed by Marvin Rosen, came under intense scrutiny. Fundraising froze, leaving unpaid a $10 million debt incurred by the party during the campaign.

By the summer of 1997, it had become clear that something needed to be done to reinvigorate the party, not to mention pay down the huge debt. I received an invitation to a meeting of the Democratic National Committee to address the party's financial condition. President Clinton, Vice President Gore, the leadership of the Democratic National Committee, and the party's largest fundraisers convened in the ballroom of the Mayflower Hotel in Washington to plot a path forward.

As I entered the Mayflower ballroom that evening, joining some fifty or sixty party officials and fundraisers, the mood was somber. I found my place card at the narrow head of a very long rectangular table. There was room for just a few chairs at this end. President Clinton was in the center and I was directly to his left. It's an honor to be seated next to the President of the United States, but on an occasion like this, I knew it was also the hot seat.

The president arrived late. Everyone stood as he entered. Even Clinton, who could light up ten ballrooms at once if he chose, looked tired. After shaking hands along the way, he arrived at his seat next to me. I'd seen him a few times since that morning meeting at the White House a few years earlier, and I was always impressed by his ability to treat everyone he met like he'd known them forever. "Good to see you, Hassan," he said with a warm handshake.

Steven Grossman, the Democratic National Committee Chair, launched the meeting. The committee had made mistakes, he conceded, but now we needed to move forward. His immediate concern was retiring the existing $10 million debt. He welcomed suggestions and encouraged candor.

The next two hours were among the longest and most unproductive I'd ever spent. It was a gripe session. No one spoke about solving the existing problems, just continued to reiterate the same problems in ever more dire terms. Had I not been sitting next to the president, I honestly might have gotten up and left.

I finally leaned over to Clinton and said, softly, "Mr. President, this is insane. We're just attacking each other. We won the election, the other side lost. The rest is just noise."

"You're right," responded Clinton in his sandpapered voice. "But we Democrats always need to beat ourselves up before we get back to fighting the other guy."

The man on the other side of Clinton was Peter Buttenweiser, a longtime donor from Philadelphia. Generally a soft-spoken man, he now launched into a blistering attack on the Democratic

National Committee and the lack of ethics that had caused our problems. When Buttenweiser was done speaking, I scribbled a note on the pad in front of me. I handed the note to Buttenweiser, asking him to pass it down the table to the chairman of the meeting. "Call on me last," is what the note said. I'd not been intending to speak, but I felt I had no choice.

A short while later, after a few more people had aired their grievances, the chairman turned to me. "Before we finish, do you have something add, Hassan?"

"I do."

Addressing the whole room now, I repeated more or less what I'd said to Clinton. "Look, the Republicans are attacking us because we won. They're attacking us because there is no other way to attack the president right now. Make no mistake, they mean to weaken the party so that the vice president is critically wounded and becomes a weaker candidate in 2000."

All of our griping only served their purpose, I said. We needed to stop talking about what was wrong with the party and figure out how to fix it. I quoted something a teacher had said to me years earlier that stuck with me: "You showed me the problem, now show me the solution."

"If this were a company," I concluded, "the largest shareholders would be asked to buy stock in the company through a rights offering, to show support for management. The people around this table represent the largest shareholders in the party. We need to show our support by making a commitment to retire the existing debt." Each of us, I proposed, should immediately commit to raising or giving $100,000.

When I was done, Clinton leaned over. "Thank you for that, Hassan. You said what needed to be said."

If I'd been inclined in that moment to muse on the irony of my situation, I might have noted that even as I was being congratulated by the President of the United States for proposing a solution to the Democratic Party's debt, my own debt was continuing to mount.

16

NO HARM, NO FOUL

I SPOKE ABOUT MY FINANCIAL DIFFICULTIES to no one. Nor, frankly, did I spend a great deal of time worrying about them. I saw them as challenging but not insurmountable. I still had assets in excess of my debts, and my experiences in Iran and the United States, in which I'd so often come out on top after making difficult or risky decisions, had given me a false sense of security, even invulnerability. I'd survived my father's death, a revolution, difficulties with partnerships, and horrendous economic markets. I was confident that I could handle my current situation, also. Then, too, there were the ever more alluring distractions of politics to take my attention away from money woes.

One night at a fundraising event at the Fairfax Hotel in Washington, Vice President Gore stopped by my table and leaned over. "Let's talk after everyone leaves." A short while later, as other guests filed out, Gore and I found some chairs in a far corner of the room and sat. Gore was lost when it came to small talk, but when he had something on his mind he was laser focused. He leaned in. "I'm wondering if you've given any thought to public service, Hassan." I told him that I had indeed thought about it. Not only would it be an honor for me personally, but I believed it would be salutary for Iranian Americans to see one of their own serving in the government.

"Good," said Gore. "I'm going to have Peter Knight call you." Knight was Gore's former chief of staff and one of his closest confidantes and advisors.

A few days later, Knight did indeed call me. He asked whether I might be interested in an ambassadorial post. I responded, quite candidly, that no assignment in government interested me more. As I mentioned to Knight, I'd grown up in the home of a diplomat. My father had considered diplomacy among his greatest satisfactions, second only to building the hospital in Shiraz. Furthermore, some years earlier, I'd had the distinct pleasure of accompanying the U.S. ambassador to Egypt, Frank Wisner, on an inspiring nighttime tour of the City of the Dead in Cairo. He'd made me appreciate what an American ambassador could be—a representative of American interests who also represented the best of America. "I'd jump at the chance," I told Knight.

■ ■ ■

As 1996 wound down, my land loan in Houston was coming due again. I had indications from Great Western that it did not wish to renew the loan and wanted to be repaid. This presented a real problem for me. I was personally liable for the loan. I could not walk away without real material consequences. Nor did I have any real hope of selling the land for a profit. The Houston real estate market was still anemic, suffering from a drop in world oil prices to $12 per barrel, a low not seen for some 10 years. I needed to refinance the loan or prepare to lose a great deal of money.

I flew to Houston and called on my contacts in the banking industry, trying to induce another bank to take over the loan and pay off my existing lender. Not a single Houston bank was interested in the idea of lending money for an inert plot of Houston real estate. I was about to give up hope when a friend put me in touch with a banker at Nation's Bank, based in North Carolina. Nation's Bank—which later merged in to Bank of America—had entered the Texas banking market into the depths of the last banking crisis and had purchased one of Texas' largest bank holding companies.

I explained the situation to the banker: I needed a real estate loan to take out my existing lender. The banker was familiar with the property and fully aware of conditions in the Houston real estate market. Nonetheless, he indicated that Nation's Bank would be interested in establishing a banking relationship with me. He offered to prepare a term sheet to memorialize the proposed deal. I gave him the go-ahead.

When I returned to New York, a fax from the bank was waiting for me. The proposal was not quite what I'd been looking for. I'd requested a real estate loan—a non-recourse real estate loan, to be collateralized by the eight acres of undeveloped land in the Galleria. What the bank offered me instead was a $10 million personal loan. I could use the proceeds to pay off the existing loan and have funds in reserve, but it was fully guaranteed by me. I would solve my existing problem by taking the loan, but I would further increase my personal liability. Given the lack of attractive alternatives, I decided to accept the bank's terms.

To complete the loan application, I was required, like any individual or business applying for a loan, to provide financial statements listing my assets. My practice had always been to avoid giving personal financial statements, or if I was required to do so, as in the case of a home mortgage, to understate assets, as I was wary of providing too much disclosure. I gave Nation's Bank a partial financial statement. A short while later, I received a call from the private banker working my account. The loan would not be problem, he said. He just needed a little more detail from me, and higher assets as collateral.

What I gave back to the banker was not false or fraudulent. It was an accurate list of equities and other assets I owned. Accurate up to a point, that is. The valuations I gave were high—best-case valuations, that is. A number of the assets I listed were equities in the telecom industry, which were going gangbusters but were, as time would tell, quite volatile. I gave them high valuations because I genuinely expected to sell them high, but that was a wish more than a sure thing. Projecting high valuations based on anticipated stock performance is not illegal, nor uncommon. But it's not good practice, either.

According to the valuations I gave, my assets were worth between $50 and $100 million. Had the banker insisted on seeing my tax returns or other documents, he would have discovered that these were high-end projections. The reason I suspect he did not ask is that he wanted to make the loan as much as I wanted to receive it.

There were a number of red flags waving around this transaction that should have given me pause, had I been inclined to notice them. The first had to do with my ability to believe my own exaggerations; I'd convinced myself that the valuations I gave were not only expedient but accurate, thus fooling not only the bank but myself about my prospective net worth. The second was that banks were happy to give me money, and as long as I made my payments on time—as I always did—they were happy to keep giving. In the short term, the greed and credulity of banks worked in my favor. In the long term, it ushered me to my ruin.

■ ■ ■

The valuations I gave for the Nation's Bank loan represented my first step down a slippery slope. But I'd not yet crossed any legal or ethical line. That came some months later.

It was the bank that initially proposed stepping-up the amount I could borrow, to a $35 million line of credit. Of course, I took the loan, and that was entirely my mistake. My hope in doing so was that I could completely pay off the land in Houston, then arbitrage the additional funds to put my finances back into shape. I had a number of potential investments that were very promising and could, with a little luck, turn a quick and tidy profit. This may have been wishful thinking, again, but it was not criminal.

What made it criminal was my decision to inflate my assets beyond best-case valuations and into fraudulent claims. To win approval for the line of credit, I needed to show higher assets than I owned. Inventing what I did not have was not just another step down the slippery slope; it was a big leap over the line between legal and illegal, and between right and wrong.

Even worse was my decision to seek the assistance of Sheila's younger brother, Shahin Kashanchi. A talented computer expert, Shahin had graduated from Tufts University with a degree in Computer Science. He had worked in our back office at First Capital some years earlier, then had moved to Telluride, where he lived in our house and set up his own computer consulting business.

Shahin's parents had remained in Iran after the revolution, so when he'd first come to the United States as a teenager, Sheila and I had acted as his surrogate parents. He trusted us completely. Of everything that I did wrong in years to come, my betrayal of his trust is the most egregious. The only excuse I could later offer for bringing Shahin into my own fraud was my sincere belief that, because he was not aware of what I was doing, he could never be accused of involvement in my actions. That turned out to be a false assumption.

I told Shahin that I needed his assistance for a project I was working on. I asked him to use his skills to recreate the formatting of F.C. Financial Services, our broker dealer. This was one of the companies I'd owned through First Capital Asset Management and affiliated companies; I'd held onto it even after dissolving my business with Gerry Angulo. Having no reason to question what I told him, Shahin faithfully produced the necessary forms and statements, including a three-page security document showing mostly U.S. Treasury bonds. This document was not a complete fabrication. I did in fact own U.S. treasuries, but I greatly inflated the amounts I held. With Shahin's unwitting assistance, it was simple to create what I needed. This may be one reason I found it so easy to avoid contemplating my legal risks and moral culpability.

I had always preached to my children, my friends, and anyone else who came to me for career advice, that your greatest assets are your character and integrity. What flaw in my character allowed me to sacrifice these? I've wrestled with this question hundreds, if not thousands, of times. No answer is adequate. But when I reach back and try to recollect my self-justification at the time, I'm struck by how successfully I convinced myself that I wasn't doing anything seriously wrong.

I suspect that living and doing business for six years in Iran accounted in part for my attitude. In Iran, financial rules and laws had been so arbitrarily applied, depending more on the whims of the Shah and his court than on the rule of law, that one tended to take them with a grain of salt. The great majority of the Iranian business community neglected to declare profits or report assets in strict accordance to rules. I'm not blaming my bad decisions on Iran or on the Shah—they are fully mine to own—but I do sometimes wonder if my time in Iran, for all it gained me in experience, might have undermined my respect for laws.

And then there is this: it never occurred to me that I'd get caught. Intellectually, I knew I was breaking the law, but I saw my transgression as provisional and transitory. I did not doubt for a moment that I would soon make all right and pay off the loan and put everything back as it was. It would be as if none of this had ever happened. No harm, no foul.

17

ARGENTINA

Near the end of that summer of 1997, I was invited to the home of my friend Peter Livanos in Greece. Peter's father, like mine, had been a shipping magnate. Unlike my father, Peter's father had stayed in the business. Peter had then expanded and made the business even more profitable. I joined a number of other guests at Peter's magnificent estate on a peninsula overlooking the Aegean Sea, near Heliopolis. At the center of the estate was a grand modern house, and scattered around it were a number of small villas for guests. Each villa was equipped with a golf cart for transportation back and forth to the main house.

One evening, I was getting dressed in my villa, about to drive up to the main house for cocktails and dinner, when my cell phone rang. Cell service was new and spotty in the 1990's, so it was a surprise to hear my phone ringing on this remote peninsula in the Aegean. Even more surprising was the number I saw illuminated on the screen. A 202 area code—Washington, D.C. I recognized the prefix, too. The call was coming from the White House.

I picked up. On the other end was a woman who introduced herself as Marsha Scott, the deputy director of presidential personnel. She told me she was calling on the president's behalf to inquire whether I might have any interest in being considered for the position of ambassador to Argentina.

Since my conversation with Vice President Gore, I'd had a few potential appointments dangled before me, including an ambassadorship to Morocco, but none of these had amounted to anything. An ambassadorship to Argentina, by contrast, was an extraordinary opportunity. Argentina was a fascinating and important country, one that deeply interested me. Although my direct experience with Argentina had been somewhat limited, I'd traveled to Latin America extensively, knew well the economic issues facing the region, and believed that I could contribute meaningfully to the relationship between Washington and Buenos Aires. I did not speak Spanish, but I was more than willing to learn it. The president's decision to consider me for the appointment was thrilling.

"We're glad you're interested," Marsha Scott said. "When you get back to the States, come to Washington to visit us. We can move forward from there." The way she said it made it all sound simple.

■ ■ ■

There are several thousand political appointments made by the president. Probably no more than a few hundred, at most, are reviewed by the president himself. Ambassadorships are among these. In the Diplomatic Corps, about 40% of the ambassadorial positions are generally reserved for political appointments. These positions are often given to supporters of the president, and they often come from the fundraising community. This is true for Republicans as well as Democrats, and has been the practice almost since the founding of America. For just as long, it has been condemned—always by the political party not in power—as a form of spoilage, somewhere on the spectrum of political sins between unsavory and corrupt.

I'd argue that it's not as bad as it looks. Yes, political appointees who become ambassadors are generally not professional career diplomats. But they are hardly amateurs. Most are highly competent and accomplished men and women. If they do not have the training or experience of career state department professionals, they bring skills, knowledge, and personal contacts that state department professionals do not have. This is not to denigrate career diplomats, merely to state an obvious but overlooked truth: the country is often well served by political appointees. For the appointees themselves, the job is the opposite of spoils. Private citizens who become ambassadors put aside lucrative careers and place assets into blind trusts. They also submit themselves to a process that is time consuming and, as it was in my case, emotionally grueling. And if appointed, they often reach into their own pockets to subsidize the costs of running an embassy.

I went to Washington and met with Marsha Scott and her immediate superior, Bob Nash, the director of presidential personnel. It was an encouraging meeting, but I soon learned that the White House, by offering me the position of ambassador to Argentina, did not mean the position was mine for the taking.

The position had been unfilled for some time. James Dobbins, serving on the National Security Council staff with responsibility for Latin America, had been the president's first choice, but apparently had run afoul of Senator Jesse Helms, the Republican chair of the Senate Foreign Relations Committee. Helms had thus far been unwilling to hold a hearing on the Dobbins' nomination. The administration had not given up on getting Dobbins through the Senate. Nor did Dobbins have any interest in withdrawing his name; he was prepared to fight it out in the Senate as long as the president backed him. I had been brought in, it turned out, to be available in the event that Helms proved intractable and Dobbins had to withdraw. I further discovered that I was not the only or even the leading alternative nominee to take Dobbins' place.

I learned much of this from my conversations with Terry McAuliffe. McAuliffe was to become an invaluable ally and confidante in my selection and nomination. He was, and still is, a unique character in American politics. Originally from Syracuse, New York, he'd moved to Washington to attend Catholic University Law School. He'd made his name in politics as a relentless campaigner for Jimmy Carter, doing whatever needed to be done to raise money for Carter, even if it meant going to Florida to wrestle an alligator (quite literally) in return for a pledge. He'd worked for Dick Gephardt in the 1992 primaries, but when Gephardt lost to Clinton, he became Clinton's chief financial aide and raised more money than anyone in the history of the Democratic Party. After the 1996 election and the Democratic National Committee financial crisis, McAuliffe almost single-handedly kept the financial operations of the party viable.

There was a lot to like about Terry, including his good humor and sunny disposition, but what I found most impressive was his honesty. Most people in Washington know less than they pretend to know and tell you what they think you want to hear. Terry knew everything, and he gave it to you straight. Regarding the Argentina appointment, he was very frank with me. Dobbins had to drop out voluntarily, and the president would not pull the rug out from under him. Furthermore, Bob Miller, the Governor of Nevada, was the president's first choice after Dobbins. He owed Miller politically and felt this might be a good opportunity to clear a political debt. At best, then, I was third in line. This was far from what I had been led to believe from my interactions with the White House, but it was good to know the truth.

■ ■ ■

The Park Avenue apartment was quieter and emptier now. Kamyar had followed Yasmine off to Deerfield, where Yasmine was now a senior. Layla, our only remaining child at home, made sure the place was never *too* quiet. She had not slowed down a bit. She had boundless energy and enthusiasm.

I managed to put Argentina out of my mind for a few months, but one afternoon I was called by the White House Protocol Office and asked if I would accept the president's invitation to be a member of the United States Delegation to the World Cup in Paris. Was this invitation a sign that my candidacy was still alive? Or was it a consolation prize? I called McAuliffe. "So am I being thrown a bone?" He laughed. "No. Do the delegation. You should have some news about Argentina soon." I was glad I took his advice. Our delegation spent an unforgettable week in Paris. The American team did better than expected, losing by only one goal. Unfortunately, we returned home before we could attend the biggest match of the tournament for the American team, against Iran.

Jim Dobbins finally decided that it was futile to continue to pursue his nomination as Ambassador to Argentina as long as Jesse Helms was chair of the Senate Committee on Foreign Relations. The administration withdrew his name. McAuliffe called to let me know that I was still being seriously considered for the post.

A month later, on a warm June day, I was walking down East 54th Street in New York, on my way to lunch, when my cell phone rang. I recognized the number as coming from the White House. "Hassan, it's Marsha Scott. The president asked me to call you to see if you would be willing to serve as his Ambassador to Argentina."

At exactly that moment, before I could utter a response, my phone dropped out. Manhattan was filled with cellular dead zones in those days, and I'd just walked into one. I was frantic. I hadn't said yes. Moments later, Marsha called back, and I was able to accept. President Clinton called that evening to make it official. "I envy you," he said. "It's one of our most beautiful embassies. There're going to be a lot of challenging issues facing you, but you're going to love it. I'm looking forward to working with you."

I immediately called McAuliffe. "Brother, I don't know what took them so long to call you," he said with a laugh. "The president decided this a week ago."

I then called Richard Holbrooke for advice. Holbrooke was married to a friend of ours, Kati Martin, whose son had been a schoolmate of Kamyar's. He'd served in the State Department as an Assistant Secretary of State, as well as Ambassador to Germany, and brokered the famous Dayton Accords, bringing peace to the former Yugoslavia. Having been nominated by President Clinton to be the United States Ambassador to the United Nations, he'd just gone through the vetting process himself. He told me what to expect. Among other things, I'd have to fill out a form that was almost 100 pages long and included dozens of questions delving into my business and personal affairs. My paperwork would be reviewed by the State Department, the White House Counsel's office, and finally the Senate Foreign Relations Committee. Holbrooke recommended a Washington law firm to assist with the process.

With the help of attorneys, I pulled together the necessary paperwork. The questionnaire, known as Standard Form #86, was even more daunting than Holbrooke had warned. I had to list every country I'd visited over the previous fifteen years, including the dates of my travel, and any other foreign contacts. Any company in which I owned more than a 5% interest had to be listed as well. All of this information was difficult to track down; in the case of foreign contacts, for example, the number was nearly countless. Still, it had to be done, and it had to done accurately. Any deception or failure to disclose on S.F. #86 was considered a felony and could land the nominee in prison. I decided to be completely candid. I knew that if investigators shared my S.F. #86 with my bank I'd be in trouble, but I preferred that kind of trouble to committing perjury on a federal form.

Not long after completing the form, I received a call from the State Department advising me that I was scheduled to be interviewed by agents from the department's Bureau of Diplomatic Security. When the time came for the interview, I was a bit nervous, but my anxieties were soon allayed. The agents were thorough but professional and focused—this was not at all a fishing expedition. Dozens of friends and family members were also interviewed by Diplomatic Security to see if there were any facts in my background that might be disqualifying or embarrassing to the president and the State Department. Apparently there were not. My paperwork was soon approved and sent to the White House Counsel's Office.

We'd said nothing to the children about my appointment. We did not want them to become anxious about a move that might not occur, so we'd decided to wait until things were more definite before broaching the subject. Nothing in New York stays confidential for long, though. Layla heard about my appointment from one of her schoolmates at Spence, who heard the news from her father, a friend of mine who had been interviewed about me by the State Department. The next thing we knew, Layla was calling home from the nurse's office at school, crying hysterically about leaving her friends and moving to Argentina.

Kamyar also learned the truth by accident. He was walking down the street and ran into Richard Holbrooke, who asked him if he was looking forward to living in Argentina. Kamyar, always a cool customer, didn't miss a beat. "Sure," he said.

■ ■ ■

Once it was clear that my nomination was on track, I enrolled in an intensive course at the Berlitz School to begin learning Spanish. I was also asked by the State Department to participate in a two week "ambassadorial school" at the department's training facility in the outskirts of Alexandria, Virginia. Over two weeks, I took seminars in public speaking, crisis management, and

Spanish, trying to cram into my brain as much of the language as I could in a short period of time. One afternoon, we took a trip to Fort Bragg to watch a very realistic hostage rescue operation, a reminder of the seriousness of the job. By the time I left the school, I was impatient to begin.

My papers were forwarded to the Senate Foreign Relations Committee the first week of January 1999. Coincidentally, the president of Argentina, Carlos Menem, arrived in Washington for a visit a few days later. Menem's visit highlighted the awkward fact that the United States had not had an ambassador in his country in over a year. Although I was not yet confirmed, the White House invited me, as ambassador-designate, to a state dinner in Menem's honor.

The night of the dinner, Sheila and I were heading out the door of the Hay-Adams, me in black tie, Sheila in a gown, when the concierge stopped us. She insisted we allow the hotel limo to drive us. "You can't walk—that's no way to arrive at the White House!" It was only a block away, but we agreed she had a point, especially since Sheila's gown and heels made it difficult for her to walk any distance. So we took the limo and were dropped off under the portico on the north side of the White House. As we entered the Grand Foyer, a Marine announced our names, and we went directly to the receiving line to greet the Clintons and the Menems.

Waiting in line, I reviewed Spanish phrases in my head—I wanted to show President Menem that I had at least a passing facility in his language. Clinton grinned when he saw me and put a hand on my elbow. "Mr. President, I'm delighted to introduce you to your new American ambassador, my dear friend Hassan Nemazee, and his lovely wife, Sheila." The Spanish came out fairly fluently as I introduced myself and Sheila to the president of Argentina.

Not many events in the United States compare to a White House state dinner, an affair of unequaled elegance and formality that also manages, at least in my limited experience, to be a fun evening. After a cocktail reception, we moved into the State Dining Room for the dinner. I found myself seated next to Rosemary Tenet, the wife of the Director of Central

Intelligence, and Salma Hayek, the actress, both enjoyable dinner companions. As the meal ended, Presidents Clinton and Menem each gave generous toasts that underscored the longstanding friendship between America and Argentina. Clinton, as usual, was extemporaneous, witty, and charming.

The president then invited his guests to the ballroom. The ballroom had an orchestra, a dance floor, and seats to accommodate all the guests in a large semi-circle. Sheila and I were assigned front row seats immediately next to President and Mrs. Clinton. The president took the microphone to announce a special performance of the tango in honor of President Menem. The lights dimmed, and out came Robert Duvall, the actor, and a beautiful young woman who turned out to be Duvall's wife. They performed a magnificent set of dances for the guests. President Menem then got up and asked Hillary to tango with him. The place went wild. Hillary was a good sport, and not a bad dancer, either. The president watched his wife swirl around the floor with a look of pure wonder and pleasure.

■ ■ ■

Victor Manuel Rocha[7], the Deputy Chief of Mission and my proposed number two at the Embassy, brought to my attention that I needed to get out in front of a developing issue before my nomination could be confirmed. This was my Iranian heritage and how it was perceived by Argentinian Jews. There had always been a thriving Jewish population in Latin America, and Argentina in particular had a Jewish community that was large and vibrant. But it was also deeply concerned about its safety. In 1994, a Buenos Aires synagogue had been bombed, killing nearly 85 Argentinians, mostly Jews, and injuring hundreds more. The evidence seemed to suggest that Iran had been behind the bombing. Now the Argentinian papers were filled with speculation about the hidden meanings of my appointment. Was Clinton sending a message to Iran? Was Clinton sending a

---

[7] In June 2000 Rocha was appointed U.S. ambassador to Bolivia. In December 2023 Rocha was arrested and charged by the FBI in a complaint stating that he "secretly supported the Republic of Cuba and its clandestine intelligence-gathering mission against the United States by serving as a covert agent of Cuba's intelligence services." It has been called the worst breach by Cuban intelligence of the U.S. government in history.

message to Argentina? To Israel? In fact, there was no message. I just happened to be of Iranian heritage, no more, no less.

I called my friend Alex Fusina of Morgan Bank, who had worked in Buenos Aires in the past. He arranged for me to meet with Julio Wertheim, a leading Jewish banker in Argentina. Wertheim and I met and got along so well that he publicly supported my nomination in the Argentine press. I then met individually in New York with Abraham Foxman, National Director of the Anti-Defamation League, Malcolm Hoenlein, Vice Chairman of the Conference of Presidents of Major Jewish Organizations, and David Harris, Executive Director of the American Jewish Committee.[8] To all I explained that I had lived in Iran for six years prior to the Iranian Revolution and had been forced into exile as a result of my association with America and the Shah—in short, that I was far from an apologist for the current Iranian regime.

Having settled this matter, I began to prepare for my Senate confirmation hearings. I knew it would not be easy. The chairman of the Foreign Relations Committee was the powerful and proudly obstructionist Republican Senator from North Carolina, Jesse Helms. Helms had already signaled that the confirmation hearing for Richard Holbrooke would be contentious. Likewise with Bill Weld, the former Republican governor of Massachusetts, who had been nominated as Ambassador to Mexico. "The only way Weld will get to Mexico," Helms famously quipped, "is as a tourist."

None of this boded well for my own hearing. I hoped that I might get lucky, though, in light of an unlikely contribution I'd given several years earlier to none other than Jesse Helms. How I came to contribute to the conservative Republican from North Carolina is a long story, but the short version is that Hushang Ansary had asked me to do it. Now that Helms was the chairman of the Foreign Relations Committee, my contribution might seem to have been money well spent, if not cynically deployed. In fact, though, I'd made the contribution long before he was the chairman or I was a nominee.

---

[8] Twenty years later, in a happy quirk of fate, my youngest daughter, Layla, and David Harris's son, Josh, would marry. I wish I could say that my meeting with David laid the groundwork for this, but it was pure amazing coincidence.

The State Department encourages nominees to request meetings with the senators reviewing their nominations. Much to the surprise of my handlers at the State Department, Senator Helms invited me to his office. We sat in his private sitting room, filled with North Carolina memorabilia, and talked about Argentina. Senator Helms asked me when I planned to depart for Buenos Aires. "As soon as I get confirmed," I responded. Helms smiled and said, "Well, I don't see any reason why this nomination doesn't go as smooth as a hot knife through North Carolina butter."

Jim Dobbins had waited eighteen months and never gotten so much as a face-to-face with Helms. I couldn't help but wonder whether my political contribution helped my prospects. I knew for a fact that it irked some Democratic Senate staffers, who did not appreciate my financial support of a conservative Republican.

It's bad enough to have Republican senators sharpening their knives for you when your nomination comes to the Senate. It's much worse to have Democratic staffers sharpening theirs.

Over the next few weeks, I met with senior officials in nearly every federal department or agency. My handlers at State were astonished when I was invited for a sit-down with Larry Summers, the deputy secretary—and soon to be secretary—of the Treasury Department. A meeting with leadership at Treasury was an honor not usually bestowed on ambassador-designates, and certainly not on ambassador-designates to Argentina. The Treasury Department had extensive interactions with the Central Bank of Argentina and generally kept the State Department out of the loop. I intended to change that. The fact that I knew Summers personally through my work in the Democratic Party was a significant advantage to me, and a good illustration of why political appointments are not necessarily bad. Still, even I was surprised when Summers agreed to work through me in future interactions between Treasury and the Argentinians.

■ ■ ■

Two days before my scheduled hearing, I got a surprise of another sort. Janice O'Connell, a senior staffer on the Senate Foreign Relations Committee, called to ask me to come in at once to answer some questions that had arisen regarding my nomination. O'Connell was Senator Chris Dodd's representative on the committee staff and, I believed, an ally. I knew an urgent meeting two days before my confirmation hearing was not a positive development, but I was not overly concerned. I assumed that the Republicans had ginned up something at the last moment to delay my confirmation and that O'Connell and I would strategize how best to respond.

I immediately went over to the Senate with my State Department handler and a young lawyer from O'Melvany and Myers, the firm that had helped me prepare my S.F. #86. O'Connell was joined by ranking senior legal counsel on the Committee on Foreign Relations. We met inside an office in the Russell Senate Office Building.

The meeting got off to a contentious start. In a somewhat accusatory tone, O'Connell announced that she'd asked me to come in to give me another chance to assure the committee that I'd fully disclosed all relevant issues that might prove "problematic." I responded that, yes, we had provided the committee, the White House, and State Department with all necessary and pertinent information. I also reminded her that I'd been thoroughly vetted by Diplomatic Security and the White House counsel. My response did not seem to satisfy O'Connell. She turned the meeting over to the committee's ranking legal counsel, who began to ask me a series of questions regarding one of my companies in the First Capital Group, called F.C. Advisors.

While some of the information he referred to was public and had been made available to the committee and the State Department by my lawyers, other facts he asked about were privileged. He drilled in on very specific issues that had come up during the lawsuit brought against First Capital several years earlier by Robert Shea, the disgruntled broker. That suit had been thrown out by the presiding judge and then sealed, meaning that only participants were permitted access to its documents. What was odd about the ranking lawyer's questions was that they were clearly drawn from the suit. Where had he gotten his knowledge of it?

And then it dawned on me: Sohrab Vahabzadeh, the Iranian-American man I'd sued after he breached his contract with us.

Vahabzadeh had gotten access to the documents of this earlier suit during the discovery process for my suit against him. He was the only possible source of the documents now evidently in the hands of the ranking lawyer. I knew that Vahabzadeh had borne a grudge against me since our legal fight. He must have decided to seek his vengeance by handing the documents to the committee and throwing a wrench in my nomination.

Before the lawyer could get too far with his questions, I interrupted him. I reminded him, first, that I had been on the winning side of both the Shea suit—which had been dismissed with a summary judgment—and the Vahabzadeh suit, for which I'd been awarded damages of $4.5 million. I also warned the lawyer and Janice O'Connell that they were clearly in possession of documents they were prohibited from seeing. The ranking counsel looked taken aback. "Okay," said Janice O'Connell, sounding flustered, "But can't you make this go away?"

"To repeat, all this was resolved in two separate federal court cases in my favor," I responded with some heat. "Would you have me vacate a $4.5 million judgment?"

Later that afternoon—my 49th birthday, as it happened—I was informed by the State Department that my hearing had been postponed by the Foreign Relations Committee. I was staying at my sister Susie's house in Bethesda, expecting Sheila and the children to come down for my birthday and to attend the confirmation hearing. It was awful to call home and tell them not to come after all. Still, I assumed that after looking into the allegations more thoroughly, the Senate staff would put my hearing back on the schedule and this would amount to just another delay. When I called Chris Dodd, whom I'd come to consider a friend, he told me not to worry. I just needed to endure some further vetting, he said. He'd make sure that my confirmation was back on track soon.

■ ■ ■

At first, the only notice of my postponement in the press came in a brief *Washington Post* item. Two weeks later, though, a freelance writer called to inform me that he was writing an article for *Forbes* on me and my nomination. He had some questions he wanted to ask me about First Capital. After he gave me a brief preview of his questions, I responded, truthfully, that while I'd very much like to speak to him, I was prevented from doing so by State Department rules. I put him in touch with my lawyers.

The general tone of his questions added to my impression that a vendetta had been orchestrated to scuttle my nomination. He knew things he could not have known unless someone with inside knowledge of our legal entanglements at First Capital had told him. Again, I suspected Vahabzadeh. He was the only one I could think of who had the motives and means to do this.

I met with Bob Nash, of presidential personnel, at the White House. I explained that I needed to rebut the accusations leveled at me, which meant speaking to the press. He was very sympathetic and promised to talk to the State Department about lifting their prohibition.

In March 1999, the *Forbes* article came out. It was a hatchet job, accusing me of all the allegations that had been made in the First Capital lawsuits, as well as an assortment of other stories meant to malign my character and integrity. Much was factually incorrect and easily refutable. But as I was never released by the State Department to speak to *Forbes*, I was left with writing a letter to the editor, a pretty ineffectual response.

The damage had been done. Senator Helms' senior staff advisor, Admiral Nance, called my attorney, A.B. Culvahouse, to advise him of the obvious: I had a problem. He told Culvahouse that Senator Helms was still willing to support the nomination, but to do so, he needed to see much more visible support from the White House and Democrats in the Senate.

After the *Forbes* article appeared, I began to suspect a leak in the Foreign Relations Committee. I assumed it was coming from the Republicans. At the suggestion of my attorney, I hired a local private investigator to determine who was feeding this misinformation to the press. The investigator hired a freelance reporter in London, who called the Foreign Relations Committee, purporting to be writing a story on me for the *Financial Times*. He asked for information, on background, from the committee. It was given, and it was mostly derogatory. No surprise there. The shocker was who it came from: none other than Janice O'Connell, the foreign policy advisor of my good friend Chris Dodd.

I asked to meet with Dodd. He adamantly denied that his staff was anything but supportive. The problem was entirely lack of White House support, he claimed. He also suggested that Helms was being duplicitous and in fact opposed the nomination. Hushang Ansary, a friend of Jesse Helms', called me to say he had spoken to Helms and had been personally assured that the senator supported my nomination.

As the weeks turned into months, I found myself at the center of a kabuki dance of finger-pointing, as my supposed allies in the Senate and my supposed allies in the White House each accused the other of failing to push the nomination forward. It was now August of 1999. Eight months had passed since my original confirmation hearing date. Two years had passed since the phone call in Greece informing me of the president's interest in naming me ambassador to Argentina. My life had been put on hold. I'd removed myself from any day-to-day involvement in my business. My family was up in the air about where we would be living. It was an impossible situation.

The White House Chief of Staff, John Podesta, and his deputy, Steve Ricchetti, called me in for a conversation. Podesta told me they were willing to keep pushing the nomination if I wanted to keep trying. But the writing was on wall, and I was capable of reading between the lines. I decided to withdraw.

For me, it was a deep disappointment. I felt I'd been sabotaged and poorly treated. I blamed myself mostly—it had been my decision to get involved with a character like Sohrab Vahabzadeh, and my decision to press a lawsuit that made him my vindictive enemy. Sheila was relieved and blamed Dodd and his staff for hanging me out to dry. As for Layla, she'd come around to the idea of moving to Argentina, so she may have been the most upset of all of us. She'd cried when she found out we were moving to Argentina, and now she cried again when she found out we were not.

18

RECOUNT

It was Al Gore who brought me back into political fundraising. As soon as he decided to seek the Democratic nomination to succeed President Clinton, he asked me to join his New York finance committee. Still bruised from the experience of my ambassadorial nomination, I told him I needed some time to think about it.

I consulted several friends in Washington, including Terry McAuliffe and Tony Coelho, a former member of Congress who was one of Washington's most experienced and wise political thinkers. Both McAuliffe and Coelho urged me to stay involved. Put the ambassadorial experience in the past, they counseled, and move forward, using the experience as a building block for the future. I decided they were right.

Again, in light of what came later, it is fair to question my motives? Had I allowed politics to become an indulgence? Was I using it to create an illusion of power over my circumstances?

The truth, at least in part, is that I believed the work to be valuable and found it gratifying. I had educated a small but significant section of the Washington decision-making establishment on Iran. I was creating an example for Iranian Americans, and my own children, that public service was open to all. I had been the first Iranian American appointed by any president to a high-level federal office, even if I did not ultimately obtain that office. While I may have let politics take too firm a hold on me, I was drawn to it because it made me feel as if I was a part of something larger than myself—something that I believed was good not just for me, but for my country.

In the meantime, I was asked by the White House to join the president's Foreign Intelligence Advisory Board (PFIAB). Created by President Eisenhower to advise the president on all aspects of American intelligence, PFIAB was the most meaningful of all of the oversight boards and commissions that were available for presidential appointment. It had oversight of the Central Intelligence Agency, the National Security Agency, and the intelligence agencies of the military branches. The position was a presidential appointment and, thankfully, did not require a Senate confirmation. Nonetheless, it did require another full background check. I submitted my papers to the White House and began the FBI vetting process.

■ ■ ■

I'd begun to invest with my old friend Alan Quasha on a more regular basis, hoping to put myself into a position to pay off my loan and get back onto the positive side of the ledger sheet, if not the right side of the law. After the liquidation of the First Capital group of companies, I'd moved my office into a shared space with Alan, in his townhouse between Park and Lexington. This was close enough to my apartment on Park Avenue that I could walk home for lunch occasionally, something I'd rarely done before.

Together, Alan and I found a number of opportunities in the telecommunications industry and put together a portfolio that included such companies as ARC Wireless, Netbeam, Global Broadbrand, and Millenium. These investments turned out to be timely, as the whole technology and communications sector was about to experience explosive growth. We bought stocks at five cents to twenty-five cents per share and saw the values increase to prices as high as $4 per share. Often the stock was restricted, precluding immediate sale. I watched it rise, but I could not touch it until the restrictions lifted.

I also invested in companies that Alan did not invest in. One of these was Medibuy, an internet auction site for medical equipment. I had taken a $1 million stake in an early round of financing that was later joined by some of Silicon Valley's premier venture capital firms, such as Kleiner Perkins, Sequoia, and others. Medibuy gave all signs of being one of the best investments I'd ever made. The company received an astronomical valuation from First Boston, which planned to take it public. Based on First Boston projections, my position had risen to a value of $30 million. My total communications portfolio had an equity value in excess of $100 million on paper.

All of this was occurring in the fall of 2000. My plan was to hold my positions until the restrictions were lifted in the spring of 2001, and then sell, yielding myself a sizeable liquidity event in the spring of 2001. I could pay off my loan and put the remaining cash back to work in the markets and elsewhere.

The bank I owed money to was no longer Nation's Bank. That bank had been acquired by the much larger Bank of America, which had assumed my debt. Just as I'd done for Nation's Bank, I provided Bank of America with quarterly statements and full financial disclosure every year. At no time was there ever an issue raised. On the contrary, Bank of America was so satisfied with me as a client that it came back several times with offers to raise my line of credit. By late 1990's, the line was up to $100 million. With little effort—simply by handing over a few pages of fabricated documents a few times a year—I had become one of the bank's largest private clients.

■ ■ ■

Vice President Gore chose Tony Coelho as his campaign chair. Given my friendships with Coelho and Peter Knight, I was well situated in the Gore organization. The key to success for any fundraiser is access to the principal candidate for events. I was able to get the vice president to attend the events I scheduled for him in New York. I quickly raised my first $250,000, and after that continued to raise sums that put me in the ranks of the most successful fundraisers in the country.

As we headed into the summer of 2000, Al Gore was running behind in national polls against the Republican candidate, George W. Bush. Gore was by any measure the more qualified and competent candidate, but Bush had money and a superb organization. Fortunately, the Democratic National Convention that August put matters right. Gore emerged with a significant lead in the polls.

The first inkling of serious concern in the campaign came after Gore's first debate with Bush, in Boston. From my seat in the front row, Gore seemed to handle himself very well. But those of us inside the hall failed to notice how his frequent sighs of exasperation played on television. The reviews were devastating.

Gore won the debate in substance but lost the spin room, and the late-night comics killed him.

The polls tightened after that. Some showed Gore ahead, others showed Bush leading. A few days before the election came news of Bush's unreported DUI arrest years earlier in Maine. Coelho called to tell me he thought it would hurt Bush badly. It did not.

I decided not to go to Gore headquarters in Nashville on election night. A good choice, as it turned out. I stayed in New York and invited friends over to watch the returns. When the networks called Florida for Gore, effectively giving him the election, Sheila and I cheered loudly. I always suspected that our guests, the Chartounis and the Ishams, were closet Republicans; their reaction was far more muted.

And then the craziness began. A couple of hours after calling Florida for Gore, the networks put the state back into the undecided column. Later, after our guests left, Fox called Florida for Bush. I was heartbroken. I couldn't believe we had lost. I went to sleep, like all of America, thinking it was over.

I was still in bed the next morning when Ralph Isham called. "No need to rub it in," I grumbled before he could say anything. Ralph laughed. "Turn on your TV, you won't believe what's happening."

The national drama of Palm Beach's butterfly ballot, thousands of votes erroneously cast for Pat Buchanan—instead of Al Gore—and the contested recounts with the "hanging chads" had yet to unfold. But it was already clear that there had been serious problems in tabulating the vote in Florida. Al Gore had retracted his concession. The only thing I knew for sure was that my candidate was still alive.

The phone rang again. This time it was Peter Knight. He had two very specific requests. First, he asked me for a $50,000 donation to the "Recount Fund." I agreed at once. He then asked me to call my contacts to raise additional funds for the recount. I and a handful of other Gore loyalists quickly raised the necessary funds to give the campaign the resources it needed to order a county-by-county recount, as well as to file the legal papers and carry out a hundred other actions required for the recount.

The next several weeks were a roller coaster of emotional ups and downs for the country, and even more so for those of us intimately involved in the campaigns—on both sides. In early December, the United States Supreme Court overturned a decision of the Florida State Supreme Court and halted the recount. Gore ended the drama by giving a very gracious and elegant concession speech. It was a frustrating and sad conclusion for all of us on the Gore team, but primarily for Al Gore himself, who had lost to a man he considered totally unprepared to be president of the United States. As collateral damage, my appointment to the President's Foreign Intelligence Advisory Board went by the wayside. President Bush, by custom, would appoint his own board. Another opportunity gone, but *c'est la vie*. Only a fool makes long-term plans in Washington.

■ ■ ■

I urged Peter Knight to ask the Vice President to come to New York to thank all of his New York supporters. Gore refused at first. Devastated by his loss to Bush, he grew a beard, put on weight, and went into self-imposed exile for several months.

Finally, in June of 2001, Peter Knight called to say that Gore would come to New York, and that his first reception would be at my apartment. I invited all of Gore's major New York supporters. It was a pleasure to host this event, but bittersweet. Gore was still deeply affected by his loss, and he seemed to carry the weight of the world, along with the extra pounds, with every heavy step. He was uncomfortable making small talk at a cocktail party, and it did not help that our air conditioning had gone on the blink just before the party. A profuse sweater in the best of circumstances, Gore suffered through it without a peep of complaint, but it was painful to watch.

Al Gore was a decent and intelligent man. But even George W. Bush, for all of his faults, was a more natural politician. Gore loved the policy, the issues, the intellectual side of governing. He did not enjoy the fundraising, the glad-handing, the human element. Gore was better suited for policy, Bush for politics. The reality is that most politicians are either Gores or Bushes. Very few are Clintons—brilliant policy wonks who are also world-class extroverts.

After our party, Gore asked me to visit with him at his home when I was next in Washington. I took him up on his invitation. I was shocked to see how small his house was. Many people, including myself, assumed that Gore was wealthy. His father had been a U.S. senator. Al had gone to St. Albans and Harvard—expensive private schools. Yet his family was not wealthy at all. Americans are understandably cynical about politicians, but as I discovered time and again, it is generally vanity, not greed, that drives politicians. I think most Americans would be surprised by how modestly the men and women who represent them generally live.

Much of our conversation during my visit focused on his future plans. Like many of his friends and supporters, I urged him to consider running again in 2004. I felt certain that the party would back him and that Bush would prove to be a one-term president. But Gore expressed his desire to move forward and beyond politics. And unlike some politicians after a tough loss, he seemed to really mean it. He was done.

He was also done being middle-class, it turned out. In coming years, he would co-found a cable television channel and an asset management business focused on green energy and become a very wealthy man.

Bill Clinton had run his last race. Al Gore was out for good. But there was one member of the old Clinton team yet to try politics.

I would be there when she did.

19

THE BUBBLE BURSTS

In the spring of 2001, I was invited to breakfast by Frank Wisner. Since meeting in Egypt during his ambassadorship, Frank and I had maintained contact and become friends, conferring often about events in Iran. Frank was the epitome of the disappearing breed of Washington Wise Men, advisors who had no agenda other than to provide America's leaders with the benefit of their wide experience and knowledge of the world.

In the dining room of the Knickerbocker Club on Fifth Avenue, Frank told me about his involvement in track-two diplomacy that was being "unofficially" conducted by various former senior foreign service officials such as himself and Tom Pickering, former Under Secretary of State, to maintain a dialogue with Iran. He asked me if I knew anything about a think tank called the American Iranian Council. He was on the council's board, along with Pickering and a friend of mine, Lucio "Lu" Noto, Vice Chairman of Exxon-Mobil. The board represented the cream of American industry and the foreign service. That said, it lacked input from the Iranian-American community. My membership on the board of AIC would be a tremendous asset for the council, said Frank. He asked if I would consider joining. I was hesitant at first, but Frank is a persuasive diplomat, and I eventually came around.

Shortly after my appointment to the board, I received a call from my cousin Mehrdad. Mehrdad was a close childhood friend of Reza Pahlavi, son of the late Shah of Iran. He asked me to come to Washington to meet with Pahlavi to discuss the AIC.

At the time of the revolution, Crown Prince Reza Pahlavi had been an Iranian Air Force pilot receiving training at a U.S. air base in Texas. After the death the Shah in 1980, Iranian monarchists, including some who lived in the United States, considered Reza the heir to the Peacock Throne. Reza was now 40 years old, living in a large but not ostentatious house in the suburbs of Washington, with the hope of someday fulfilling the monarchists' dreams and returning to take his rightful place as leader of Iran.

We met for lunch in Washington at the Hay-Adams. Unlike his father, the young Shah was a naturally genial man. After a general discussion of Iran, he got to the point. He told me that the AIC was an organization affiliated with and supported by the Islamic Republic, and that Americans on the board were being duped into supporting a discredited regime. I was taken aback. I told him of my long friendship with Frank Wisner and Lu Noto, both men of impeccable reputation and experience; I seriously doubted that they would allow themselves to be manipulated by the mullahs. Nonetheless, I promised to take what he told me into account.

I immediately called the founder and chairman of the council, a Rutgers professor named Hooshang Amirahmadi. In previous encounters, I'd found Amirahmadi to be energetic (good) and a self-promoter (not so good). Now, when I asked him for information regarding AIC's finances, Amirahmadi promised me full disclosure.

■ ■ ■

While I waited for this to materialize, the AIC held its annual conference at the Ritz-Carlton in San Francisco. I was invited to join a panel of speakers, and given the freedom to address a topic of my choice. I decided to raise the issue of Iranian-American involvement in U.S. politics. Or, rather, the nearly total lack of Iranian-American involvement. I was the last on the panel to speak.

I began by pointing out that more than twenty years had passed since the Iranian Revolution of 1979. Iranian Americans had assimilated well into the United States and risen to the top of numerous fields—medicine, business, law, sports, the academic world. The only sphere in which we had not successfully participated was politics. I asked the audience to raise their hands if they were American citizens. Almost 100% of the audience put up their hands. I then asked how many in the audience voted in the last election. Now about half raised their hands. "And how many of you have contributed to a political candidate or party?" This time, it was fewer than 10%.

"Look at the American Jewish community," I said. "Look at the Cuban American Community. Each has achieved significant political power. The reason the Jewish community and Cuban community are powerful and influential is that they engage in the American political process. They vote, and they contribute to candidates. As a result, they have a voice and a platform. I challenge you to involve yourselves. If you care about your civil rights. If you care about family reunification and immigration policy. If you care about how Americans of Iranian descent are perceived by decision makers in Washington. Engage!"

I was given a standing ovation. Afterwards, a number of people approached me to take up my challenge. Many confided that they wanted to engage but did not know how to do so effectively. As I flew back to New York the following day, I began to think about how to achieve what I'd discussed years earlier with President Clinton in my first White House breakfast—that is, how to involve Iranian Americans more deeply in the American political process. Before the plane landed in New York, I knew what to do. I would form a political action committee, or PAC, to support candidates of Iranian descent and bring the same into the political process.

Through the AIC I'd come to know two Iranian-American businessmen, Akbar Ghahary and Faraj Alaei, who shared my vision for greater inclusion of Iranian Americans in U.S. politics. Together, we founded the Iranian American Political Action Committee (IAPAC). Our objective was simple: to focus on issues of importance to the Iranian-American community. We agreed to avoid direct involvement in U.S.-Iran relations. There was to be no foreign policy position taken by IAPAC, and the PAC would contribute identical amounts to Democrats and Republicans. We would focus on issues of common importance to Iranian Americans, such as civil liberties, immigration reform, voter registration, and electing Iranian Americans to local, state, and federal office.

I raised the necessary funds, hired counsel to advise on election law, and hired our first political director, a young Iranian American named Morad Ghorban. We created a board of directors representing the geographic areas of the country where we established IAPAC chapters—Northern & Southern California, Washington D.C. and the Mid-Atlantic, the New York Tri-State area, the Northeast, and the South. As a goodwill demonstration of non-partisanship, I hosted a fundraiser in my home for an Iranian-American woman, Goli Ameri, running for Congress as a Republican.

Goli ultimately lost her election but was appointed to serve in the Bush administration as an Assistant Secretary in the State Department. Other members went on to significant roles in government: Cyrus Amir-Mokri, a member of IAPAC's board of directors, for example, would serve in the Obama administration as an assistant secretary in the Treasury Department. IAPAC hosted numerous events for Republican and Democratic candidates running for the House, Senate, and the Presidency. Within a short period, the Federal Election Commission's publicly available information showed IAPAC as one of the country's most significant contributors by total dollar amounts.

I owed my idea for IAPAC to the American Iranian Council—I may never have conceived of it but for the speech I gave at the AIC conference in San Francisco. Nonetheless, I decided to resign from the council's board. The financial information I'd requested from Amirahmadi had never been provided. Furthermore, I began to question Amirahmadi's personal ambitions after he told me that he planned to run for President of the Islamic Republic of Iran, which struck me as close to delusional. I shared my decision with both Frank Wisner and Lu Noto. Both also resigned from the board as a result.

Alas, I did not leave soon enough. My involvement in AIC would come back to haunt me, as fringe elements in the Iranian-American community accused me of being an "agent" of the Islamic Republic. This was an absurd misrepresentation of my views and actions, but that did not stop certain websites, claiming to represent "Islamic students," from accusing me of attempting to influence my Democratic friends to reestablish relations with the Islamic Republic. This was my first taste of the brave new world to come, in which vicious rumors flourish on the internet to the point where they overwhelm fact.

Meanwhile, some of the actual facts of my life were unpleasant enough. And early in 2001, my own delusions met with a large dose of reality.

■ ■ ■

I planned to sell my technology and communications portfolio as soon as I was legally able to do so. Most of my portfolio, now worth over $100 million, was in private placement investments that called for six-month restrictions on sales of securities. Medibuy, the business-to-business medical auction site, was scheduled by First Boston for a multi-billion-dollar IPO in the spring of 2001. After that happened, I would be in a position to put my finances back in the black and extricate myself from the loan I'd received on my inflated asset claims.

Despite occasional predictions of a correction in the so-called "tech bubble," the bull market continued to rise, and so did my portfolio. Medibuy promised to rise even higher after the company decided to take its IPO out of the hands of First Boston and give it to Goldman Sachs. The imprimatur of Goldman, the veritable king of IPOs, strongly boosted the chances for a successful offering. To ensure the results it expected, Goldman decided to wait until the spring of 2001 to take Medibuy public. The delay caused me some anxiety, because it meant I'd have to wait longer to take my money out. But it also meant I'd probably have more money to take out when the time came. And then, all at once, the tech bubble collapsed.

Nothing can prepare an investor for the kind of correction that hit the stock market in 2001. And what the stock market as a whole suffered was nothing compared to the bloodbath in the "small cap" tech sector where my portfolio was concentrated. Market valuations were reduced by as much as 90% in a heartbeat. ARC Wireless went from more than $4 per share to less than 25 cents in weeks. Covalent plummeted from a high of $12 per share to $2. And Medibuy, my great hope, shriveled like a punctured balloon. Goldman decided to pull its IPO and wait for better conditions. Those never came. A company that had been valued at $3 billion the previous winter was now practically worthless. My portfolio, which had achieved a market value of well in excess of $100 million, was suddenly reduced to $5 million. My paper losses were staggering.

Adding to this disaster was the fact that I'd used borrowed funds for the investments, that is, from my fraudulent line of credit at Bank of America. Using borrowed funds for investment purposes will yield excellent leverage when the market is rising, but when the market reverses, it's a brutal experience. I was paying the bank my quarterly interest payments, and now I suddenly found myself not only with growing debt, but also with assets drastically reduced in value, if not completely wiped out. My exit strategy had become a sinkhole.

It seemed that the only solution was to try, once more, to invest my way out of my debt. But to do so, I would need to borrow more money.

■ ■ ■

I was still absorbing my losses that September when the events of 9/11 dramatically overshadowed my personal troubles. I was in our apartment on Park Avenue when the first plane hit Tower One at 8:46 that morning. I was still watching CNN when the second plane hit at 9:03, and suddenly we all knew we were under attack.

That afternoon, I was scheduled to meet a business associate for lunch at the Racquet Club on Park Avenue. Walking to the club, I had a clear view downtown. Far in the distance, a thick cloud of smoke and dust hovered under an otherwise stunning blue sky. My lunch guest never showed up, so I ate alone. I will never forget looking up to see a man—a member of the club—enter the lobby that afternoon. He was dressed in a suit and clutching a briefcase, but entirely covered in white dust. Like many who worked downtown near the World Trade Center, he'd fled north on foot. Because subways and other transportation were out of service, he'd walked the entire way. The club was the first place he could stop and rest and drink some water before heading back out and continuing home. Throughout the afternoon, members who had made the trek from near Ground Zero straggled into the club, looking like dazed ghosts.

Given the magnitude of 9/11, I could hardly mourn my own losses, which were insignificant compared to the personal grief so many faced that day. That said, the further collapse of the stock market after 9/11 did not help my situation. I was living on borrowed money and borrowed time.

20

THE NEXT PRESIDENT OF THE UNITED STATES

I WAS PLAYING GOLF on a course in Arizona one afternoon when my cell phone rang. I stepped away from the green to take the call. "Hassan, it's Joe Biden. You got a minute?" When I explained that I was on the seventh hole of a golf course in Arizona, he laughed. "Well, finish playing. Let's talk soon."

A week later, I flew to Washington for my first meeting with Senator Biden. Over time, he was to become my closest friend in the Senate, but my first impression of him never changed. Honest, open, loyal, and humorous, he was exactly the man he appeared to be. I liked him immediately.

The story of Biden is well known by now, but I found it quite moving when I first met him. At 29, Biden had been one of the youngest men ever elected to the Senate. Shortly after his election, but prior to his swearing in, his wife, driving with their three children to buy a Christmas tree, collided with a truck. She died, as did their daughter. Biden's two young sons, Beau and Hunter, survived. Joe was engulfed in grief but somehow found the strength to move forward. He immersed himself in the work of the Senate during the days, and every night commuted home to Delaware to be with his sons, and eventually he remarried. By 1988, he was one of the Democratic Party's rising stars, and he ran for the Presidential nomination against Dukakis and others. He was unsuccessful in that bid, but he was resilient. He was also, despite his genuine decency, fiercely ambitious. He returned to the Senate and rose in seniority in the Democratic Party.

Biden now wanted to put together a more substantive finance organization than he had ever had. An incumbent in a reliably Democratic state, he had never required large sums of money in order to be reelected. It became clear, as we spoke, that Joe was not interested in raising money for his Senate reelection. He still harbored bigger ambitions. And he recognized that if he wanted to run for president again, he would need a superior national finance organization. He asked me to be part of his core financial group, with responsibility for fundraising in New York. I told him I would think about it—but under one condition. "Joe, my reputation was tarnished as a result of my experience in the confirmation process. If you want me to become involved in a significant fashion, I want your Senate staff to review my entire file to determine to your satisfaction that there are no issues. I want you to be comfortable." He agreed at once to have his senior legal counsel review my file.

As Bush's popularity rose after the 9/11 attacks, some Democrats, who had considered running in 2004, reconsidered. One of these was Hillary Clinton, now Senator Clinton. I'd raised quite a bit of money for her senatorial race in New York and was eager to see her jump into the Democratic primaries. But after feeling the waters for a while, she decided to serve out her term in the Senate. Biden was now well positioned, but he was conflicted. His gut told him to run, but his wife, Jill, was firmly opposed. As I told Alan Hoffman, Biden's chief of staff, I was certain I could organize the necessary finance operation to support his candidacy should he decide to go for it. I thought he had a good chance of winning.

Biden made a pilgrimage to the Clintons' home in Chappaqua, NY, to consult with Bill Clinton. Upon his return to Washington, we met in his Senate office. "Clinton told me I could win, and he showed me how," Biden announced, sounding like a kid who'd just discovered a treasure map. He handed me a yellow legal pad. The pages were filled with single-spaced, hand-written notes of his meeting with Clinton. It was difficult to divine much from Biden's scribbles, but apparently they detailed Clinton's analysis of how he could get the nomination and win the presidency. I was pleased that Biden was confident and ready to go.

Alas, a week later, Joe called. The moment I heard his voice I could tell that he'd changed his mind. He'd had a long discussion with Jill, he told me, and had decided not to run. Too bad, I thought as I hung up, he probably would have made a good president.

PERSIA, POLITICS & PRISON

■ ■ ■

No sooner did Biden drop out than Peter Maroney, John Kerry's finance director, called to ask if I'd meet with the senator on his next visit to New York. I told Peter that it would be my pleasure.

Senator Kerry came to my office in midtown one afternoon in the autumn of 2002. He'd been making the rounds in New York, and it was late in the day. Looking exhausted, he asked for water, loosened his tie, and dropped into a chair. "I'm beat," he said. After a few sips of water, he revived a little. "I'm running for president, Hassan. I'd like you to be part of my finance team. What do you say?"

With his lantern jaw, patrician elocution, and background (St. Paul's, Yale), Kerry certainly looked and sounded and acted like an American president, but he lacked the kind of chummy warmth that born pols like Clinton and Biden exude in their sleep. Like most politicians, he had strengths and weaknesses. If his aloof demeanor was a strike against him, his productive tenure in the Senate and his exemplary military service during the Vietnam War were pluses (though, incredibly, the war would end up being used against him, as we'd come to learn).

I liked Kerry. He was gracious and quite witty. I thought his argument for his candidacy was a good one, too. By the time he circled back to his initial question—would I consider joining his national finance team?—I knew my answer. I agreed to meet with Bob Farmer, his national finance chair, and Peter Maroney, his finance director. And in short order, I also agreed to co-lead—with Orin Kramer and Blair Effron—the New York Finance Committee.

In part due to our fundraising success, John Kerry was soon anointed the frontrunner among the Democrats. Frontrunner status is both a blessing and curse. It's a help to fundraisers initially, as many supporters want to get on the bandwagon. But sooner or later, the press gets bored with the frontrunner narrative and creates an alternative story. In 2003, that story became Howard Dean.

The governor of Vermont, Howard Dean was by no means well-known nationally before the run-up to the primaries. His candidacy was a long shot when he announced. But with the liberal wing of the Democratic party up in arms over the war against Iraq, Dean's anti-war platform, along with fawning press attention, earned him a surprisingly large following. By July, he was the Democratic frontrunner for the nomination. To add insult to injury, when the fundraising totals were announced, it turned out that Dean had significantly out-raised Kerry, the presumed establishment candidate. Alarm bells were going off in Boston and Washington. In New York, too.

For some time, the leading donors, myself included, had been vocal about the lack of organization and formal structure in both the political and fundraising parts of the Kerry campaign. We were concerned that Jim Jordan, the campaign manager, was in over his head as he tried to run his first national campaign. Bob Shrum, a senior advisor to Kerry and the voice he most trusted, advised Kerry to make fundamental changes, but it was months before Kerry was able to make the decision to remove Jordan. The fact that Kerry seemed hesitant to make hard decisions worried me. I would have several conversations with Kerry regarding the state of the campaign, and the specific problems, only to find decisions I thought he'd agreed to were never implemented.

On the fundraising side, Dean had tapped into the internet in a new and hugely successful way. The anti-war movement spawned MoveOn.org, and the site was used to raise unprecedented amounts for Dean. These donations were in small dollar amounts, usually less than $200, but enormous in the aggregate, dwarfing amounts that either John Kerry or John Edwards were able to raise by conventional means. Kerry made a decision to bring in Louis Susman as the new National Finance Chair, effectively demoting Bob Farmer to National Treasurer. Maroney then called to ask me to take over New York as the sole chair of the New York Finance Committee. This meant more work and more responsibility, but I was convinced that Dean was a flash in the pan and that ultimately Kerry would prevail. I happily accepted the challenge.

Raising money for Kerry definitely *was* a challenge in the fall of 2003. Not only was the momentum with Dean, but there were rumblings that General Wesley Clark might join the race, and do so with the backing of the Clintons. Indeed, when Clark finally announced, many Clinton supporters joined his finance team.

Kerry made two dramatic decisions that greatly helped him. First, he took out a $5 million loan against his home in Boston. Though married to one of the richest women in America, Teresa Heinz, he could not legally access her fortune. Putting his own money into the campaign was a testament to his belief in his candidacy. Kerry also finally fired Jim Jordan and replaced him with Mary Beth Cahill. The money gave the campaign the necessary oxygen for the final push to Iowa, and Mary Beth brought much needed organizational skills.

The campaign went from being written off as dead in December of 2003 to winning the Iowa caucus in January of 2004. After Howard Dean's infamous post-Iowa rant—"the Dean Scream"—effectively torpedoed his campaign, Kerry came roaring back from near oblivion to recapture frontrunner status. Money began to pour in. Following another victory in the New Hampshire primary, our website nearly crashed with internet donations, a welcome problem to have. In short order, Kerry had the nomination in a lock.

Lou Susman called to tell me John would be coming to New York in early March. I suggested a dinner to introduce him to the major New York donors, those who had been early supporters but also the finance leadership of competing campaigns. We hosted a seated dinner at our apartment at 770 Park Avenue for forty guests, including Alan Patricof, Stan Shuman, and Pete Peterson.

This was the first opportunity most of our guests had to meet Kerry in person, so it was important that everyone get a chance to know him. The senator had a tendency to park himself and settle into serious conversations, but I encouraged him to keep moving and spend equal time at each of our tables. Whenever he stayed too long with one group, I put a hand on his shoulder and nudged him along. After the dinner, I gave a brief introduction and then Kerry stood and answered questions from guests. The small setting suited him well, and he was superb.

A month later, I chaired the largest finance event in the history of the Democratic Party—a reception at New York's Sheraton

Hotel, followed by a performance at Radio City Music Hall. We raised in excess of $8 million, more than had ever been raised for a political candidate at a single event. As I introduced John that night from a podium at the Sheraton, I took a moment to savor the overflowing crowd of 2,500. I'd come a long way from my first meeting with Al Gore in 1994. Here I was 2004, introducing the man I believed to be the next President of the United States.

The Shah attends the Iran Foundation Dinner, Waldorf Astoria, New York, 1949
(My father third from the right)
Hassan Nemazee Personal Collection

The Shah and Queen Soraya at the inauguration of the Nemazee Hospital
Hassan Nemazee Personal Collection

Mohammed Nemazee, my father
Hassan Nemazee Personal Collection

Fakhri Dehesh Nemazee, my mother
Hassan Nemazee Personal Collection

School Days (I'm second from the left)
Hassan Nemazee Personal Collection

The Owl Club, Harvard, 1971.
(I'm top row, third from the left)
Hassan Nemazee Personal Collection

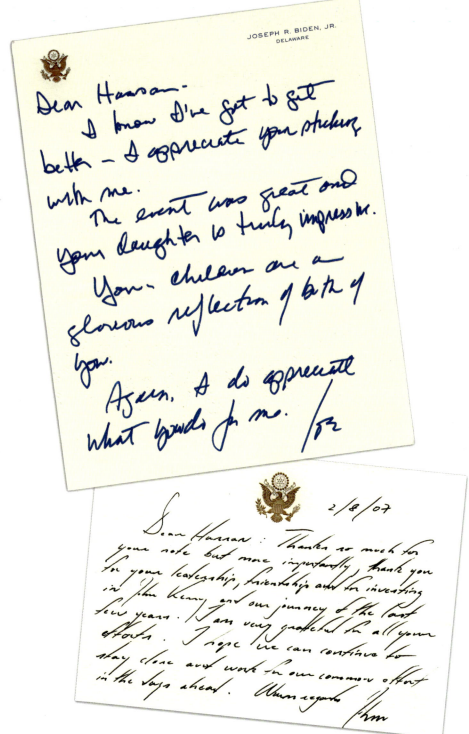

Personal notes from Joe Biden, John Kerry and Bill Clinton
Hassan Nemazee Personal Collection

WILLIAM J. CLINTON
9/29/08

Dear Hassan—

I'll never be able to thank you enough for what you did for Hillary. This tie is from the collection Hillary and I have had for many years. I want you to have it as a small expression of my lasting gratitude. In her campaign you were a rock, and lion-hearted.

Best,
Bill

THE WHITE HOUSE

Office of the Press Secretary

For Immediate Release   December 30, 1998

PRESIDENT CLINTON NAMES HASSAN NEMAZEE
AS U.S. AMBASSADOR TO ARGENTINA

The President today announces his intent to nominate Hassan Nemazee to be
U.S. Ambassador to Argentina.

Mr. Hassan Nemazee, of New York, New York, currently serves as Chair and CEO of Nemazee Capital Corporation. He has been an investor in public and private equity markets since 1972 and also has experience in real estate development. From 1979 to 1987, Mr. Nemazee was involved in developing properties in Houston, Texas and suburban Washington, DC, including a 300,000 square foot office building designed by I.M. Pei. Mr. Nemazee is also very active in the academic community and in 1996 was honored as a John Harvard Fellow. He currently serves on the Harvard University Visiting Committee for the Center for International Affairs and is a former member of the Harvard University Middle East Advisory Committee. Also in conjunction with Harvard University, Mr. Nemazee is a member of the Board of Trustees of the Aitken Neuroscience Institute, was a member of the Board of Trustess of the Spence School and is a member of the Board of Directors of Columbia University's affiliate Encylopedia Iranica.

Mr. Nemazee was born in Washington, DC, and received his A.B. degree with honors from Harvard University in 1972. He and his wife, Sheila, reside in New York City with their three children, Yasmine, Kamyar and Layla.

-30-30-30-

White House press release announcing me as U.S. Ambassador to Argentina
National Archives

VII

With President Bill Clinton at the White House State Dinner for the President of Argentina
Photo: Barbara Kinney/William J. Clinton Presidential Library

With President Barack Obama
National Archives

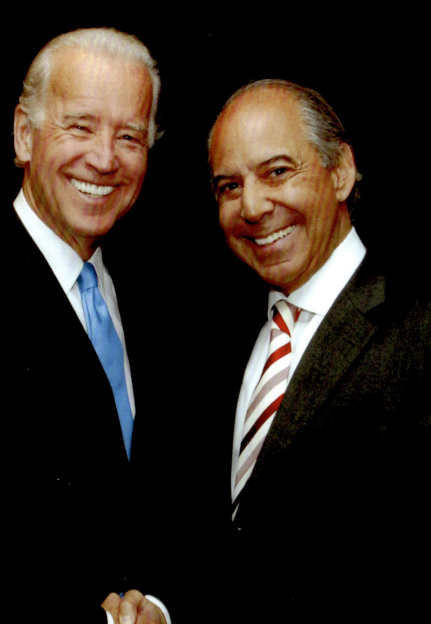

With President Joe Biden
National Archives

With Secretary of State Hillary Clinton
National Archives

With Vice President Al Gore
Hassan Nemazee Personal Collection

With Senator Ted Kennedy and President Bill Clinton
Hassan Nemazee Personal Collection

With Senator John Kerry
Hassan Nemazee Personal Collection

With House Speaker Nancy Pelosi
Hassan Nemazee Personal Collection

Outside the courtroom
Photo: Brendan McDermid/Reuters/Redux

The original manuscript for this book, written in prison
Hassan Nemazee Personal Collection

FCI Texarkana
The two men on the right, Wayne Jaegers and
Martin "Doc" MacNeill, both died in prison
Hassan Nemazee Personal Collection

FCI Otisville Camp
Inmate 62625 054
Hassan Nemazee Personal Collection

FCI Cumberland Camp
Nazie enters my life, January 2019
Hassan Nemazee Personal Collection

My children and grandchildren
My wife Nazie and I on our wedding day May 1, 2021
Hassan Nemazee Personal Collection

Hassan Nemazee
Photo: Jonah Markowitz/New York Times

21

LESSONS

New York is the key to fundraising in America. Nearly 30 cents out of every campaign dollar raised nationally comes from the tri-state area. As a result, there was enormous pressure on my staff to produce the necessary dollars for the Kerry campaign. I went out of my way to bring in the leading donors who had supported the now defunct Dean, Clark, Edwards, and Gephardt campaigns. Many were personal friends I knew from the Clinton and Gore campaigns. I hoped to make them all feel welcome in the Kerry effort.

Historically, after the conventions, candidates accepted federal funds for the general election, forgoing any further fundraising. As a result of our unprecedented success on the internet and the support of energized Democratic donors, we questioned the wisdom of taking federal funds. Why limit our resources when so many were in the offing? We knew Kerry would take political heat if he opted out, but this was offset by the opportunity to raise two, three, even four times the amount of the federal funds.

Lou Susman called a meeting of the finance chairs. I represented New York at the meeting. Alan Solomont represented the Northeast, Mark Gorenburg flew in from Northern California, and Bill Singer came from Chicago. A few others were present, too. With Lou's encouragement, we engaged in an open discussion on the pros and cons of opting out. The finance leadership, myself included, unanimously favored doing it, even though we recognized how much more time, effort, and responsibility we would be taking on. Our vote was relayed to Kerry. He mulled it for a few days, but in the end took our advice and opted out. The press killed us, as expected, but it was the absolutely correct decision.

The Democratic National Committee scheduled a gala victory dinner in Washington to celebrate Kerry's nomination. This was meant to bring together all of the candidates, as well as Bill Clinton and Al Gore, to show the unified front of the Democratic Party. I was seated at the head table, with John Kerry and Teresa Heinz. One by one, the other candidates spoke. Then Bill Clinton came to the podium. His job was to introduce Kerry. He extemporized, as usual, without notes or teleprompter. His theme was "send me". Working off the fact that John Kerry had always volunteered for the hard and dangerous duty, going back to his Vietnam service and the medals he had won for bravery, Clinton kept coming back to his refrain—"send me!"—and it became more powerful every time he said it.

It was a great speech. Unfortunately, the real star of the performance was not Kerry but Clinton, who simply could not help his tendency to outshine everyone else in the room. You could say of Clinton what people used to say about Teddy Roosevelt—he needed to be the corpse at every funeral, the bride at every wedding, the baby at every christening. You never wanted to follow him onto a stage if you could help it.

I happened to be sitting next to Kerry and could tell that he was growing uncomfortable as he realized that Clinton was upstaging him. Halfway through Clinton's speech, Kerry leaned over to me. "Get Shrum," he whispered. Bob Shrum was at the next table. I ducked over to him and told him Kerry needed him. Shrum came to our table and crouched next to Kerry. For the next few minutes, I watched the two of them go over Kerry's speech, trying to coax a little more life into it.

Shrum's last minute tweaks notwithstanding, Kerry's speech fell flat. After Clinton, he sounded tentative, lacking conviction and passion. Nothing could change who John Kerry fundamentally was as a person and politician. But one lesson that we could and did learn after that event was quite simple: never put a Kerry speech after a Clinton speech again.

Missteps aside, that summer of 2004 was a good one for Kerry. Whatever his flaws as a politician, he was a compelling and plausible candidate. And as Kerry's fortunes rose, I could not help feeling that mine were rising, too.

■ ■ ■

Some years earlier, I had transacted business with Julius Baer, a private bank in Switzerland. At Baer, I'd worked with a capable and energetic young banker. He had left Baer and was now working for Citibank's Private Bank, focusing on high-net-worth clients. Not long after arriving at Citibank, he got in touch with me. He undertook an aggressive campaign to encourage me to open a banking relationship with Citibank. I explained to him that I already had an arrangement with Bank of America for a $100 million credit facility and found this sufficient. He persisted. He pointed out that the Bank of America line of credit had to be renewed every year. All it took for me to lose it was a decision by Bank of America to lower its credit exposure. Should that happen, I'd suddenly have nothing to borrow and would be scrambling for a loan. Wouldn't it make sense, as a matter of security, to set up a side-by-side credit line at Citibank?

It was a compelling argument, given how much I'd lost in the markets and how dependent I'd become on credit. The fact that he made the argument suggested he had a hunch about my dependence on credit. Later, it would occur to me—and to others around me—that my bankers were not entirely fooled by me. The strange truth is that, despite my fraud, I was an ideal client for banks. I made them a great deal of money in fees, and I never defaulted on a single payment. As long as I made my payments, they made their money and were willing to overlook certain red flags.

This leads to a larger strange truth: it's a lot easier to borrow $100 million than to borrow $100,000. A bank is likely to conduct more due diligence on a small client than on a major client. If you are middle class and want to borrow money to buy a house, you will have to go to a bank and convince it to loan you the money. If you are wealthy and want to borrow a fortune—or even if you *don't*—the bank will come to you and sell you on the idea. For the small loan, you will have to provide significant disclosure, and this will be non-negotiable. For the large loan, a few official-looking documents will probably suffice, and if the bank asks for more, you can refuse. You'll probably get your loan anyway, because the bank wants your fees.

Once again, we went through a due diligence process with the bank's legal department and risk management experts. Once again, I provided fabricated materials and refused to hand over tax returns. And once again, the bank approved the loan without hesitation.

Given my fraud, it's fair to ask why I continued to maintain a high-visibility profile in my political work. Not only was I exposing myself to scrutiny, I was potentially tainting politicians who associated with me. My only answer, again, is that I rationalized my actions with the expectation that I would repay my debts, with no adverse impact on me or others. Of course, I understood at some level that I was taking a risk, but the longer I took this risk—the more routine it became—the easier it was to live with it.

■ ■ ■

After Kerry decided to opt out of the campaign finance structure, even greater responsibility was placed on my shoulders. Lou Susman came to New York to meet with Jamie Whitehead, my finance director, and me. He needed to be absolutely certain that we could deliver. I had a practice of under-promising, and over-performing, but I assured him we could. And we did. New York would lead the Kerry fundraising effort month after month.

One of our challenges was booking Kerry for events. There's always a tension in a campaign between the political operation and the finance operation. The candidate only has so much time in his day. The political operatives want it for political functions, the finance people want it for fundraising functions. The operatives often turn up their noses at fundraising, forgetting that none of them would have jobs without it. That's why it's so critical that there be a strong and respected National Finance Chair capable of arguing for the candidate's time. Susman fulfilled that role. When I called Susman to tell him I needed Kerry for an event, he would go to bat for me. He assisted me, too, in securing surrogates for smaller events. I organized multiple receptions with special guests such as Wesley Clark, Al Gore, Richard Holbrooke, Ted Kennedy, John Edwards, Joe Wilson, and Madeline Albright. Donations were always highest when the principal attended, but a marquee name was the next best thing.

I'd learned a great deal about the art of fundraising by this point, thanks in large part to Terry McAuliffe. He went out of his way to make the experience as enjoyable for the donors as possible, inviting them to share in the honorable mission of getting a good candidate elected. This mission included asking donors to go out and find new donors. Increasingly, the key to fundraising was converting donors into "bundlers."

I never liked that term. The press tended to use it pejoratively, as if there was something distasteful about soliciting donations from a wide circle of friends and acquaintances. The truth is that after the passage of McCain-Feingold bill in 2002, bundling became a necessary feature of campaign finance. Donors were limited in how much they could give. No longer was it possible for a single donor to write a check for $100,000 or $250,000, as had been the case in the past (and, frankly, is the case today, in this era of big money super PACS), so it became important to find a greater number of donors. Campaigns became dependent on fundraisers who had networks and the ability to raise significant amounts from their social and business contacts.

Other than his decision to opt out of the campaign finance structure, Kerry's biggest decision was his choice of vice president. There had been an attempt by Kerry and others to convince John McCain to join the ticket, in a bipartisan attempt to move the country forward. The McCain play was not popular inside the campaign, but it demonstrated Kerry's determination to do what was best for the country. McCain, himself a man capable of putting country over self, was interested, but in the end it was just impossible for him, as a staunch Republican, to join a Democratic ticket.

Bob Shrum made a strong push for John Edwards. I'd never been a fan of Edwards. I felt he was an empty suit and questioned his ability to be loyal to Kerry—Edwards was always mainly interested in Edwards. He was also totally indebted to the trial lawyers for having almost single-handedly financed his campaign. Putting in my own two cents, I argued for Joe Biden. He'd been a close friend of Kerry's in the Senate, and they had a warm personal relationship. He was a good man, a loyal man, and he had support in the states Kerry would need to win in November—Pennsylvania and Ohio. Needless to say, I lost the argument. Edwards was chosen.

■ ■ ■

My family accompanied me to the convention in Boston in late July of 2004. We had a wonderful time. We went to a game at Fenway Park, sat on top of the "Green Monster," and watched Kerry throw out the first pitch. Then we went to a concert of the Black Eyed Peas and danced until three in the morning.

We also watched a young unknown candidate for the Senate from Illinois, Barack Obama, give the stirring keynote speech at the convention. This was the speech that would catapult Obama to stardom and, eventually, to the White House.

When it came to oration, Kerry was no Obama—and no Clinton—but he gave one of his best, a memorable acceptance speech invoking his service in Vietnam. He was joined on the platform with members of his Swift Boat crew that had served with him in Vietnam. It was a great end to a very successful convention. We came out of Boston with a bounce in the polls that showed us leading Bush by five points.

In retrospect, it's astonishing how unprepared our campaign was for the attacks that immediately followed the convention. A group called Swift Boat Veterans for Truth began to air spots on cable news programs calling into question Kerry's military service. The hypocrisy of this was breathtaking. Kerry had received several medals for valor in combat in Vietnam. Neither Bush nor Cheney had served in Vietnam at all. Shamelessly, the Republican attack machine went to work to destroy Kerry's character and challenge his military record. As the charges came from an "unaffiliated" group, the Bush campaign could retreat behind plausible deniability. The Kerry campaign hesitated to fight back. Bob Shrum argued that to respond would be to legitimize the accusation. In fact, the opposite was happening—the ads were gaining traction by the hour.

After a few days of this, I'd had enough. I called Lou Susman. He agreed that the campaign needed to respond immediately. This was an opinion shared by almost everyone I spoke to in the finance leadership, as well as donors. But for ten days the Kerry campaign took incoming without mounting any defense, allowing the impression to build that there was truth to the allegations. By the time the campaign did respond, it was too late. The damage had been done. Bush pulled ahead in polls.

The Swift Boat episode was a painful lesson in hardball politics, one that Democrats learned the hard way: when you are hit, hit back. Fast and hard.

The debates in the fall helped pull Kerry back into a statistical tie with Bush. As Election Day arrived that first Tuesday in November, Kerry's chances seemed good. I flew up to Boston on the private plane of a friend and Kerry supporter, Glen Hutchins of Silver Lake Partners. As we touched down, I opened my Blackberry to receive a message from a friend in the White House: "Congratulations."

At 4 p.m., private exit polls of both our campaign and the White House indicated that John Kerry would be the next President of United States. Bob Shrum went to see Kerry at his Beacon Hill home at 5 p.m. "May I be the first to call you Mr. President," said Shrum. But Shrum had been too late on Swift Boat, and now he was too early.

We gathered that night at the hotel where Kerry and the campaign had its headquarters to watch the returns. We were all in a celebratory mood. I attended an early cocktail reception hosted by Terry McAuliffe, who was chair of the DNC at the time and who introduced the main speaker, Senator Ted Kennedy. Both gave victory speeches as though the results had already been counted.

As the night wore on, I could tell things were not going as predicted. I ran into Steve Elmendorf, a senior campaign official. He looked ashen and could barely look me in the eye. I went to Susman's suite. He was composed as usual, but his concern was evident. "It all comes down to Ohio," he said. "If we win there, we win the election. If not, it's over." Exit polls had predicted that Kerry would carry Ohio, but as the night wore on, Bush continued to hold a small but steady lead. At 11 p.m., the networks began calling Ohio for Bush.

I went back to our hotel room in a daze. I was crawling into bed around 1:00 a.m. when the phone rang. It was Susman, asking me to come to an emergency meeting. I dressed again and went back down to his suite. There were a dozen of us, the entire finance leadership of the Kerry campaign. Susman asked us if we could raise the necessary dollars for a recount if a decision was made to contest the outcome. This was a desperate but completely unserious proposition, one that fizzled out almost immediately. By the time I got back into bed, Kerry had called Bush to congratulate him on his victory.

Within 24 hours, I learned a fact that I found almost impossible to believe. The Kerry campaign had $17 million in unspent money in the bank. It is beyond comprehension that a presidential campaign would not spend every last penny, especially in a closely contested election. If anything, a hard-fought campaign often ends with a debt that is paid off after an election. To my knowledge, prior to this, there had never been an instance in the history of politics when a presidential campaign ended up with a *surplus*.

All along it had been clear that the election was going to be decided in Pennsylvania, Ohio, and Florida, and whoever won two out of three of these states would win the election. Florida had always been unlikely for Kerry, and Pennsylvania was a near certain win. That left Ohio. Had the $17 million been used to bring out the vote in Ohio, John Kerry would have been president.

■ ■ ■

Four days after the election, on November 8 2004, my mother died in Paris. She'd been unwell for quite a while. I'd gone to visit her in late October. She had been very weak, but I was hopeful that she would recover. She never did.

My mother had lived a long and productive life, and in her last years had been deeply involved in the lives of her children and grandchildren. Having lost my father too early, I considered myself fortunate to have had her in my life for as long as I did. Not a single day did we fail to speak to each other by phone or in person. She was as supportive and loving as a mother could be.

We arranged for her body to be flown to New York. Ever since her midnight conversion in Crans fifty years earlier, when she'd asked God to spare me, she'd remained a committed Catholic. And so, just as she wished, we laid her to rest in a Catholic cemetery, not far from my country home in Katonah.

22

AUDACITY, HOPE, AND OBAMA

John Kerry came to New York in December to attend an event I organized to thank his many supporters. Gore had taken almost nine months after his loss before coming to the city. Kerry came after just a month. Granted, his loss had been less tortuous and grueling than Gore's, but his willingness to face his supporters took courage.

We had a large reception at the Regency Hotel, followed by a small dinner at the restaurant Jean-Georges on Central Park West. I rode with John and Teresa to the dinner in the back of an SUV, awkwardly squeezed between the two of them. Gone were the full Secret Service details and the police escorts.

The drive across the bottom of Central Park was less than a mile, but it felt like a century. No sooner were we in the car than Teresa began scolding John for refusing to litigate the results of the Ohio election. She was convinced, as were many on the left of the party, that irregularities had occurred in several voting precincts. As we crept through holiday-season traffic, her voice grew sharp—the reception, the first they'd attended since the election, seemed to have stirred up strong feelings, and she sounded genuinely angry. Kerry remained calm, but he was adamant that he'd done the right thing. His attorneys had looked at the facts and concluded there was no basis to contest the outcome. "There is nothing more we can do, sweetie," he said. I was caught in the middle of a domestic squabble, albeit one regarding events of national significance.

I felt for Kerry. I'm sure he was no more inclined to concede the election than his wife and supporters were. But he also knew he had a responsibility to the American people to not drag them into another bitter fight about election results. Like all worthy American leaders and patriots, Kerry put the country ahead of himself, and the country was better for it. His own wife and some supporters may not have appreciated this yet, but many of us did.

The moment we stepped into Jean-Georges that evening, the diners recognized Kerry and broke out into spontaneous applause. Kerry smiled and waved as we made our way to the table I'd booked near the back of the restaurant. Sheila was already there, sitting with Coco and Arie Kopelman, old and close friends of the Kerrys. Despite the friendly welcome, the dinner would have been morose and uncomfortable had it not been for Arie. The chairman of Chanel in America, Arie was a world-class raconteur. He single-handedly made the dinner enjoyable by telling jokes and injecting levity into the evening.

■ ■ ■

The weeks after a losing campaign are deflating time for all involved, not just the candidate. My own feeling after that evening was that I'd had enough of politics. I was exhausted, both physically and emotionally. And after worrying about Kerry's finances for so long, I knew I needed to focus on my own, as I probably should have been doing all along.

Alan Quasha identified an investment opportunity that I was eager to participate in. He'd negotiated the purchase of one of New York's oldest asset management businesses, Carret, which had been established by Phillip Carret in the early 1960's. After Carret's death, at the age of 101, the company had been purchased by a well-known New York leveraged buyout organization called Castle Harlan. They had done a poor job of managing the business. As a consequence, we purchased Carret at a very attractive price. Alan became chairman, and I became co-chairman. Among those we recruited to work with us was Terry McAuliffe, who joined our organization after resigning as the chair of the DNC. Terry would remain with Carret until December of 2006, when he left to become chairman of the Hillary Clinton Presidential Campaign.

In addition to pursuing business opportunities, I became involved with the Asia Society. This was a natural fit for my interests, and I was pleased when Richard Holbrooke, a long-time board member, asked me to join the society's board of trustees. Holbrooke also ushered me into the prestigious Council on Foreign Relations, another great honor. I would devote a good deal of time to both the society and council in the years to come.

My plan to take off time from politics was soon interrupted. After chairing the New York finance effort for Kerry, I was sought by nearly every major Democrat running for office. A steady stream of candidates and would-be candidates came knocking at my door in 2005, sometimes to comic effect.

One amusing situation involved the race for attorney general of New York. Mark Green, the state's former public advocate, had decided to run for the office. He asked me to be his finance chair. I told him I had no time to devote to it. Green suggested that I allow him to use my name as finance chair but take no responsibility for any fundraising efforts. I liked Green, and this seemed a reasonable solution that cost me nothing, so I agreed.

A week later, I got a call from Mario Cuomo, the former governor of New York. A very effective surrogate speaker for Kerry, he'd been very helpful to me during the campaign and we had become friendly. He now asked me to support his son, Andrew, who had also decided to run for attorney general. I explained my arrangement with Mark Green to the former governor. "I understand," said Cuomo, "but can Andrew call you?"

"Of course."

Andrew Cuomo had been Bill Clinton's Secretary of Housing and Urban Development. He was smart, aggressive, and accustomed to getting his way. He came to see me in my office and pressed the argument that I should be his finance chair. Again, I explained my arrangement with Mark Green. "Well, okay," said Cuomo. "How about being the finance chair for both of us?"

"The finance chair for two competing campaigns?"

"Sure," said Cuomo. "Why not?"

"I'm flattered. But that's impossible."

I finally agreed to be finance chair for *neither* campaign. I also agreed to give an equal amount of financial support to each.

Several months later, I got another call from Andrew. He noted that I had not yet given him any money. "Remember I told you I'd give you exactly the same amount as I give Mark Green? Well, I haven't given Green a penny."

■ ■ ■

It was Chuck Schumer who brought me back, once more, into serious fundraising. He did it by making me an offer I could not refuse. He asked me to be National Finance Chair for the Democratic Senatorial Campaign Committee (DSCC).

Schumer had a well-deserved reputation as the Senate's most relentless fundraiser. He was aggressive and committed. At the behest of Senate Minority Leader Harry Reid, he had become chair of the campaign committee for the 2006 cycle. In taking on this assignment, Schumer put himself in a powerful but difficult position. It was his mission to regain Democratic control of the Senate. This was no easy task after the 2004 election. The Republicans held the Senate with a comfortable majority.

Schumer assured me that I would be given significant resources to compete with the Republicans. He had chosen a very smart and aggressive woman, Julianna Smoot, as his finance director. She would later go on to become finance director of Barack Obama's presidential campaign.

By accepting Schumer's offer, I knew I would be working on a truly national scale for the first time, which excited me. I also knew that a big part of my challenge would be working with Schumer. I'd already done some fundraising for several of his earlier campaigns, so I knew that he could be extremely prickly.

Schumer's first task was to recruit strong challengers to compete for open Senate seats. He was incredibly successful. Claire McCaskill in Missouri, Amy Klobuchar in Minnesota. Sheldon Whitehouse in Rhode Island, Jon Tester in Montana, Tom Udall in New Mexico, Ken Salazar in Colorado, and Jim Webb in Virginia—of all of these superb candidates, only Webb was not recruited by Schumer.

My responsibility was to raise the necessary funds from a pool of national donors to augment the candidates' own local fundraising efforts. Schumer was brutally efficient at dispensing these funds. He would not allocate money to any candidate who did not hit fundraising targets set by him. Moreover, he would not give DSCC funds to campaigns that didn't need support or appeared doomed to lose. This upset a number of his colleagues who were accustomed to handouts from the DSCC irrespective of their needs. Those days, under Schumer, were finished.

Our fundraising efforts were complicated by the unintended consequences of the McCain-Feingold Campaign Finance Reform Act. The law not only capped contribution limits to individual candidates, but it also placed a dollar cap on the total amount that an individual could contribute, in any given cycle, to candidates, the national party, congressional committees, and political action committees in aggregate. Schumer as chair of the DSCC, Rahm Emanuel as the chair of the DCCC (Democratic Congressional Campaign Committee), and Howard Dean as the chair of the DNC were all competing for essentially the same dollars.

■ ■ ■

So much for taking a break from politics. I was in deeper than ever, and just in time for the presidential campaign of 2008. The Democratic field was taking shape by the summer of 2006. Likely candidates included Hillary Clinton, Barack Obama, Joe Biden, Bill Richardson, John Edwards, Mark Warner, Tom Vilsack, and Chris Dodd.

John Kerry, too, remained viable. I was in Nantucket that summer for a DSCC event when John asked me to visit him at his home on the island. On the porch overlooking the ocean, John told me that he wanted to run, and he wanted to recreate his finance team. He asked me if I would be his National Finance Chair.

I very much wanted to run the finance operation of a national presidential campaign, and I was well positioned to do it. I knew everyone in the New York donor community. I'd gained national exposure and national relationships. I'd also forged a number of important and unique relationships in the emerging ethnic donor communities—Indian, Pakistani, Turkish, and Greek, and, not least, Iranian. I felt a great deal of loyalty to John, too, and would have welcomed a chance to help him become president. However, I did not think the party would welcome another run by him. I told him I was honored but thought he should take his time before announcing a decision.

As it happened, his candidacy ended before it began. He botched a joke while giving a speech that fall of 2006, when his attempt to ridicule President Bush's war in Iraq came off sounding like an insult to U.S. military troops. There was no coming back from that, and Kerry was smart enough to know it.

Not long after that, I received a call from Joe Biden. I'd long wanted Biden to consider running for the presidency and had even hosted a lunch to introduce him to the core New York donors. He now invited me to his home for a meeting with his staff and a small core of donors to discuss his candidacy.

I took the train to Wilmington, where I was met at the Amtrak station by Dennis Toner, Biden's long-serving finance director, who drove me to Biden's home outside of Wilmington. Having been a public servant for most of his adult life, Biden was not a wealthy man, but he liked big houses. This one was at the end of a long drive and surrounded by a wide lawn that ran down to the edge of a small lake. We initially met with Biden and a few members of his family in the large eat-in kitchen, clearly the command center of the house, then moved to his study near the back of the house, and finally, as our numbers grew, into a large dining room. We ended the day in a local restaurant.

Typical of Biden, the meeting had a homespun feel to it. About half of those present were members of his family. This included his sister Valerie, who had served as his campaign manager for his Senate campaign, and both of his sons, Beau and Hunter. His 90-year-old mother was present for much of the afternoon, as was his wife, Jill. Also in attendance were Tom Donilon and Ted Kaufman, both former aides to Biden.

Given that the point of the discussions was to discuss the viability of a Biden candidacy, I was struck by the paucity of major donors at the table. Other than me, the only donors in attendance were Bill Singer, Mike Adler, and Mark Angelson. This seemed inauspicious. As Jill Biden herself noted during one of her cameos, the entry fee to a presidential race was $40 million. When Mark Angelson suggested that getting to $40 million would not be a problem—all it was required was 40 people to raise $1 million each—I caught Bill Singer's eye and we both smiled. Bill was very experienced and knew pie-in-the-sky when he heard it.

Raising $100,000 is relatively easy, but very few people can raise $1 million. To get there, you need a wide network, and you need to be convincing and persistent. Finding forty people who could manage this was a significant challenge.

It fell to me to be the skunk at the garden party. I pointed out that while Joe was fantastic at retail politics, he would require a whole different set of tools to run for president in the current environment. He did not have a national network, and there would be fierce competition for national donors who could not only give their own donations but, more importantly, bring in other donors. Perhaps with more honesty than tact, I added that I was frankly disappointed by the turnout for this meeting, as it indicated to me that there really was no national network. One would have to be built from the ground up. It could be done, I said, but it would require a huge commitment of Joe's time.

On the train back to New York after a long day in Delaware, I felt conflicted. I was far closer to Joe than to any of the other candidates, including Hillary, but I was worried he was unrealistic about what he needed to do in order to compete in 2008. Before leaving, I'd pulled him aside to express my concerns. "We need to talk more before I can commit."

Later that week, the very smart and highly-respected New York Democratic fundraiser, Blair Effron, called me at my office. "I just spoke to Joe Biden. He tells me you're on board." I was taken aback. I called Dennis Toner and asked him to please explain to Joe that I'd not yet committed and did not want to do him a disservice by publicly contradicting him. Joe subsequently called to apologize for the misunderstanding.

■ ■ ■

The next candidate on my dance card was Hillary Clinton. Terry McAuliffe had committed to a major role in a Hillary campaign. If she ran—and that was still a big if at this point—he would choose the person to run her finance operation. From our private conversations, McAuliffe knew I was interested in the role. He arranged for Hillary to come to my office for a talk in December of 2006.

Hillary has a reputation of being cold and standoffish. She is quite the opposite. She is warm, kind, humorous, and curious about people. She does not have her husband's natural political gifts, but few people do. Walking into my office, she paused at a series of large framed photographs hanging from one of the walls. One was an image of the Three Gorges Dam in China, another of the ruins of Persepolis. She asked me about the photographs, which led to a conversation about my family's background—Shiraz, Bombay, Hong Kong—which then opened up a two-hour chat about everything under the sun, from family history to gossip about mutual friends to politics. We touched on the position of National Finance Chair, but only lightly, and neither of us made any commitment, one way or the other. Whether I ended up as her finance chair or not, I felt comfortable with the thought that she might someday be President of the United States.

And then there was Obama. I'd only met the junior senator from Illinois briefly at a few DSCC events where he was a guest speaker. He had captured the imagination of many Democrats who thought he was the future of the party. But would he decide to run after being in the Senate for only two years?

My first sustained interaction with Obama occurred shortly after my meeting with Hillary Clinton, when I was invited to an event for the young senator at George Soros' office. I recognized friends from the Kerry campaign, including Orin Kramer and Robert Wolfe, but the attendees were not the usual group of New York donors. Obama came into the conference room after meeting in private with Soros. He took off his jacket, went around the room to introduce himself, then began a discussion that lasted over an hour.

I had to leave to attend an event for my staff at the DSCC, but before departing I asked Obama what I expected to be the core question if he ran: "Senator, given the fact that you've only been in the Senate for two years, and don't yet have the experience of some of your potential rivals, what would compel us to support your candidacy versus those of folks like Biden or Hillary?" Obama gave a long, circuitous, and dispassionate answer that revolved around the fact that he had been a lawyer and would talk to the American people like a lawyer addressing a jury. It sounded exactly like the answer of a good lawyer. As the answer of a man running for president, though, it was inadequate.

I excused myself and left to attend the DSCC event. There I ran into one of Obama's close friends, Brian Mathis, who had also been at the Soros event. Mathis told me that Barack was not satisfied with the answer he'd given me and would be following up soon to clarify his remarks. Indeed, the next morning, just as I was finishing breakfast, my cell phone rang. It was Jenny Yeager, Obama's New York staff aide. "Mr. Nemazee, I have Senator Obama for you."

Obama opened the conversation by apologizing for his response to my question. He realized that it was a threshold question and he needed to answer it better than he had. The real rationale for his candidacy, should he decide to run, he said, was his belief that judgment was more important than experience. It would be a central theme of his candidacy.

The fact that he called me to make this clarification was more telling than his revised answer. He was very attentive to detail, and had an excellent staff that insured his follow up—very impressive for a man only two years in the Senate.

■ ■ ■

Our family took a ski trip to the Italian Alps over the 2006 Christmas holiday and into the New Year. We rented an apartment in the Alpine village of Cortina d'Ampezzo, where we were joined by my younger sister, Susie, and her husband, the British diplomat Sir Peter Westmacott. Both Susie and Peter had been previously married and divorced. They were thrilled to have found new love in middle age.

Cortina offered a nice break from politics, and the bracing alpine air helped me clarify the options I'd face when I returned home. I'd now gotten feelers from virtually every Democrat considering a run for the nomination, including Bill Richardson, Tom Vilsack, and John Edwards. I liked Richardson personally but questioned whether he had the legs to go all the way. Obama intrigued me, but I continued to worry that he was too young and unseasoned. My real choices, as I saw it, came back to Joe Biden and Hillary Clinton.

We were still in Cortina when Terry McAuliffe called to tell me that he'd agreed to chair Hillary's campaign. He planned to talk to Hillary soon about the position of National Finance Chair.

Almost immediately upon my return to New York, I felt pressure to make a decision. Some of this pressure came from the candidates themselves, but mainly it came from the press. Nearly every day a reporter called to ask whom I intended to support. Having little else to write about in the early days of the campaign, the press tended to look to donor preferences as a leading indicator of which candidates had the best shot. The fact is, for better or worse, the first primary in any national race is the money primary.

One afternoon, my assistant, Ziba Mahdavi, buzzed me to announce that Senator Obama was on the line. Obama and I exchanged pleasantries briefly, then he got to the point. He'd decided to run and wanted to invite me to be part of his finance leadership team.

"Senator," I said, "may I speak frankly?"

"Of course."

"We really don't know one another. My allegiance is to Hillary. We've been friends since the Clinton Administration, and her husband was very supportive of me." I reminded Obama that I'd run John Kerry's New York finance effort and had just finished my term as Finance Chair of the DSCC. "My assumption is that you've already chosen someone from your Chicago network. But the only position I'd consider would be as your Finance Chair."

Obama was silent. He'd clearly not expected me to cut to the chase so quickly. "Okay," he said after a moment. "Pitch me."

"With all due respect, Senator, it usually works the other way."

He chuckled. "I very much appreciate your input, Hassan. I'll get back to you." The next call I received from Obama would be after he had defeated Hillary in the primaries.

■ ■ ■

With Obama's decision now leaking to the press, Hillary realized that she did not have the luxury of waiting. As demonstrated by his call to me, Obama was already making a serious run at the top Democratic donors. Lou Susman, Kerry's former Finance Chair, was firmly in Obama's camp and was reaching out to all of Kerry's finance leadership on behalf of Obama. Hillary needed to move fast if she hoped to secure her own roster of top donors.

Shortly after Hillary Clinton announced her candidacy in January 2007, Terry McAuliffe called to say that the campaign had decided to hold off on naming a Finance Chair until after the first quarter, at the earliest. McAuliffe knew I wanted the position. I assured him that, after careful consideration, I'd decided to commit to Hillary in any case. The campaign immediately leaked my decision to the *New York Times* and *Wall Street Journal*.

I soon received a call from Hillary herself. She was, as always, gracious and good humored. We spoke of the upcoming campaign. I told her that I already had two events lined up for her. She was delighted.

One of these two early events was in Los Angeles. As it happened, this was Hillary's first official fundraiser for the campaign. The guests were predominantly Iranian American and proceeds were close to $400,000, way above my or anyone's expectations. I then hosted the New York event, with Bill Clinton as my special guest. This time we raised $500,000. By the end of the first quarter, I'd raised nearly a million dollars, far more than any other Hillary fundraiser.

McAuliffe had told me that Hillary would make a decision about her Finance Chair after the first quarter. But it became clear to me that the campaign, and Hillary in particular, did not want to appoint a single Finance Chair, as doing so would risk alienating everyone who wasn't appointed. Hillary's decision made a certain amount of sense, but it would ultimately come back to haunt her.

■ ■ ■

Chuck Schumer's task had been to flip the Senate to Democratic control in 2006. He'd done this, despite considerable odds. My own role, as chairman of the Democratic Senatorial Campaign Committee, had been to raise the funds to help him to achieve this, and I'd delivered. I should have called it quits at this high point, but Schumer asked me to stay on as finance chair of the DSCC, to prepare for the next round of senatorial elections. I made it clear to him that I wanted to be finance chair for a presidential campaign and would probably take on such a job if it were offered to me. Fine, said Schumer. But stay anyway. You can do both.

At this point, as I say, I'd seen enough of Schumer to know that he was a difficult character. I'd witnessed him be extremely tough on his finance staff, tearing into them, for example, when they failed to meet certain fundraising goals. I pitied his staff but maintained a decent personal relationship with him myself. Then one day in the early summer of 2007 I found myself on the receiving end of one of his tirades.

I'd given him a list of donors to call. These were people I'd already spoken to and convinced to donate to the DSCC. Schumer's part was to close the deal. Many politicians, even the best, are uncomfortable with this aspect of fundraising. Bill Clinton, for example, never minded making calls, but he routinely neglected to make the ask. Schumer had no such scruples.

On this summer day I had him call a wealthy woman in Los Angeles. In my conversation with her, she'd indicated that she would give $25,000. I relayed this to Schumer. He called her, chatted her up for a while, and then made the ask. For reasons having more to do with her decorous way of conducting business—she did not like to talk money—than with second thoughts or reneging on her commitment to me, she gave him a noncommittal response, then wished him good day.

Schumer immediately called me. He was yelling. I'd wasted his time putting him in touch with this woman, he told me. Furthermore, he fumed, I was not giving enough of myself to the DSCC recently—and this was just another example of how I'd let him down. And so on.

Having overheard Schumer verbally abuse his staff, I was not totally shocked. But his staff at least got paid to take the abuse. I was doing my fundraising work for free and, by the way, had raised enormous sums for him. And my staying on as DSCC chair had been at *his* insistence—I'd warned him that my heart was in presidential politics.

I gave him a minute to vent, and then I interrupted. "Hey, Chuck," I said. "Go fuck yourself." I hung up the phone.

Half an hour later, one of his staffers called me to apologize for the boss. Chuck was in bad mood, the staffer said, and had lost his temper. "I understand," I said. "But that was unforgivable." The following day, his Senate office called me to make an appointment for Schumer to come by my office and apologize in person. He did so a few days later. If Schumer was unaccustomed to people telling him to go fuck himself, he was even less accustomed to eating humble pie. "I accept the apology," I said when he was done. "But I won't be doing any more fundraising for you."

"I hope you'll reconsider, Hassan."

"I won't," I said.

I probably earned Schumer's eternal wrath in saying this, but I meant it. I never lifted another finger or raised another dollar for him.

■ ■ ■

Well, there are bad days and then there are the good ones. That summer of 2007, I was invited to a Clinton Foundation weekend retreat in beautiful Aspen, Colorado. The foundation held this annual retreat every year for its major supporters and potential supporters. Days were spent in seminars, where attendees learned about the work of the foundation and the Clinton Global Initiative; nights went to receptions and dinners.

One afternoon I was invited to golf with the president. I'd never played with Bill Clinton, or any president for that matter, and was quite nervous. But Clinton, as always, put those around him at ease, which tended to bring out the best in people. It definitely brought out the best in me that morning: on my first shot, I hit a spectacular drive down the center of the fairway, a good two hundred and fifty yards. Clinton did not congratulate me, but he was impressed enough that he asked to borrow my driver, a brand new Titleist. When his first tee shot sliced, he took another shot. This one hooked. He chuckled and handed the club back to me.

My next shot, from the fairway, was probably the best second shot I'd ever played on a par 5 hole. It landed just ten yards in front of the green, and rolled to the back fringe. I was on in two, and ended up birdieing the hole. I was ecstatic. Clinton said nothing. I called over to him. "Mr. President, I've just hit the best two shots of my entire golf career. How about some acknowledgement?" He roared with laughter.

■ ■ ■

As the campaign moved into the fall of 2007, Hillary was well ahead in the national polls. Obama and the rest of the field were often as much as 30 points behind. But the reality on the ground was quite different than these polls indicated.

In December, Sheila and I joined Alan and Susan Patricof, along with Robin Duke, an 80-year-old former ambassador to Norway, on a visit to Iowa. We wanted to see the Iowa organization for ourselves, and spend the weekend canvassing for Hillary. The best thing to come out of the trip was an article in the *New York Observer* by a reporter who trailed us as we went door to door canvassing for Hillary on a day when temperatures hovered around 13 degrees. His fish-out-of-water story, featuring wealthy Manhattanites trudging through an icy middle-class Iowa neighborhood, trying to sway voters, was good natured and hilarious. Hillary called to say it was the first good laugh she'd had in a while.

On a more serious note, though, were the alarming omens we saw in Iowa. In Ames, a university town, we counted many yards plastered with signs for Edwards and Obama but very few for Clinton. The Ames office, which should have been packed and bustling on the eve of a major election, was strangely quiet.

The results in Iowa turned out to be even worse than we'd feared. Despite having spent over $25 million, Clinton came in third in the caucuses, behind Obama and Edwards. She was suddenly in dire trouble. Obama's poll numbers shot up, and so did heart rates among Clinton stalwarts. Were Obama to win New Hampshire, he could effectively knock us out of the race. More alarmingly, Obama had substantially out-raised us. This was the last thing the campaign had predicted. We were supposed to have been the "Clinton money machine." There was near panic in Washington headquarters.

The day after Iowa, McAuliffe called me. "Hassan, it's yours if you want it. Will you become National Finance Chair? Better late than never."

"Yes," I responded. "Of course."

Minutes later, Hillary called to thank me, and to assure me that the race was far from over. She was right. Five days later, on January 8, 2008, she won New Hampshire, stopped the Obama momentum, and set the stage for a slugfest that would last until June.

■ ■ ■

Immediately after Iowa and New Hampshire, the Clinton campaign held an emergency meeting in Washington for the National Finance Committee. On the train down from New York, I found myself in the same compartment as Bill Clinton and his entourage of aides and security, also headed to the meeting. Clinton stopped by my seat, and we talked briefly about the campaign. Despite the setback in Iowa, Clinton was energized and glad to be engaged in promoting his wife's run.

The meeting and dinner were to seek commitments from individual members of the finance committee to raise funds for the next 30 days. As chair, I committed to raising $250,000 by the end of the month. I knew this would be a significant challenge in a three-week window, but I also knew it was important to lead by example. The Obama campaign was out-raising us every passing week, and the time had come for Clinton supporters to go all in.

After the dinner, I joined Bill Clinton and a group of friends in his suite for a game of cards. Clinton loved to play Oh Hell, a combination of Hearts and Canasta. I was new to the game, and Clinton took it upon himself to teach me, mainly by leaning over and playing my hand as well as his. Meanwhile, he entertained the table with endless stories and jokes, plus occasional forays into more serious topics. At one point, someone raised a question about future potential appointments in a Hillary Clinton cabinet, and Biden's name came up. "Biden is underestimated," said Clinton. "He should be on everyone's short list. I think Joe would make a good choice as vice president." As usual, Clinton's political instincts were prophetic.

As luck would have it, I ran into Clinton again on my return to New York. I was seated on the New York shuttle, with an empty seat beside me, when he boarded the plane moments before the door closed. He settled down next to me. On the flight back to New York, we talked about the campaign and what needed to be done. Ted Kennedy and John Kerry had recently endorsed Obama, and endorsements were becoming politically significant to both campaigns. The president knew I was close to Bill Richardson, the former governor of New Mexico, who had just withdrawn from the race. Clinton asked me to call Richardson and try to secure his endorsement for Hillary. I said I would do so immediately. I also promised to call Biden.

I called Biden first. He told me that he planned to be available to both Hillary and Obama for foreign policy advice but had decided to endorse neither. He was firm in his answer. I then called Richardson. I told him about my conversation with the president and asked him to endorse Hillary. Richardson heard me out and said that he would get back to me. I called him several times again over the course of the next several weeks, anxious to get his answer before I departed on a long-planned visit to the Middle East.

Richardson finally got back to me. "I have some good news to tell you," he said. "It will have to wait a day or two as I make some calls here in New Mexico, but you can tell the president and Hillary that they will be happy." I thanked him and immediately called the president and emailed Huma Abedin, Hillary's chief aide, to give them the good news. Several weeks later, in Cairo, I picked up an English language newspaper to learn that Richardson had just given a full-throated endorsement for Barack Obama.

■ ■ ■

The intrigues of U.S. domestic politics did not end at America's borders. I was still in the Middle East when I learned this lesson from Zbigniew Brzezinski, one of the masters of international diplomacy and Washington gamesmanship.

My visit to the Middle East was on behalf of the RAND Corporation, a for-profit think tank and consulting firm that worked closely with the U.S. defense and intelligence communities. I'd agreed to serve on RAND's Middle East Advisory Board, chaired by Brzezinski. I cleared the trip with McAuliffe prior to leaving. As long as I kept my affiliation to the Clinton campaign out of it, he had no problem with the trip.

We enjoyed a fascinating whirlwind of a week. Before it was over, I would visit Mecca in Saudi Arabia, the Wailing Wall in Jerusalem, and the Church of the Nativity in Bethlehem—the most iconic and revered religious sites, respectively, of Islam, Judaism, and Christianity. We also met a number of Middle Eastern leaders and learned a great deal about the region from those who were determining its future.

One of our last stops was Syria, where we met with President Bashar al-Assad. The United States did not have an ambassador in Syria at this time, but we did have a functioning embassy. The staff was anxious to brief us before our meeting with Assad, and even more eager to hear our impressions afterwards. Since succeeding his father in 2000, the Syrian leader had been an enigma to much of the West.

Assad received us in a new palace on a hill, overlooking Damascus. There was an enormous receiving room, with couches along three walls and two large chairs at the head of the room. Assad and Brzezinski sat in the chairs, side by side. Brzezinski was the highest-ranking American official or ex-official to have traveled to Syria in several years.

I expected the visit to be a superficial meet and greet, with little real discussion or substance. I was mistaken. We were with Assad for over an hour and a half. The conversation, as they say in diplomatic speak, was frank and candid. Assad was far more intelligent and engaged than we had been led to believe, and less patently evil than he would eventually reveal himself to be. Brzezinski was the consummate smooth-as-silk statesman and made sure to include all of us from RAND in the conversation.

One of the most interesting aspects of the trip was getting to see Brzezinski in action. He was well into his 70's, and the trip was a nonstop itinerary of travel and meetings and dinners, but he was always energetic and intellectually prepared. He was also tactically prepared to defend his turf and do what was necessary to win on his terms, as he'd shown years earlier, during the Iranian Revolution. Back then, as the brusque and sometimes belligerent National Security Advisor to President Carter, he'd supported a hard-line stance against the Ayatollah while masterfully undercutting the more dovish positions of his nemesis, Secretary of State Cyrus Vance.

As we left Assad's palace after our long meeting, we were surrounded by Syrian television crews and reporters. A podium had been set up. Brzezinski was livid, as he'd expected this to be a private and off-the-record visit. He was a senior foreign policy advisor to Obama and did not want to become a pawn in Assad's public relations efforts, as this might rebound negatively on the Obama campaign and his own reputation. Given the circumstances, he had no choice but to speak to the press. He cut it as short as possible, and we beat a hasty retreat to our hotel.

The next day, precisely as he'd feared, Brzezinski's visit to Assad was picked up by the Western press. There was a hue and cry from pro-Israeli journalists who demanded to know why Brzezinski, a foreign policy advisor to Obama, would meet with the despised Bashar al-Assad.

Giving little thought to the kerfuffle, I went off with our group to see the sights in Damascus. That night, I received a call from Ziba, my assistant. A reporter had just reached out to ask whether it was true that I was in Damascus meeting with President Bashar al-Assad. What, the reporter wanted to know, was Hillary Clinton's National Finance Chair doing talking to Assad? Mystified, I asked Ziba to call the reporter back and find out where he'd heard of my visit to Syria. Ziba soon got back to me. The reporter had been informed by someone from Brzezinski's office.

I'd become quite friendly with Brzezinski on the trip. We'd spent hours together talking about Iran and American politics. Given his own wish to keep RAND business distinct from the presidential campaign, I could not believe he would sell me out so easily. The next morning, I confronted him. "Yes, I told them," he said with a shrug. "What did you think? I wouldn't tell them there was a senior Clinton person here after they slammed Obama because of me?" He gave me a wolfish grin. "Welcome to Washington, Hassan."

In fact, we were thousands of miles from Washington. But I got his point.

■ ■ ■

The Clinton campaign experienced its worst month while I was in the Middle East. February 2008 was dominated by caucuses and primaries in states that Hillary's campaign manager, Patti Solis Doyle, had ignored. David Plouffe, Obama's campaign manager, had done exactly the opposite, opening field offices in states that were small and easily overlooked. The wisdom of Plouffe's strategy became evident that February. We lost eleven primaries and caucuses in a row.

Our own strategy had called for Hillary to win Iowa and New Hampshire, as Kerry had done, and then use her superior financial advantage to eliminate any competition going forward. When much of that failed to materialize, though, we had no plan B. The Clinton organization had not comprehended the impact of the Democratic Party rules regarding proportionality of delegate selection. Gone were the days when the winner of a primary or caucus took 100% of the delegates. Now, delegates were awarded proportionately, by percent of the vote. It was a game of math and rules—rules that had been written, as it happened, by a DNC controlled by the Clintons.

Hillary was a terrific candidate. Hard-working, disciplined and dedicated. Unfortunately, she was poorly served by her campaign leadership. So were Clinton's fundraisers. We raised all the money the campaign asked us to raise. The problem was how the money got spent.

Super Tuesday was supposed to be the day that would vault us to the finish line. We did in fact win the major states, but we lost a number of small states by a large margin. In the game of proportions, these losses added up not only in the delegate count, but also in financial terms. Funds had been allocated in a way that made little sense. For example, we'd spent $10 million in New Jersey and won the state by 10%, which gained Clinton a net total of twelve additional delegates. Obama won Idaho, where he spent just $500,000 but also netted himself twelve delegates, thus cancelling out our New Jersey victory for 1/20th the cost.

Hillary continued to win in the large states—Pennsylvania, Texas, and Ohio—but we could not close the delegate lead that Obama built up in February.

By June of 2008, it was all over. Hillary had done all she could, as had those of us who remained loyal and committed to the end. I am convinced that Hillary would have become president of the United States had she chosen her campaign leadership more wisely. She would be back, of course. But by then it would in 2016, and I would be in no position to help.

23

THE END

OVER THE SUMMER and early fall of 2008, as Barack Obama and John McCain clinched their respective parties' nominations, the U.S. economy went into free fall. Mid-September brought a cascade of once unthinkable disasters. The legendary investment bank Lehman Brothers declared bankruptcy on September 15, 2008. That same day, Merrill Lynch, to avoid its own bankruptcy, allowed itself to be purchased by Bank of America. The next day, the Federal Reserve effectively took control of AIG, the company I'd gone into business with years earlier in Iran.

Across the country, panicked Americans pulled tens of billions of dollars out of bank accounts and money markets, fearing they would lose everything. Many more Americans found themselves in suddenly worthless homes with large mortgages. The stock market plummeted to record lows. Characteristically equanimous men like Ben Bernanke of the Federal Reserve and Hank Paulson, secretary of the treasury, warned that the country was on the verge of total economic collapse.

Surprisingly, none of this had an immediate effect on my own finances. I was relatively well insulated from the market turmoil, because I was no longer heavily invested in public companies. Some years earlier, after losing so much in the collapse of the tech bubble, I'd made a calculated decision to focus on private equity investments, including a number that I'd purchased with Alan Quasha. Two of these, Carret and Brean Murray, were asset management companies that had managed to stay above water through 2008. Even better was an abundantly profitable company that Alan and I had purchased in Nigeria called HydroDive. Operating off the west coast of Africa, HydroDive specialized in underwater maintenance of offshore oil rigs. Our clients included major oil companies such as Shell, Chevron, and Exxon. We had purchased the company for about $50 million and saw profits grow to $35 million, with an expected $50 million in net profits due in the coming year. We were looking to expand into Angola and elsewhere in Africa, and had high hopes for a lucrative exit in the not-too-distant future.

Still, it took a good deal of wishful thinking, if not outright self-deception, to look at my financial situation with anything but despair. My debt was now nearly $200 million. And while my assets had survived the financial crisis intact, it was not at all clear that my debt would remain viable. The financial crisis had been precipitated by bad loans made by banks that were more interested in collecting fees than in performing due diligence. As a consequence, there was a great hue and cry about the lax practices and foolish risk-taking of banks, many of which had now fallen into the control of U.S. government regulators. I had to wonder what all this would mean to my loans.

My concern was not so much getting found out and suffering legal consequences, as having the banks drop me and seeing my funds suddenly cut off. The focus of my concern was my Citibank loan. The bank's enormous parent company, Citigroup, had been hit hard by the financial crisis. Its stock had dropped to about a dollar a share, and it seemed quite possible, for a time, that the bank would collapse completely.

■ ■ ■

Even in the midst of all this, I continued to spend. In addition to the duplex on Park Avenue and the house in Katonah, I'd purchased a loft in Tribeca for my children, a house in Telluride, Colorado, and an apartment in Rome. I took a fractional ownership of a plane and fractional ownership of yacht. I also continued to send checks, as I had done for many years, to old friends who had been devastated by the revolution. Altogether, my monthly expenses continued to grow at an alarming rate.

My spending may be hard to understand or forgive, given my situation. Clearly, these were extravagances that I should not have indulged in. I doubt any amount of reflection or psychotherapy could unpack the full range of motives, conscious and unconscious, that contributed to my behavior. I acknowledge that, at least in part, I continued to spend because I was intent on keeping up appearances. The Greek shipping magnate Aristotle

Onassis—a man who got himself in and out of debt more often than most people get in and out of bed—used to say that the key to success was to never let your banker see you without a suntan. Downgrading my life would have signaled the banks that I had financial problems, and that was the last thing I wanted to do. Now was not the time to call my own bluff.

At a deeper level, pride and fear surely came into play. My identity had been so long tied to my wealth, and to my good name, that I could not let go of the pretense—not to banks, not to my friends and family, not to the politicians I raised money for. I continued to practice my fraud not only on banks and everyone else, but on myself. I continued to believe that all of my loans would be repaid, and that life would go on with no harm done to anyone. Was this delusional? Detached? Naïve? Arrogant? The answer is yes. All of the above.

■ ■ ■

Now that Obama's victory over Clinton was sealed, I'd come around to feeling positive about him. I was treated warmly at his convention in Denver, where I enjoyed meeting some of his senior advisors. I especially enjoyed meeting Valerie Jarrett, who surprised me with the news that she'd grown up on the grounds of Nemazee Hospital in Shiraz. Her father had been a doctor at the hospital and her mother a nurse.[9]

Following the convention, in the late summer of 2008, we went to our apartment in Rome. As I had after John Kerry's loss in 2004, I hoped to get a breather from politics. While I found the work energizing and exciting when I was in the middle of a campaign, I always felt a little depleted when the campaign ended, particularly when it had not gone the way I'd hoped.

My cell phone rang at about 2 a.m., Rome time, awakening me from a deep sleep. I saw the area code was 312. Chicago. I picked

---

[9] Jarrett's father, Dr. James Bowman, was a notable example of the kind of physicians my father attracted to Nemazee Hospital. Dr. Bowman was a highly regarded pathologist whose chances of advancement in 1950s America were poor, due to the fact that he happened to be African American. Dr. Bowman became head of the pathology department at Nemazee Hospital, where Jarrett was born in 1956.

up the phone and heard a deep baritone. "Mr. Nemazee, this is Reggie Love. I have Senator Obama on the line."

I didn't bother to explain to Obama where I was, or what time it was. He was cordial and gracious. He began by acknowledging all that I had done for Hillary and the party. He then got to the point of the call. He asked me to come on board and play a "meaningful" part in his fundraising effort. I promised that I would do my best.

Before we hung up, I raised the issue of the debt Hillary had incurred near the end of her campaign, which came to millions of dollars. "Senator, if you were to indicate to your people your desire to see this debt reduced, it would make it easier for me to raise funds from the Clinton world for your campaign." Essentially, I was asking Obama to help erase a debt that our campaign had built up while trying to beat him.

"I hear you," said Obama without pause. "I'll talk to our people."

From Rome, we traveled to Puglia, on the southern tip of Italy. We were staying at a lovely old converted convent, owned by an eccentric English lord, when my phone rang again. This time it was Bill Richardson. We had not spoken since he backed out of his commitment to support Hillary Clinton. That episode had rankled me, as I'd been the one to convey his supposed endorsement to the Clinton campaign and had been embarrassed when he endorsed Obama instead. But his real problem now was not with me. It was with the Clintons. You might think such seasoned politicians as the Clintons would be philosophical about a betrayal like Richardson's, chalking it up to politics and not taking it personally. Not so. The Clintons never forgot a slight—especially not a slight from someone like Richardson, who owed his political career to Bill Clinton.

Richardson was calling to say he wanted to repair his relations with the Clintons. To make amends, he suggested that he host an event for Hillary in New Mexico to help pay down her debt. He told me he would personally raise a minimum of $250,000.

I knew it would not be easy to convince Hillary or the president to forgive Richardson, but $250,000 was a meaningful commitment, and, candidly, we were having great difficulty raising any money to pay down the debt. I called McAuliffe to tell him of Richardson's offer. He protested at first but ultimately agreed to run it by Bill and Hillary. Within hours, Hillary called me. Being more realistic than angry, she agreed to attend Richardson's fundraiser.

One more call came while we were in Italy. This one was from Joe Biden. He apologized when he heard I was on vacation, but he had a serious problem and needed my help. His campaign treasurer has stolen upwards of $300,000 from his campaign account. Biden now had to raise the money and realized that it would be a very difficult task. I told him not to worry; I'd call his finance director, Dennis Toner, and we'd find a way to take care of it.

When I returned to New York, I organized several events for Biden, including a speech he gave to a conference held by one of our companies, Brean Murray, on Chinese investment opportunities. I also quickly organized several events in New York, California, and Texas for Obama's general election campaign. The campaign reported my "bundler" total as in excess of $500,000. In fact, the total I raised for Obama was $956,000. That was in three months—July, August, and September. Not bad for a Hillary supporter.

■ ■ ■

The last major fundraiser I hosted for Obama was in September of 2008. It was at our home in New York, featuring Hillary Clinton as our guest of honor. This was Hillary's first and only dinner for Obama's campaign in New York, and a magnanimous and important gesture. Her presence at the dinner would signal to her supporters that the time had come to pull together for Obama.

The *New York Times* contacted me to ask if I would allow their political reporter, Michael Luo, to do a major piece on fundraising on the part of Hillary Clinton's finance organization for Obama. I was willing to participate, and the Obama campaign raised no objection, so I let Luo sit in my office for several days, watching and listening as I made call after call to potential donors. Re-reading the *Times* article now, I am reminded of how difficult the Hillary dinner was to pull off in the middle of a global economic crisis. The per-couple price of the dinner, $28,500, was a significant ask when many New Yorkers were watching their wealth decline by the hour—"hunting for hefty checks at an inauspicious time," is how the *Times* described my mission. Even putting the economy aside, it was late in the season to raise money, many donors having already maxed out their per person limit under campaign finance law.

Fortunately, after nearly fifteen years of practice, I knew how to do this. As the *Times* noted, I began with a long, handwritten list of names, some seventy people I considered persuadable, even if they had been strong Clinton supporters. Near the phone I kept a "fundraising bible," a thick sheaf of printouts from a contact list on my computer. I had names, numbers, and a record of previous donations the person had given.

There was a method to my calls, though it was more art than science. I persisted, but I did not push. I listened. I commiserated—genuinely—about the economy and Hillary's loss, but I reminded my potential guests that the price of losing the nomination was nothing compared to losing the White House after eight years of incompetent Republican rule. I heard "no" far more often than I heard "yes", but slowly I went down my list and soon I had twenty guests, to which I added a few more donors who could not attend but were willing to send checks anyway. Right up until the afternoon of the dinner, as the waiters set up the dining room and Mr. Yeung prepared his famous Peking duck in the kitchen, I worked the phones to bring in a few more. By the time we sat down with Hillary in our dining room that evening, we had a full house and nearly half a million dollars in donations. Hillary was her most charming self, and Mr. Yeung's duck was better than ever.

The economy, and particularly the financial sector, was in free fall as the campaign entered September. McCain, expecting to focus on foreign policy, was totally unprepared to deal with the economic collapse facing the country. Obama won easily. Sheila and I attended the inauguration in January 2009. It was an amazing scene, both moving and uplifting. Although Obama had not been my candidate, he was my president now, and I could not help but share in the joy of the crowd.

■ ■ ■

That spring of 2009, as Obama took the reins of government, the economy began to recover. My investments with Alan were doing well, and I still had plenty of credit to draw on. I continued to have some concerns about my loans, but as the economy improved, those concerns diminished. I certainly had no interest in taking out a new loan. Not until HSBC came calling.

In 2007, my banker at Citibank, who had also previously done some banking for me at Julius Baer, moved to HSBC. A do-not-compete contract had prevented him from pursuing his Citibank clients for a year. The moment that year passed, in the fall of 2008, he came to me. He suggested that I consider taking out a line of credit with HSBC.

It's worth repeating that the bankers always came to me—they were the pursuers, I the pursued. At first, I had little interest in the loan HSBC offered. As I explained to them, I already had two lines of credit, one at Bank of America and the one at Citibank that had been set up some years earlier, and found these adequate. What I did not say was that I had little interest in subjecting myself to the approval process for a new loan. The first round of approval was the most arduous and brought the most scrutiny—why put myself through that?

HSBC's bankers were as persuasive as they were persevering. They invited me to consider the possibility that my other lines of credit might vanish. Bank of America was in good shape—it had survived the crash intact and had just purchased Merrill Lynch—but Citibank still looked shaky, even after receiving a $500 billion bailout from the federal government. HSBC had a better balance sheet than Citibank, they argued, so my loan would be more secure there. And I could easily use the HSBC loan to pay off Citibank and then start over, in firmer hands. I had to admit that their pitch made a certain amount of sense, but still I hesitated.

As the spring of 2009 turned into summer, Citibank continued to have difficulties. In exchange for bailing out the bank, the government had imposed a number of restrictions and requirements, and bank officers were going through existing loans with a fine-tooth comb, looking for red flags. HSBC was right: Citibank could pull my line of credit at any moment. So could Bank of America. It was a new world of banking, and I could all too easily imagine my two existing lines of credit evaporating and leaving me high and dry. I called HSBC and told them I'd decided to take the their loan.

In early August, I had lunch with the head of private banking at HSBC. We agreed on a $100 million credit facility on the same terms and conditions as I had with my existing lenders. We negotiated some fees, which were fairly negligible in the scheme of things, and I gave them the same documentation of my assets that I'd given to my other lenders.

Needless to say, most of this documentation was fake, but no one at HSBC raised an eyebrow. They did not demand tax returns and I did not offer any, nor did they check up on any of the assets I'd listed as collateral. The due diligence was negligible, and that suited me just fine. When I told them I intended to leave for Rome near the end of the month, they promised to have my line of credit in place and ready to use before I left.

■ ■ ■

Sometime in early August, while I was still in discussions with HSBC, I received a call from Citibank. The caller was a credit officer for the bank. Her call, I later came to realize, was the beginning of the end. A question had come up regarding the custody account supporting my credit facility, she told me. As a result of the financial crisis, the bank was reviewing all of its major credit facilities. It was likely that someone from the bank would need to speak to someone at Pershing, the financial firm I'd named as custodian for most of my assets.

None of this should have been any surprise—in fact, this was exactly the scenario that had inspired me to pull the trigger on the new credit line at HSBC. The timing of Citibank's inquiry, coming at the very moment I prepared to sign for the new credit line, confirmed that I'd been right in taking the loan from HSBC. It also confirmed that I had good timing. I now had a way to pay off Citibank.

In the meantime, though, I did not want Citibank to call Pershing. While I did have an asset portfolio at Pershing, my holdings were nowhere near what I'd represented to Citibank. Furthermore, the contact I'd given them at Pershing was fake, as was the midtown office address I'd provided. Incredibly, over fifteen years, no one at Citibank had ever suggested calling Pershing before. Now that they were proposing to do exactly that, and I had to stop or delay them.

This turned out to be fairly easy to do. I told Citibank that if they had any concerns about my collateral, I would happily pay off my debt at once and move my account elsewhere. My veiled threat had exactly the effect that I hoped it would have. My private banker at Citibank called me later that day to ask that I not close the account. They would resolve the issue internally. No need to trouble ourselves with phone calls to Pershing.

Sometimes I allow myself to indulge in hypotheticals about the past, those what-ifs around which we can imagine our whole lives pivoting. For example: what if I'd gotten the HSBC loan a few weeks earlier that summer? Had I done so, I probably would have paid off Citibank immediately, which would have short-circuited the series of events that unfurled in August. None of what happened later that month would have come to pass. But—to carry this speculation a little further—would that have been better in the long run? Would it have allowed me more time to dig myself out of my debt, or would it merely have delayed the discovery of my fraud? If the latter, would that have been better for me, or worse?

Of course, we don't live in the world of what-ifs but of what-wases and what-ises. And in that world, I had a long-standing invitation, set for mid-August, to lunch with the newly installed president of Citibank Private Bank. The lunch, so far as I knew, had no agenda and no connection to the earlier call from the Citibank credit officer. It had been scheduled well in advance and was merely a courtesy extended to me to meet the newly installed president.

We met at Cipriani, on Fifth Avenue in midtown. I liked the new president, and our lunch was pleasant and friendly. We talked about business, politics, and summer plans. At some point, I mentioned that I was going Italy for a yachting excursion later in the month. He made it clear that Citibank was pleased to have me as a client and that everyone on his team looked forward to working with me in the future.

Only as lunch was ending, almost as afterthought, did he bring up the matter of my custodial account at Pershing. "Oh, by the way, Hassan, when you get a chance..." Almost apologetically, he told me that he was getting pressure from pesky regulators to show more documentation for loans. It would be very helpful to him, if I wouldn't mind terribly, to have Pershing send him a letter attesting to the assets in my account. The letter need not be anything complicated—in fact, his office would send me a template for what they needed—but it would get the regulators off his back and he'd really appreciate it. "Would you be able to do that?"

It is hard to say no to a man who just bought you lunch at Cipriani. So I said yes, and then immediately regretted it.

■ ■ ■

I could have saved myself a lot of trouble if I'd called my personal banker at Citibank later that afternoon and said something to the effect of, "I've reconsidered, and I don't want to do the letter after all, and by the way I've decided to close the account," and then done just that. But that's another "what if?" The truth is, I felt bound to send the letter after promising I would. Not sending it might prompt Citibank to call Pershing, and I wanted to avoid that at all costs.

Over the next few days, I had my brother-in-law create a letter on letterhead stationery purporting to be from a senior official from Pershing. Again, Shahin had no idea that he was doing anything illegal. He took my word for it that this was just a formality and a convenience for me. I delivered the letter to Citibank on Wednesday, August 19. I personally fed it into the fax machine, and my secretary later mailed the original. Even as the fax machine sucked it down, I wanted to grab it and pull it back.

I heard nothing from Citibank on Thursday, which I considered a good sign. The following day, Friday, August 21, I finalized my loan with HSBC. Then I drove out to our house in Katonah for the weekend. The house was empty, Sheila and the kids having gone ahead to Rome. I had a quiet weekend, handled some upkeep issues on the property, then had dinner Saturday night with our caretaker. Early Sunday afternoon, I drove back into the city to pack before my flight to Rome that evening.

■ ■ ■

My flight was on Delta, from Newark Liberty Airport, direct to Rome, where I would meet up with my family to travel together to Sardinia. I took my usual car service to Newark. On the ride out, I was feeling relaxed and relieved. I'd been looking forward to this excursion for some time. Along with our children, we had invited some friends from Texas, as well as a Turkish couple, the Ongors, who had hosted us several times in Bodrum. Also joining us would be Oliver Westmacott, eldest son of my brother-in-law, Peter Westmacott. A number of summers earlier, during a family sailing vacation off the Turkish coast with my sister's family, my daughter Yasmine and Peter's son Oliver had fallen in love. The relationship had grown quite serious over the years, and Oliver had become an important part of our family. Both Kamyar and Layla were also bringing their significant others. It promised to be an extraordinary week of sailing through the Mediterranean with family and friends.

As I looked forward to all of this, my concerns of the previous week no longer weighed on me. The letter I'd given to Citibank had apparently satisfied the bank's requirements. I'd heard not a peep from them since. The new loan from HSBC had closed without any last-minute complications. As soon as I got back to New York, I would pay off Citibank with the newly available funds from HSBC and put that issue to rest.

What I did not know as we sped south on the New Jersey Turnpike was that earlier that Sunday, while I'd been packing for my trip, a meeting had taken place in a suite of offices on Foley Square in Manhattan. A meeting that would determine the next dozen years of my life.

Not until many years later, when I read Preet Bharara's memoir of his tenure as U.S. Attorney for the Southern District of New York, would I come to learn how the events of that day came together. It is fascinating to read what Bharara put in his book, but also to consider what he left out. For example, he writes of me as if he'd never heard my name before that Sunday afternoon, though in fact we'd met a number of times when he'd worked as lead counsel for Chuck Schumer in the Senate. But more on that later.

Here is what Bharara says happened that Sunday: He was just ten days into his job as U.S. Attorney, sitting at his desk in his new office, still getting his feet wet, when his deputy walked in urgently. "We have a situation," announced the deputy. He told Bharara that a few days earlier, Citibank had called the FBI to report their suspicion that a client name Hassan Nemazee had committed a large bank fraud. Bharara does not mention what triggered Citibank's call to the FBI and I have never been told, but I am sure it was the letter I'd sent on Wednesday, purportedly from Pershing but fabricated by me. Maybe something about the letter looked fishy. Or maybe someone at Citibank finally picked up a phone and called Pershing.

As for how the FBI learned the next bit of important information that Bharara's deputy told him—that I was booked on a flight to Rome that very evening—this must have come from Citibank. I'd mentioned it during my lunch with the bank executive, and he must have passed it on. It was this fact that gave urgency to the matter, because it raised the question of whether I was going on a pre-planned trip or whether I was, as Bharara puts it, "hinked up and fleeing." In fact, I was far from "hinked up" as I contemplated our cruise around the Mediterranean. Laid back was more like it.

■ ■ ■

Newark Airport was unusually quiet that Sunday night. I suppose anyone who had anywhere to go that last week of summer had already gone. My driver helped me get my duffel out of the trunk and deliver it to a porter on the sidewalk. I told the driver I'd see him again in a week, then I followed the porter through the airport doors and across the atrium to the Delta counter. I saw my greeter waiting near the counter. She was a woman we hired to expedite our passage through airport security and customs. She was smiling as I approached. "Good evening, Mr. Nemazee. Is Mrs. Nemazee coming too tonight?" Before I could answer, another voice spoke to me.

"Hassan Nezamee?" It was a woman's voice, coming from behind. She had the wrong name but I knew she was addressing me. I turned around.

Preet Bharara writes in his book that the two agents who first approached me were men. In fact, one of them was a woman—Special Agent G. Dalynn Barker—she's the one who had spoken. Bharara also writes that they approached me only after I'd gone through airport security, "to make sure he had been screened for weapons." I had not yet gone through security. I'd just entered the airport.

"Nemazee. Hassan Nemazee," I said to the woman. "Who are you?"

The agents were dressed in nondescript civilian clothing. The woman took another step. She was young, with long auburn hair. She held out something in her palm. It was a laminated shield with an FBI logo. The moment I saw it, I knew why they were here. "Special Agent Barker, FBI, sir. We'd like to ask you some questions."

She seemed friendly enough. The man with her did not. He looked pissed off about having to spend his Sunday evening at the airport. She did most of the talking, while he glowered. Good cop, bad cop.

"I'm on my way to Rome. What's this about?"

"Just a few questions, Mr. Nemazee."

"All right."

"The collateral you're claiming for your Citibank loan. There's an issue about a letter you recently submitted."

"What's the issue?"

I was surprisingly calm. Perhaps because at some level I'd known this day would someday come, I was psychologically prepared for it. My heart was not pounding. My mind was not spinning.

Agent Barker asked about the origin of the letter written to Citibank. The origin, I told her, was Citibank itself. The bank had sent me a draft of what they wanted, and this was almost precisely what they were given. I pulled my Blackberry from my pocket and brought up the email from Citibank containing the draft they had prepared as a template. I told Agent Barker that I had simply forwarded that to the custodian, Pershing. "I didn't write the letter. I simply provided it."

"Okay, thank you. That's helpful."

"Are you telling me there is no money in my account? Because if so, that's news to me."

"Well, that's what we need to determine. To do that, we'd like you to put off your flight to Rome."

"Am I under arrest?"

"No. But we'd prefer you to remain in the United States until we can determine the facts."

Here is what Preet Bharara wrote of my encounter with the FBI agents: "The hope was that one of three things would happen... Nemazee would lie to the FBI, so they could arrest him; he would incriminate himself by making some admission, so they could arrest him; or he would decide voluntarily to stay in the country while we sorted it all out."

I've been asked over the years why I chose option three. Why did I not simply refuse to comply with their request and board the flight? What could they have done to stop me? Maybe nothing. Possibly they had a federal judge on standby to issue an instant warrant if I tried. But as Bharara himself admits in his book, they had little to base a warrant on, just an unverified accusation from Citibank. Not a very firm pretext for a warrant to arrest a man whose rap sheet included nothing more than a few speeding tickets.

Many of the same people who ask me why I did not just ignore the FBI and leave for Rome also wonder why I'd not set aside any money abroad—a few million in a Swiss bank account, say—in anticipation of this moment. The premise of that question is that a man smart enough to defraud sophisticated banks of hundreds of millions of dollars over fifteen years is surely smart enough to plan for his eventual escape. But smart had nothing to do with any of it, and the fact is I'd never given a moment's thought to fleeing the United States. Arrogant and deluded, perhaps yes. But a criminal mastermind I was not.

"We'd like you to come and see us tomorrow morning," she said, handing me her card. "Could you do that?"

"Sure."

She thanked me, and the male agent grumbled something. As I pulled out my phone to call the car service to summon back my driver, the two agents walked over to a wall perpendicular to the Delta counter. Four men, also clearly FBI, appeared from behind the edge of the wall. Clearly, they'd been lying in wait in the passage I would have passed through on my way to security and the departure gate. They were going to keep me off that plane one way or another.

Twenty minutes later, I was in the rear seat of the same car I'd come in, speeding north on the Turnpike, heading back to the city. I looked over my shoulder to see if anyone was following. I figured the FBI might want to make sure I didn't turn around and try board the plane after all.

But I had no intention of going back to the airport and trying to escape. I had a better plan, one that formulated quickly and clearly in my mind. As soon I could, I would do what I should have done weeks earlier. I'd transfer funds from my new HSBC account into the Citibank account. I'd do this first thing in the morning. It would be simple—pull money from my new credit line, pay off Citibank, then watch them withdraw their accusation. A few months down the road, they'd probably be back in touch, begging me to take another loan. I'd escaped tighter spots than this. I'd get out of this one, too.

Part III

Prison

24

NIGHTMARE

In the early morning hours of Wednesday, August 26, 2009 I found myself on a lumpy cot on the bottom of a bunk bed in a small concrete cell. Above me, a young Puerto Rican man snored quietly. Every few seconds, a drop of water fell from the faucet into the stainless steel sink bolted into the wall across the cell. Beside the sink was a toilet, also stainless steel, no seat. The door of the cell was steel, with a small rectangular slot cut out of the center. Hours earlier, I'd backed my hands into the slot to have shackles removed from my wrists by a guard on the other side. Later, a tray of food had appeared in the slot—dinner—but I'd refused it. Also through the slot drifted men's voices—someone yelling in Spanish, someone else telling him to shut the fuck up—and odors of human sweat and decay. A fungal rot seemed to exude from every pore of this place.

I was inside of a nightmare. But there was no waking from this nightmare, because sleep was impossible. What time was it? Close to 2 a.m., possibly 3:00. I closed my eyes. It would be morning on the Mediterranean, the sun rising over the decks of the *Ocean Emerald*, the sea glimmering below it. My family would be sitting down to breakfast, wondering where I was.

■ ■ ■

My encounter with the FBI had taken place just two nights earlier, but already it seemed a lifetime ago. I'd still inhabited some version of my old life back then, still believed I might find a way out of trouble. Still held onto whatever delusions had gotten me here in the first place.

First thing I needed, I'd realized that Sunday night as I headed back into the city, was a good attorney. From the back of the town car I called Pat Oxford. Pat was managing partner of the highly respected Texas law firm, Bracewell LLP. Years earlier, he'd represented J.C. Helms, until Helms flipped out and Pat decided he'd had enough. Since then, Pat and I had become good friends, and he'd often represented me in civil matters. He did not handle criminal cases, but I was sure he'd know someone who did.

Pat picked up on the first ring. "There's been a mistake," I told Pat after describing my ordeal at the airport. "I need to get this worked out." Pat was very understanding and reassuring. "Give me a few minutes," he said. "I'll make some calls."

Waiting for Pat to get back to me, I sent Sheila an email from my Blackberry. I didn't want to worry her, so I mentioned nothing about the FBI. I'd missed my flight, I told her. They should start the cruise without me. I'd catch up to them in a day or two.

A few minutes later, Pat called back. He'd spoken to Marc Mukasey, the head of his firm's litigation practice in New York and the son of Michael Mukasey, former Attorney General of the United States. Marc had been an Assistant U.S. Attorney for the Southern District of N.Y. for many years and was smart as hell. He was expecting my call.

I called Mukasey and gave him the broad outlines of what happened. "I'll see what I can find out," said Mukasey. "In the meantime, forget about going into the FBI tomorrow. You don't need to do that." I took heart from his forceful tone. I was in good hands.

Later that night, back in the apartment, I had a conference call with Marc and Pat. Marc had made some inquiries since we spoke in the car. His contacts in the Southern District informed him that my case had already been referred to the U.S. Attorney. He advised both the FBI and the U.S. Attorney that I would not be submitting to an interview the following morning. "If and when you do meet them, I'll be with you," Marc told me. "Before that happens, tell me what's going on."

In the next few seconds, almost reflexively, I made a fundamental mistake. I told Pat and Marc that there had been an error on the part of Citibank, or maybe on the part of Pershing, the custodian of my assets. The clear impression I gave them was that I'd done nothing wrong. Bad move. The cardinal rule in dealing with counsel is to tell them *everything*. Even if it's embarrassing or confirms your guilt, give them the full, unvarnished truth.

Under attorney client privilege, they can't and won't divulge anything you reveal to them, and the more they know, the better they can advise and defend you. I should have known this—I *did* know this—but I dissembled anyway. Having lived my deception for so long, I was not able to come clean, even when it was to my advantage to do so.

Somehow, with a little help from Ambien, I fell asleep that night. The next morning, Monday, I woke early and went to the office. I had one thing on my mind, which was to immediately pay off the Citibank loan and try to make the problem go away.

Had I done this a few weeks earlier, when I first thought of it, I might have avoided the mess I was in. But to do it now—to make a wire transfer under the nose of the FBI—was reckless and self-defeating. Nonetheless, the moment I arrived at the office I asked my assistant, Ziba, to draft a memo to order the immediate transfer of $75 million from my HSBC credit facility to Citibank. Ziba executed this with her usual efficiency. I signed the letter and she faxed it to Citibank. If HSBC was surprised by my request to drain three quarters of my credit line just days after its approval, they gave no sign of this. Before noon, $75 million had moved from HSBC to Citibank.

I called Pat Oxford and Marc Mukasey to tell them what I had done. Again, I left out the critical fact that I'd made the transfer using another banking relationship based on false collateral. They knew only what I told them, which was that I'd decided to cut ties with Citibank.

Mukasey called back a few hours later to inform me that the FBI had asked him to secure my passport. It was a pro forma request in cases such as mine, he assured me, and best to comply without argument. He suggested we meet for dinner that night to make the hand off and discuss my case. As it happened, the electricity at 770 Park was due to be shut off by Con Edison that night to make repairs. I'd already made arrangements to spend the night at the Hôtel Plaza Athénée on 64th Street. I told Mukasey to meet me at the hotel's restaurant.

That evening, after checking in I ate dinner with Mukasey and a young associate from his law firm. In retrospect, I'm amazed that I had the composure to eat and chat that evening. On some level,

I knew I was in serious and unavoidable trouble. I understood that the moment FBI agents got around to checking my assets—or simply visited the address of the fake office I'd given for my brokerage accountant—they would learn the truth. Somehow, though, I managed to carry on as if I were an innocent man. "So, Hassan," Mukasey said to me as our meal ended, "anything else that might be helpful for me to know?"

"No," I responded without missing a beat. "Nothing."

■ ■ ■

I was still in bed at the hotel the next morning—Tuesday, August 25—when my cell phone rang. The moment I saw Mukasey's number I had a bad feeling. "They have a warrant for your arrest," said Marc when I picked up.

I have no memory of my response to this, if I made one. I only recall sitting on the edge of the bed, feeling like I'd just taken a punch in my gut.

"I told them we'd do this the easy way," said Mukasey. "We'll pick you and up and go down in a car. The sooner the better. We'll get this over with and have you home tonight."

Forty-five minutes later, I was in the back of a town car with Mukasey and his associate, heading down Fifth Avenue. I'd not brought a full change of clothes to the hotel, so I was wearing the same pants and shirt I'd worn to dinner, fully expecting, per Marc's assurances, to be back in my apartment that night.

Mukasey warned me that there was likely to be press in front of the building on Foley Square, but he'd worked out an arrangement to avoid them. When we got to Foley Square, we turned into an outdoor lot, then descended into an underground parking garage. As my eyes adjusted, I saw Agent Barker, the woman who had questioned me at the airport. She was standing in the gloom of the garage with another agent, waiting for me. I stepped out of the car and she approached me. "Thank you for coming in, Mr. Nemazee. You are now being placed under arrest." She read me my Miranda rights, then asked me to place my hands behind my back and slipped a pair of handcuffs around my wrists.

■ ■ ■

I entered into what I can only describe as a timeless vortex—a fugue-like state that would last, in a sense, for an entire year. As Mukasey left me to go upstairs to work out the conditions of my bail, I went into a dark tunnel—quite literally. I spent the day shuffling through a warren of windowless passages and enclosed bridgeways. I recall an interminable series of humiliating tasks buffered by vast stretches of sitting on hard benches. I was fingerprinted, photographed, strip-searched, and given numerous forms to fill out. Agent Barker ushered me through all this with as much decency and courtesy as possible.

But there was no softening the reality: I was under arrest, and my life as I'd known it was over.

Sometime early that afternoon, still in handcuffs, I was taken upstairs to a room with a table. Mukasey was in there, waiting for me. He looked grim. "You haven't been telling me the truth, Hassan," he said as soon as we were alone and the door was closed.

He quickly filled me in on what he'd learned from the prosecutors. They had strong evidence that I'd committed bank fraud at both Citibank and Bank of America. They also knew about my HSBC loan and believed that had been fraudulently obtained as well. And they knew about the transfer I'd made the previous day to close out the Citibank loan. By making the transfer, Mukasey told me, I'd added a count of wire fraud to the already considerable number of charges they intended to file against me. "If I'm going to defend you, I need the truth. All of it."

So I confessed to him. I told him everything. The financial statements claiming assets I did not have. The fraud, going back a decade. The version I gave him was brief but accurate. When I was done, Mukasey shook his head, still angry. "You can never keep anything from me." Not only had I hamstrung his defense of me, I'd also embarrassed him personally by letting him give representations that were clearly false. I swore to him I'd be completely honest and candid going forward, and I was. As of that moment, my lies were finished forever.

Mukasey and I entered a courtroom for my bail hearing. As a magistrate judge presided, a young prosecutor from the Southern District of New York (SDNY) demanded that my bail be set at $25 million. I don't remember much from that day, but I distinctly recall what the magistrate judge said as he shook his head, apparently as astonished as I was. "I've never seen a bail this high." In fact, as I came to learn, it was one of the highest bails ever set in the Southern District. By contrast, Bernie Madoff, arrested a year earlier for swindling *billions* of dollars from *thousands* of innocent investors, had been given a bail of $10 million. I had voluntarily given up my passport before my arrest and voluntarily surrendered. And yet I'd been given a bail more than double Madoff's.

It began to dawn on me that I was going to be singled out for harsh treatment. I had a pretty good idea why. Preet Bharara, the newly installed U.S. Attorney, had been Chuck Schumer's chief counsel. Schumer had recommended Bharara's appointment to the position of U.S. Attorney, the most visible and prestigious prosecutorial position in America short of Attorney General of the United States. I was Bharara's first big case and he obviously intended to make an example of me. All the better, for his purposes that we came from the same political party—I was his opportunity to demonstrate his political independence from the Democrats. Who could say he was beholden to Schumer if he stuck it to me?

Actually, as time went on, I began to wonder if I had it wrong—that maybe he *was* beholden to Schumer, and it was for precisely that reason that he targeted me. I can't prove it, but given the animus Schumer felt for me, and the harsh treatment I started receiving immediately from SDNY, I think it's a distinct possibility. Am I suggesting that Chuck Schumer might have been so vindictive as to sic Bharara on me simply because I'd told him to fuck off a few years earlier?

Yes, that is what I'm suggesting.

I spent a few more hours waiting in various cells, then Mukasey reappeared to deliver some more bad news. I was going to need a home monitoring device placed in my apartment before I'd be allowed to return home. Unfortunately, it had gotten too late in the day for this, so I was going to have to spend the night in detention.

"I thought I was going home tonight."

"That's usually how it works. But they won't budge. You're going to have to do a night in MCC. Bad luck, I'm afraid."

Bad luck? Or intentional malice? I believe the prosecutors knew exactly what they were doing when they sent me, and others, to MCC. They were scaring us into submission.

■ ■ ■

The Metropolitan Correctional Center (MCC) is attached to a vast multiple-building structure that comprises the Federal Court and prison system in downtown Manhattan. The facility is meant to be a temporary holding cell for suspects and convicts in federal custody. In fact, a number of prisoners have been locked up for long periods at MCC, which is the very definition of cruel and unusual punishment.

Some years later, MCC would become infamous around the world as the hellhole where Jeffrey Epstein hanged himself with a sheet while guards napped a few yards away.[10] Already in 2010 it was grimy, vermin infested, damp, dark, and altogether awful. The only place worse in the federal system—as I'd eventually learn firsthand—was the federal holding facility in Brooklyn known as MDC (Metropolitan Detention Center). For the time being, though, MCC was the foulest place I'd ever set foot into.

I was shackled and escorted through more passages, each seeming to get darker and grimier by the step. We entered another set of rooms and holding cells for more processing, almost a complete duplication of what I'd gone through earlier in the day. Fingerprints, photos, DNA swab, another strip search. Then a quick physical by a prison doctor and psych evaluation by a prison psychologist. When I mentioned that I was only in for one night, the psychologist shrugged. One day or a thousand—it made no difference. Everyone got the full treatment.

At some point, my clothes were taken from me, and I was told to put on the orange jumpsuit they handed to me. Then I was offered the use of a phone to make a call—one call. I stood in front of the phone and stared at it. I seldom dialed anyone's number, as all the important ones were stored in my phone, and

---

[10] Based on details in press reports, I believe I had been placed in the very cell where Epstein died.

now I drew a blank. I could not remember the number of Sheila or any of my children.

In fact, as it turned out, I did not need to tell my family what had happened because they already knew. Preet Bharara's office had released a statement to the press earlier in the day. Because this was Bharara's first big case since taking over SDNY, he was going to make damn sure the world knew about it. *Hillary Clinton National Finance Chair and Major Democratic fundraiser arrested for bank fraud*. A number of international news organizations picked up the press release. CNN put it on a ticker at the bottom of their screen. My family was sailing out of Sardinia when friends began to call in disbelief.

■ ■ ■

Sometime that evening, I was escorted down one more long corridor to the Special Housing Unit inside of MCC. I could smell it as I approached—that indescribable odor of fungal rot. Something small and dark moved along the concrete wall beside me—a cockroach, the first of many I'd see that night. The guards placed me in a cell, shut the door behind me, and told me to back up to the slot if I wanted my handcuffs removed.

My cellmate was a young Puerto Rican. He volunteered that he'd been rearrested on a parole violation. I told him I was 59 years old and needed the bottom bunk. "Okay," he said. "But then we make a deal. You give me your mattress." The mattress I ended up with was as lumpy and hard as a bed of rocks. It didn't matter. No chance I was sleeping anyway.

25

THE GAUNTLET

"YOU READY FOR THIS?"

It was late Wednesday morning. Guards had come to my cell early to offer breakfast and a shower. I'd not eaten since dinner at the hotel Monday evening, but what I'd seen of the food at MCC killed my appetite. And what I'd experienced of the place so far did not make me want to go anywhere near the shower. I just wanted to get out.

I was shackled and taken to a large holding pen with a few dozen other men. After a few hours of waiting, I was given several forms to sign, one to get my clothing and other possessions returned to me—watch, wallet—and another agreeing to conditions of my bail and home confinement. In the office of the U.S. Marshal an officer instructed me to lift my pants cuff so that he could attach a plastic strap around my ankle. The strap held a rectangular plastic transmitter that would ride over my foot for the next year, monitoring my movements and ensuring that I obeyed the conditions of my home confinement. Eventually, I'd grow so used to the ankle bracelet as to not feel it, but for the moment it felt alien and uncomfortable.

After all of this, I was ushered before the magistrate judge who had seen me the previous afternoon. With Marc Mukasey back by my side, the judge went over the terms and rules of my release and asked me if I understood. I said I did, and then I was free to leave. Though free was not quite the word.

Mukasey and I now paused in the cavernous lobby of the courthouse. Through the windows of the gold-framed doors, we could see the press outside. Camera crews, photographers, and reporters with notebooks formed a gauntlet along the stairs. New York's press needs a steady diet of rogues and villains to satiate it, and I was apparently today's feast, offered fresh by SDNY.

Mukasey had tried to arrange for me to be picked up in the same garage where I'd been dropped off, but the prosecutors had refused this time. The fact is, in the case of a high-profile arrest, a perp walk—or in my case, a reverse perp walk—is good publicity for prosecutors. Preet Bharara was not about to let this one go. The only way we were leaving the building was out the front door. Fortunately, Mukasey's office had arranged for a car and driver to pick us up. We could see the car idling in front of the courthouse, beyond the press and across some twenty yards of flagstone.

The answer to Marc's question—"You ready for this?"—was no, I was not ready. But there was no alternative. "Hold your head up," said Marc. "Look straight ahead and ignore their questions."

He plowed through the revolving door and into the crush, and I followed. "We have no comment now," Mukasey responded to the shouted questions and the snapping cameras. "We're going home."

■ ■ ■

My family returned that evening. I met them in the front hall of the apartment as they came off the elevator. Surrounded by luggage after a long flight, they looked exhausted and bewildered. Since learning of my arrest less than 24 hours earlier, they had raced through a tortuous journey by sea, air, and road, to be with me.

For a few moments, we just stood there and hugged. And then I told them the truth—the truth I'd been hiding for years—right there in the front hall, then more of it later in the living room. I could see in their eyes that they did not want to believe me—it could not possibly be true—and yet it was. "I'm guilty," I told them.

I had lectured my children about the importance of character, integrity, and family. I'd preached the value of word and reputation, pointing to my own father as an example of how honor is integral to success. There were other values, too, that I'd imparted to them over the years. The importance of accepting responsibility. The need to provide security and protection to your family and others dependent on you. Now, I admitted to them that I'd failed to live up to my own values. But I wanted them to understand that, while I had screwed up monumentally, I was still the man they knew. Still the father who loved them and cared for them. And I was sorry—sorry beyond words—for the pain I knew I was causing them.

They had every reason to respond with anger and resentment. Unlike me, they'd had no hand in bringing this about and no warning that their entire lives were about to be upended. But they only told me they loved me and would be there for me, no matter what.

■ ■ ■

Marc Mukasey visited us that night. We gathered in the living room. "Look around this room," said Marc. "In a month, all your friends will disappear. This is all you will be left with. Each other."

Marc's prediction made sense. I had every reason to expect the worst from people who had put their trust in me. Business partners who would be harmed by my actions. Politicians who would be attacked for taking money I'd raised. Board members who had served alongside me at various organizations that could be tarnished. Friends who had believed in me. All had been deceived, and some would be injured by my deceit. But Mukasey turned out to be only partially right. A few did turn on us—but very few. Most of our friends would be incredibly supportive. The depths of their generosity would be one of the revelations that came from all this and one of the few things that would redeem the experience.

It's hard to overstate how much we depended on our friends from the start. The government froze all of my assets, including all of my bank accounts, both personal and corporate. They also attached my wife's and children's accounts, including credit cards, on the assumption that some of the money in these came from ill-gotten gains. Beyond the cash in our pockets, we were all essentially broke within a week or two of my arrest. We had some valuables in the apartment that we might have sold, except the government froze our ability to do this, too.

As my family absorbed the initial shock of my arrest, they then had to deal with a more immediate problem: there was no money to pay for anything. Not for the maintenance fee for the apartment. Not for food. Not for utilities.

Friends stepped in at once to help. Charlie Parker, a former lawyer of mine in the Texas and now a good friend, took it upon himself to set up a trust account for us. He put in some of his own money to keep us afloat, then invited other friends to contribute. This gave us enough to buy food and keep the lights on.

There was only so far kindness could take us, though. It took us a few weeks to grasp the scope of our problems. We were in a catastrophe that kept expanding. We owed money on credit cards, mortgages, utilities, and other assorted obligations. Clubs had to be quit, memberships un-renewed, subscriptions canceled. Then I had to complete the task of writing letters to the boards and organizations that I belonged to and tender my resignation. Not because they demanded I do so, but because it was the right thing to do. The Asia Society. The Council on Foreign Relations. The Brain Trauma Foundation. The RAND Corporation. Various committees at Harvard.

Worst of all, staff had to be let go, including household staff, our caretaker at Old Apple Farm, and Ziba, my office assistant for 35 years. All had been with us for years and were like family to us. Every one of these conversations was excruciating.

■ ■ ■

On the last Monday that I was at my office—the day before my arrest—I'd told Pat Oxford that I would transfer money to his firm's account to pay for my legal fees. Not to worry, he told me then. We could deal with that later. Now that my accounts were frozen, I had no means to pay Bracewell LLP.

A few weeks after my arrest, Pat told me his firm could no longer represent me. This had nothing to do with my ability to pay. The problem was that Bank of America was one of Bracewell's largest and oldest clients, creating a classic conflict of interest. Pat was extremely concerned for me, and Mukasey did not want to leave the case, but there was nothing to be done. I had to find new counsel.

Several friends helpfully put together a list of attorneys in New York who specialized in white-collar criminal litigation. Given its high profile, my case had a certain attraction to criminal defense attorneys, and a number were interested in representing me. I interviewed five, finally settling on Paul Shechtman. Paul had worked for the U.S. Attorney's office in the 1980's, rising to become head of the criminal division. Paul and his partner, Charlie Stillman, were among the most highly sought "old school" white-collar criminal defense attorneys in the city.

Now I had a lawyer but still had no way to pay my legal fees. I was extremely fortunate that my old friend and partner Leo Linbeck came to my aid and lent me the necessary funds to retain Paul Shechtman. I'd met Leo in 1974, when he and I formed our partnership, Linbeck Iran. Later, I'd hired Leo's firm to construct my Houston office building, and we'd remained friends since. Had it not been for Leo, I don't know what we would have done. It was pure decency and generosity on his part.

With thick wavy hair and a perpetually ruffled suit, Paul Shechtman was a large bear of a man. He combined a keen intelligence with a low-key manner, and I liked him immediately. Sheila and the children felt the same, and Shechtman was soon a nightly fixture in the dining room of our apartment, talking strategy and eating pistachios. Paul's consumption of pistachios became a running joke in the family. We did not have much money to spend on inessentials, but we always made sure to have pistachios in stock for Paul.

These regular pistachio sessions were an opportunity for my family to express their ideas about the case, which Shechtman listened to respectfully, even if he did not agree. Sheila and the children were particularly insistent on addressing the negligence and culpability of the banks that had given me the fraudulent loans. They proposed a defense based on the banks' willful negligence, the theory being that the three banks were so focused on generating interest income and fees that they disregarded the most basic due diligence. It was inconceivable that they did not suspect—and inarguable that they never took the most basic steps to discover—the truth of my finances. They were as morally and legally culpable, argued my family, as a drug dealer selling to an addict.

Paul acknowledged that it was a legitimate strategy. But it was risky. Given the way the U.S. judicial system works, if we were to take the case to trial and make this argument and then lose—which we were likely to do, Paul told us—I would be penalized by the point system utilized by federal courts to determine a sentence. Almost inevitably, this would result in a much longer sentence than one I'd obtain from a plea agreement.

In Paul's opinion, there was no good defense for my actions, and suggesting there was risked antagonizing the judge in whose hands my fate resided. As it happened, we'd drawn Judge Sidney H. Stein, a Clinton appointee. He was known as a middle-of-the-road jurist. Neither overly liberal and lenient nor overly conservative and punitive, Stein was viewed as fair and reasonable. He was a good match for us, but Paul felt that we needed to be careful not to do anything to alienate him. A defense based on blaming the banks could backfire.

"If you go to trial and lose, taking federal minimums into account, you're looking at a possible 21-year sentence. You'd be 80 when you got out."

"And if I plead guilty and cooperate?"

"We're talking fifteen years, max. We can probably get that down to ten or less."

Paul's strategy was straightforward: unilateral surrender. Rather than fight the charges, I would plead guilty, then bend over backwards to cooperate with the prosecutors and the banks. All my actions would be aimed at mitigating my sentence. I did not like the sound of ten years in prison. But I liked it a lot better than 21 years.

■ ■ ■

Paul's first task was to have the conditions of my release improved. On the day of my arrest, the court had consigned me to 24/7 home confinement. I was permitted to leave the apartment only to attend court hearings or for pre-approved visits to my doctor and attorney. Paul negotiated a relaxation of my confinement to allow me one hour in the morning in the gym in our building, as well as unlimited daily visits to my attorney and a three-hour block of free time each day or night. All of this made home confinement slightly more bearable but did nothing to help my overall situation.

At the time, it seemed that the best thing I could do was stay out of prison as long as possible, to delay incarceration and enjoy what time I had beforehand. The terrible fact, though, was that I was incapable of enjoying any of my time in home confinement. And not one day of it was going to count toward my sentence. Only later would I realize that the best thing I could have done was to begin serving my sentence at once.

26

THE LOST YEAR

I WISH I COULD GIVE a better account of my home confinement. The truth is that it was the most wasted year of my life. I shut down completely and became nearly catatonic. I continued to go through many of the motions of life, but without feeling, intent, or motivation. What this meant in practical terms is that, while we had many serious problems confronting us, I did nothing to solve any of them.

Every day presented new challenges. Money was the greatest of these, but merely cooking dinner was hard. A long-delayed renovation of our kitchen had been started just before my arrest. The workers had torn out virtually everything, including our stove and most of the cabinets and counters. Now our kitchen was in shambles, and the work had completely stopped. After a while, we managed to get our refrigerator and microwave hooked up again, but home dinners, which had once been a pleasure, were now a chore.

Compared to the millions of Americans who go without even the basics of housing and food, we were still fortunate in many ways, but it did not feel that way at the time. And though our apartment was large and luxurious, it felt suffocating to me. I left every weekday, rain or shine, to visit Paul Shechtman's office at Park and 54th Street. Paul's firm had provided me with one of their spare rooms, with a desk and phone. It was small, but I could breathe more freely there than in my home.

Ostensibly, I was in the office to review documents that might pertain to my case. Marc Mukasey's associates had gone to Old Apple Farm and retrieved nearly 100 boxes of material, all filled with documents I'd been saving since 1979. I was supposed to look through these boxes for exculpatory evidence, but I could not motivate myself to do it. The boxes remained stacked up against the walls, unopened. I was reminded of the urgent visit I'd taken near the end of 1978 to the office of the minister of justice in Tehran, where I'd found him surrounded by boxes of banking documents. My task felt nearly as Sisyphean as his.

As the weeks passed, I declined cognitively and physically. I'd been a voracious reader most of my life, but now I could not concentrate on books or newspapers. At Shechtman's office, I dawdled and accomplished little. At home, I spent much of my time watching television, mostly the kind of mindless garbage I'd avoided in the past. Having always treated time as a precious commodity, I now wasted day after day of it. I began to drink more heavily, too—often several vodkas on the rocks, followed by one or two bottles of red wine. I had a good cellar of Italian and French wines, and I was determined to empty it before I went to jail. This was just about the only goal I made any progress in reaching, though I did it with more determination than pleasure.

I also ate poorly—pizza and other takeout—and exercised very little. Shechtman had gotten me the privilege to use the gym in our building, but I seldom went near it. I did not realize how much weight I'd gained until we were invited to a wedding that fall. I could barely squeeze into my tux. When I sat down, the seam split.

The worst manifestation of my mental state was my emotional unavailability. I did not give my family the support they needed. I'd brought all this upon them, and it was my obligation to do all I could to help them handle it. Having experienced a few emotional cataclysms in my young life—my father's death when I was still in college, the turmoil and fear of Iran in 1978—I knew better than most what they were going through. In the end, they all handled it with remarkable grace and strength, but I was unable to help them.

A good friend, Steve Roth, lived in our building. One of New York's most successful real estate investors, Steve was not only very smart, he was also wise. He knew I liked to play backgammon, and one evening he showed up at our door with a board in his hand. It was clear within a few moves that Steve had not come to play backgammon. He was here to talk.

"Hassan, you need to take control of your situation," he told me. "No one—not your attorney, not your wife, not your friends—can do it for you. You need to take full ownership. You don't want to wake up one day, a year, maybe two years from now, and say, 'I wish I'd done this differently'."

His advice was absolutely correct. Unfortunately, I never followed it.

■ ■ ■

It was no surprise that the majority of my old political friends ran for the hills after my arrest. Overnight, I'd gone from being one of the Democratic party's most highly courted fundraisers to persona non grata. Later, in prison, I would write to a few of those I'd been close to and apologize for any harm or embarrassment I'd caused them. I never heard back from most, although, some years later, I would get a message from a friend of Bill Clinton's. The former president wanted me to know that I was "forgiven."

Of course, Bill Clinton knew something about sin and redemption. He was profoundly human and had a soft spot for fallen angels, being one himself. There were a few others like him. I recall a completely unsolicited phone call from the Governor of New Jersey, Jon Corzine, and another from the Governor of New York, David Paterson. I knew both men through Democratic circles and considered both friends, but I'd done little fundraising for either. Neither owed me anything or had anything to gain by calling me. "I want you to know I come from a culture imbued with forgiveness," Corzine said to me. "I remain your friend." Paterson told me how much he appreciated what I'd done for the Democratic Party and wished the best for me. Both of these men, like Clinton, had endured hard times and scandal. They knew something about human frailty and human forgiveness.

One day my phone rang, and it was Terry McAuliffe. I looked at the phone, considered answering, but could not bring myself to do so. I couldn't bear the shame. Of course, I only compounded the shame by not taking the call and then failing to call Terry back. I later learned that he was calling only to tell me that he was thinking of me and wishing me well.

Terrible events, either self-inflicted or not, are clarifying. The calls from people who had no reason to be kind—old friends from Landon, for example—were incredible. I'm sure they were all amazed that I had gotten himself into such hot water and needed to hear it from me to believe it, but they all wanted me to know they were there for me. And they meant it. Several would later visit me in prison.

Most amazing was my family, not just my immediate family, but my sister and my brother. They stuck with me far above the call of duty and family. Cousins, too.

We had a tradition of gathering in New York for the Thanksgiving holidays. I knew this would be the last holiday I'd share with my family and friends for a long time. My sister Susie and her husband came from Paris, where Peter had been recently begun serving as the British Ambassador to France. Susie's daughter, Safieh, came from Houston with a new beau. My half-brother, Manucher, came with his daughter, Pamela, and her husband and children.

Soon after Thanksgiving, we celebrated Yasmine's 30th birthday. She decided to have a party at our apartment. The Nemazees were famous for throwing great parties, and this one was no exception. Fortunately, none of our close neighbors were in town, or they would have been kept awake by the music and dancing that went on until 4 in the morning. For a few hours, I forgot my circumstances and simply had fun. It was glorious. We followed this with a low-key Christmas at home. As always, I bought a tree, and we decorated it together. We all understood that this ritual would not happen for many years, if ever again. It was bittersweet.

That January, the start of 2010, I turned 60. I had no interest in any kind of celebration. At the last moment, though, two of my good friends, Edgar Cullman and Anders Brag, organized a dinner for me at one of New York's finest steakhouses, in a private, wood-paneled dining room. Twenty-five of my friends attended. It was a wonderful evening, topped off by my son's toast. Kamyar rose and thanked Edgar and Anders for hosting the dinner, then recounted Marc Mukasey's prediction. "He told us within a month, we would be bereft of friends," said Kamyar. "Tonight is a testament to how wrong he was. All of you here, and so many others, have been so supportive in so many ways." There was hardly a dry eye in the room. It was one of the best evenings I'd had in years.

But the happiest occasion of that mostly bleak year was the day of my daughter's marriage. Yasmine's boyfriend, Oliver, had been with the family in Sardinia on the boat when the news of my arrest first became known. He had been wonderfully supportive since. His business had him living in Iraqi Kurdistan for three out of four weeks every month, but he came as often as possible to New York to see Yasmine, who had just finished her year as Chief Resident at New York University Hospital. Both were extraordinary young people, high achieving and truly decent, and they were very much in love with each other.

Yasmine wanted me to be part of her wedding. As there was not enough time to organize a proper wedding before I left for prison, she and Oliver decided to hold a civil ceremony, for family only, in June in New York. They would follow this with a larger wedding the following spring in Paris, at the British Embassy, to be hosted by Oliver's father and my sister Susie.

When the day came, we all dressed in our formal best. We held the ceremony at our apartment. Yasmine and Oliver had booked an officiant, licensed by the state of New York, to perform the vows. Peter and Susie flew in from Paris, and Oliver's mother, Angie, flew in from London, and my half-brother Manucher and his daughter Pam flew in from Florida. All of our family was present. As I walked Yasmine down the stairs of our duplex—our version of an aisle—I thought of nothing other than her happiness. Afterwards, we all shared in a dinner and made toasts to the bride and groom. It was a perfect day.

■ ■ ■

Paul Shechtman began negotiating in earnest on my plea agreement in the early spring of 2010. The government had charged me with three counts of bank fraud. It dropped the wire fraud charge but added one count of identity theft—this last because I'd fraudulently used the name of a Pershing employee in my deception. Paul believed the identity theft charge was bogus, but it was no joke. It carried a mandatory 2½-year sentence, to be added to the sentence for the other charges. At one point, the government proposed dropping the identity theft but adding a "leadership" charge, on the absurd claim that I was the leader of a "group" that committed these crimes. As the only other person involved was my brother-in-law, who was totally unaware and innocent of complicity in any crime, it was an outrageous claim.

As I came to learn, the government was not interested in merely charging me with the crimes I'd committed. It wanted to send me to prison for the rest of my life, even though I was fully cooperating and doing nearly everything it asked of me. When I say "it," I mean of course U.S. Attorney Preet Bharara and the man he'd assigned to the case, an assistant U.S. Attorney named Daniel Levy. I could not have drawn a worse prosecutor. This was Levy's first major case, and he pursued it with a breathless zeal that took Paul by surprise. He seemed to be driven by some kind of personal vendetta or blind ambition—or both.

A hard fact you quickly come to understand when you are on the receiving end of the federal criminal justice system is that arriving at the truth is of marginal importance to the prosecutor. Especially in high profile cases such as mine, the public narrative and the political angle take precedent over truth.

It was clear to me at the time, and remains clear to this day (judging from what he writes about me in his 2019 memoir) that Preet Bharara had an idea of me and my crime that conveniently allowed him to place me in a box that suited him better than it fit me. This is not to excuse my crimes, merely to point out that Bharara's representation of me as a mini-Madoff, involved in a "Ponzi scheme" (as he writes in his book) or someone who might get "hinky" and flee, was ridiculous on the face of it.

My victims, it is worth recalling, were three of the most sophisticated financial institutions in the world, not the sort of individual investors and charities ruined by Madoff. Moreover, a Ponzi scheme as commonly understood involves taking money from multiple investors and repaying some with money from others. I suppose my last-minute transfer from HSBC to Citibank was meant to qualify me for this dramatic description, but the truth was more banal than Bharara wanted it to be. By putting me in the same box as Madoff, Bharara not only got to portray himself as the great avenger he so badly wanted to be, but he also rationalized the extraordinary punishment he and his henchman wished to impose on me. Daniel Levy aimed to send me away for no fewer than 17 years and as many as 23. I would not be eligible for release until I was 83.

The sentence Levy sought was based on federal guidelines imposed by Congress. In the past, federal judges had been given total discretion to determine criminal sentences. But in 1987, when the issue of federal prison sentences was a hot topic on both the left and right, Congress altered the law and imposed mandatory guidelines for federal crime. Liberals like Ted Kennedy wanted to lessen the perceived disparity in time served between whites and minorities. Conservatives wanted a system that was perceived to be hard on crime. They both got the bill they wished for, but the net result was a huge increase in the number of prisoners in the federal system and, consequently, a huge increase in prison spending. The Supreme Court loosened the guidelines in 2005 and returned more discretion to judges, but the basic calculations still applied, and none of them were good for me. For crimes that would have earned me seven years in, say, 1997, I was now looking at a possible two decades in prison. Moreover, parole was no longer given in the federal system, so when you were sentenced to 20 years, you had to serve at least 85% of it (with one exception, which I'll get to later).

Paul tried to negotiate my plea down, but Levy and his colleagues at the U.S. Attorney's office would not budge. All the power was in the hands of prosecutors, and they wanted blood. If we did not agree to their terms, Levy told us, they'd add an identity theft charge, with a mandatory minimum sentence.

People who have never dealt with the federal criminal justice system may be unaware that 98% of all federal cases are settled through a plea agreement and never go to trial. This is in the interest of the government, because the court system cannot handle all the cases charged, and plea deals are a good way to dispense with the vast majority of cases. Even better for the government, it can claim victories without ever having to spend resources arguing its case before a judge. For defendants, though, plea deals are a kind of gun to the head. To avoid the risk of losing at trial, defendants have a powerful incentive to take a plea deal, even if it means pleading guilty to crimes they did not commit.

Of course, that was not an issue in my case. I was not innocent. But then again, I was not guilty of all the charges the government wanted to convict me of. Nor did I deserve to be harshly treated for the sake of Preet Bharara's ego and advancement. I was willing to take my punishment, but only what I deserved.

To force me to take its deal, the government not only threatened additional charges if I refused its offer, Levy also threatened to go, first, after Sheila (he backed off of that), and then, second, after her brother (a threat on which he carried through). If I failed to take the deal offered, the government promised to find a way to make life more unpleasant for my family than it already was.

The larger point is not about me. It's about the way the federal justice system works. Anyone who thinks the system is actually in the business of justice should think again. Federal prosecutors are in the business of winning. The primary metric they care about it how many cases they can claim as victories and for how many years they can send people to prison. Guilty pleas and long sentences—those are the "W's" on their scorecards.

■ ■ ■

Paul counseled me to take the deal Levy offered and hope Judge Stein would give me a reduced sentence, based on factors such as my background in charity and community involvement, as well as the fact that I fully accepted responsibility and was highly unlikely to repeat the crime. It was a difficult call for me. By either fighting too hard or giving in to easily, I could end up spending the rest of my natural life in jail, and it was not clear which was the better bet—complete surrender or risk all for the best outcome. I ultimately agreed to Paul's advice to take the government's offer and put my fate in the judge's hands.

My plea hearing was on Thursday, March 18, a sunny morning with a hint of spring in the air. The hearing in Judge Stein's courtroom was mostly a boilerplate affair. I pled guilty to three counts of bank fraud. "I am deeply ashamed of my conduct," I told the judge. "I accept full responsibility for my actions." I agreed to forfeit all my bank accounts, my properties on Park Avenue and in Katonah, as well as those in Rome and Tribeca. I also agreed to a sentencing guideline that put the range of my prison term between 15 years, 8 months and 19 years, 7 months— essentially 16 to 20 years—in hopes that the judge would reduce this.

Then came a most unwelcome surprise. After asking me a long series of questions to assure that I'd entered into the plea knowingly and willingly, Judge Stein turned to the prosecutor and asked him why the government was not seeking to have me remanded—that is, why they were not asking to have me sent directly to jail. The answer to that question was that my deal with the prosecutor stipulated that I remain in home confinement until my sentencing. The judge's admission that he thought I was a "good candidate" for remanding did not bode well for me. For the moment, his question required Levy to twist himself into a pretzel to explain why he was not demanding even harsher treatment of me than he'd already sought. Not many things gave me amusement in those days, but watching Levy stutter and fumble before the judge put a smile on my face. In the end, the judge announced that he was going to think about the issue of remanding. For the moment, I was free to go back home.

Shechtman quickly composed a brief in which he laid out reasons why I should not be remanded. For one thing, I was not a flight risk. I had long-standing ties to my community and close relationships with my children, all of whom lived in New York. Furthermore, my actions since my arrest attested to my intention to cooperate and accept my punishment. It was a good, well-argued brief, and Judge Stein decided in my favor.

At the time, this felt like a victory. Looking back, though, remanding might have been the best thing for me. As mentioned earlier, my time in home confinement was totally wasted and did not count toward the sentence I would eventually have to serve. All the effort to keep me out of jail only prolonged my agony.

■ ■ ■

I was not yet officially on the road to prison. The next step was to submit myself to a pre-sentencing investigation—better known as a PSI—to be prepared by Court Services for Judge Stein. This was significant because it would result in a report, called a PSR, that would recommend either an upwards or downwards revision of my sentence relative to the guidelines. Paul made it clear that it was important to have a favorable PSI.

The best advice I got about the PSI was not from Paul, though. It came courtesy of Sam Waksal. As most of the world knew at the time, Waksal was a former pharmaceutical executive who had been sentenced to eight years in federal prison for insider trading in a highly publicized case involving Martha Stewart.

Before I ever spoke to Waksal, I'd met with a so-called prison consultant recommended by Paul Shechtman. As good a lawyer as Paul was, he, like most criminal defense attorneys, knew very little about the experience of prison, having never gone to one himself. So, in a well-meaning effort to prepare me, he set me up with this consultant. Turns out there is a whole cottage industry of ex-cons and ex-prison officials who make decent livings telling anxious men and woman on their way to prison what to expect and how to prepare. I'm sure there are some notable exceptions, but on the whole it's a racket that preys on people who are at their most frightened and vulnerable. Little of what I heard from the consultant would have any bearing on my actual experience. The money I spent on him—money I did not have to spare—was wasted.

Sam Waksal, on the other hand, charged me nothing, and nearly everything he said was invaluable. He came up to the apartment one afternoon at the suggestion of my old friend Alan Patricof. We sat in my study and talked. This was a few days before my PSI, and the timing could not have been more fortuitous. Waksal told me he'd had a bad experience with his PSI, which resulted in his having a sentence at the upper end of the guidelines. He cautioned me to be forthright, honest, and not to have an "attitude." It was good advice.

Waksal then asked me whether I had a drug problem. Taken aback, I told him candidly that I'd never done any recreational drugs.

"Too bad," he responded. "How about alcohol? You drink?"

Again, candidly, I told him that I'd developed a pretty serious drinking problem during my year in home confinement. Of course, I had no intention of sharing this information at my PSI. I figured it would not gain me any favor with the investigator.

Waksal set me straight. "Make sure you let them know about it. That kind of drinking might qualify you for RDAP."

He explained that the federal system, while it offered no parole, did have one mechanism for reducing sentences. It was called the Residential Drug Abuse Program—RDAP for short. Inmates who were eligible for RDAP could reduce their sentences by a year.

Incredibly, before Waksal told me about it, I'd never heard of RDAP. As I later learned, many of the men who served with me had never heard of it either, and by the time they did they were already in prison and it was nearly impossible to qualify. Knowing that I needed to come clean about my drinking in the PSI, rather than hide it, was one of the best pieces of advice I ever received.

A few days after meeting Waksal, I went downtown to Foley Square for my PSI. The investigator spent almost four hours with me, going over my history, my crime, and my life after my arrest. When he asked about drug and alcohol use, I was completely honest. I told him I'd had no experience with drugs and too much with alcohol.

■ ■ ■

While we waited for the result of the PSR, Paul asked Sheila to reach out to family and friends to solicit letters to be submitted to Judge Stein attesting to my character. He pointed out that all the judge knew of me at this point was what the prosecutor told him. It was important that he learn there was more to me than my crime.

We were overwhelmed by the response. More than 150 letters flowed into Paul's office, including a number that were unsolicited. It was truly touching. I was particularly moved by the letters from people I'd not expected to hear from. One letter was from a woman whose brother I'd helped on an immigration matter after reading an editorial about him in the *New York Times*. A political refugee, the young man was about to be deported to Iran by U.S. Immigration. He feared for his life if returned to Iran. I was able to have Senator Clinton's office intercede to stop the deportation. The woman wrote to say it meant the difference between life and death for her brother.

Another letter came from Nazie Eftekhari, one of the board members of IAPAC, the political action committee I'd founded years earlier. The CEO of a healthcare business in Minneapolis who had been born and raised in Iran, Nazie ran a charity that assisted mortally ill children in need of high-quality healthcare. In her letter to Judge Stein, she related how, even though we did not know each other well, she'd once called me in tears. She was having trouble obtaining a visa for a two-year-old Iranian baby who needed to be transported to America for an emergency heart operation. The visa had been denied by the American consulate in Dubai, and Nazie was desperate. Could I help? As she told it in her letter, I responded at once. I called Senator Schumer's office, told them this was a high priority matter, and within 24 hours the baby girl was on her way to America. That child owed her life to Hassan, wrote Nazie. "He who saves a child," she wrote, quoting scripture, "saves the world."

It was an extraordinary letter that—many years later—would come back to have an even more extraordinary impact on my life. At the time, I just hoped that it would help Judge Stein see me as a person whose life was defined by far more than the crime I'd committed.

■ ■ ■

The PSR result came in that May. It was disappointing in some respects, as it did not recommend a downward revision of the sentence. But it did recommend the RDAP program, meaning that I could lower my sentence by a year. Before you serve a long sentence, the length of time can seem so great that a year is almost unimportant. But the moment you are in and counting not just years, but months, weeks, and days until your release, you realize that it matters—every second of it. I was incredibly fortunate to qualify for RDAP.

As the sentencing hearing approached, we were all sensitive to the power of the court to decide my fate. Judge Stein had it within his power to sentence me to a term in prison that could well be a life sentence, even with RDAP. I was 60 years old. A sentence at the upper end of the guideline range, or above the guideline—which was within the judge's power to deliver—could be higher than 20 years, effectively a life sentence for a man nearing sixty. We took heart in knowing that Judge Stein was considered a fair judge. Still, there were no guarantees. Anything could happen.

The day of my sentencing—Thursday, July 15, 2010—was sunny and hot. My family attended with me. We took two town cars down to the courthouse on Pearl Street. Reporters were already gathered in front of the courthouse when we arrived, and they descended on us as we stepped out of the car. Shechtman led the way into the scrum, and we walked through the shouted questions, heads high but mouths shut. We climbed the stairs to the courthouse and pushed through the brass-framed revolving doors. The large courtroom was already packed and warm. Several friends of mine were there to lend support, as were a number of our children's friends. At least two dozen reporters sat together near the front, notebooks out. A courtroom artist was off to the side, a sketchpad on her lap. I sat at the defense table with Shechtman. My family took the row behind us. Everybody was jittery, but I was more numb than nervous.

None of us knew what to expect. Shechtman hoped for leniency but believed we were probably looking at something in the neighborhood of 10 years. One of our friends overheard the press pool discussing a wager among themselves; the over-under was eight years for me.

The press was focused on this case not because of me or my crime against major financial institutions, but because of my friendship with so many major Democrats, including Bill Clinton, who had appointed Judge Stein. Whatever sentence Stein imposed would not just get the usual line or two in an obscure law journal. It would be covered in all the major media. Stein would feel pressure not to appear lenient, lest he be perceived as compromised by politics. On the other hand, I hoped he would take into account the totality of my life and values.

Judge Stein opened the hearing to say he had read each of the 150 letters written to the court. It was clear from his comments that he really had read and absorbed every one. He went on to say he was impressed by my accomplishments and those of my father. He talked about the lives that I had clearly impacted. He even read into the record a part of the letter that Nazie Eftekhari had written. "His punishment will be greater than whatever the court sentences him to serve," she informed the judge. "His punishment is the fact that he has tarnished the name and reputation of his family."

"You've done a great deal of good in your life," said Judge Stein, addressing me directly. "On the other side of the ledger, this crime is breathtaking in its brazenness and scope."

He laid out the three questions he asked himself when determining a sentence. First, had the defendant accepted responsibility? Second, was the defendant likely to commit the crime again? Third, what would be the likely effect of the sentence upon general deterrence?

We should have known this last issue was going to be addressed. My daughter Layla had looked up some of Stein's recent decisions and found that he was particularly interested in the issue of general deterrence as a sentencing criteria—that is, how a punishment for a certain crime might, or might not, deter others from committing the crime.

Layla had brought this to my attention, and I'd brought it to Shechtman's. Paul appreciated Layla's research but thought deterrence was too vague a standard for him to argue one way or the other. Instead, he decided to focus his pre-sentencing brief on the 150 letters addressed to Judge Stein. It was an eloquent brief that argued for leniency based on decency and good works, but it did not at all consider the issue of general deterrence. Now in court, when Judge Stein raised the issue and put it to the defense, Paul seemed stymied. His oral response was initially weak and unfocused. He rallied to improve the argument, but clearly he had not anticipated a relatively easy question.

I was given a chance to speak. I stood up. I looked Judge Stein in the eye. Prior to the hearing, I'd thought about what I wanted to say to the judge, but the words that came out now were not scripted or memorized. They came to me as I spoke. "The guilt and shame that I bear will remain with me long after I finish prison," I told him with perfect frankness. "For the rest of my life, I will seek to atone for the actions that have brought me before you."

After I sat, Stein did something quite unusual. Declaring that he needed time to think, he announced a fifteen-minute recess, then stood and retired to his chambers. What did this mean? Was this an indication that, given his genuinely positive comments about me, he might be prepared to give a significantly lower sentence? The courtroom stirred and murmured. The press chattered softly. Generally speaking, judges come into sentencing hearings knowing exactly what they intend to do. Why the second thoughts? I turned back to look at my family and try to give them some indication of hope.

That's when I saw Preet Bharara standing in the back of the courtroom with his arms folded. He'd not been there earlier, so he must have crept in during the hearing. It was rare for the United States Attorney to appear personally in the courtroom. Evidently he'd dropped by to enjoy the spectacle of my sentencing—or was it, rather, to signal the judge that his office was deeply invested in my prosecution? To this day, I wonder if Bharara's appearance influenced Judge Stein's decision.

Judge Stein reentered. We all stood and the courtroom hushed. The judge took the bench, adjusted his glasses, and folded his hands. "I've given this sentence a great deal of thought." He paused. "Mr. Nemazee is clearly a man who is repentant for his crime. He is unlikely to commit this crime in the future. He has done some very good things with his life, including his involvement in the American political system. However, I cannot overlook the substantially large fraud he perpetrated on these major financial institutions. I cannot ignore the magnitude of the crime, nor the length of time that he continued in this criminal behavior." He looked directly at me. "Mr. Nemazee, I'm going to issue a downwards departure from the federal guidelines and sentence you to 144 months in prison, plus restitution."

He continued to speak after that, but I have no idea what he said. I was doing the arithmetic: 144 months divided by 12 months equals 12 years. So that was it. Not eight years or ten years, but 12 years of prison. This was a five-year downward departure from guideline minimum of 17 years, but it was an onerous sentence nonetheless.

I heard a few gasps and sobs behind me as my family absorbed it. Friends were muttering. I held my tongue and turned back to my family. I wanted them to know I was okay. "Listen," I said softly. "We're going to get through this."

Almost at once, Assistant U.S. Attorney Levy jumped to his feet and motioned that I be remanded—taken into custody, that is—by U.S. Marshalls to begin serving my sentence. The request seemed to puzzle Judge Stein. "At the plea hearing, Mr. Levy, you told me you agreed to not remand. Now you want to remand? I see no reason to believe Mr. Nemazee is a greater flight risk now than he was then. Motion denied." Judge Stein ordered me to self-surrender in six weeks—on August 27, 2010—at a prison to be designated by the Federal Bureau of Prisons.

Despite the chiding from the judge, Levy was triumphant. I was a feather in his cap—the first big fish he'd ever caught. Later, I came to learn that Levy purchased one of the sketches of me made that day by the courtroom artist. No doubt he framed it and put it on his wall next to his diplomas, like a trophy.

■ ■ ■

The federal prison system has four basic tiers of incarceration, from "supermax" security, for the most dangerous and violent offenders, to minimum security, for those deemed the lowest risk to society. Because my crime was not violent and because I was a first-time offender, I was theoretically a good candidate for a minimum-security prison, or "camp," as they are generally known. Unfortunately, one of the conditions for assignment to a camp is that the inmate have no more than ten years to serve. My sentence of 12 years made me ineligible. I would first have to serve time in a low-security prison, one tier up from a camp.

When he sentenced me, Judge Stein asked the Bureau of Prisons to place me in the nearest low-security prison possible. There were several within a few hours of New York City, such as the Federal Correctional Institute (FCI) in Danbury, Connecticut, a mere 70 miles away. But that is not where I ended up. A few days after the hearing, I was informed that I'd be going to a prison in Texarkana, Texas, 1,400 miles from my family.

There is no way to prepare yourself to leave your family to go to prison for a lengthy period. As I look back on that time, I feel as though I wasted an opportunity to truly maximize my time with my family. I think we all understood that we were saying goodbye not just to each other, but to what remained of our family as we knew it. The young lives of my children would move on, through new jobs and romances and adventures and marriage and children of their own—through all the challenges and excitement that young people experience—and I would not be there. I felt a deep sense of loss for the years I would miss. Not of my life, but of my children's lives.

Many good friends came to say goodbye in those last weeks. Some were emotional; all were supportive. We drank the last of my wine and smoked the last of my cigars. It was my friend Edgar's idea that he and few other friends should accompany me to Texarkana. He understood that going alone would be awful and that going with my family would be unbearable. Soon a few other good friends signed on for the trip.

So it was arranged. Edgar Cullman, John Bernbach, Fouad Chartouni, and Kim Fennebresque would all fly down with me. We'd enjoy my final night of freedom together. And then I would begin my long journey as Federal Inmate #62625 054.

27

TEXARKANA

At the start of this book, I described my self-surrender. Those last 24 hours before I went in. The flight to Texas with my friends. The last supper in the mall steakhouse. The cigars under the portico of the chain hotel. And then arriving at prison on a hot Friday morning and feeling not despair or fear but rather, unexpectedly, a weight lifting off my shoulders and the shadows that had haunted me the past year slipping away. Instead of focusing on the almost inconceivable amount of time I'd be in prison, I decided to live every day as productively as possible.

I was fingerprinted, photographed, searched, given endless forms to fill out and a set of prison clothes. All of this took a few hours. Time moves glacially in prison, as I'd learn, and no one does much to speed it up.

At the end of my processing, one of the assistant wardens brought me into his office. A bland looking white guy with close-cropped graying hair, he blended into the grays and tans of federal prison décor. In his hands he had my file and he knew everything about my case. "Listen," he said to me, "about those political friends of yours. Best for you to keep your association with the Clintons and the rest to yourself, okay? It'll be easier all around."

"Sure," I said.

I was given sheets and blankets, then escorted down a hall by a corrections officer. As we left the air-conditioned administrative offices, the temperature rose dramatically. We arrived at a long, narrow two-story building. "This is B-unit," he said. "You're in 303." He pointed to a set of stairs. "Second floor." He did not intend to climb the stairs with me. He turned and headed back to the cooler air.

I was sweating by the time I made it up the stairs. I was in poor physical shape, and the air felt like it weighed a hundred pounds.

A man in khakis—another inmate—pointed me down the hall to #303. "On the left," he said. "Welcome to Texarkana."

The number was painted on the wall. It wasn't really a room or even a cell, but more of a glorified cubicle. There were no doors and no bars, just an opening in the wall. About 10 feet long and 6 feet wide, it had cinderblock walls and a linoleum floor.

The air was hot, but I could feel a fresh breeze coming in from the open window. Through the window, across a lawn and over a high fence, I could see a water tower. On the side of the tank was a large purple cougar looking back at me. The mascot of a local high school, I guessed.

Having spent that one horrible night in prison a year earlier, I was pleasantly surprised to see how clean and well-lit the place was, a far cry from the grim, dank cell at MCC. It was also relatively private. As I'd come to learn, I was lucky to land in B-unit. Other housing units at Texarkana were dormitory style, with up to 120 men in a large gymnasium-sized room. Even the relatively small units had four, five, and even sixteen-man rooms. The two-man room set-up of B-unit gave me a semblance of peace and quiet. Of course, as with most things in life, there was a trade-off. Because B-unit was an older building, it had no air conditioning. I would be in for some brutal nights before autumn came to East Texas.

A bunk bed stood against the wall to my right. I could see that the bottom bunk was already taken. I began to make up the top bunk, laying the sheets and blankets I'd been given over the thin mattress. Just as I was finishing, a man walked in. He was white, middle-height, with thinning gray hair and gray eyes. "You did that wrong." He stepped up on a rung of the bunk ladder and pulled the lower sheet down, then demonstrated, deftly and swiftly, how to tie the two corners together, first at the head, then at the end, to secure the sheet tightly over the mattress. "Like that," he said. "Keeps it on with a good fit."

"Thanks. Good to know."

"I'm Walt." He put out his hand and we shook. I introduced myself. "Yeah, I heard about you. You're from the Big Apple." He had a slight Texas twang.

"Yes."

"I hear you're pals with the Clintons." Before I could answer, he grinned. "Don't worry, we all done things we're ashamed of."

It turned out that whatever the assistant warden may have wanted, the whole floor already knew pretty much everything about me, including my political affiliations, my crime, and the length of my sentence. Correction Officers had seen my report. COs, as they're commonly referred to, come in all shapes and sizes, but one thing they have in common is that they like to gossip as much as inmates do, and gossiping is pretty much *all* inmates do. Ironically, some of the facts that had been circulated about me turned out to benefit me. Outside, a long prison sentence won't earn you any respect, but inside it's a badge of honor.

For the moment, though, I was just trying to figure out what was what. It had been a long while since I'd been the new kid on the block, but those first few days I had to get up to speed on dozens, if not hundreds, of new rules and protocols and codes. I did not even know where the bathroom was when I first got there. In fact, I was just about to ask Walt to point me in the right direction when a voice on a PA system boomed out three words that meant nothing to me. "Four o'clock count!" Walt stepped into the middle of the room.

"What's going on?"

"We're getting counted. Stand here."

As I came to learn, "counts" are one of the constants in federal prisons all across the county, no matter where they are or what level of security they might be. The world outside could be burning to the ground, but the count goes on. There are five per day. The 4:00 p.m. and 10:00 p.m. counts are known as standing counts, because you have to stand for them. For the other three counts—Midnight, 3:00 a.m., and 5:00 a.m.—you just have to be in your cell. At each count, two COs come by, first one then the other, and count every single prisoner in their unit.

This was the first of some 20,000 times I'd be counted, and it was not an auspicious start. "All right if I go to the bathroom?" I asked the first CO who came by our cell.

He looked over and glared at me as if I were a piece of excrement that had just attached itself to his shoe. "You're new here."

"Yes."

"I'm gonna let this pass this once. But don't ever talk to me again while I'm doing the count or I'll write you up. Understand?"

I nodded and the CO moved on. I looked over at Walt. He was grinning. "The deal is," he whispered, "when they count, we shut the fuck up."

Walt was about as good a first "celly" as I could have asked for. Nearing the end of a ten-year sentence for low-level organized crime, he was scheduled to leave Texarkana in three weeks to complete his sentence at a minimum-security camp in Florida. But in those weeks he took me under his wing and guided me through the mysteries of prison life. He was a quiet man and watchful—his eyes, I noticed, never stopped moving—but he carried himself with authority and was well liked and well respected. A good man to have by my side.

■ ■ ■

Soon after that first count, it was time for dinner. (It turns out that everything happens early in prison. You rise at dawn, eat lunch at 11:00 a.m., dinner at 4:30 or 5:00, lights out after the 10:00 p.m. count.) The mess hall was a large cafeteria that would have fit into any mid-sized public high school. By example, and with a word here and there, Walt taught me the rules of the mess hall, which are the rules of prison generally. Don't crowd other men. Wait your turn. If you accidently bump into someone, immediately apologize. Don't touch another inmate; don't invade his space.

There is more etiquette in prison than at a Park Avenue dinner party. If none of this is written down in an Emily Post-style handbook, it's every bit as codified. In society, etiquette is mainly a test of class and background. In prison, it's about keeping the peace.

We sat with two other men, friends of Walt's, on hard round stools bolted to the base of our table. We ate with plastic forks and knives off plastic trays. All the food I'd consume over the next decade would be eaten off plastic trays with plastic utensils.

Glancing around, I noticed that the dining hall was segregated along racial lines. Without exception, blacks sat with blacks, Mexicans with Mexicans, whites with whites. Between bites of lasagna, Walt explained that within races there were further divisions. Mexicans raised in America, for example, sat apart from Mexicans born in Mexico. But of all the divisions in the mess hall—in the entire prison system, in fact—none was stricter than the one among whites. There were two classes. There were the whites who were there for general crimes—drugs, white-collar, mob—and there were the chomos.

As Walt explained, chomo was short for child molester. This included anyone found guilty of any type of sex crime. Most were not here because they tried to have sex with a minor but rather because they accessed child porn on the internet. They were a strange group, socially awkward, timid. They were also, for some reason, almost entirely white.

Whatever got them into trouble, chomos were the untouchables at every prison, state or federal. In higher security prisons, they were in danger of getting beaten up, but at low-security prisons like Texarkana they were generally left alone, so long as they did not attempt to mix in with the general population.

"What happens if a chomo tries to sit over here?"

"Never happens," said Walt. "They're not stupid."

After dinner, Walt gave me a tour of the yard. The yard was centered by a large grass field surrounded by a track. In one corner of the field was a baseball diamond, and alongside this were two netless tennis courts, several netless basketball courts, an area of free weights where a group of men were lifting, a horseshoe pit and a bocci pit.

Again, much of it looked as if it could have been imported from a typical American high school, except for the fact that whole thing was surrounded by a thirty-foot-high fence crowned by concertina wire. Beyond the fence ran a circular road, about ten feet wide, and on the other side of this was another fence, this one higher and—as Walt told me—electrified. In the distance, through the two lines of fence, I could see a field bordered by scrubby trees.

It was still scorching hot at 5:00 p.m., but there was a lot going on out here. Men were walking or jogging around the track, others playing basketball or handball or lifting weights at the piles. The activities were generally segregated by race, but more loosely than in the mess hall. The chomos, again, stuck completely to themselves, off to one side of the yard in the evening shadows cast by nearby structures.

"You play bocci?" Walt asked. "Come on, I'll show you."

■ ■ ■

The Bureau of Prisons is run like the military. At every federal prison, there's a warden and one or two assistant wardens who oversee the entire prison. Below them is a captain, followed by several lieutenants who supervise the correctional officers. It's the CO's job to keep the peace, oversee the daily movements of the inmates, and perform the counts, to make sure everyone is where they are supposed to be. Altogether, a staff of 300, spread out over shifts, oversaw some 1,400 inmates.

If your idea of a CO is a thug with a baton, you will find some at a federal prison who fit that description. Just as there is the occasional knucklehead inmate, there is also the mean and vindictive officer. That's just a fact of life. But generally speaking, in my experience, CO's and other staff were decent enough. In nearly all cases, if you didn't give them trouble, they didn't give you trouble.

A few staff members were exceptional and went out their way to treat you humanely, even kindly. I will never forget, for example, Miss Dickerson at Texarkana. A pretty African-American woman who held the position of Assistant Warden, Miss Dickerson was delighted that I knew Hillary Clinton—"I love Hillary!" she exclaimed, not a common sentiment in an all-male East Texas prison. She even took me over to introduce me personally to the white male warden of the prison. He was Miss Dickerson's opposite in every way—cold, rude, detached—and wanted nothing to do with me. He literally turned and walked away from me when Miss Dickerson tried to introduce us. Not a Clinton supporter, I guess.

Parallel to the organization of prison staff was a separate chain of command among inmates. As I mentioned earlier, age and length of sentence conferred status and authority, but also, as in any group, there were men who naturally earned deference. There were hierarchies within hierarchies, mostly arranged along ethnic and or racial lines. The men known as "shot callers" were the most important voices representing their respective groups. In every unit, the whites had one, the blacks had one, and the divergent Hispanic groups had theirs. Shot callers were especially important when disputes arose between groups and required mediation.

None of this was written down on a flow chart or spreadsheet, but everyone in prison quickly comes to learn who is in charge and who is owed what in terms of respect and seniority. You are expected to wait your place in line not just literally, as at the mess hall, but figuratively in all sorts of ways.

The TV rooms presented a perfect example of this. There was one main TV room, with five TVs, where primarily white inmates sat, and a few smaller rooms with one or two TV sets, divvied among blacks and Hispanics. Each TV was set on a different channel. You watched the channel you preferred by listening through earphones plugged in a small transistor radio (every inmate bought his own) that carried the audio. The right to sit in one of the plastic chairs in the TV rooms was a privilege. Newbies like me could not just walk in and sit down, because all of the chairs were already claimed by men who got there first. You needed to be invited by one of the chair owners to use his seat when he was not there. Eventually, you would inherit a chair of your own. Unless you were a chomo, that is. As in all other aspects of prison life, the chomos were excluded. They were not even allowed in the TV room, much less in a chair. The only way they could watch TV was to stand behind a glass partition in the busy corridor that ran alongside the TV room.

One of the few places where sects and castes were set aside was the library. This was a small but pleasant room filled with newspapers, magazines, books, and several computer terminals connected to law databases. Races and ethnicities, and even chomos, came and went without aspersion or fear. The library would become a great getaway for me. Books would be a place to escape to. They'd let me step into worlds far outside of prison and to recall things that were in short supply inside, such as beauty and adventure and the feeling of freedom.

That first evening in Texarkana I grabbed a paperback from the display table. It was an autobiography of Andre Agassi, the tennis player. I'd met Agassi a few times, back when he was one of the greatest players in the world. He was part Iranian, and we'd had some interesting conversations about our backgrounds. (His father, Emmanuel, had competed as a boxer for Iran in the 1948 and 1952 Olympics.)

I'd seen Agassi play several times at the US Open in New York, which, as it happened, was commencing the very same week I entered Texarkana. I took Agassi's book to my bunk that night and dived in. Reading it took me back to wonderful summer evenings years earlier, when all I'd had to worry about was watching a yellow ball streak back and forth across the net at Center Court.

28

TIME

Shortly before I left for Texarkana, my friend Peter Georgescu came to see me. The former chairman and CEO of Young & Rubicam, Peter is a remarkable man with an extraordinary personal story of grit and determination. In 1947, as a eight-year-old boy in communist Romania, he'd been separated from his parents, then arrested and sent to a prison work camp with his brother and grandmother (his grandfather having been murdered by the communists). He was finally freed and reunited with his parents in 1954, thanks to the intervention of the Eisenhower administration, but only after seven years of separation and untold hardship. Peter arrived in America with no English and only limited education but went on to graduate, with honors, from Princeton.

"Hassan, you're probably looking at the next decade as a punishment of time," Peter told me as we sat in my study. "I suggest that you think of it as a gift of time. Consider this as an opportunity to do all of the things you've always wanted to do but told yourself you'd do later, when you had more time. Exercise. Read. Write. Think. Teach. Now is the time to do all of this."

I took Peter's advice seriously. From day one, I was determined to use my time as well as possible. I promised myself to begin with a disciplined exercise regime to lose the 30 lbs. I'd put on during my year of house arrest in New York. The afternoon after my arrival at Texarkana, I did three laps around the track, or one mile. I'd eventually get this up to thirty laps, or 10 miles, per day, plus exercise classes, weight lifting, and yoga.

I also promised myself to take advantage of my time in prison to read the books I'd always wanted to read but had never found time for. The library was decent but limited. There were good books and recently published books but not enough to feed my voracious appetite. At my request, family and friends began sending me books every week. I'd read them, then pass them on to anyone else who might be interested. Some were light reading—spy novels and mysteries—but I also devoured history, biography, and current events, along with literary novels and a number of classics I'd never gotten to. (Where better to read Dostoevsky's *Crime and Punishment* than a federal prison?) I started reading an average of three books per week. Very soon I was up to five to seven books per week. Ultimately, I would read 2,652 in eight years.

As in the case of books, the Bureau of Prisons (BOP) generally provided free but minimal necessities. If you wanted a wider or finer selection, whether of books or food or toilet paper, you had to acquire it on your own. One option was the prison commissary. Every prisoner was assigned a day a week to shop at the commissary, where you could buy food, snacks, sodas, radios, toiletries, or clothing such as boxers, long johns, sweats, and shorts. To purchase the items, you needed money in your commissary account. One way to get this was through a prison job. Another source was contributions, via Western Union, from family and friends. The BOP limited the amount you could spend to $320 per month, which was more than enough to cover staples.

Then there was a whole other world of buying and selling, where the real prison economy occurred. Just about every inmate had a hustle, either something he sold or something he did to make a few bucks—though bucks is not really the word. It was not U.S. dollars you earned from your side hustle, but rather U.S. postage stamps—30-cent U.S. postal stamps to be precise. Each book of stamps consisted of twenty 30-cent stamps, for a value of $6 per book. These stamps were not for sale in the commissary and were no longer supplied by the U.S. Postal Service, but a number were in circulation at Texarkana to be used as an alternative currency.

You could get pretty much anything you wanted with the stamps. What most of the men wanted, it turned out, was better food, especially fresh food. There was a thriving business in smuggling goods out of the kitchen. The primary agents of this operation were the men who worked in the kitchen, where they skimmed prized items such as onions, bell peppers, tomatoes, bananas, and apples, and sold them—for stamps—to fellow inmates. The going rate for an onion was three stamps. Three stamps also got you two bananas.

Most of this black-market commerce was tacitly condoned by the CO's, who turned a blind eye to it. But some contraband absolutely was *not* condoned. Cell phones, cigarettes, drugs, and booze—these were the big four. It was downright stupid to possess any of these, and yet, inmates being inmates, they could be found for a price, as could pretty much anything you might desire. And it wasn't just goods—services, too, were available. If you knew the right guy, and you had some stamps at your disposal, you could hire pretty much any kind of helper you needed.

This was where J.P. came in handy. I wrote earlier that the prison consultant I'd hired earlier in the year was a waste of money. That is not entirely true. There was one very useful thing he told me. He suggested that when I got to Texarkana, I look up a guy named J.P. When I asked Walt and a few others if they knew J.P., it turned that *everybody* knew J.P.

One afternoon in my first week at Texarkana, I came back to my cell to find a guy waiting for me. He was white and in his late 30's, with a crew cut and huge forearms. He looked like he could crush a can or two of spinach in his hands if he wanted to. "I hear you've been looking for me," he said as I approached him, a little wary. "I'm J.P."

J.P. turned out to be one of the friendliest people I met in prison. He was also one of the savviest (until he wasn't, which I'll get to later). Contractor, middleman, salesman of goods and services, and not least, prison bookie, he was the hustler of hustlers—the guy who knew everybody and everything and could hook you up with whatever you required. Like many inmates I'd meet over the years, he was more naturally gifted, and harder working, than most people on the outside.

I made a number of arrangements through J.P. For example, I hired another inmate to do my laundry. I did this not out of an aversion to doing my own laundry, but because I'd been warned by Walt that the laundry room was a place where fights broke out. The best way to stay out of trouble in prison, Walt preached, was to avoid situations where trouble was likely to occur.

More importantly, J.P. became the middleman and contractor for some improvements to my cell. For example, when I wanted a desk installed, J.P. set me up with an inmate who had excellent carpentry skills. The carpenter installed a collapsible desk hinged against the wall, supported, when open, by two rods. J.P. also found me an electrician who installed a reading lamp over my cot. I paid both men in stamps. Such improvements were not technically permitted, but the CO's on my run made no objection. Now I could write and read in private pretty much whenever I wanted. J.P. also fixed me up with a better mattress than the prison-issued back-breaker I'd been sleeping on. Where he got the mattress I did not know and did not ask.

While I can't say that I ever came to feel at home at Texarkana, I did, after a bit of renovating, feel comfortable. Prison cells are never more than sterile and plain, but at least my cell was functional and quiet. It was also clean. In fact, cleanliness was the rule in Texarkana. The bathrooms, for instance, were well maintained and sanitary. They were nothing like those prison bathrooms you see in movies or on television, where men shower in foul communal showers while Bubba lurks nearby, ready to pounce if they drop the soap. Each unit had four private shower stalls. Unit orderlies cleaned the showers, toilets, and sinks two or three times a day. Nobody was named Bubba.

Perhaps the most surprising thing about prison from the start was how generous I found most of my fellow inmates. On the first day, I'd been visited by a "greeter" who made sure I had everything I needed to get started, from toothpaste to clean clothes. I learned that inmates take turns playing this role for newbies at every prison (I'd play it myself later) and generally look out for one another, particularly within various races or religious groups. Most inmates were polite and well behaved, so long as certain codes and hierarchies were observed. With Walt's counsel, I did my best to respect these. If I had to stand in the TV room for a few days, so be it. Respect begets respect. Very soon, a few inmates were inviting me to sit in their chairs, and soon after that, I had a chair of my own.

Which brings me to another surprise, one I found rather amusing. As you might expect in a male prison, there were plenty of sports on the TVs—football, basketball, baseball, and all the NASCAR you could want—but nearly as popular were romantic comedies, or "chick flicks." It turned out that we men, even the most hardened and brawny among us, wanted to see these movies as much as any "chick" did. All the more so, I suppose, because we lived in such a sterile place, so devoid of romance and beauty.

■ ■ ■

Walt left three weeks after my arrival in Texarkana. We exchanged addresses and shook hands and promised to stay in touch. His final words to me: "Be smart and keep your head down." I was sorry to see Walt go, but my knees were pleased, because the lower bunk now became mine. No more painful climbing up and down the narrow rungs of the metal ladder. And since no one else came in to replace Walt, I had the cell to myself for a while.

The weeks passed and began to accumulate into months. Before I knew it, we were in October. The air turned cooler and the days shortened. I walked three hours daily, first in the morning from 7:30 to 9:30, then again in the afternoon for an hour. When I wasn't exercising or reading, I did my prison job, teaching English to non-English-speaking inmates. My days were full but repetitive. Other than the gradual change of weather, the coming and going of inmates, and the five-week rotation of meals in the mess hall, life in Texarkana was the carceral version of *Groundhog Day*.

What kept it interesting was getting to know different people. Like military service, prison puts you in the company of people you'd never meet otherwise. Some of these were among the most interesting and intelligent men I'd ever known.

Among my first and best friends at Texarkana, after Walt left, was Wayne Jaegers. Wayne occupied a cell a few doors down the run from me. I always call Wayne by his name, but most people knew him as the Mayor. With his shaggy silver hair and long sideburns, Wayne bore an uncanny resemblance to Captain Kangaroo, the host of a children's television show back in the 1950's. He'd been in the unit for longer than anyone else, ten years into a twenty-year sentence, which gave him seniority and authority—hence his nickname—but he never lorded this over anyone. In fact, he was the most genial and jovial man you'd ever want to meet. It was a surprise to learn, then, that he'd been involved with the St. Louis mob and had been convicted of money laundering. Harder to believe still, he'd been an accomplice to a grisly murder in which the victim's body had been chopped into small pieces. To his credit, Wayne felt badly about it.

Among his winning qualities, Wayne was a great storyteller, and often as we walked around the track together he would regale me with his colorful past, hinting at various atrocities he'd committed on behalf of his boss. I was never sure whether Wayne's stories were entirely factual, but their entertainment value was worth gold. Later, when I had a chance to check out some of Wayne's stories, I learned that virtually everything he told me was verified by press accounts.

Wayne's particular talent was cooking, and he was generous with sharing. Soon I was eating several meals a week with him. He would make a sauce for spaghetti bolognese that was as good as any I'd had. It was amazing what he could create with relatively meager ingredients. Everything was prepared in a microwave. Pizza, nacho bowls, burritos, quesadillas, pasta, cakes, and puddings. We'd eat at my desk or in Wayne's room, joined by one or two others, a huge improvement from the mess hall in all respects.

■ ■ ■

It was Wayne who introduced me to Martin MacNeill, better known as Doc. Doc became another close friend. With degrees in both law and medicine, Doc was extremely well educated, and as well read and informed as anyone I'd meet behind bars. We had many good conversations about books and current events. That said, there was something a little off about Doc, as if part of his mind was perpetually occupied with something else. Though blandly handsome in appearance and low-key in demeanor, he seemed like a man who had deep and troubling secrets. Which turned out to be the case.

As I came to learn, Doc had been convicted of identity theft. But his story was far more complicated and weirder than that. Before his life took a dark turn, he'd been a devout Mormon and a practicing physician in Pleasant Grove, Utah, where he lived with his wife and seven children—four natural and three adopted. His wife was a pretty former beauty queen, Doc was a successful physician, and together they seemed to have a picture-perfect life.

What happened to them I gathered in part from things Doc told me and in part from newspapers and television shows on which Doc was featured. As the story was told, Doc encouraged his wife get a facelift. She agreed to this, albeit reluctantly. After the surgery, Doc took it upon himself to medicate her with painkillers. One afternoon, when he came to check on her, he found her dead in a warm bath. The medical examiner pronounced the death as a freak heart attack brought on by the surgery. No inquiry or autopsy was ordered.

A few weeks after his wife's death, Doc invited a young woman to be the nanny for his seven now motherless children. A few of the older daughters figured out pretty quickly that the new nanny, known as Gypsy, was in fact Doc's girlfriend, with whom he'd been having an affair for some time. Moreover, it turned out, Doc had used the Social Security number of one of his daughters to create a bank account for the girlfriend. It was for this crime that Doc was sentenced to four years at Texarkana.

But, as Doc told me, the identity theft charge was the least of his worries. While he'd been in jail, his daughters had become convinced that he intentionally overdosed their mother with painkillers then drowned her in the bathtub. They'd brought their suspicions to the attention of the local police and the press. Nancy Grace of CNN's Headline News network had done a show on Doc and the alleged murder. *People* magazine had run a multi-page spread. Doc was due to be released in a few months, but he talked like a man headed to the gallows. Immediately after his release, he expected to go on trial for first-degree murder.

■ ■ ■

One day I heard a voice from the cell across the hall singing a Marvin Gaye song. I said there was no beauty in prison, but that's not quite true—this voice was a thing of beauty. It turned out to belong to an African-American man who went by the name of Slice. Usually in prison you resent people who make noise, whether singing or whistling or loud talking, but no one resented Slice. When he sang, people stopped in their tracks to listen.

Slice and I became friends. We spent time talking when we were both on "the run"—as the corridor was called—then he invited me to lift weights with him. Slice was 47, but between his weight lifting and intensive cardio workouts he maintained the body of a 27-year-old. He became my unofficial trainer.

Everybody liked and respected Slice. He was the shot-caller for the black men in our unit, as well as the "commissioner" of the prison basketball league, no small job given the important role basketball played in the lives of many inmates. He assigned the teams, arranged the playoff brackets, and appointed the refs. Slice's family was originally from Belize, where his mother was a highly-educated and successful tax attorney. Slice himself was one of the smartest people I met in prison. Not just street smart, but book smart. Not many convicts have read Sun Tzu, Machiavelli, and are fully conversant and knowledgeable about nutrition.

Originally from Los Angeles, Slice had been arrested in the early 1990's for conspiracy, money laundering, and drug dealing. He began serving his 17-year sentence in a U.S. penitentiary—the highest-level security—before being transferred to a medium and now a low to complete his sentence.

Slice was a good role model for anyone looking at significant time in prison. He told me how angry he'd been at first. That he was his own worst enemy. An older inmate told him that if he didn't calm himself down, he would never survive, never return to his wife and five children, his mother and father. Slice pulled himself together, became motivated, and started to play a positive role in prison. Given better opportunities and a greater respect for the law, Slice would have made a great CEO. He was a natural motivator and leader. He also now had the discipline and skills to succeed once he was out of prison. I had no doubt he *would* succeed and *stay* out.

The same could not be said for Rattler. I'm not sure I'd call Rattler a friend, but he was certainly a constant and amusing presence in my life at Texarkana. Rattler—he got his nickname on account of his love of rattlesnakes—was an odd fellow. You'd hear his feet slowly shuffling and scraping the floor as he approached your room, then his pale chubby face would appear, surrounded by a massive head. Most men in prison kept their hair short.

Not Rattler. He kept his in a ponytail that flowed down to the middle of his back. His calves were the size of a normal person's thighs and covered in tattoos, including one of Pope John Paul sporting, for some reason, horns and a dagger.

Rattler was enormous, probably in excess of 350 lbs. When he showed up at my cell, he'd fill the entire entrance with his bulk. Crossing his legs and leaning his head against the wall, he'd gaze off into space as if he were poet beholding the moon. Finally, I'd look up from my book. "Can I help you, Rattler?"

"I'm sooo hungry," Rattler would purr. "I ain't eat nothing all day. You got any honey buns?" We'd had this conversation many times before. Rattler loved honey buns. It was nothing for him to eat seven at a single sitting. He often prowled the run looking for honey buns.

"Sorry, Rattler."

"Awww, shit."

Disconsolate, Rattler would shuffle off somewhere else, then reappear a short while later eating a honey bun and drinking a Diet Dr. Pepper and happy as could be.

Now in is mid-forties, Rattler had been behind bars—county, state, and federal—for most of his adult life. His crime was addiction, and his drug of choice was meth. His arrests were always for possession, never distribution. He needed help, not punishment. As a consequence of his prior drug offenses, though, he was now serving a fifteen-year sentence. When I asked about his plans for the future, Rattler truthfully admitted that he didn't know if he'd be able to resist drugs when he was finally released. Like many men in prison, he'd spent so much time inside that he had no tools to make it on the outside. As sure as I was that Slice would never return to prison, I was even more sure that Rattler would never leave.

■ ■ ■

Other than Wayne and Doc, my best friend at Texarkana was Richard. He was one of a small handful of people I met in prison who did not deserve to be there. Quiet and reserved, Richard Hicks was a farmer from East Texas. As a young man, he'd gone to Vietnam with the army, then returned home and married his high school sweetheart. They had four children and lived a relatively normal life. All that went off kilter after a difficult divorce. Richard began to drink and found himself in trouble with local law enforcement. He led cops on a few chases in his pickup truck, nothing too serious but enough to put him on the radar of law enforcement. When a local police officer was shot to death in his squad car, Richard, through a series of unfortunate coincidences, was falsely accused of the crime. In a trial by jury in state court, Richard was found innocent. Case closed. Except not quite.

During the trial, a witness for the defense testified to how well Richard had raised his sons. In doing so, this witness described Richard taking his son bird shooting. It was that friendly testimony that got Richard into trouble. After his divorce, Richard had been subject to a restraining order that, among other things, prohibited him from possessing a weapon. When the Feds heard the friend's testimony, they decided to charge him with violating his restraining order. In an odd twist of federal law, the judge gave Richard a fifteen-year sentence, essentially overthrowing the state court's verdict and concluding that the jury had been incorrect in finding Richard innocent of murder. It sounded almost impossible to believe, but after I mentioned Richard to my daughter Layla, she sent me a copy of several stories she found in the newspaper about the great injustice of his case. All to no avail. Richard had served ten years and had another two and a half to go.

It's hard enough to do time when you know you're guilty; I can't imagine how you do it when you know you're innocent. Richard had suffered more than most anyone I met in prison. At the beginning of the sentence, he'd been sent to a federal penitentiary populated by violent and hardcore offenders. As a result, he was far slower to engage with other inmates. Trust is not easily earned in prison, especially not in someone who has been in a maximum security facility, but slowly we became friends. We began to lift weights together every day. Richard was better than any private trainer I'd ever worked with on the outside. With his help I got into the best shape of my life.

■ ■ ■

In mid-November, I weighed myself and discovered that I'd lost 30 pounds since arriving in Texarkana. I had not been so trim and fit since Landon. I went into that first Thanksgiving feeling homesick and remorseful, but also pleased that I'd handled my first three months positively and productively.

Holidays are never fun in prison, but I'll say this for the BOP—they try to make them as painless as possible. We had a traditional Thanksgiving dinner and it was surprisingly good. All my exercise had given me a good appetite, so I enjoyed every bite.

Still, time is always slow in prison and it comes to a crashing halt over the holidays. Many of the activities, including prison jobs, were canceled. More free time meant more opportunity to miss my family. Christmas was the same, but even worse because it lasted nearly a week and because the memories of the holiday were more piercing.

I stayed in contact with my family through phone, letter, and email. It was not easy for them to visit, since I was far from New York and even farther from Europe, where Kamyar had moved for a new job, but they came whenever they could.

One day a large envelope arrived for me at mail call. Inside I found a sheaf of official looking documents that turned out to be divorce papers prepared by Sheila's lawyer. I was surprised but not shocked or angry.

My crime had affected Sheila and my children on multiple levels. Although the government quickly recognized that Sheila and my children had no knowledge of my actions, it had seized all of my personal assets. As a result, Sheila was limited to assets that were in her name prior to my original crime, purchased from money that had not come from loan proceeds. Sheila had some difficult decisions to make. Among these, I suppose she concluded that she had no choice but to protect herself and her assets by filing for divorce.

As this was happening, the government was slowly dispensing my assets to repay the banks. As I stated earlier, the metric the government used in handling cases was not how much justice or compensation they won for victims but rather how much punishment they doled out to the perpetrator. The way the government handled my assets was a good example of this.

Theoretically, the government was trying to pay back my ill-gotten gains to my victims. According to the government, I owed $292 million to the three banks I'd defrauded. The government had immediately recovered $101 million in unspent dollars. This included the $75 million I'd transferred just before my arrest from HSBC to Citibank. It also included money the government made by selling my assets at absurdly low prices. The market value of our Park Avenue duplex was about $27 million, but the government sold it for $17 million. My share in HydroDive, one of dozens of companies in which I owned a significant interest, was worth about $100 million, but the government sold it for a pittance.

The extraordinarily poor effort to get a reasonable price for my assets not only meant that the banks did not get repaid (which really was not an issue anyway, as they'd receive insurance payments for their losses), but it imposed a higher restitution on me than was warranted. As part of my sentence, I was obligated to give 15% of every dollar I made to the government, until the entire amount of my fraud had been paid back. According the government's calculation, I still owed $191 million. I was never given—and to this day have not been given—any accounting of how much the government sold my assets for or to whom it sold them.

■ ■ ■

Even in Texas, winters got cold. Some days the weather made it impossible to go outside. The BOP provided us with coats, but these were too poorly insulated to withstand real cold and useless against precipitation. Still, I did my walking whenever I could, inside if not outside, putting together miles from countless circuits through the runs of B-unit. At the end of each day, I wrote down how much exercise I'd done and what I'd read. I was racing through nearly a book a day now.

Spring was pleasant but brief, and then it was a summer again and boiling. My cell was a steam bath at night. I purchased two fans from the commissary, then two more, which only doubled the ineffectiveness of the first two. Many nights were simply too hot for sleep.

When I could, I continued to exercise in the yard, very early morning only before the heat turned brutal. On days when the temperature rose above 100—black flag days, as they were called—the yard was closed to prevent anyone going out and embarrassing the BOP by dying of heat stroke. Then I'd walk inside again, doing my hamster-wheel laps around the unit. By retreating to the air-conditioned email room and the library I could get some relief during the days. But nights were back in the swelter of my cell.

■ ■ ■

One afternoon, following another hot sleepless night, I looked up from my book to see a tall, awkward-looking kid in the doorway of my cell. He mumbled something.

"Sorry?"

"I'm Jacob. I'm assigned to this room."

I'd not had anybody in my cell for months. But every Thursday afternoon brought a new busload of incoming inmates, and it was the luck of the draw who you got. If you were lucky, you got no one. If you were unlucky, you got Jacob.

Actually, that's unfair. He was not a bad cellmate. Just extremely awkward. He was about 6'3", chubby, freckled faced, with receding strawberry-colored hair. He'd been assigned the top bunk, and it was painful to watch him try to maneuver himself up there with his lanky and clumsy limbs.

Jacob was on the quiet side—which was good—but we chatted a bit. Suddenly, with no prompting, he blurted out, "I'm here for wire fraud." He did not elaborate and I did not pursue it. I was a bit suspicious, though. He was only in his twenties and did not strike me as a particularly savvy young man. Wire fraud is pretty complicated. I doubted he even knew what it meant.

Later that night, Jacob came back into the room and said he needed to talk. He'd spoken to the Mayor, he said. The Mayor—Wayne—had told him that it was the kiss of death to lie about your crime in prison and to then be found out. So Jacob wanted to come clean. "It wasn't wire fraud," he said quietly. And then, quietly and haltingly, he told me the truth.

It turned out that Jacob had been sentenced to thirteen years for possession of child pornography. His crime was downloading over 600 images of underage girls. I asked Jacob if he'd ever had sex. He had not, he admitted. He was a virgin. He'd spent all of his time on the computer and had ultimately turned to pornography.

In an era before computers, Jacob would have been buying girlie magazines and going to peep shows. Today he's a sex offender and will have to register as such wherever he lives for the remainder of his life—assuming he makes it through prison in one piece and has any life to look forward to. He was clearly a very sick young man, but it was hard not to pity Jacob. Clearly he had not asked to be made this way—no one would.

Jacob soon moved out of my room, and I never saw him again. I still wonder how someone so clueless and awkward could make it through 13 years of prison.

■ ■ ■

Whatever happened to Jacob, I'm sure he ended up in a better place than my yoga instructor did. If you have a picture of a yoga instructor in your mind, the person you're imagining is probably the opposite of the guy who taught my yoga class at Texarkana. You see a lot of brawn in prison, but this guy was in a class by himself, with boundless muscles that should not have been able to stretch, much less perform some of the maneuvers he led us through. Sometimes on hot days he took off his shirt, revealing not only more of his muscle but also his numerous tattoos. It was disturbing to see that some of these identified him as a member of the Aryan Brotherhood, an incredibly violent white supremacist gang that operates inside many U.S. prisons. Although the Aryan Brotherhood makes up a tiny percentage of the prison population, they commit as much as a quarter of all murders in prison. The AB also runs drugs and engages in other criminal enterprises, including murder, all from within the prison system. No group is more ruthless.

One day, the yoga instructor disappeared. Because everybody in prison gossips, including both staff and inmates, secrets in prison do not remains secret for long, and soon everybody came to learn what happened.

As it turned out, some AB members in Texarkana had learned that the yoga instructor was not the man he pretended to be. He was not serving time for a drug crime, as he claimed. He was in for pedophilia. As Wayne had warned young Jacob, you do not lie about your crime in prison, and you definitely don't lie if you are in for pedophilia. Getting ostracized as a chomo is bad, but pretending not to be a chomo and then getting found out is far worse.

The yoga instructor had made the ultimate mistake. He'd lied about being a chomo to the Aryan Brotherhood. When he was found out, he begged to be sent to another prison to avoid the punishment he knew was coming. But there was no avoiding punishment. The AB was everywhere, in nearly every prison, and when they found out where he'd been sent—which they could easily do—they would send a "kite," or message, to their chapter at that prison. The punishment would be extreme. They would not just severely beat the yoga instructor; they would remove, by knife, the AB tattoos on his chest.

It was hard to feel pity for a member of the Aryan Brotherhood. But I pitied the yoga instructor.

■ ■ ■

Prison is filled with people who have sad stories to tell, and sometimes they make them sadder by their actions in prison. By definition, people who wind up in prison are risk takers and rule breakers, and some of them can't fight those tendencies even behind bars. My first celly, Walt, was one of the smart ones, and I followed his good advice—keep your head down and stay out of trouble. I had no intention of adding so much as a day to my sentence or making my time behind bars any harder than it had to be.

But not everyone was willing or able to do this. They fought, they drank, they crossed one too many lines and put themselves in worse trouble than they were already in. The Mexican-American guy who did my laundry stabbed another guy over an argument about whose turn it was to use the dryer. He was placed in solitary, shipped to a higher security prison, and given additional time on his sentence. Over some wet clothes. Stupid.

A young Jewish kid whom I befriended—one of just two Jews in the entire prison—was the kind of handsome and smart son every Jewish mother dreams of, except that he was too smart for his own good. He got himself a gig working in a prison warehouse, where he made a contact on the outside to smuggle in cigarettes. He hid the packs in prison walls and sold them through runners in every community—the whites, the blacks, the Mexicans. Inevitably, one of his runners got caught and turned him in. The next morning, we saw him get dragged away in handcuffs. We all knew where he was headed: a higher security prison, and a longer sentence. Utterly not worth the few dollars he'd made with his scheme.

Perhaps the saddest tale of all, at least for me personally, was what happened to J.P. It was to J.P. that I owed my desk, my lamp, and my other creature comforts. He'd also become a good friend. I admired his sharp mind and can-do attitude. But I worried about his judgment sometimes. He generally operated in the gray areas of prison rules, providing goods and services that were not strictly legal but were tacitly condoned. But sometimes he stepped over the line and engaged in foolishness. Making or buying "hooch"—homemade booze—for example, or dealing in cell phones. Both were serious infractions.

In the fall of 2011, J.P. was close to release, just a few months to go. He had a daughter he adored and desperately wanted to see, and he was looking forward to putting his talents to use on the outside. I had no doubt he'd succeed. First, though, he had to make it out of prison.

One of J.P.'s hustles was operating as the Texarkana bookie. Sports betting was popular in Texarkana, as it is at most prisons. Many of the bets went through J.P., who took them and set the point spreads. The administration generally ignored low-level gambling among inmates, but bookmaking was not tolerated, and J.P. was taking a serious risk.

One afternoon towards the end of that football season, J.P. and I took a walk around the track. "Think about what you are doing, J.P.", I said. "It makes no sense. You're out of here in a few months. Why would you do this? It's not worth it." J.P. did not disagree with me, but neither did he commit to pulling back.

In fact, as the play-offs began, he embroiled himself even more deeply in bookmaking.

A few Sunday evenings later, J.P. stumbled into my cell. He was clearly drunk. I could smell booze on him, and he was grinning, almost laughing. He'd gotten himself into a heap of trouble, he told me. A number of bets had turned against him. The Giants play-off game had killed him. He owed over $5000 in stamps and he had nowhere near enough to pay this.

"I'm fucked," he laughed.

"You got to get out of here, J.P."

"Exactly. That's what I'm doing. They'll put me in the SHU when they find me like this. Only place for me to go right now that's safe."

This term I knew. The SHU, or special housing unit, is usually reserved for disciplinary cases or extremely violent prisoners. It was a euphemism for solitary confinement.

"I mean you need to leave my cell. You can't be here." If they found J.P. drunk in my cell, I'd be guilty by association. That's how it worked.

So J.P. stumbled away. Later than evening, he got caught, breathalyzed, and sent to solitary, just as he wished. And then, without warning, the BOP moved him to another prison, higher security, to finish out his sentence—a sentence that would now be a good while longer, since any good time he'd earned in prison would be retracted. I never got a chance to say goodbye to him and never saw him again after that drunken visit to my cell.

If J.P. hoped that going to another prison would protect him from the men whose bets he'd failed to honor, he was sadly mistaken. The problem, again, was that anyone on the outside could easily find out where he'd gone. And so J.P. was located. A kite was sent, this time by a few of the black guys who were owed money by J.P. I later heard what happened through the grapevine. J.P. was beaten to a pulp. Stupid and sad.

∎ ∎ ∎

There's not a lot of good to be said about prison. As I've suggested, though, it's not all bad, if you use your time productively. Perhaps the best thing prison gave me was the opportunity for constructive reflection. About my fellow inmates. About myself.

I thought a lot about the quirks and flaws of personality that landed us in prison. The irrational tolerance for risk we shared. The unhealthy tendency to delude ourselves and rationalize our actions. The failure to anticipate the damage we might inflict not just on ourselves, but on our families. We'd all done bad things, stupid things, but we were not all bad or stupid men. Among us was as much kindness, generosity, good humor, and raw intelligence as you'd find in any population of a thousand men. And yet.

I often wondered how I'd ended up there. I'd grown up with respect for law and authority. I was the kind of young person who got along well with teachers and adults—far from a delinquent. I suppose as I got older I felt a pressure to live up to my name, my legacy, and when my financial decisions turned against me, I not only believed that I'd work my way out of them, but also—worse—I could not accept the shame that might accompany admitting failure. My years in Iran had seemed to change me. My respect for law had diminished in proportion to my growing confidence in my ability to seize opportunity and escape catastrophe. I came from a long line of men who had done the same, and I fooled myself into believing I was only following in their footsteps. As I tried to trace my road to prison, my mind began to go back—to my childhood, to Iran, and even further back to the grandfather I'd never met, who had left his family in Shiraz and gone to Bombay to strike it rich.

On New Year's Day of 2012, I woke up, as always, very early. Because it was a holiday, the usual activities were canceled, and it was too cold to go outside. I propped up the small, hinged desk in my cell that J.P. had arranged to have built for me. I pulled out a pen and pad of paper and I began to write this book.

29

DETOUR

One Tuesday morning in April of 2012, I met with my counselor at Texarkana, a middle-aged white woman named Miss Lindsey. Rather like a guidance counselor at a high school, her job was to oversee my progress through Texarkana, deal with any issues that came up during my stay, and arrange any physical movements I might make, from doctor's appointments to transfers. We met that morning to discuss an upcoming visit by my son, Kamyar, who was flying from Europe to see me. As I started to leave her office, Miss Lindsey called to me. "Oh, by the way, you've been designated. You're going to a camp. Just what you wanted. Otisville."

I was stunned. My original request to transfer to Otisville had been denied by the Bureau of Prisons, and I'd not expected another chance to apply until the following September. So this was great news—extraordinary news, in fact. And it got better. I'd assumed it would be weeks, if not months, before I would actually be transferred, but five days after hearing from Miss Lindsey, I got a message from R&D—Receiving and Discharge—to have all of my personal belongings packed up so they could be shipped to Otisville. I'd be leaving Texarkana in a matter of days.

I was looking forward to moving to a minimum-security prison, but my emotions were mixed. Texarkana had not been all bad. As I thought back on my 18 months there, I was astonished by what I accomplished. I looked over the logs I'd kept and counted more than 530 books I'd read, more than 4,000 miles I'd walked, and, just in the previous few months, more than three hundred pages I'd written. I felt healthier, more energetic, and more clear-headed than I'd felt in years. I had pride in my achievements and control of my life—an irony for a man in prison, I admit, where you control so little.

As news of my imminent departure circulated, people came by my cell to say their goodbyes. I reflected again on what an interesting, colorful, strange, and in some cases inspiring group of men I'd come to know in Texarkana—men I would never have met, much less befriended, outside of prison walls. Slice and Rattler, of course, who lived in my unit. And guys like Hillbilly, Stiles, Armadillo, Wilson, Montez, Bruce, Dave the Cardinals fan, Stan, Johnny, Dennis, Jerry, Gary, Billy, Potter, Brunson, Geno, One-Eyed Jack, Scott, Steve, Wayne H, Mansfield, Haney, and many, many more. Black, white, Hispanic. I'd miss them all. Most of all, I'd miss Wayne, Doc, and Richard. Amazing how you can develop friends in the most peculiar of places. I ate many a good meal with Wayne, exercised with weights every day with Richard, and walked with Doc every weekend. Of these men, two were almost certainly guilty of murder, while the third, Richard, was an accused cop killer. I almost had to laugh when I considered that these were my closest friends. We took each other as we found each other here.

We promised we'd see each other again on the outside, but of course we never did. Wayne would die in prison a few years after I last saw him. Doc would be convicted of murdering his wife in 2013; a few years after that, he'd hang himself in prison. Only Richard would make it out alive, eventually moving back home to the small town in Texas where he'd been born and raised.

■ ■ ■

The BOP communicates with inmates on a strictly need-to-know basis. It's true that inmates come into a lot of information by way of loose-lipped CO's and fellow inmates, but this is mostly useless gossip. About the things that actually matter—such as when and where you are going to be transferred—you hear nothing in advance. Ostensibly, this is for security reasons, lest a prisoner use the information to plan a jailbreak or hatch some other nefarious plot. The general effect on those of us who had no such plans was to treat us like pallets of cargo or livestock.

At about 3:00 a.m., on April 20, 2012, with no warning, a CO flicked on the light in my cell and woke me. "Nemazee, let's go! R&D! Now!"

I got dressed quickly and grabbed a small bag with the few items I'd not already packed up and sent to Otisville. I took one last look around my cell and headed down to R&D. The moment I got there, I was placed in a holding cell with twenty other inmates who had come into Texarkana the night before. This wasn't quite the dramatic exit I'd imagined, but by now I was used to these sorts of unexplained holding patterns. The only thing to do was give in and let time pass. By the end of the day, I'd be in Otisville. That was all that mattered.

Finally, several hours after my abrupt waking, it was time to go. We were shackled, hands and feet, and shuffled outside to a BOP bus. By the time we got moving, it was late morning.

The prison bus was an old converted yellow school bus. There was a driver and two armed guards, one in the front, the other in an enclosed cage in the back. The bus's shocks had blown out long ago, and the hard seats registered every pothole and bump between Texarkana and Oklahoma City. I did not care. I was just happy to be moving. The countryside was flat and drab at first, but then it got hillier and greener as we drove up into Indian country. It was early spring, and the trees were coming alive with bright, delicate looking leaves, and along the road wildflowers and fruit trees bloomed. In an earlier life, I might have found the five-hour drive monotonous, but now I enjoyed every minute of looking out the window—live oak and mesquite, meadows in the distance and cows gazing back at me, then a farm house, then a muddy creek gushing under a bridge we passed over. We drove up the Indian Nation Turnpike through the reservations of the Choctaw and the Cherokee, where the U.S. government had moved the tribes during the infamous Trail of Tears in the 1830's. After a few hours of this, we began to see more houses and other buildings, and suddenly we were on the outskirts of Oklahoma City, and airplanes were ascending and descending overhead.

FTC Oklahoma City is housed in a large building adjacent to the Will Rogers World Airport. FTC stands for Federal Transit Center. It's the hub of the BOP air system. Imagine an airport waiting lounge combined with a prison and you get the idea. Armed guards escorted us off the bus. The air was thick with the noise of plane engines and the odor of jet fuel. Inside, we were placed in a single large holding cell. Hours passed as we waited to be processed. At last, I was called to the desk by a CO. He barely looked up from his papers.

"You're going to be placed in seg, so hold tight."

"Seg?" I'd never heard the term.

"Yeah, Seg. The SHU."

"Why am I being put in the SHU?"

"Prison policy. All high-profiles go into seg."

"You're kidding me." He looked up and peered at me through thick glasses, trying to decide if I was about to become a problem. "I'm not high-profile," I said "Nobody gives a shit who I am."

"I'm just telling you the information I have. If you don't like it, you can take it up with the lieutenant." He looked back down at his desk and scratched something on a form.

"When?"

"He'll be back Monday. Good luck." He was done with me. He called up the next inmate.

It was Friday. Apparently, I was spending the weekend in the SHU. It turned out to be a bit longer.

I watched as the other inmates who had accompanied me from Texarkana were taken upstairs to the general population area. I was then put in handcuffs and escorted to the SHU.

Other than the fact it was less grimy, the cell here was similar to the one I'd spent the night in at MCC. It was a small room of concrete and steel, 10' x 8', with a sink, toilet, and shower. A tall, thin window let in gray light; the glass was so thick and frosted that I could see nothing through it and could barely tell if it was night or day. The only time I could leave the cell and see actual sunlight was one hour a day to walk in a sort of dog run on the roof of the SHU. This was nothing more than a 12' x 12' cage, and I had to wait until Monday to see it—there is no exercise on weekends in the SHU.

When I asked to place a phone call so I could tell my family where I was, a CO informed me that I was only permitted one call every 30 days. In other words, I'd have to be here a month before I could call anyone.

Even in a well-managed prison, solitary confinement is an incredibly unpleasant ordeal, and even a brief stay is interminable.

The isolation, the feeling of being trapped, the lack of natural light, all are enough to challenge any man's sanity. And because the SHU is where the most violent and truly crazy inmates go, there is always shouting, wailing, and screaming—the feral noises of anger and desperation that pierce the cell door. So you are alone, but you have no peace.

Within 24 hours, I felt myself getting edgy and depressed. I understood why some men are never the same after long stretches in the SHU. But I knew what I needed to survive: books. Every time a CO came near I called out to ask for books. Finally, a few paperbacks appeared in my slot. Dog-eared trash mostly, but better than nothing.

My requests for an interview with the lieutenant came to nothing. But one afternoon a few days in, I was reading on my cot when I heard voices—men and then a woman, which was unusual. I went to the slot and looked out. I saw white shirts, indicating high-ranking prison officials, and then a woman—well-dressed, attractive, black. My eyes widened when I realized I knew her—it was Miss Dickerson, the assistant warden from Texarkana who had once confessed her love of Hillary Clinton to me.

"Miss Dickerson!" I called out.

She stopped. She came over to the door. She motioned to someone to open it, and a second later Miss Dickerson was standing before me, smiling quizzically.

"Nemazee? What are you doing here?"

"I'm being transferred. What are *you* doing here?"

"I'm the warden here now."

I explained to her what had happened—how I'd been on my way to Otisville, had gotten thrown into solitary for being 'high-profile,' and was desperate to get moved.

She interrupted me. "Look, I'll give you my word, if you aren't on next flight out I'll have you moved out of the SHU." She explained that the paperwork to have me moved for just a day or two would make both of our lives difficult; better if I could stick it out in the SHU.

"Okay," I said. "Deal."

I thought of a book written by a friend, Haleh Esfandiari, who had been corresponding with me for the last year. She was an Iranian-American Scholar who had been arrested and imprisoned while visiting Iran a few years earlier. The mullahs of the Islamic Republic had put her in solitary confinement inside the notorious Evin prison in Tehran for 110 days. If a frail elderly woman could survive 110 days in Evin, I could handle two more days in the SHU of FTC Oklahoma City.

■ ■ ■

They came for me, at last, early on the morning of the sixth day. I was again shackled at my hands and feet and frog-walked with a group of inmates up a long hallway. Then we were led down a jetway that extended directly from the prison to an awaiting plane.

An antique-looking Boeing 727, the plane was already nearly full when we boarded. Entering from the front, we shuffled through the women's section first—such a sullen-looking group of women you have never seen—and were taken to seats in the back. Everybody was shackled. A few looked up, but most ignored us. We were deposited in our assigned seats. And then we performed that activity that inmates learn to master or else go mad: we waited and waited, and then waited some more.

The plane was owned by the Justice Department. It was one of several in the small federally-operated fleet commonly referred to as "Con Air," more officially known as the Justice Prisoner and Alien Transportation System (JPATS). The 1997 Nicolas Cage movie *Con Air* shows a plane outfitted with all manner of chains and cages and decks. In reality, Con Air planes look pretty much like any other 727s, except there is no first class and no kitchenette, and instead of flight attendants you get a dozen federal marshals armed with pistols and long guns.

Another amenity you don't get on Con Air is the reassuring voice of the pilot informing you of your destination and expected time of arrival. Such details you learn only after you land.

■ ■ ■

I could tell from the direction of the sun that we were flying to the northeast, as I expected. This was confirmed when we landed at an airport to drop off and pick up inmates. Through the window I saw a dozen well-armed guards on the tarmac, but also a few signs that told me we were in Memphis.

We continued to the northeast through the afternoon, then at last I felt the plane start to descend. When the plane banked, I saw a wide green river below—the Hudson. We touched down at Stewart Airport, just outside Newburgh, New York. I recognized the airport because I had landed there once before, years earlier, when diverted from Palm Beach on a NetJets flight. Newburgh was about 70 miles north of New York City. More importantly, it was about 30 miles due east of Otisville.

As soon as we landed, the plane was surrounded by armed guards and BOP buses and vans. Still shackled, we were removed from the plane. I was directed to a bus. After a while, the bus began to move. It was late afternoon now, the sun streaming in from the west, where I expected us to soon be headed.

It did not take long for me to realize that I was mistaken. The bus merged onto a highway. We should have been driving into the sun, but the sun was to my right. We were headed south— but where? A roadside sign confirmed that we were on Interstate 87, the New York State Thruway. The Thruway ran more or less parallel to the Hudson, north from New York City to Albany and beyond. Or, in our case, south, toward the city.

When we crossed the George Washington Bridge into northern Manhattan, my worst fears were confirmed. For a while, I thought I was being taken back to MCC, the hellhole in lower Manhattan where I'd spent my first night in prison several years earlier. So I was relieved when we turned into a tunnel, exiting Manhattan. Wherever we were going, it could not possibly be worse than MCC.

Wrong again. There is a federal prison worse than MCC. It's known as MDC—the Metropolitan Detention Center. A holding facility of the Bureau of Prisons located in Brooklyn, MDC is usually reserved for pre-trial inmates who have been denied bail, often non-American detainees, including terrorists and hardened criminals.

For the moment, I had no real knowledge of any of this. I only had questions: Why was I here? How long would I be here? What about Otisville?

When I finally met a counselor, he explained the situation. There were no beds available in Otisville at the moment. I was going to be held here until one opened up.

"And when will that be?"

He shrugged. "It'll probably be a minute."

■ ■ ■

As it turned out, my minute would stretch to nearly three months. These would be the worst three months of my entire incarceration, and among the worst three months of my life. If the MCC in Manhattan is the second-worst prison in the federal system, that's only because MDC in Brooklyn takes the prize as #1 hellhole. Regularly in the news for beatings, riots, and cruelties that occur inside its walls, MDC was a prison that would have been at home in Iran under Ayatollah Khomeini.

Inmates were not supposed to be kept at MDC for more than 30 days. In fact, though, just as at MCC, many were warehoused in MDC for months, even years in some cases. Later, I'd come to share a bunk with a man who spent six and a half years at MDC. I don't know how he came out sane.

I was placed in a unit that housed approximately 100 people. Known among inmates as "the dungeon," it was a large dorm-style unit. Imagine a high school gymnasium, but instead of the bleachers and basketball hoops, you have row upon row of bunk beds. Off to one side was a section for showers, toilets and sinks, and in another section was a kitchen that dispensed meals. The only other distinct area was a small exercise room, approximately 20'x20' in size. There was no outdoor space, no fresh air, no sunlight. As long as I was at MDC, the inside of the dungeon was all I'd see of the world. For three months, I never saw the sky.

Inside the dungeon, the conditions were disgusting. Bathrooms were filthy and moldy. Misdirected urine puddled around toilets. Showers were filthy and, at least on one occasion while I was there, had been defecated in by inmates. The food was almost inedible. Sleep was nearly impossible, as lights were kept on throughout the night.

Sleep was especially difficult for me during the first week I was there. I'd been assigned a lower bunk on account of my age, but the bunk was directly next to a bank of televisions, all of which stayed on 24/7. As in Texarkana, men listened to the TVs through radios and earpieces, so the volume of the programs wasn't the problem. Rather, it was the vocalizations many of the men made as they watched, laughing, shouting, swearing, and otherwise responding loudly to anything on the screen.

Asking my fellow inmates to keep it down seemed ill-advised. The inmates in MDC were more tightly wound, and a lot less friendly, than at Texarkana. Most were here awaiting trial or, like me, in transport to another facility, so no one felt much need or desire to form bonds or be charitable. As mentioned earlier, there were prisoners at all levels of offense here, including some recently off the streets for violent crimes. Many of the non-Americans were drug traffickers from the Dominican Republic and Colombia. Some were from Pakistan, Bangladesh, and India.

One was from Iran. His name was Ali. Middle-aged and mild-mannered, he could not have been more out of place. He told me he'd emigrated to America before the revolution and settled in Virginia, where he'd somehow become involved in the opium trade. Ali was helpful to me in many ways. He gave me detergent for my wash, sandals for the shower, and cooked me a Persian meal, quite decent given the limitations of the supplies at hand.

After several days near the televisions, I was fortunate to be moved to a quieter area. One of the benefits of the move was that it brought me close to an interesting character by the name of Henry. That was his real name anyway. "Call me Black," he told me soon after we met. "Everyone does." Given that Henry was African American and I was not, it felt a bit strange to call him by his nickname. Then again, I'd pretty well gotten used to the bluntness with which race is addressed in prison, and so I obliged.

Henry had been in the entertainment business, with a sideline in the drug business. He was arrested, denied bail, and became a cooperating witness in a major drug trial of a well-known hip-hop personality. He told me that among his prior involvements, he'd been a producer on the movie *Precious* before his life went off the rails. Henry was kind, polished, and cultured, and having him at my side put me at ease.

Even with Henry's friendship, though, Brooklyn MDC was a terrible experience. We were stuck in a closed space that felt smaller by the day. The options for exercise were limited, we never got so much as a sniff of fresh air, we never heard natural sounds—birds, wind, rain—and never experienced quiet. When you confine 100 restless men in a single enclosed space, there is no such thing as quiet. Which means there is no such thing as a good night's sleep.

Placing people in an environment like this, even briefly, makes no sense. Prison is not meant to be pleasant, but it's difficult to see how it's in the interest of society to undermine the mental and physical health of people who are probably going to return to the outside world someday. The BOP not only does prisoners harm by keeping people there for extended periods—it does society a disservice.

As the weeks passed, I lost weight and muscle. I became extraordinarily tired from sleep deprivation and generally felt as low and lethargic as I'd been since my arrest. Because my razor had been shipped to Otisville and I did not want to spend more time in the bathroom at MDC than I had to, I stopped shaving and grew a beard, which came in gray and thick and made me look even older than I felt. In a few weeks, I'd aged a few years.

■ ■ ■

The only glimmer of good news during this dark time concerned Shahin Kashanchi, Sheila's younger brother. The prosecutor in my case, Dan Levy, like a modern-day Inspector Javert, had continued to pursue Shahin for the previous two years, despite the very obvious fact that Shahin was totally innocent and ignorant of my crime. Even after my brother-in-law verbally agreed to a plea agreement of a misdemeanor with no jail time—just to get the matter behind him and get on with his life—Levy put together 30 exhibits to try to prove that Shahin *should* have known that I was committing a crime, and therefore must be held accountable and jailed. In the end, the judge gave Shahin just one year of probation, rather than the year of jail time that Levy had sought.

It is truly hard to understand Levy's motive for doing this to a young man whose only crime was assisting me. Ten years later, the U.S. Attorney in New York would essentially admit this when it tried to deny my request for early termination of my supervised release (a post-prison probation that I will have more to say about later), arguing that my brother-in-law had been an "innocent victim duped by Mr. Nemazee." This begs a disturbing question: If the SDNY knew Shahin was an innocent victim, why did Levy spend so much effort trying to put him in prison and branding him a felon for life?

As I've written, my conduct regarding Shahin Kashanchi is among the most unforgivable of my crimes. I abused his trust and innocence to assist me in manufacturing documents to perpetrate my crime. The thought that he might spend any time in jail was something that hung over my head during the previous two years. I can hardly express how relieved I was when Sheila told me the judge's decision.

Not long after hearing about Shahin, my own deliverance finally came. In the early morning of July 12, at around 3 a.m., I was woken up by a guard and told the words I'd been waiting to hear for months: "Get dressed. You're leaving."

No one had told me that I was going to be moved. I'd had no time to pack, no time to say goodbye to Henry and Ali. But I didn't waste any time gathering my few belongings. After 83 days, I was finally leaving the dungeon and on my way to Otisville.

30

OTISVILLE

Eighty miles northwest of New York City, on a high clearing in the southern foothills of the Catskill Mountains, lies Federal Correctional Institution, Otisville. To the east, farmland and small towns slope toward the Hudson River. To the west is nearly uninterrupted forest, clear to the Delaware River—some twenty miles distant—and into Pennsylvania. Arriving late on a bright but cool July morning, following a two-hour van ride from Brooklyn, I was stunned by all the lush green of countryside and the blue skies overhead. I'd lived inside a gray cube for nearly three months.

We turned off the state road onto curvy Two Mile Drive, passing a sign for FCI Otisville then wending our way upwards through a corridor of birch, oak, and spruce, finally arriving at the prison. FCI Otisville is really two separate facilities on one campus. The larger of these, enclosed by a high fence crowned by concertina wire, is a medium security prison for serious offenders. Adjacent to this is the minimum-security facility, Otisville Camp.

Nearly all of the inmates on the van from Brooklyn were bound for the medium security prison. Only I and one other man—Lonnie, a tall black guy with a ready smile—were headed for the camp. Lonnie and I spent the morning inside the medium security prison with the others, undergoing the usual round of forms and evaluations, then we were given our prison uniforms, green pants and shirts, and told to report to the camp. The CO pointed at the door to the outside. "Head out to the left and go on up that way. Stay on the left. Go past the baseball diamond, then take a right at the warehouse. Camp's at the top of the hill. They're expecting you."

And so out we went, out under the EXIT sign and into the sunshine and air. We took the cement path to the asphalt road that ran around the medium security prison. We walked alongside the high perimeter fence, but we were on the outside of the fence, and that felt different than being inside. We came to a road that forked off to the right. There were a couple of warehouse and barn-like structures but no sign of fences, chains, bars, barbed wire, or even guards. A few men in green prison uniforms stood at the back of a panel truck, unloading boxes. When they saw us they waved and pointed to two buildings another hundred yards beyond. We thanked them and headed up the hill.

The first and smaller of the buildings, as I came to learn, housed the administrative offices for the camp, along with a small dormitory, the education center, the visiting room, and a few other functional spaces. The farther, larger structure was the main building of the camp, where we'd been told to report. Inside were a couple of small offices and a busy common room, which turned out to be the central living area for the inmates and included the dining and living areas. The layout was airy and open. Surrounding the common room were semi-enclosed cubicles with walls that ran about as high as the top bunk. The atmosphere was dorm-like, but this was nothing like the dungeon at MDC. Natural light poured in through the windows, the air was fresh, and the volume was low and soft as men calmly went about their business.

A single CO was on duty. A chubby young guy, he sat in a small office with a large glass window that looked over the common room. He greeted us politely, then handed us a sheaf of papers to fill out. Just then, a young man approached from across the common room, grinning broadly and waving his hand. "Hassan!"

It took me a second to remember the face, and then it came to me—Ezra. I'd met Ezra a few times when he worked at a hedge fund run by a friend of mine. I don't know how he recognized me, as I'd not shaved in three months, but he greeted me like a long-lost brother. He immediately offered to assist me with anything I might need, then started introducing me to other inmates. Soon a small crowd was gathered around. It seemed they'd been expecting me, and hands were offered to shake, along with words of welcome and more offers to help me settle in.

Shortly, I was approached by a man I recognized instantly: Ken Starr. Not the Ken Starr of the Clinton impeachment—the other Ken Starr, the former accountant and financial consultant who the press had taken to calling another "mini-Madoff" after trying, briefly and unsuccessfully, to stick that label on me. Even if you did not know him personally, Ken was not hard to recognize, given that his face had been plastered all over the media after he was arrested for allegedly bilking his celebrity clients—Uma Thurman, Natalie Portman, and Al Pacino among others— of millions of dollars. Ken and I had met a number of times through mutual friends. Although he and I did not have much in common, it was nice in these early days to see familiar faces. I was not home, but I was closer than I'd been in a long while.

It was clear from the start that Otisville was going to be a completely different experience than any I'd had yet in prison. In fact, Otisville is different than any other prison experience in America. One striking clue to this was the high percentage of men who grew beards—very long beards in many cases, much longer than my own relatively novice effort. The beards signal one of the anomalies that make Otisville so unique, which is the large number of Jews at the camp. Jews comprised about 40 or 45% of the population when I arrived and more than 50% by the time I left. This number included secular and Reform Jews, but it also included many Orthodox and Hasidic Jews who, along with their impressive beards, grew payots—side-curls that hang over the sideburns—and wore tzirzit, a kind of fringed shawl, beneath their green shirts.

There are not a lot of Jews in the federal prison system as a whole. As I mentioned earlier, there were just two in all of Texarkana when I was there. But if you are Jewish and are convicted of a white-collar crime, Otisville is where you seem to end up. At least, it is where you *want* to end up. The prison accommodates Jewish religious needs as no others. A room is set aside in the administration building to serve as a *shul*, where the more devout Jews can eat and pray, and where a Torah scroll is kept under lock and key. Other signs that you are in Otisville include the kosher vending machines and a small kosher kitchen in the main building.

It wasn't just the Jewish presence that made the demographics of Otisville unusual. There was also the matter of race and age. In most federal prisons, the demographic is about 40% black, 30% Hispanic, and the remainder white. Here it was about 80% white and 20% black and Hispanic combined. And the population was much older. In Texarkana, where the average age was probably 30, I'd been a prison elder. At Otisville, where there were nearly as many canes as beards, I was practically a spring chicken.

For the moment, my focus was less on demographics and food than on the physical environment. After my week in solitary in Oklahoma and the three months in MDC, the freedom of movement and the access to fresh air and nature was simply amazing. We had as much access to the outdoors as we could possibly want, day or night, and the only thing that hemmed us in were birch trees and pines.

That first evening, I sat out under stars for first time in two years. The only sound was of crickets and birds and the breeze passing through the tree branches. I slept better that night than I'd slept in many months.

■ ■ ■

Most of the camp inmates slept in the main building. This housed 100 men in two-man cubicles with bunk beds. There were no free beds in the main building when I arrived, so I was placed with about 20 other men in a small dorm in the administration building. I would have preferred the more private cubicle arrangement of the main building, but compared to what I'd been subjected to in Brooklyn, the living arrangements were more than adequate.

The morning after my arrival, I got up early, awoken by the unfamiliar but not unpleasant symphony of thousands of chirping birds. I grabbed a banana from the mess hall and went outside. The grass sparkled with dew. Birds hopped around, pecking at the ground, as the rising sun lit the tops of the pines. These were all perfectly normal things, but having been deprived of them for close to two years, they all looked like little miracles to me.

A few men were already out walking or otherwise exercising. I saw Ken Starr come striding down a path. He waved when he saw me and invited me to join him. I took my first walk—of many, many hundreds—around the camp grounds at Otisville.

There was no track at Otisville. Instead, a path wended around the perimeter of the camp. It was not long—maybe a third of a mile for the whole loop—but it felt long enough that first time. We passed a small chapel, then a tennis court, then curled around the bottom of a small soccer field and came back up on the opposite side of the field, along the edge of the forest. We passed a Quonset hut that served as the gym—I'd spend a lot of time there—then turned again, toward the warehouse that marked the boundary between the camp and the medium security prison. As Ken told me, we were not to go beyond this unless expressly permitted to do so.

Ken and I did a few loops, and by the time we were done the sun had burned off the dew and the day was turning hot. When I got back inside, I found that the items I'd shipped from Texarkana three months earlier were waiting for me. It was good to be reunited with my clothing, my books, and the rest of my personal possessions. Best of all was a black knit cap that had been given to me by Doc as a parting gift. Most prisons do not allow headwear, but Otisville, because it allowed skullcaps, could hardly object. Doc's cap would serve me well when cold weather came to Otisville.

Among the items I'd sent from Texarkana were my toiletries, including my razor and shaving cream. But my beard was now too thick for me to shave myself—I needed a barber. I was pleased to learn that the camp had an in-house barber, a middle-aged black inmate who ran a small shop in the administration building, complete with a barber chair and an arsenal of scissors and buzzers—everything but the striped pole. I secured an appointment and soon found myself smooth-chinned and fresh faced. When the barber shaved my grizzled beard, he also shaved a decade off my apparent age. It was good to have it gone.

My next task was getting back in shape. After nearly three months without real exercise, I'd loss muscle tone and stamina. Walking the circuit around the camp would help put me back on the road to physical fitness, but I wanted to resume weight training, too. With advice from Ezra, I got a great guy named Hector to work with me as my trainer.

Hiring Hector introduced me to another idiosyncrasy of Otisville. In Texarkana, the currency to pay for goods and services had been 30-cent stamps. Here in Otisville, it was small foil pouches of mackerel—yes, the fish—that you could purchase at the commissary. Only in Otisville.

■ ■ ■

The grass, the forest, the absence of fences and barbed wire. The turkeys that paraded by in the mornings on the edge of the woods. The deer that nibbled the leaves right outside the windows of the dorm. It was almost possible to forget you were incarcerated sometimes.

It was still prison, though. The prison's famous nickname—Club Fed—suggests that inmates enjoy four-star comfort. Actually, while the setting at Otisville was superior to most prisons, the amenities were far from posh. The infrastructure was classic drab federal, circa 1970's, and was scarred by decades of deferred maintenance. The famous tennis court where Otisville inmates ostensibly whiled away the hours lobbing balls was, in reality, a minefield of tripping hazards and ankle twisters, the whole thing sloped so precipitously to the west that you had to factor the wonky grade into your shots. The soccer field was similarly lopsided, one of the goals a couple of feet closer to sea level than the other. The basketball court was a minefield of pitted asphalt, perfect for tearing up middle-aged Achilles' heels and ACLs. This was nobody's idea of a club.

There were still plenty of rules, too. As at every other federal prison, the day was divided into five counts. For each of these you needed to be at your bunk, the only exception being during visiting hours on weekends, when you could be counted in the administration building. And though there were no fences or bars, there were strict boundaries we had to observe. We could not just walk off into the woods (though some did now and then, as I'd learn), and we still had to wear our green uniform, for most of the day. Prisoners who broke rules faced serious punishment, including the likelihood of being kicked out of Otisville and sent somewhere worse.

The BOP staff that ran Otisville was skeletal compared to those of other prisons, but it was arranged much the same. At the top was the warden, who ran the entire prison, both the medium security part and the camp, and under him were assistant wardens. The camp had its own administrator, counselor, and case manager, as well as a few correctional officers who rotated through. At any given time there was seldom more than one CO watching over the whole camp, and never more than two.

For the most part, the camp was self-regulated. The inmates quite literally ran this asylum. We did all the cooking, cleaning, and much of the maintenance work, including groundskeeping. It was camp inmates who plowed the snow on Two Mile Drive in winter and cut the grass in summer. Inmates enforced most of the rules, too, without need of official intervention. Mostly, as at Texarkana, this came down to quietly enforcing social norms of respect and manners. Needless to say, 120 men sharing close quarters experienced tensions and tempers sometimes, my own included. But that was about the extent of it. Physical altercations were very rare. No one carried a shiv, as some men had done at Texarkana. The closest thing to a weapon in Otisville were the canes wielded by the arthritic old rabbis.

The most serious disputes in Otisville were in fact mainly among the old rabbis. The more Orthodox they were, the more they argued. Mainly they argued about who should be the Gabbai. The Gabbai ran the shul where they worshipped, settled disputes among the various sects, oversaw the distribution of kosher food, and was de facto top Jew at Otisville. For much of the time I was there, the Gabbai was Meshulem Jacobowitz, a rabbi from a prominent Hasidic family in Williamsburg, Brooklyn, who had been convicted of fraud and bribery. Another rabbi, named Pinter—he was doing time for mortgage fraud—was constantly trying to outmaneuver Meshulem and get himself elected Gabbai. And then there was a rabbi, the former head of a Yeshiva, who was married into a prominent New York real estate family. The rabbi had been arrested after forcing some bad husbands to issue *gets*, or divorce decrees, to their wives. You could not blame him for coming to the aid of long-suffering wives, but the method he used to induce the bad husbands to cooperate was problematic: he tortured them with a cattle prod.

For all their internecine battles, the Jews closed ranks when it was in their interest to do so. They'd achieved amazing political leverage by doing this and, as a result, enjoyed remarkable accommodations from the BOP regarding both clothing and diet.

It was quite amazing to see what the BOP permitted, especially on Shabbas—Friday evening through Saturday evening—when the Jews brought in feasts of fresh salmon, chicken, vegetables, and fruits—far better than the usual federal fare—along with Jewish delicacies such as gefilte fish and potato kugel. No one held it against the Jews for getting better food, in part because they were so generous to the non-Jews, always saving some of their bounty to share with the rest of the camp.

The most remarkable displays of Jewish solidarity came when a fellow Jew was perceived to be mistreated. An example of this occurred early in my time at Otisville when a new CO, who did not quite understand how matters stood at Otisville, busted Rabbi Naftali Schlesinger for possession of a blender. A Hasidic Jew of Hungarian origin, Schlesinger was about 85 years old, but he was one of the toughest and most argumentative men in Otisville. He passed a lot of his time barking at fellow Jews for being too lax in their practice. Anyone who disagreed with him about anything, gentile or Jew, he accused of anti-Semitism. One evening not long after I arrived at Otisville, Schlesinger was gnawing on a banana in the shul when a fellow Jew came in to play the guitar and sing some religious songs. Schlesinger objected to the music. When the guitar player ignored him and kept strumming, Schlesinger started pelting him with pieces of banana.

This brings us to the blender. Bananas were about all that Schlesinger could eat, because he was pretty much toothless. To help with this, his family had smuggled in a blender so that he could pulverize his food. Blenders were contraband under prison rules, but this was the sort of thing the administration generally turned a blind eye to—or so it had, until this officious newbie CO came in, saw the blender, confiscated it, and immediately wrote up Schlesinger with a SHOT—a form that would in most circumstances result in some time in solitary confinement.

Except that was never going to happen. The CO had yet to learn the unwritten rule at Otisville: don't mess with the Jews. No sooner did the SHOT get written up than calls started going out from the pay phones at Otisville to the outside world. Then the calls started coming into the warden—from irate rabbis, strong-arming politicians, aggrieved family members. Inmates took bets on how much time would pass before the SHOT got ripped up.

The odds-on favorite was half an hour. It took about 25 minutes. The new CO was reprimanded for being an idiot, Schlesinger got his blender back, and life went back to normal.

■ ■ ■

After a few months of dorm life in the administration building, I was moved to a cubicle—or cube, as we called them—in the main building. I had more privacy and a space, albeit small, to call my own. My bunkmate was Eduardo, born in the Dominican Republic and raised in New York City. It was Eduardo who had spent six and half years at Brooklyn MDC before getting transferred to Otisville. Somehow he not only survived the experience, but came out a sane and decent guy.

Just as I had at Texarkana, I fell into a routine at Otisville that centered around exercise, reading and my assigned work shift. (My first job was setting up the visitors' room, but that did not amount to much, as the man who already did the job preferred to do it alone.) In the evenings I watched the news and some other television, then went back to reading. Many men passed the time playing cards, but I avoided this, along with other games, even chess and backgammon. I saw too many men get upset when they lost, especially if they had money riding on the outcome. Not worth it.

I tried to mind my own business and stay out of conflict. I commandeered a plastic chair in the chapel, a small building across the lawn from the main building. I had it mostly to myself during the week, when I went there to read the papers in the morning. Later, friends began to call on me there, and we'd talk about the news of the day and prison gossip or anything else that came to mind.

One of my best friends at Otisville arrived a short time after me. His name was Walter Forbes. I'd met Walter years earlier on a golf course in Scotland. Seven years older than I, Walter had been CEO of Cendant Corporation before his arrest for conspiracy to commit securities fraud. Chris Christie, U.S. Attorney for the District of New Jersey at the time (and later governor), came down hard on Walter. He was sentenced to 12½ years and a $3.3 billion restitution, the largest in history until Bernie Madoff's

$170 billion restitution. After serving the first half of his sentence in Allenwood, Pennsylvania, Walter had come to serve the last half at Otisville.

Walter was a great guy who had been pilloried by an ambitious politician, a fact he handled with an admirable lack of bitterness. While he did not deserve to be in prison, his arrival at Otisville improved my life immeasurably. We had a number of mutual friends and mutual interests and lots to talk about.

■ ■ ■

Forbes was someone I might have been friends with on the outside, but many of my friends in Otisville were folks I never would have met had it not been for prison. One of these was Sal Romano. Sal and his brother Vincent were both in Otisville—one of several pairs of brothers in the camp, as it happened. Their family, from Long Island, had run afoul of the law for selling rare coins to collectors for wildly inflated prices; four Romano brothers altogether were convicted of fraud. The oldest brother, Joe, was doing life in maximum security prison after attempting to hire a hitman to kill, by beheading and other mutilation, the judge and prosecutor who put him in jail. Unlike his psychopathic older brother, Sal was a sweetheart, as kind and generous as a man could be. Sal took over my weight training after Hector left Otisville. He got up with me every morning at 7:00 to lift. He would accept no money—or mackerel, or anything else—as compensation. During our workouts we got to know each other well and became close.

Another of my friends was known to me only as K. I never knew K's full first name or his last name. He was one of numerous Russians at Otisville. He never told me exactly what he was in for, and I never asked, but over time it came out that he had been some kind of enforcer for the Russian mob. He knew martial arts and looked like he could take down an oak tree if he cared to.

But the strongest guy in Otisville camp, hands down, was Russell. Born in Israel, Jewish, but not too serious about it, Russell was a huge mass of muscle covered in tattoos. He was also smart, funny, and one of the most generous men at Otisville. One of his acts of goodwill was helping out an inmate named Levi

Deutsch. Deutsch had cerebral palsy and needed assistance but did not want to get transferred to a BOP medical facility, where his life would be greatly diminished. (BOP medical facilities are to be avoided at all costs.) Russell's goodwill helped this man to stay in Otisville.

Some men end up in prison because they are just plain awful human beings. There were a few of them in Otisville. One guy in particular comes to mind. Covered in eczema, his lips perpetually turned up in a snarl, he was always on the verge of losing his temper and was rude by default. Once, when he was being especially obnoxious, I told him he was a "lying rat motherfucker." I'm not proud I said it, but it happened to be a pretty accurate description of the man.

Usually, though, the men were more like Russell, which is to say: complicated. The general public may not have time to distinguish among the various levels of wrongdoing of men who end up in prison, but those of us who have served time know there is at least as much human variety inside as outside. One of the things I did to keep myself entertained in prison was take notes on the men I met, one-page thumbnail sketches I wrote down in a marble-covered notebook. When I look through these notes now, I see the phrases 'heart of gold' and 'dumb as a rock' or 'total rat' appear pretty frequently. Otisville had every manner of nut job, bullshit artist, and sleazebag. But we also had warm and generous and even brilliant men that you'd be happy to know in any context. Sometimes all these qualities appeared in the same man.

■ ■ ■

Because we were a relatively mature prison population, and mostly non-violent offenders, we were calmer and better behaved than a general prison population. We were lucky to be in Otisville, and few of us took chances that might get us kicked out. That said, some men did take risks. Small risks, mostly. A few ounces of smuggled prosciutto, for example, or Parmesan cheese or salami. Families would hide the contraband in the woods below the soccer field when they came to visit, and later, after dark, an inmate would stroll down the road and grab it.

Most of the CO's ignored this sort of thing, but one CO was an exception to the rule. His name was Fiela, but everybody called him Fife behind his back, as in Barney Fife from *The Andy Griffith Show*. A reedy-looking guy with a shrill voice, he resembled Fife to a T, and he had the same eager-beaver approach to fighting crime. The greatest infraction in Fife's view was smoking. He loved nothing more than creeping around the side of the gym to bust guys trying to cop a smoke there. There were tales of Fife hiding in the woods, lying in wait to catch someone lighting up. The funny thing about Fife was that he himself smoked. We'd see him furtively sucking on a cigarette in the parking lot when he thought no one was looking. His clothes always reeked of tobacco.

Fife's behavior was ridiculous, but not as ridiculous as the behavior of some of my fellow inmates. The same tendency to self-sabotage that I'd witnessed in Texarkana was apparent in Otisville, where it was even more inexplicable. Since we all knew we were lucky to be there, behavior that could get you thrown out made no sense.

It was hilarious the way Fife snooped after smokers, but cigarettes were no joke—they could get a man shipped—and yet a number of inmates smoked them anyway. Stories of alcohol entering camp circulated now and then, too, though I never saw booze or smelled it on anyone's breath. The penalty would have been automatic solitary, followed by transfer. Same with cell phones. I remember one sad case who missed his wife and kids terribly. He got caught with a cell phone he'd procured to talk to them. He was shipped out, now to serve a longer sentence in far worse circumstances.

Even sadder was what happened to Russell, the muscle-bound, tattoo-covered Israeli. One visiting day, Russell helped a fellow prisoner known as Doc smuggle in some food that had been brought by Doc's family. Inside the bag of food, unbeknownst to Russell, was a vial of pills meant to help Doc with his chronic constipation. Smuggling in food was one thing; smuggling in an unapproved medication, even a benign one, was quite another. Russell was just being a mensch and acting as lookout when the hand-off was made in the camp parking lot. Unfortunately, the transaction was done right in the sightlines of a security camera, which recorded the whole thing. The bag was searched, the medication was discovered, and everyone involved was sent to the SHU and eventually shipped out, Russell included.

The story of those who got caught red-handed would not be complete without the sorry tale of Big Red. An African American with a reddish complexion that gave him his nickname, Big Red had a pretty girlfriend he adored. The two of them could not get enough of each other, and the physical separation was intolerable for both. So Big Red's girlfriend started driving up to Otisville for covert trysts. After the 4:00 p.m. count, Big Red would sneak off the camp (not hard to do if you were dumb enough to try it) and duck into her car. They'd go and have sex in the car or in some fleabag hotel, then have a meal together, and then the girlfriend would drive Big Red back to a drop-off spot near the camp, and he'd sneak back in before the 10:00 p.m. count. Six hours of bliss with his girl. What could go wrong?

What went wrong was this: one evening while driving Big Red back to the camp, the girlfriend ran a stop sign. A local police cruiser happened to be there and pulled her over. As the cop asked for her for license and registration, he noticed that Big Red was wearing grey sweatpants. Being a local cop, he recognized the sweats as similar to the sweats that inmates wore at Otisville. So the cop asked Big Red for his ID, too. When Big Red replied that he did not have any ID on him, the cop decided to take the couple to the station to sort things out.

I can imagine the panic that must have gone through Big Red's mind as he watched the clock on the wall close in on 10:00 p.m. and realized he was going to miss the count. As Big Red knew, there are screw-ups the BOP will forgive and even treat with human understanding. Sneaking out of camp and missing the count is not one of them.

We never saw Big Red again.

■ ■ ■

Two facts about the American prison system stood out above all others for me: first, prisoners behave in illogical and self-destructive ways—which is how they (we) end up in prison in the first place, and why so many can't ever seem to get out—but are generally not terrible or disposable people; and second, the entire carceral system is unnecessarily cruel, absurd, and counterproductive.

So much about the system—the plea deals that determine overly long and onerous sentences, the punitive rather than rehabilitative effect of incarceration, the use of arbitrary rules and solitary confinement to discipline prisoners—make no sense as a matter of social policy, much less as a matter of justice. It's not just me saying this—most prison wardens would quietly tell you the same. Failing to give prisoners the tools to survive on the outside by isolating them and demeaning them, for example, is foolish and almost certain to result in high rates of recidivism. Of course—as some wardens will also secretly acknowledge—recidivism is probably not a bad thing from the point of view of the BOP and the various private contractors it hires to oversee inmates. The greater the number of people in prison, the larger the budget of the BOP and the more money the private contractors make.

One of the biggest absurdities I observed was the imprisonment of old people. This was particularly hard to miss in Otisville, with its cane-wielding octogenarians, but it was true in every prison in the United States. U.S. prisons were overpopulated with men who had committed crimes and served reasonable time for them and were now just growing old on the taxpayer's dime. It made sense on every level to let them out of prison to serve out their sentences at home with their families.

From the moment I entered Otisville, I began to ponder this. Though I was still relatively young and in good physical shape—the best ever, in fact—I could see myself in some of the men growing old around me. They were men, like me, who deserved reasonable punishment. But they did not deserve to die alone, far from their families. And the American taxpayer did not deserve to bear the extraordinary cost of supporting people who in many cases eventually required high-priced medical care. One number stood out to me: The average cost to the U.S. taxpayer is $35,000 per year to house and feed an inmate. The average cost for an inmate over the age of 50 is $70,000 per year.

There was a law on the books regarding the compassionate release of aging inmates. Unfortunately, it was a law that only emphasized the absurdity of the federal penal system. An inmate could be released to home confinement if he was older than 70 years of age and had served either 75% of his sentence or ten years—whichever was greater. The law made it nearly impossible to qualify for release.

One afternoon I was talking to Rabbi Jacobowitz about this when he told me I needed to meet a visitor who was coming to see him the following week. The visitor's name was Rabbi Moshe Margaretten. He was a young Hasidic firebrand who was devoting enormous energy to prison reform. Interestingly, like many Orthodox Jews, he was a Republican. Prison reform was no longer just a liberal issue; in recent years many conservatives had joined the cause. I met Rabbi Margaretten, liked and admired him, and we started to work together.

One element I could bring to the table was my contacts in Democratic circles. Margaretten had already hired some Republican lobbyists focusing on prison reform. I offered to see what I could do on the Democratic side. I got in touch with a leading Democratic lobbyist, a man I'd known in my previous life, and convinced him to join the effort. I also put the rabbi in touch with sympathetic donors who generously aided the cause.

Then we began to look at the language of the bill that had been passed a few years earlier. It turned out that one of the sponsors of that bill was Senator Rob Portman, a Republican from Ohio. When Portman was shown the language of the bill as it pertained to the elderly, he agreed that it made no sense.

It should have been an easy fix after that. Barack Obama was president and wanted prison reform, the Democrats in the House and Senate wanted it, and now many Republicans wanted it, too. A new bill, known as the Sentencing Reform and Corrections Act, was proposed with bipartisan support in 2015 and made great headway. In the end, though, Mitch McConnell and the Republicans decided to kill it, more for reasons of politics than policy. They did not want to pass a bill that Obama could sign into law and claim as a victory.

We'd have to try again. Little did we know that our success would depend on the improbable election of an ultra-conservative, pro-prison president by the name of Donald Trump.

■ ■ ■

The entire time I was in prison no one ever cared or even brought up the fact that I was of Iranian descent. Not the good old boys in Texas, and not the Orthodox Jews in Otisville. They may have hated the Iranian regime, but they did not lump me into their negative feelings.

I can't say the same about the fact that I was a Democrat. Everybody seemed to know my political affiliation, and many would joke about Democrats in a humorous and bantering way. As the elections of 2016 heated up, I took an informal poll at Otisville. I discovered that more than 75% of inmates, and nearly 90% of staff, wanted Trump from the start. Granted, the residents of Otisville were not a cross-sampling of the American population, but the enthusiasm for Trump was so overwhelming I knew it could not be dismissed. Hillary Clinton had her work cut out for her.

The night of the election, as it became clear which way things were going, the CO on duty—a big Trump supporter—got on the PA system to razz me. "Hey, Nemazee, get used to it! President Trump! President Trump! President Trump!" The words were hard for me to say. But good things sometimes happen in mysterious ways.

31

CUMBERLAND

THE FOG PRESSED UP TO THE WINDOW, so thick that I could hardly see the tree line ten yards away. I looked at the clock again: it was just after 8:30 a.m. Kamyar would be close to Otisville by now, off the interstate and into the back roads. Soon he'd be driving up Two Mile Drive and pulling into the parking lot across from the main prison, arriving to pick me up at 9:00 for our long drive to Cumberland. Rather than find me waiting for him as planned, though, we'd both be staring at the fog and waiting.

Seven hours. That's what the BOP had granted me—a 7-hour furlough on this Monday in autumn to complete, according to MapQuest, a five-hour drive. In essence, this was seven hours of freedom. Originally, I'd been granted 9 hours, but then the warden, in his infinite prickish wisdom, had decided that was two hours too many and cut it back. Still, seven hours away from prison was nothing to scoff at. Seven hours with no rules, no counts. Seven hours to chill with my son. The only catch: I had to self-surrender at Cumberland at 4:00 p.m. This time was non-negotiable—a minute late, I'd be counted as absent. The sooner we left Otisville, then, the more time we'd have together.

And then came this damn fog. Weather could be dicey at the top of the hill at Otisville, bringing snow squalls, freak hailstorms, rain torrents, and, often, fog. Of all these, fog was the worst, and autumn was the worst season for it. When fog rolled in, the warden shut down the entire prison, including the camp, the way a lifeguard shuts down a swimming pool at the first reports of lightning. The problem with fog from the warden's perspective was that it made inmates hard to see, so the CO's lost visibility of inmates outside. Therefore, no one could go outside until the fog lifted. And every minute the fog lasted cut into the hours with my son.

"Looks like it's a clearing a little." This was Morales, the CO on duty. Slight but wiry—he competed as a triathlete in his free time—Morales was one of the good ones. In part, this was probably because his own father had served some time on Rikers Island, the notorious jail in New York City, so he had some empathy for inmates. He was no pushover, but Morales treated us with fairness and kindness. Now he peered out the window from his desk. "As soon as we get the all-clear, I'll drive you over." The distance was only a few hundred yards, but Morales knew that every minute mattered to me.

"I appreciate that."

"No problem. Just send us a postcard from Cumberland."

■ ■ ■

Cumberland had been a long while coming. I'd now done five years in Otisville, and it was time to get my Residential Drug Abuse Program (RDAP) done with, so I could qualify for my one-year sentence reduction. Because Otisville did not offer RDAP, I had to go to a facility that did. There were about 80 of these in the country, but only 20 or so were minimum security camps. I'd originally set my sights on the prison camp in Miami, figuring that I might as well do RDAP in a warm environment after enduring five Otisville winters. But just as I was starting to fill out my request, a man who had been at Otisville before transferring to Miami wrote to a friend at Otisville. The program in Miami was awful, he wrote, and the camp was even worse.

Around this time, a Russian named Isaac arrived at Otisville, having just completed RDAP at FCI Cumberland. Isaac recommended Cumberland highly, both the prison and the RDAP. Many RDAPs were known to be grueling, but Cumberland, said Isaac, was a piece of cake. Near the western edge of Maryland, Cumberland was no Miami weather-wise, but it was a lot closer to home, a mere five-hour drive from New York City. I started my forms over and this time requested transfer to Cumberland.

After my approval came through, I applied and was granted a furlough to travel from Otisville to Cumberland. The BOP often granted brief travel furloughs to low-risk prisoners serving long sentences. When the furlough came through, my son, Kamyar, volunteered to make the drive. Five hours of driving time, two extra hours to have a meal or otherwise enjoy freedom with my son. Assuming, that is, the fog ever lifted.

At last, it did, suddenly dissolving into the trees. An announcement on the PA system told us we were clear to go outside. The time was a quarter to nine. I lifted my bag and Morales stood. "Let's get you out of here."

■ ■ ■

At the bottom of Two Mile Drive, Kamyar paused at the stop sign and handed me a thin rectangular wafer of brushed steel and glass.

"What's this?"

"It's an iPhone."

The iPhone had been come onto the market a year before my arrest but had been a pretty rare commodity in 2010, when my Blackberry was the closest thing to a smartphone I'd seen.

"The girls want to FaceTime you."

"FaceTime?"

Kamyar laughed. He took the phone back from me. "You're going to like this." He touched the screen, and a few seconds later I saw my daughter Layla smiling back at me from her apartment in London.

"Hi, Dad," she said.

Over the next half hour, driving through the back roads in the passenger seat of the rental car, I got to see and talk with both of my daughters, as well as laugh with Yasmine's three children— two girls and a boy—all of whom had been born while I was in Otisville. It was an incredible experience.

Kamyar and I fell back into our usual easygoing, bantering relationship. We did not speak about anything serious. We were just happy to be together. Sitting side by side in a car for hours took away the pressure imposed by official prison visits, when time was limited and everyone felt a need to fill it. We crossed the Delaware River and drove through the pretty countryside of western Pennsylvania, through Scranton and Wilkes-Barre.

We made it to Cumberland with an hour to kill and parked in the downtown pedestrian area. We walked a little to stretch our legs, then found a table at a pleasant outdoor café. I don't remember what we ate or what we talked about, and it did not matter. Every minute was pure pleasure. And then, all too soon, it was time for me to surrender myself back into custody. We got into the rental car, and Kamyar drove me to the front door of the main prison.

A few years earlier, saying goodbye would have been torture, but we were both old hands at this now. Furthermore, I was heading into the last stretch of my sentence. The light at the end of the tunnel was still distant, but it was getting brighter.

■ ■ ■

Like Otisville, Cumberland was a minimum-security camp adjacent to a higher security prison. Also like Otisville, Cumberland had no bars or fences around the camp. But there were big differences. Physically, the buildings at Cumberland were newer and more substantial. And the culture at Cumberland was worlds away from Otisville. This became clear to me that very first day, when I walked into the central courtyard of the camp and saw a group of young black men smoking cigarettes. No one would have dared smoke in the open at Otisville. I was stunned.

Later, I'd see other things that surprised me at Cumberland, such as open consumption of alcohol and wide use of cell phones. The men in Cumberland were younger and more cavalier than the inmates of Otisville and far more willing to do what they pleased, damn the consequences. As I'd come to understand, the administration here was laxer and the staff was lazier. This laziness would become especially apparent when I began the RDAP program.

I'd hoped to begin RDAP immediately upon entering Cumberland, but that was not to be. There were three overlapping classes per year, each lasting about nine months and comprised of about 30 inmates. My expectation was to enter the session commencing in October. Unfortunately, this session turned out to be over-subscribed, so I had to wait until the next one began in January.

While I waited to go into the RDAP program, I was assigned to a cube in a section known as P-Building, filled mostly with young men serving time on drug convictions. The cubes at Cumberland were larger than at Otisville; rather than one bunk and two men, my cube had two bunks and four men. Sharing a small space with three other men was not ideal, nor was the unit of the prison where I was assigned. The prevalence of young men meant loud voices and less than perfect hygiene.

I immediately resolved to occupy my time productively, just as I had done in Texarkana and Otisville. According to my logbook, the day after my arrival I walked four miles, did 30 pull-ups and 100 push-ups, and read the entirety of an odd little book called *In the Garden of Martyrs*. My logbooks were how I measured time; and time, according to my logbooks, began the day I entered prison. On the top of every page I wrote the year, starting my first full day at Texarkana—Saturday, August 28, 2010—and the week. I was now in week five of year seven. Which made it the last week of September of 2017.

Along with staying busy I tried, as always, to steer clear of conflict and trouble. This proved difficult. Fairly early into my stay, I had an encounter in one of the TV rooms that could have gotten me thrown into the SHU, if not into the infirmary.

It occurred when I tried to watch a Yankees playoff game on TV. As a new arrival at Cumberland, I had no seat in any of the TV rooms, but a black inmate I'd become friendly with—his name was Big Mike—offered me his seat so I could watch the Yankees. When another inmate, known as Fat Tony—he was about as wide as Big Mike was tall—came in and saw me sitting in Big Mike's seat and watching the Yankees, he turned to me and said loudly, "What the fuck are you doing in Big Mike's chair watching this shit?"

Like Big Mike, Fat Tony was from Baltimore, and apparently not a New York fan. I don't know if it was my mere presence in the TV room that filled him with fury, or if Fat Tony just hated the Yankees, but it looked like he was ready to come at me with his considerable heft. I stood up. I had no intention of getting into a fight over a baseball game; on the other hand, I'd defend myself if I had to.

Fortunately, it did not come to that. Big Mike had overheard Fat Tony yelling at me and came into the TV room. The two men were not only fellow Baltimoreans; they were also co-defendants in whatever drug case had brought them to Cumberland. Big Mike was clearly the alpha in this duo. "What the fuck you shouting at?" he shouted at Fat Tony. "Shut the fuck up and let my man Hassan watch the game. He's my *guest*."

Fat Tony looked at Big Mike, then he looked at me. "Why the fuck didn't you tell me?"

"I was trying—"

"Everybody just shut the fuck up," Big Mike interjected, "and watch the damn game."

That was one near miss. Another came a few weeks later, when I woke up in the middle of the night to see a dim blue glow in our cube. I traced the source of the light to a small chair next to my cot. It was coming from under a jacket. When I lifted the jacket, I saw a cell phone. The phone was plugged into an outlet, charging. The hairs went up on the back of my neck.

As lax as Cumberland seemed to be about contraband, a cell phone on a chair in a cube was practically begging for attention. If a CO saw it, he would likely throw all four of us in the SHU while the administration sorted out whose phone it was. I'd seen this movie before: everyone gets punished, and if someone does not come forward and take the blame, the punishment is equally applied to everyone. We'd all be in the SHU for weeks, and I'd almost certainly be thrown out of RDAP and facing an extra year in prison.

You have four options in a situation like this. You can ignore the phone and go back to sleep and hope for the best. You can snitch to a CO and get someone in trouble. You can quietly unplug the phone, find somewhere to toss it, and then pretend you never saw it. Or you can do what I did, which was get out of bed and walk down to the other end of the unit and wake up Gennario Blaylock.

Despite a name that made him sound like a character in a spy novel, and despite being younger than most of the men on the floor, Blaylock was the shot caller in the unit. He was strong, cool, charismatic, and respected by all. We'd become friendly after I gave him a book he enjoyed about the history of Jeff Bezos and Amazon. Then I gave him one on Google, which he liked even more. I knew he was the guy to handle this.

Blaylock was in his cot, top bunk, asleep. I tapped his shoulder and he opened his eyes. I did not want to wake up his cube-mates, so I just motioned for him to come with me. He got out of his bunk and climbed down. "There's a fucking cell phone in my cube," I said quietly when we were out of his cube.

When we got to my cube, I pointed at the cell phone. Blaylock understood at once. He took the phone and dealt with it. Later, he told me he was grateful that I did not go with option three and toss the phone, or option two and get someone in trouble. Generally, cell phones like this, although owned by one man, were passed around and used by many others, for a small fee. It gave inmates a way to talk without time restrictions or worrying about the BOP listening in on their calls. Cell phones were dangerous contraband but they were highly valued.

The cell phone, as it turned out, had been borrowed by the older black man who occupied the lower bunk across from mine. He was good guy, and seemingly sensible, but this was a stupid thing to do, and I told him so. He swore up and down that if he'd gotten caught, he would have taken the blame.

"Sure," I said. "But by that time, we'd all have been in the SHU for a week. You want to put yourself in that position, that's up to you. But you can't put the rest of us in there with you."

■ ■ ■

After a few months in Cumberland, I had the good fortune to fall into a good work assignment when I met the inmate who ran the camp library. He told me he'd just lost an assistant and asked me to assume the evening shift, 4:30 to 8:00. Eventually, after he left, I took over as head librarian. It was an ideal prison job for me. For one thing, it came with a desk. This was a great place to read when things were not busy, or do some writing. The job also gave me command of the remote for the library television—if I wanted to watch CNN, no one could complain. Best of all, the job provided an opportunity to meet and get close to some of the younger men in the camp, who normally would have kept a distance from me. The library was a neutral space where people lowered their guards and dropped their tribal identities for a while. It was a kind of safe space.

Funny thing in Cumberland, as I came to discover, was that many of the young black men assumed I was Italian mafia. They thought my last name was Italian—DiMasi—and took me for an "OG", or original gangster. This was not necessarily a bad thing, as it got me a certain amount of respect, but it tended to make them wary. Gradually, though, some of them came to know me. A young guy would come into the library, and I'd ask him what he was looking for. Sometimes it was a book about the law, but more often it was a book about business, such as the books about Amazon and Google that I'd given to Blaylock. What the outside world usually fails to recognize about inmates is that many of them are not only smart, they are curious and ambitious. Sometimes their ambitions outpace their educations, but they are willing to be educated. Many of them, especially the ones in for drug operations, are essentially misdirected entrepreneurs. They fell into drug dealing because it was the only business available to them.

One of the young men I got to know in the library, funny enough, was Fat Tony. He and I had gotten off to a rocky start in the TV room, but later it turned out neither of us was quite the asshole we mistook the other for. Tony had an interesting dream for what he wanted to do when he got out: he planned to buy up some real estate in Baltimore and get others in the neighborhood to invest. Tony figured he and his friends could acquire delinquent houses for pennies on the dollar, fix them up, then rent them cheaply, not only bringing back families to the neighborhood with good affordable housing, but allowing Tony and his crew to become legitimate businessmen, doing good and doing well at the same time. It was an admirable if quixotic scheme. I told Tony what I knew of real estate and steered him to resources that could help.

■ ■ ■

RDAP finally commenced in February of 2018. The program required participants, some 90 of us, to live in a distinct residential section, separated from the rest of the prison population. Fortunately, I was moved into another wing of P-Unit. This was an improvement, quieter, calmer, and cleaner.

The following Monday, I met with my incoming "class" at 7:00 a.m. for my first session of TC, or Therapeutic Community. We sat in several rows in a large U-shaped formation. Front and center, looking back at us, was the director of the program, a middle-aged white woman whose flat greeting and humorless disposition immediately clued us into the fact that she had better places to be. She read some literature to us in a soporific drone, then handed out some booklets that we were to use for our homework. The only part of her presentation that she got animated about was letting us know the penalties for screwing up.

Later, we separated into smaller groups for PT—Program Therapy. This would be the daily schedule—first TC in the visiting room, then PT in the chapel, then lunch. That was the schedule in theory, anyway. But it turned out there was a wide space between RDAP in theory and RDAP in practice.

Nominally, RDAP is run on an approach called Cognitive Behavioral Therapy, or CBT, that treats unhealthy mindsets and behaviors. It's based on the assumption that the best way to catalyze positive personal growth is to change thinking patterns. The therapy begins, at least as employed by RDAP, with critical self-analysis. You are made aware of certain patterns of "distorted thinking" that contribute to both your addiction and to your crime (RDAP tended to see these as manifestations of the same problem). Supposedly, by becoming aware of the flaws in your personality—narcissism and self-aggrandizement being the two biggest—you can cure them. The BOP purports that this is all "evidence-based" and results in a 15% reduction in recidivism.

It all sounds pretty reasonable in theory. Based on my experience, though, there are some problems in practice. These start with the staff who run RDAP. Outside of prison, CBT is generally administered by highly-trained psychologists. In prison, it's more often implemented by BOP employees with only a rudimentary understanding of, much less interest in, human behavior. Inmates I know who have undergone RDAP have often experienced the therapy as an almost sadistic effort to break them down by raining verbal abuse on them. This can be belittling and humiliating. It's also coercive, since participants have no choice but to take the abuse and pretend that it's helping. They could quit RDAP, of course, but then they'd be looking at an extra year of prison. So in effect a prisoner's inability to react as required to the therapy would result in additional time served.

I never saw the extreme cruelty in Cumberland's RDAP that I heard about in other RDAPs, but the rules of the program actually *required* participants to criticize each other. Every day we had to give fellow group members "push-ups" and "pull-ups." A push-up was a compliment—a high five for doing something positive, such as helping another inmate. A pull-up, on the other hand, was a criticism. It might be calling someone out for butting in line, say, or for walking on the grass, or something worse, like smoking or drinking. We were told that anything we said would stay within the confines of the group, but no one really believed this. In any case, no one wanted to rat out fellow inmates. Push-ups were easy; pull-ups were hard. According to the rules of RDAP, we had to give equal numbers of each. As always, the penalty for failing to comply was expulsion from the program. We came up with a way around the pull-ups. We agreed in advance of meetings on some minor offenses to toss at each other. Thus, we met our quota of pull-ups, but no one got hurt.

All in all, though, this was therapy by coercion, which completely derailed any possibility of trust between the patients and the therapists. If RDAP really worked as well as the BOP claims, then I'd say fine, it's worth it. A 15% reduction in recidivism is not great, but it's something, and any reduction in addiction is hard to argue with. Based on my admittedly limited experience, though, I suspect that the whole program is a boondoggle erected on a foundation of bullshit.

In part, the problem is built in. Because RDAP is the only way to reduce sentences in federal prison—there is no parole, no reduction for pursuing an education or learning a skill— inmates and lawyers have learned over decades to game it. The great majority of participants could care less about the therapy— they just want to get out of prison. You can't blame the inmates for this. If the federal system offered any other legitimate ways to reduce prison terms, RDAP would immediately have more credibility.

Worse than convicts taking advantage of RDAP, though, was prison officials taking advantage of it. I can only speak of what I learned from fellow inmates and experienced myself; there may be a facility somewhere in America using the RDAP program successfully. But the sad truth seems to be that some prison officials take advantage of it as a way to collect easy paychecks.

RDAP is supposed to take 500 hours to complete. I counted no more than 50-70 hours of program time at Cumberland. I understand that this is not the case in other RDAP programs; and, frankly, it was my good fortune that the Cumberland program was so easy. Better a lazy RDAP instructor than a sadistic one. But from a societal point of view, the crime was how tax dollars were wasted by the BOP.

■ ■ ■

All of this brought me back to focusing on prison reform, and especially about reform regarding elderly inmates. Like so much of what the BOP did, incarcerating older men and women who were not violent offenders and had served a considerable portion of their time made no sense. Overhauling the entire federal prison system was necessary but not likely to happen anytime soon. Changing smaller pieces of it was entirely possible and well worth the effort.

It is often the case that a liberalizing reform that has no chance during a Democratic administration finds fresh life in a Republican administration, and so it was under Trump. Considerable numbers of conservatives had started joining liberals in embracing prison reform. A new bill, called the First Step Act, had been proposed in Congress with bipartisan support. The main player behind the First Step Act inside the White House was Jared Kushner, President Trump's son-in-law. Kushner had a personal interest in the issue, as his own father had served 14 months in federal prison for tax evasion and other crimes. As I learned from Rabbi Margaretten, with whom I'd stayed in close contact after leaving Otisville, Kushner was working hard behind the scenes to influence his father-in-law, while quietly lobbying conservative politicians on the Hill to pass the First Step Act. For the first time in years, there was real hope of change.

Meanwhile, quite unexpectedly, an extraordinary change occurred in my personal life.

32

FIRST STEPS

In March of 2018, Morad Ghorban drove out from Washington, D.C. to visit me in Cumberland. Morad was the political director at IAPAC, the organization I'd co-founded in 2002 to promote and fund political involvement by Iranian Americans. Years earlier, I'd brought Morad to work at IAPAC and never regretted it for a moment. We'd stayed in touch during my incarceration, and I always enjoyed hearing his updates on the work of IAPAC. Now, that Sunday in early spring, we sat in the visiting room and talked about our lives, politics, and of course about IAPAC. I asked Morad to fill me in on the current board of directors.

This is how Nazie Eftekhari's name came up. Nazie, as mentioned in an earlier chapter, was a prominent businesswoman from Minneapolis, founder and CEO of a highly successful healthcare company. Some years earlier, Nazie had joined the board of IAPAC. This was coup for IAPAC, as she was not only politically engaged and connected but was from the Midwest, a region of the country under-represented on the board. Nazie and I had met a few times in person, at board meetings and various other IAPAC functions. I'd enjoyed talking with her and found her warm and engaging, not to mention attractive, but we always met in a strictly professional way.

And then came my arrest, my lost year at home, and my trial. When my lawyer suggested that we gather letters of support from people who knew me, my family reached out to members of the IAPAC board, including Nazie. She responded with her extraordinary letter—one of the letters that Judge Stein focused on and found so moving that he read an excerpt of it into the record.

"Wait," I interrupted Morad when he mentioned Nazie. "I never thanked her. I need to do that." Eight years had passed since my trial. Nazie had probably forgotten she'd even written a letter, but she was one of those people for whom I had real gratitude. It was never too late to say thank you. "Do me a favor. Find her address for me when you get back to D.C. and email it to me. I'd like to write her."

That same evening, Morad sent me an email with Nazie's address in Minneapolis. The following morning, I wrote my letter. "Dear Nazie," it began, "I have been remiss." I went on to tell her how much her letter of support had meant to me and how grateful I was to her for writing it.

According to prison rules, I had to indicate on the envelope that my letter came from inside FCI Cumberland. Nazie later admitted that when she received a letter from a prison, she was nonplussed. But then she recognized my name and opened it with interest. In my letter, after apologizing for the delay in thanking her, I told her how much her letter to the judge had meant to me. I followed this with a brief description of my life in prison, ending on the news that I would be released within the year.

I had not expected a response, so it was a nice surprise when I received a letter from Nazie a couple of weeks later. I immediately wrote back, then Nazie immediately responded again. A few letters in, she asked me if I had access to email. I added her to the list of people with whom I could have email correspondence and we began emailing. Emails in and out of prison take a lot longer than emails on the outside, because each one, outgoing or incoming, is subject to review by the BOP. Still, email was a lot quicker turnaround than snail mail. We could communicate more frankly and immediately. I told her about life in prison—what I'd learned from my fellow inmates, the challenges, but also the unexpected rewards of my life, and my hopes for when I was released.

"I'm not sure I remember what your voice sounds like," Nazie wrote in one of her emails. "Can we talk on the phone?"

A few days later, we spoke. There is no calling *into* a prison, so I placed the call. Nazie still remembers that first phone call, starting with a jarring recorded message that informed her she was receiving a call from a federal inmate. But after I came on the line, our voices were familiar to each other at once, and we spoke easily and comfortably.

Nothing more unexpected had ever come my way. Nazie was a gift from heaven. We talked about everything under the sun that spring and summer. Our lives. Our childhoods. Iran.

Nazie had grown up in Tehran but, like many children of affluent Iranian families, had been sent to boarding school in Britain at young age. She'd done a year of schooling in Shiraz at Pahlavi University before coming to the United States to finish her education. Nazie was five years younger than I, so we'd been in different social circles, but our worlds and interests had overlapped in numerous ways. I learned that Nazie had been married and divorced years earlier and had two wonderful adult children. I learned about her business and her struggles to become the extremely successful CEO of her own company, and I learned about her deep investment and interest in American politics.

Our daily talks became my greatest and most constant source of pleasure. So when Nazie told me she'd like to visit me at Cumberland, I could not have been more pleased.

■ ■ ■

Her first visit came on a weekend in September. She flew into the Greater Cumberland Regional Airport from California, where'd she been doing business, and spent the night in a local chain hotel. By now we'd spoken many times on the phone and had exchanged many more emails, but this would be our first in-person contact since before I went to prison some ten years earlier.

The morning of her visit I waited in my cube to hear my name on the PA letting me know that she'd arrived. Visiting hours began at 8:00 a.m., but at 10:00 a.m. I was still waiting to hear my name. Then I had to stay in place for the count. Still no Nazie. I began to wonder if something had gone wrong. Had she decided not to come at the last minute?

Finally, before 11:30, I got the call. I went to the visiting room, and there she was, waiting for me, smiling, looking every bit as beautiful as I'd recalled. I did notice, though, that she was wearing an unusual outfit that included a baggy skirt over leggings.

"Sorry I'm late," said Nazie. "But it took you eight years to write me, so I guess we're even."

She explained what had happened. She'd arrived early that morning, but when the female CO in charge of the visiting room saw her leggings, she told Nazie that she was not appropriately dressed for a prison visit. In fact, as Nazie politely tried to the point out to the CO, there was nothing at all inappropriate about the leggings, as they were covered below the hips by a long shirt. But the CO was adamant. "You can't wear yoga clothing here. Prison rules."

"It's not yoga clothing," said Nazie, adding that she'd just flown 2,500 miles to be here and wouldn't the CO please make an exception?

But the CO would not budge. Nazie went back outside to the parking lot. Fortunately, the car she'd hired to drive her to the prison was still there. Nazie jumped in and told the driver to take her back to town. In downtown Cumberland, she quickly found the only clothing store that was open early on a Saturday morning. It happened to be a Goodwill thrift store. From a rack she grabbed a used skirt that she thought might fit—price $5.00—and jumped back into the car. She returned to the prison wearing the skirt over her leggings. "Okay," said the CO when Nazie returned. "That's better."

Not the entrance she'd planned to make, but beautiful and elegant nonetheless. I don't recall what we talked about, but I remember that I enjoyed every moment of conversation. That evening, Nazie went back to her room in a chain hotel in town, then she came back the next day and spent hours with me. It was a wonderful weekend, the first of several more to come that fall.

Thus, our relationship evolved, much like a courtship between teenagers in Persia a century earlier, from written words to chaste in-person visits. The CO was our chaperone. Despite being a nitpicker about Nazie's wardrobe on that first visit, she was willing to turn a blind eye if we sat side by side and held hands, even if this pushed up against prison rules. She also allowed us an embrace at first greeting and another when we said goodbye. These embraces lingered a little longer each visit.

Before Nazie arrived, I'd pretty much tabled any hope or expectation that good things were in my future. I was in my late 60's, had spent nearly decade in prison, been divorced by my wife, and had seemingly lost any chance I had to start my life over in a meaningful way. Friends had promised to help me get on my feet after my release, but I tried to be realistic. Just as I'd seen many men over the years give in to resignation and despair, I'd seen too many let themselves become deluded. I'd heard it all from my fellow inmates: the loving wife they expected to warmly greet them on their release (but who then turned out to have filed for divorce and taken up with another man); the doting children who could not wait be reunited (but who then turned out to be completely AWOL); the elaborate business plans that would make them rich (but which were clearly desperate fantasies). I'd sworn never to give way to either hopelessness or wishful thinking. Would I end up with a job, a place to call my own? Or would I end up sleeping alone on a couch for the rest of my life? I did not pretend to know.

One afternoon that fall, as we held hands in the visiting room, Nazie turned to me and started asking me some pointed questions. "What are your work plans when you get out? Have you thought about where you'll live?" After just a few minutes of discussion, she told me she'd made a decision: she'd set me up with a job and find me a place to live. As I soon came to discover, when Nazie decided to do something, she did it.

■ ■ ■

The First Step Act moved forward haltingly that fall. The bill had passed the House of Representatives in May of 2018, and now it languished in the Senate. Trump remained silent on the bill, but I heard from friends on the outside that the White House, thanks to Jared Kushner's continued efforts, was prepared to support it. The biggest roadblock now was a contingent of conservative Southern senators, namely Tom Cotton, John Kennedy, and Lindsey Graham, who still strongly opposed the bill. Former senator Jeff Sessions also firmly opposed prison reform; he was now running the Justice Department, where he could do plenty to harm the bill.

It wasn't just conservatives who stood in the way. Although liberals are usually in favor of prison reform, many were less than thrilled with a prison reform bill that went through a Republican Senate and would hand a victory to a Republican president. Liberals also disliked the trade-offs that had been made in the bill to garner Republican support. They wanted more sentencing reform than Republicans were willing to grant.

Nazie, along with all the happiness she brought into my life, did everything she could to bring Democrats on board. She had good relationships with Nancy Pelosi in the House (Pelosi was minority leader at the time) and Amy Klobuchar in the Senate, among others. Part of the message Nazie tried to communicate to her Democratic contacts—with my urging—was that this bill constituted a once-in-a-generation opportunity to fix some systemic problems. Was it everything liberals wanted? No. But don't let the perfect get in the way of the good. Half a loaf is better than no loaf.

The midterm elections came and went, and then it was Thanksgiving break. The chances of any bill going through the Senate before the end of the year were looking increasingly slim.

As usual, Thanksgiving was hard in prison, but there was actually much to be thankful for that year. Nazie had come into my life. And even if the First Step Act did not pass, my time in prison was winding down. Adding to this, we got some good news over the holiday weekend, when Trump tweeted that the First Step Act "would be a major victory for all." Trump had spent much of his life as a tough-on-crime hardliner, but now—with a push from Kushner—he was clearly signaling to Senate Republicans that if they passed the bill, he would sign it.

By this time, I'd become the go-to conduit for information regarding the bill. Nearly every man in Cumberland was following its progress closely, including CO's and wardens, and they all came to me for updates. When there was something meaningful to report, I stood up at the start of RDAP meetings and gave announcements. I warned everybody that we'd gotten close once before, in 2015, only to have the bill die at the last minute, so we had to be careful not to get our hopes up too high. As I pointed out, some in the Republican Party were continuing to fight the bill, which made Majority Leader Mitch McConnell reluctant to bring it to the Senate floor. Given that he had only limited floor time to devote to a bill between midterms and the end of the year, the easiest thing for him to do was punt and let the bill wait till the following year.

Then, on December 11th, the dam burst. Under pressure from the White House, McConnell announced that he would allow the bill to proceed after all. The following day, December 12, 2018, Sen. Chuck Grassley of Iowa and Sen. Dick Durbin of Illinois sponsored a revised version of the bill in the Senate. Six days later, the bill passed the Senate, and three days after that, on December 21, in a triumphant ceremony at the White House, President Trump signed the First Step Act into law.

Handing Trump a win had to be difficult for the Democrats, but they had good reason to celebrate. What Trump signed was not a perfect bill by any means, but it was a good bill, and, more to the point, the best bill to be had. It gave relief to thousands of federal prisoners by easing mandatory minimum sentences, lowering sentences for non-violent offenses, placing prisoners closer to families, and adding opportunities for compassionate release.

For me, personally, it was a wonderful bill. A section of it applied directly to my case, mandating release to home confinement for non-violent inmates over 60 who had served at least ten years or two-thirds of their sentence, whichever was less. I was well over 60 and had served well over two-thirds, making me eligible on both counts for immediate release to home confinement.

The bill also recalculated the way the BOP counted good time credit. Previously, the good time credit had been 15% reduction on every year served. As anyone with a calculator knows, 15% of 365 comes to 54 days. But the BOP had found a way to reduce this to 46 days. To understand how they did this is to gain insight into the Kafkaesque mindset of the BOP. Essentially, they removed the 15% *before* they calculated the number of days they would reward. So they were calculating 15% of 311 days, rather than of 365 days. Under the bill, my sentence was instantly reduced by 93 days. My "out-date" had been February 6, 2020. Now it was November 14, 2019.

■ ■ ■

The very day the bill was signed, on the afternoon of December 21, I put in my cop-out. A cop-out was a formal request from an inmate to staff. I'd already filled in the information in anticipation of Trump's signature, including my name, my BOP identification number, and the nature of my request, namely to be released immediately to home confinement, per the First Step Act's provision for elderly release. That same afternoon, I walked my cop-out over to the administration wing of the camp and handed it to the camp administrator.

My cop-out turned out to be even more important than I anticipated when I signed it. That's because the day after Trump signed the First Step Act, and the day after I signed my cop-out, Trump, with his inimitable knack for stepping on his own toes, turned from Santa into Scrooge. He refused to sign a congressional appropriations bill because it did not include $6 billion in funding for his border wall, effectively defunding the government for what would turn out to be the longest shutdown in U.S. history.

Along with handing his foes another reason to bludgeon him, Trump gave the BOP a great excuse to keep folks like me in prison. They could claim that the shutdown made it impossible for them to implement the law. They had good reason to drag their heels, as they were not logistically prepared to abruptly release the thousands of inmates who had qualified for home confinement. Frankly, though, that was their problem, not mine or any other inmate's. To keep us in prison was contrary to both the letter and the spirit of the law.

Fortunately, I had an out. There was a provision in the bill that I'd been lobbying for among my politically influential friends and to people I'd gotten to know, such as Rabbi Margaretten. The provision was this: if an inmate was not released within 30 days of filing a cop-out, he or she could go immediately to a judge for a ruling. If there is one thing I knew about the BOP after all these years, it was that the agency would drag its feet as long as it could. It often took six months for the bureaucracy to respond to the most basic of prisoner requests. I had no doubt it would take even longer to implement the First Step Act—unless, that is, the law expressly prevented it from doing so. I like to believe I played at least a small role in making sure it did.

■ ■ ■

Over Christmas, Nazie and I spoke often about my release. She insisted on hiring me a lawyer, in the likely event that the BOP refused to release me to home confinement. This instantly gave me more leverage than most inmates, 99% of whom had no way to come up with money for a lawyer. Not for the last time I had to count my blessings. With any luck, my good fortune would redound to the benefit of other inmates who qualified for release to home confinement. If I could successfully make the case to a judge for timely release, it would set an important legal precedent.

Thirty days passed slowly. Predictably, the BOP refused to take action on my case. In late January, I filed a motion with Judge Stein, the federal judge who had heard my case in 2010.

If BOP officials had any sense, they would have read the law and realized they had no argument on their side. Still, though, the BOP fought my release, using the excuse of the government shutdown, along with a completely bogus argument that the new law did not kick in until 210 days after Trump signed it. In fact, some of the provisions in the First Step Act were on a delayed track, but the elderly release program was very explicitly *not* one of these. It had become effective the day of signing—December 21, 2018.

A few weeks later, in mid-February, Judge Stein held a hearing in his Manhattan courtroom. I was represented by the lawyer Nazie had hired, and the BOP was represented by a lawyer from SDNY. Because I was one of the first to test the new law, the case garnered some attention, including that of a *New York Times* reporter named Benjamin Weiser. Seeing my case on the docket, Weiser was struck by irony of a former bigwig Democratic donor using a Trump law to seek release. He showed up for the hearing with a few other reporters. Nazie also attended, with two friends.

I could not be there, of course, but the lawyer and Nazie later filled me in. The attorney for the Southern District began his argument by telling the judge that he—Stein—did not have the jurisdiction to decide the case. Not a smart way to begin your argument to a judge, and Stein immediately shut him down. Stein had read the law closely, he told the attorney, and the law was very clear: first, this was a case that fell firmly in his jurisdiction; and, second, the law left no doubt about the conditions for release to home confinement for inmates over 60 who had served more than two-thirds of their time.

Stein gave the BOP two weeks to either come back with a better argument for holding me or to release me. He warned the BOP that if they chose to come back to him with another bad argument, he would probably be forced to make an adverse ruling that would stand as precedent. The BOP would then be faced not just with my immediate release, but also with the immediate release of thousands of inmates who fell within the purview of the First Step Act.

On the afternoon of Thursday, March 14, 2019, shortly before the 4:00 p.m. count, I came in from exercising. As usual, I got into the shower to clean off. I'd just covered myself in soap when I heard my name on the PA, telling me to report to the camp administrator. It was a Thursday, not a visiting day, and weekday announcements over the PA seldom yielded anything good or interesting, so I took my time getting out of the shower. Before I was done, another announcement told me to go to the camp administrator's office immediately. This was either something very bad or something very good. I quickly dried off, dressed, and walked over to the administration offices.

"What took you so long?" the camp administrator asked me when I entered. She handed me a piece of paper. "Time to start packing, Mr. Nemazee. You're outta here in six days."

33

NOWRUZ

WEDNESDAY, MARCH 20, 2019, was the first day of Nowruz, the Persian New Year. Nowruz is the day Persians all around the world celebrate the hope that comes with a new spring. It also happened to be the day I walked out of prison for the very last time.

I was up early. I spent the morning much as I'd spent most of my mornings at Cumberland. After a quick breakfast, I went to the CO's desk to pick up the newspapers that had come in that morning—the *New York Times, Wall Street Journal, Washington Post*, and a few others. My position as head librarian remained in effect until I left Cumberland, and so, as always, I took the newspapers to the library and placed them neatly on the newspaper table. My own copy of the *Financial Times* I took with me to the desk in the back of the library.

My son Kamyar and daughter Layla were coming to pick me up and drive me to New York. Now, as I waited to leave Cumberland, friends came into the library to wish me goodbye and good luck. These farewells had been going on for the last six days more or less constantly, ever since word got out that I'd won my motion and was going to be released. Some of the older men came by for a few words of legal advice so that they might pursue their own releases; the younger men, ineligible for release under the new law, just seemed to hope that my good luck would rub off on them somehow.

What everyone seemed to recognize was that my victory was not mine alone. Later, there would be talk that the First Step Act only benefited white-collar white inmates, but nothing could have been further from the truth. The law applied to *all* federal inmates, and the great majority of these were non-white. My court win paved the way. Almost immediately upon my release, the BOP did what it should have done back on December 22, 2018. It released a policy statement instructing wardens to comply with the First Step Act, effective immediately.

The announcement for me to report to R&D came a little after seven that morning. With a few last handshakes and hugs, I headed out. The town driver—the inmate, that is, who had the job of driving inmates and prison officials to various appointments in one of the official prison vehicles—had offered to drive me to the main building. This was strictly ceremonial, as I could have walked over in a few minutes, but these ceremonies were important to prison life and I was grateful to participate in this one. We drove to the main building, shook hands, and then I stepped out and walked into the building to sign the forms that would complete my release to home confinement. I would walk in, walk out, and then be on my way.

Or so I thought.

"We have a problem," said the burly lieutenant overseeing my release.

Nearly an hour had passed since I'd entered the main building. I was sitting in a holding room when the lieutenant came in to talk to me. He looked somber. I'd never dealt with the guy before and instantly did not like him. He exuded asshole.

"What problem?"

"You've got two cars out in the parking lot. Both say they're here for you."

"There's just my son and my daughter. In one car."

"Yeah, and someone else in another car. You can't have two cars here for you. This is not good."

"Not good?"

"Yeah, we may not be able to let you go."

Later, I pieced together what happened. Nazie wanted me to have clean street clothes to return home in. Since she was not able to meet me in person and take me home herself, she decided to send some clothes, via FedEx, to the driver who picked her up whenever she came to Cumberland. A pair of blue jeans, a nice button-down shirt, clean socks and underwear. The driver brought the clothing to Cumberland on the morning of my release and then waited for me to appear to hand me the clothing. A few spaces away, Kamyar and Layla, having driven out the previous day and spent the night in Cumberland, also awaited my appearance. When asked by prison officials who they were here to see, both cars gave my name.

How this could have taken more than a minute for the BOP to sort out, or why this would have represented anything more than a trifling misunderstanding, is probably not worth the mental bandwidth required to think about it. In any case, the prison officials managed to turn it into a very long and anxious hour for me, as I waited in the holding cell. Finally, the lieutenant came back into the holding cell. He told me I was lucky they'd decided to let me go after all. "Be at the halfway house at 4:30."

■ ■ ■

The drive to New York with Kamyar and Layla was beautiful. It was a cool but sunny day, completely cloudless as we headed east out of Cumberland. Much as when Kamyar had taken me to Cumberland more than a year earlier, we picked up where we left off. There was a lot we could have said—a lot I'm sure my kids might have wanted to say to me—but we were content to simply be together and enjoy each other's company, without a CO in sight. Kamyar drove, I sat in the passenger seat, Layla behind me.

As we drove into the still-rising sun, I looked out the window at the budding trees of early spring, and my mind went back to those many wonderful Nowruz celebrations at the old house on Glenbrook Road, when all of Iranian Washington seemed to pack into our house and my father gave the women and children gifts, and the whole house filled with the scent of Persian spices and the melodies of Persian voices. Those were wonderful days.

But no Nowruz, ever, had been better than this one. Yes, I was still in the custody of the BOP and would remain so until the end of my home confinement, but I was as close to freedom, physically and mentally, as I'd been since my arrest in August of 2009.

"Let's get something to eat," I said after we'd gone a few hours. I was starving—starving with the kind of hunger only someone who has lived on prison food for a decade can truly appreciate.

According to Kamyar's phone, we needed five hours to drive from Cumberland to the BOP halfway house in the Bronx where

I'd been told to check in that afternoon. I had to arrive at the halfway house by 4:30 p.m. So we had a few hours to ourselves. Kamyar pulled off at the next exit and we found a diner.

I'd had the good fortune to eat at the very finest restaurants in New York. But what I'd craved most while in prison was not food from Le Bernardin or Four Seasons. I wanted a hamburger—a real hamburger, which was a very different thing than the damp gray patties of mystery meat they served us in prison. In fact, what I ended up ordering was a bacon cheeseburger, accompanied by a delicious coffee milkshake. Both were delicious. I was 30 pounds thinner than when I'd gone into prison, but I think I put a few pounds back on at the first lunch.

We still had about two and half hours to drive, and about four hours to do it, before I had to report to the Bronx. There was no rush, no pressure. But as we were finishing our meal, something odd happened. Out of the clear blue sky, an enormous cloud suddenly appeared over the diner. Everything turned dark, and then the heavens opened up. It only lasted a few minutes, but in those minutes biblical proportions of rain fell from the sky. The sun was back out as we walked across the flooded parking lot to the car. Kamyar maneuvered us back onto the highway—and right into a traffic jam.

The rain had caused an accident, and the accident caused a total shutdown of the highway. For the next hour or so, we crawled along. All that extra time I'd had to make it to the halfway house evaporated along with the rain. By the time we were on open highway again, the sun was behind us.

■ ■ ■

It was shortly before 4:00 p.m. when we turned off the thruway and drove into the heart of the West Bronx. Following the directions on Kamyar's phone, we found our way to a large, bleak tenement on Creston Avenue, catty-corner to a desolate-looking public park. Kamyar pulled to the curb across the street.

"I'll be right back."

The street was covered in late afternoon shadow. I walked up to a metal door, painted silver. I pressed the button on the wall next to it. A second later, through an intercom, a voice asked who I was. I said my name, a buzzer sounded, and I entered into a dingy foyer. A few steps led up to a landing area. To the left was an office with a few desks, enclosed in thick glass. Three or four staff were in there. I went up to the glass and put my mouth near the small metal grate. "Hassan Nemazee," I announced. "Signing in for home confinement." The man at the nearest desk barely glanced up.

"Too late. Your case manager is gone for the day."

"I was told me I had until 4:30." I pointed to the clock over his head. "It's just after 4:00."

"Yeah, she had some personal business to attend to. She'll be here in the morning."

"My home confinement is supposed to start today. Tonight."

He looked up at me, more bored than irritated. My desire to spend the night at home, rather than in this dismal halfway house, was of no interest to him. "She'll be here tomorrow morning. You have to stay here till then."

I knew arguing with him was waste of time. If the case manager was gone, she was gone.

"I need to tell my kids. Can I go back outside?"

"Sure."

I went back out to the car, where Kamyar and Layla were patiently waiting. I explained the situation. They were disappointed for my sake. I assured them that after eight years in confinement I could handle one more night. Kamyar offered to get me something to eat.

I returned to the halfway house to fill in some forms. By the time I got back to the car, Kamyar had been to a nearby Subway and gotten me a sandwich. I took the sandwich, along with the bag of clothing from Nazie, hugged the kids and then went back into the halfway house.

I needed to call Nazie. She was waiting in the apartment she'd rented for me. I had to let her know what had happened, that I would not be coming home tonight. I picked up the payphone in the lobby. It was dead—no dial tone.

I was still in the lobby when a tall white guy with a shaved head came in through the door. I did not recognize him, but he knew me. "Hassan?" And then I remembered—he'd entered Otisville just as I was on my way out to Cumberland. Now we shook hands. I told him my predicament. "Are there any goddamned phones that work around here?"

"Come with me."

Still carrying my sandwich and clothing, I followed him up a few narrow flights of stairs. We entered the small bedroom he shared. His roommate was out. He handed me a cell phone. Strictly speaking, cell phones were no more sanctioned in halfway houses than in prisons or camps, but they were tacitly condoned, as long as residents were discreet about using them. As he stepped out to give me privacy, I thanked him and dialed Nazie's number.

Nazie picked up on the first ring. When I told her what had happened, she was crestfallen that I was not coming to the apartment. She was also upset that I'd not accepted the offer she'd made to fly me home from Cumberland. Had I done so, all of this could have been avoided.

She was right, of course, but there was nothing I could do about that now. Just one more night, I told Nazie. One more night.

■ ■ ■

They put me in a small room in the back of the building on the first floor. Resigned to my night in the halfway house, I found a few books on a table in the lobby and settled down in the room to eat my sandwich. When I opened up the wrapper, I almost laughed out loud. Kamyar, clever fellow that he was, had placed a few bills—two twenties and a ten—inside the wrapper. I stuck the bills in my pocket, then ate the sandwich.

After that, I changed into the clothing that Nazie had sent to me. The shirt fit perfectly, but the pants ballooned around my waist. I realized that I'd given Nazie the waist of my prison pants, which were sized differently than normal men's clothing. My prison-trim waist was too narrow to support the pants, and I had no belt to hold them up. Well, so be it. The clothing was new and clean and pressed, and I was glad to have it. I lay down on the cot and picked up one of the books.

I'd been reading for a few hours when the door opened and a skinny black guy in a uniform entered. I had not seen him earlier, but he evidently worked for the halfway house. I looked up from my book. "It's your lucky night. You're going home."

Later, I learned what happened from Nazie. After hanging up the phone with me, she'd called a BOP inspector named Mr. Gill. She'd met Mr. Gill some weeks earlier when he'd come by the apartment she was renting. (It was usual protocol for the BOP to visit the premises where prisoners released on home confinement planned to live.) Nazie is a woman who never met a stranger, and by the time Mr. Gill left the two of them were old friends. Now she found his card in her wallet and called him. By the time she was done explaining what had happened to me, no doubt with tears to punctuate her distress, Mr. Gill was assuring her he'd work it out.

It was Mr. Gill, then, who found another case officer, a woman who was a friend of his, to come into the Bronx halfway house deep into the evening and complete the paperwork that would allow me to go. The long and short of it was that I was not spending the night in the Bronx after all, thanks to Mr. Gill and his friend. Even in a bureaucracy that could be as inhumane as the BOP, there were people who acted out of pure kindness and compassion.

The man at the desk of the halfway house was not a shining beacon of either attribute, but he did do me a favor that night. He called a car service and ordered me a ride home.

■ ■ ■

It was a beautiful spring night. We drove past Yankee Stadium on the way into Manhattan, and I remembered all the many wonderful days and evenings I'd spent there with friends and family watching games from a box seat. We joined the flow of traffic on the Harlem River Drive, moving fast on a Tuesday night, then merged into the FDR and raced along the East River, a drive I'd taken thousands of times in my prior life. The city rose before me, soaring and jeweled. I'd now seen the very bowels of the city—the darkest it had to offer—and yet Manhattan had not looked so welcoming since I'd arrived from Tehran at the end of 1978 to start my life over.

The driver turned off the FDR at 63rd Street and headed west, and a few traffic lights later I was back in my old neighborhood. The streets were crowded with people out enjoying a mild spring evening. Everything looked more or less the same as I'd left it, other than the striking fact that half the people I saw were looking down at screens in their hands. That had not been true in 2010.

The driver turned onto Fifth Avenue and pulled up in front of the address I'd given him. It was a doorman building near the bottom of Central Park. After touring a number of properties, this is where Nazie had decided we should live—in a one bedroom in a luxury apartment building on Fifth Avenue. For a guy who had woken up in a bunk bed in a cinderblock cubicle in Cumberland and then spent the last five hours in a bleak tenement in the Bronx, it was quite a change. Kamyar had given me $50. This turned out to be just enough for the car, tip included.

As I stood to rise from the back seat, I had to grab the waist of my loose pants to keep them from falling. I made a cinch with my fist to tighten the waist, then I walked up to the door of the building with as much dignity as it is possible to have while holding up your pants with one hand. A uniformed doorman nodded to me and held the door open.

"Mr. Nemazee to see Ms. Eftekhari," I told the concierge behind a high desk. He reached for the phone. "Don't call up," I said. "This is a surprise." The concierge took a look at me. After deciding that I was not a serial killer on the loose—or a convict just released from prison, for that matter—he decided to trust me.

"26-A. Elevator down on the right."

"Thank you."

Nazie was having a glass of wine with a friend when they heard the knock on the door. It was the friend who opened the door. The friend and I had never met, but she seemed to recognize me the moment she saw me, and her mouth dropped.

"Um, Nazie?" said the friend.

I could see Nazie sitting in the living room. She turned and saw me and a look of confusion flashed over her face, replaced an instant later by a smile. She rose.

"It's you!"

34

HOME

ONE SUMMER AFTERNOON in the early days of my incarceration at Otisville, I was sitting in a plastic chair outside the main building reading a book when another inmate named Weitzman drove by in a golf cart. Weitzman was tall, large framed, and Jewish, and therefore was known around camp—with the usual subtlety of prison nicknames—as "Big Jew." His job at camp was working in the warehouse, where he helped load in food that came to Otisville. This meant that he sometimes had access to a better class of food—the stuff meant for the staff, not the inmates.

On this summer afternoon, as Weitzman drove by me, he called out. I looked up, and he tossed a small dark purple orb in my direction. It took a second after I caught it for me to realize what it was: a plum. I had not seen a plum in four years. The only fruit provided to inmates was bananas and apples and maybe a bland orange now and then. I'll remember the first bite I took of that plum until the day I die. And the second, and the third—pausing a long time between each bite to make it last as long as possible. It was just an ordinary plum, but it was hard to believe anything so fine existed in the world.

That plum is what it felt like to be out of prison in those first weeks at home. It was familiar and natural, yet utterly delicious.

I remember exhaling that first night in the apartment with Nazie. Literally exhaling. A long, slow letting out of the breath I'd been holding for ten years without even knowing it. I'd adjusted well to prison, never felt afraid or anxious, but never fully relaxed either. It is not home, and you don't know how hard it is to be away from home until you are back.

It was incredible how easily Nazie and I slipped into a contented relationship in those first days of my release to home confinement. Before this, our entire relationship had been conducted through the prism of prison. All our communications and time in each other's company had been monitored, and not for a minute had we been left alone. But from that very first evening together in the apartment, as Nazie ordered in Persian food from a local restaurant while I called my kids to let them know I was out, we were comfortable in each other's company. It was as if we'd known each other our whole lives.

Nazie's home and business were in Minnesota, but she stayed with me in New York for a few weeks to help me settle. She found an office for me in a WeWork building and made me an employee of her company, with the job title of Senior Advisor to the Chairman of the Board. My salary was modest but real, and so was the job. Nazie had given it to me to help me get back on my feet, but it was meant to be more than a nominal position. I believed I could play a useful role in strategizing the future of her healthcare company and other various businesses, and I set out to do exactly that. I learned everything I could about her businesses, which included not only the healthcare company, but a number of real estate concerns as well. It was wonderful to be working again and I quickly absorbed myself in the details of Nazie's enterprises.

While I felt liberated in a hundred different ways, I was still far from free. I'd been released to home confinement, which meant I was still under the custody of the BOP. I could go out for work, to see a doctor or lawyer, and for special circumstances, but I was not permitted to walk out into Central Park whenever I felt like it, for example, or to stroll off for an impromptu visit to the Metropolitan Museum of Art. Everything I did had to be submitted and pre-approved by my case manager. Every Monday I went to the halfway house in the Bronx to meet with her. She'd look over my proposed schedule—with time filled in for work at the office, visits to the gym, appointments with a doctor—and unless anything stood out as inappropriate, would sign it.

Other than the limited approved activities, I was expected to be inside the apartment. The BOP kept tabs on me by a landline phone. During the day, calls were random. At night, they came on a schedule, the at-home version of a head count—10:00 p.m., midnight, 6:00 a.m.—to make sure I was home and had not vanished to some foreign country or crack house. For each of these three nightly calls, I had to pick up the phone and verify my name and ID number. I adjusted pretty easily and managed to fall back to sleep, but those middle-of-the night phone calls were difficult for Nazie.

A greater challenge for me, after nearly a decade away from technology, was learning to use my iPhone and the TV remote. The prevalence of cell phones—everyone gazing into their hands as they walked down Fifth Avenue—was the most striking difference between the world I'd left and the world to which I returned. The most maddening difference was how modern life now required me to master a touch screen that could perform a thousand incredible functions but seemed designed to thwart my simple desire to place a phone call. As for TV remotes—how had turning on a television and changing channels become more complicated than piloting a Cessna?

■ ■ ■

None of this, though, came close to the more basic frustrations of trying to reintegrate as a functioning member of society. I came out of prison with no official government ID other than my prison card. My driver's license had expired while I was away, and so had my passport. To get either of those renewed I needed other forms of ID to prove who I was. A prison card did not cut it at the DMV or the U.S. passport office.

It also didn't cut it at the bank. A bank account is one of the first things every ex-convict needs to start life over on release, otherwise he or she will have no way to save money or cash checks. When I went to Capital One to open an account, I was totally transparent about my situation—that I was a former inmate still in home confinement and that my crime had been nearly $300 million in bank fraud. As I was not asking for a loan, merely for a checking account into which I could deposit money, there was no risk to the bank. Initially, Capital One gave me an account, but a short while later the bank closed it.

For me, these were all minor and fairly easily solved hassles. Thanks to my education, my experience, and Nazie's help, I had resources to get over these hurdles. But my experience was the exception that proved the rule, which is that it's extraordinarily challenging for most inmates released from incarceration to re-enter society. The world is filled with traps and Catch-22s that seem almost designed to trip up even the best intentioned and best equipped ex-con. Many of these, incredibly, are laid by the government, despite the fact that it is inarguably in the interest of the government—which is to say, of the people—to have a functioning population of convicts and ex-convicts. While the success of his or her re-entry is the number one predictor of whether a convict will re-offend and end up back in prison, the vast majority of prisoners come out of prison without basic skills that would help them succeed. Federal prisons offer no training to keep them up with changes in technology, which may go through several generations of change over the course of a long sentence.

And that's just technology. Then there's the rest of life: children have been born, children have grown up, spouses have left, friends have moved on, parents have died. There may be no home to come home to when a prisoner gets released to home. It can be a very cold and unfamiliar world for ex-inmates. Many discover that the outside is even harder than the inside.

Again, I was the fortunate exception. The great surprise in my case was how easily I was able to readapt to life outside. Yes, there were some fundamental changes, but the world had not turned upside-down while I was away. Not only did I have Nazie and my children to welcome me, I had friends who embraced me warmly. A small minority of those I'd once considered friends weren't there, but they had never really been friends in the first place. Of my true friends, many had stayed in touch with me through the whole ordeal, and the moment I was out they began calling. Because my weekly work schedule always allowed me time to eat, I reconnected with them over lunches, picking up more or less where we left off.

Shortly after my release, I went to lunch with the four men— plus my son, Kamyar, and a few others—who almost a decade earlier had shared a last cigar with me under the portico of the Hampton Inn before escorting me to the doors of Texarkana. It was wonderful to see them on the other side of my dark journey.

■ ■ ■

In mid-April, three weeks after my release, I was displeased to read an article about me in the *New York Times*. The article itself was not a surprise, but the content was disappointing.

Months earlier, my lawyer had approached me with an inquiry from Benjamin Weiser, the *Times* reporter who had attended the hearing on my release in January. I'd originally declined to talk to Weiser but eventually agreed to answer some questions, provided he focus his attention not on me but on the First Step Act. I was encouraged to believe that if I did not cooperate with the article, it would be done anyway, and it would set me up as an example of how the act benefited white-collar white inmates. I did not intend to be the poster child of this misconception, nor did I want the irony of my release under a Republican administration to get in the way of the real good the First Step Act did for *all* inmates in the federal system.

Needless to say, for all the reporter's assurances to the contrary, the article turned out to be exactly what I feared it would be. It presented me as the privileged beneficiary of the First Step Act. I was not happy, but there was nothing I could do about it. And the truth is that I *was* privileged. I did not intend to sour my good fortune with anger.

■ ■ ■

One of the perks of having Nazie as my employer was that I could legitimately put down dinners—*business* dinners—with Nazie on the schedule I gave to my case manager at the halfway house. I was not pulling the wool over anyone's eyes. My case manager knew about my relationship with Nazie, and as long as I did not abuse the privilege—and as long as Nazie and I actually discussed business, which we did—she let me have a little bit of leash.

So Nazie and I began to venture out as a couple. We'd walk into restaurants I used to frequent before prison and find them not only still extant—never a sure thing in the hyper-competitive world of Manhattan restaurants—but much of the staff still in place and the maître'd's as pleased to see me as they'd been ten years ago. So much had changed, and yet so little.

In these early days, Nazie and I played it cool. We understood that our individual profiles and the way we'd met and fallen in love would make us objects of gossip. Given what I'd been through, this made little difference to me, but for Nazie's sake I wanted to keep our relationship quiet for the moment. Along with all the other pressures we were facing, we did not need to put ourselves under the spotlight.

We thought we'd been pretty successful in our attempt to keep our relationship quiet until one evening when we went to dinner at a local French bistro. We were almost done with our meal when Nazie looked over her glass of wine and saw the daughter of the Queen of Iran walk into the restaurant. A moment later, Queen Farah herself appeared, a woman of 80 now but still elegant and attractive. Soon she was followed by a young man Nazie took to be the daughter's boyfriend. The threesome took a table between ours and the door. There was no way to exit without passing right by them.

Since the fall of Shah, the royal family had been through great hardships, including financial challenges and suicides. But while the Shah was ancient history, the remnants of his family were still very much alive and, in some cases, well. Queen Farah lived mainly between Washington and Paris. I'd seen her a number of times over the years, and so had Nazie.

We had no choice but to say hello on the way out. The queen, speaking in Persian, beckoned us to sit. The boyfriend made room by taking the opportunity to go outside for a smoke. Nazie took his seat, and I pulled up another chair. We chatted for a few minutes about banalities. Then the queen turned to Nazie and said, in Persian, "Nazie, dear, you look so young. You are glowing."

"Well," said Nazie, caught off guard, "that's because I am in love."

"Yes, so I hear," said Queen Farah, looking over at me with a knowing smile.

So much for keeping secrets.

■ ■ ■

The morning after chatting with Queen Farah in a French bistro on the Upper East Side, I found myself standing in a small windowless bathroom in the halfway house in the Bronx, trying to pee into a cup as an impatient guard stood behind me, telling me to hurry it up. That's how life went in those months. I lived in a world of contrasts, traveling back and forth between the sunlit apartment that I shared with Nazie on Fifth Avenue and the grim halfway house in the Bronx.

I had to be in the Bronx every Monday to meet my case manager and go over my schedule, then four more times per month for random urine tests. The halfway house was in some ways grimmer than prison. Not grimmer than MCC or MDC, but worse than Otisville and Cumberland. At least there were rules and order and cleanliness in prison—and few if any drugs. Here men passed out in halls from drug overdoses. The moment some men came out from behind bars, they went right back to the habits that got them there.

My case manager, Ms. Ortiz, was a kind and helpful woman, but some others of the staff were not. The guy who stood behind me that morning after our dinner in the bistro was one of the latter. "Come on, man, I got things to do. If you can't do it, you gonna have to come later when you can."

Making a 70-year-old man urinate on command is no fun for anyone. To avoid being harassed by the guard for wasting his time, I'd drink a lot of water before heading up to the halfway house, but I had to be careful not to drink too much. Sometimes my bladder was so full I barely made it on time. Once, I had to tell to the Uber driver to pull over to the curb while I ran around the Bronx, restaurant to restaurant, begging to use a bathroom.

The whole thing, frankly, was an exercise in absurdity. The point of urine tests was to ensure that I stayed substance free, but as Nazie pointed out—she knew this as the owner of a healthcare company—urine analysis, while it can detect drugs in a body, is pretty useless for detecting alcohol, which can only be accurately detected by a breathalyzer. Drugs were never my problem, so making me do a piss test made no sense.

Still, I took it very seriously. I never drank so much as a sip. The closest I came was sampling a dessert made for me by the wife of an old friend. The tart was delicious. When I inquired of the woman what made it so good, she told me it was the Grand

Marnier she'd splashed into it. I was not pleased. Fortunately, no Grand Marnier ever turned up in my urine.

■ ■ ■

In addition to my one or two trips to the Bronx every week, I attended twice-weekly meetings of TDAP, or the Transitional Drug Abuse Program. This was a required post-incarceration extension of RDAP. Our meetings were held at a plain suite of offices on the second floor of a building on Broadway and 37th Street. Once a week we met alone with our counselor, and once a week in a group session with other inmates.

Like RDAP, TDAP mostly felt like a waste of time as therapy, but it was not without value to me. Our group sessions gave me insight into the resilience of some of my fellow attendees, in the face of what appeared to be insurmountable challenges. Complicated personal lives, poorly-paid jobs, crappy living conditions—it all seemed too much to bear, and yet most of the men bore it with admirable fortitude.

Ironically, one of the biggest complications in their lives turned out to be TDAP itself. I was lucky. Not only could I walk over to TDAP from my office in midtown, but I had an employer—Nazie—who was understanding about the time demands of the program. But again, I was the exception. Most of the men lived far from the TDAP office, in many cases at the halfway house in the Bronx. Getting to TDAP meant commuting an hour each way by subway. If they were lucky enough to have secured a job—not easy for an ex-convict—they had to go to their boss and ask to take off four hours, twice a week, in the middle of the workday. This in addition to the hours they had to take off to meet their case manager and do their piss tests at the halfway house in the Bronx. It was another BOP Catch-22: the agency encouraged ex-inmates to seek employment but then did everything in its power to make employment impossible. No wonder so many inmates would fall back into illegal ways to make money. The BOP was almost pushing them to do so.

To make matters worse for the men in the group with me, we had a young social worker—his name was Adnan—who seemed to think that part of his job description was being a hard-ass.

As I say, most of the men had tough commutes to get to TDAP, but Adnan imposed an inviolable rule: anyone more than three minutes late to the group would be written up as absent. No exceptions. Men would come rushing in five minutes late, after subway delays and other debacles, and be told they were being written up. This was a big deal. Anyone marked absent risked being kicked out of TDAP, which would mean his entire RDAP credit would be revoked and he'd owe the BOP another full year of prison time.

Adnan was an interesting guy. He was a good listener and showed flashes of real empathy and understanding. But he'd decided the only way to impose discipline was to be inflexible. Were he a CO at a supermax prison, his attitude might have made sense. But TDAP was meant to be a group therapy session for frank and open conversation to help men deal with serious problems they faced in their lives. The fact that Adnan was making himself the biggest problem many of the men faced had to be addressed, but fear of retribution kept most of the men from addressing it. I realized I was in a unique position. For one thing, I'd never been late to TDAP. Also, I had a good lawyer.

"Adnan, you're a nice guy," I said in the group one afternoon after he'd handed down yet another peremptory write-up to one of our group. "But you haven't decided what hat you want to wear. Are you a social worker or a prison guard? You can't be both."

The group erupted in applause and shouts of agreement. All the pent-up feelings of frustration and resentment came pouring out into the open. Needless to say, this did not go over well with Adnan.

A few days later, I was called into the office of his boss, the guy who ran the Manhattan TDAP. Before the meeting, I informed them that my attorney would be present. If they intended to punish me for saying something in a supposedly protected group therapy session—something that absolutely needed to be said—I wanted them to know I'd fight back. Clearly rattled by my mention of an attorney, the director promised me this was not meant to be an adversarial meeting.

It was a short meeting. The director clearly wanted the matter to go away. He was all smiles and conciliation. Still, I said what I came to say: "You're accusing me of being an inciter in a room where we are supposed to honestly express what we're thinking. But when we're honest, you punish us." I turned to Adnan. "You have tremendous power over us. How you use it matters."

I'm not sure these words had any effect on Adnan—he left me alone after the meeting, but he continued to be a hard-ass to others. Still, the words needed to be said and I hope they sank in a little.

■ ■ ■

The first Easter after my release, my daughter Yasmine came with her family to visit me. While I was in prison, she'd given birth to three beautiful children, two girls and a boy—Soraya, Darya, and Pasha—all total delights. I'd met the kids during Yasmine's visits to Otisville, but now we were able to spend days together without the pressures of time and prison rules bearing down on us. Nazie prepared to host my grandchildren by purchasing an extraordinary array of Easter eggs—plastic eggs of every color and size, filled with candy, and small chocolates wrapped in foil—and Yasmine's husband, Oliver, and I hid hundreds of these in the courtyard in the center of our apartment building. Then the children came out in their Easter outfits, carrying baskets, and ran gleefully around the courtyard, scooping up eggs wherever they could find them. They got most of them, but I'd bet a few remain in the courtyard, still hidden in some nook or cranny.

Through the summer and early fall of 2019, I continued to straddle my two worlds, one created for me by Nazie and my family and friends, the other forced upon me by the BOP. Going back and forth was enough to give me whiplash, but it also made me exquisitely appreciative of all I had to cherish.

For the most part, life ran pretty smoothly. But there were a few hiccups. For example, I'd come out of prison with a number of disastrous dental problems (dental care in federal prison is subpar at best) that required a minor fortune to fix. When Nazie found a dentist for me in Washington who would do the work for one-third of the best price I could get in New York, I applied for and received, after great effort, permission to travel to D.C. It was a pain to get that permission—to say nothing of the pain of the long neglected dental work—but it saved many tens of thousands of dollars.

• • •

Nazie and I changed apartments in our building that first summer, to move to a different floor. During the move, Verizon turned off the phone service in the old apartment but neglected to turn it on in the new apartment, and then the weekend came and Verizon was nowhere to be found.

For most people, this would be an annoying inconvenience. For me, it was a potential disaster. When the halfway house tried to get in touch for my thrice-nightly phone check-ins, they reached a disconnected line. Not good. Fortunately, I could speak to them by cell phone and explain what had happened. They were understanding, but only to a point. I was given a deadline to get the landline functioning—9:00 p.m. Sunday. Otherwise, I'd have to report to the halfway house.

Nazie spent hours trying to get through to Verizon over the weekend, then hours more pleading for repair, but to no avail. As a result, I had to pack an overnight bag and head out to the Bronx on Sunday night. Back I went into the dreary little room they'd put me in that first evening I'd arrived there. It was an unpleasant night, but again, like so much of life then, it reminded me of my great fortune and filled me with respect for the men who had noplace else to go.

As the end of my home confinement neared, Nazie and I began to talk about places we would go as soon as I was able to travel, including her home in Minnesota. I would not be entirely free until I'd completed three more years of "supervised released"—a kind of parole—that would follow the end of my sentence, but I would be a lot freer than I'd been since August of 2009. I could come and go from home more or less as I pleased. No more phone calls in the middle of the night. No more trips to the Bronx to pee into a cup.

November 14, 2019, was a brisk but sun-drenched autumn day. Early that morning, Nazie and I Ubered out to the halfway house to sign my release papers. Signing documents at a desk in a halfway house in the Bronx may not have looked like high drama, but to me—and to Nazie—it was an extraordinary moment marking the end of an epic ordeal. Everyone at the halfway house, including some of the staff, understood what it meant and congratulated me. My prison term was over.

I was free.

Nazie insisted on throwing a party at the apartment that evening. I'd resisted, but she won the argument, and I was glad she did. It was wonderful to bring together my old friends and my children—only Layla could not be there, due to her job in Europe—with Nazie and some of her friends, and a few friends we'd made together. By Nazie's arrangement, we had a scrumptious spread of Persian food in the middle of the room. I had my first sip of alcohol since 2010, a vodka with lemon. It was a pleasure to know I could sip a drink—not just free from the scrutiny of the BOP now, but free from whatever had driven me to overindulge in the past. The truth was that I'd outgrown my need for alcohol much as I'd outgrown my need for deceptions and delusions. There is no better freedom than that.

As I looked around the living room that night, I felt perfectly content. The struggles I'd been through—and had put others through—were not forgotten and never would be. And there would be other struggles ahead. But I'd been given a chance to start over. Like that delicious plum Weitzman had tossed to me many summers earlier at Otisville, an unexpected gift had come to me. I'd never again take a plum for granted.

EPILOGUE
LILY OF THE VALLEY

Not long after I began serving my prison sentence in Texarkana, I got a letter from Hushang Ansary. Now heading into his ninth decade of life, Hushang was still running strong and still as sharp as ever. Despite our different political views—Hushang was a committed Republican—we'd stayed close through the years. We shared memories of my father, and we shared memories of Iran, where I'd gone so many years ago to make my fortune after seeking counsel from Hushang. Likewise, we'd both suffered the revolution in 1978 and had been forced to reconstitute our lives and careers in the United States.

I'd not always followed Hushang's advice, but I'd always found it to be extremely perceptive and valuable. And now, in that fall of 2010, he sent me a wonderful letter. He began by reminding me that we'd both had to start over after the revolution, and that for those of us who had managed to do it, the experience had turned out to be not only survivable, but positive. He counseled me to look upon my time in prison not as the end of my old life, but as the start of my new life. "It is like being born again," he wrote. "Only this time, on the first day of your life you will not be a day old with no experience. You will be reborn at whatever age you are, with a good deal of experience, good, bad, or indifferent. That can serve as a jumping board to start from."

As always, Hushang was spot on. Prison, like the disruption of the Iranian Revolution, had ended a part of my life, but it had granted me a new life. My decade behind bars had been a struggle to be sure, but I had learned things about myself, and about others, that I would never have known otherwise. My arrest had been the end of a chapter, but not, it turned out, the end of my story.

■ ■ ■

After my release, I began to work in earnest for Nazie. She'd decided, for a number of reasons, that the time had come to sell her healthcare company in Minneapolis. As I discovered when I began to look into the company's finances, its value was significantly higher than Nazie had been led to believe. I was convinced that a number of prospective buyers would be interested, and that turned out to be exactly the case. As soon as Nazie put her company on the market, attractive bids came in from around the country.

In mid-February of 2020, Nazie signed a letter of intent to sell the company. Everything went well in negotiations, but just as Nazie was on the verge of finalizing the contract, the Covid pandemic struck. Markets plummeted, business froze nationwide, and the buyer had no choice but to withdraw its offer.

Like everyone else in the world, we could only wait and see where the pandemic took us. If it seemed cruelly ironic that my release to freedom should be met almost immediately by a once-in-a-century plague that forced me, along with everyone else, back into confinement, the truth is that I was probably better equipped to ride out a quarantine than most. Years of prison had endowed me with inner resources. I'd learned to find pleasure and freedom in reading and thinking, and to endure physical limits with patience and positivity.

■ ■ ■

Covid was a challenge. But the more frustrating challenge turned out to be the one inflicted on me by the Southern District of New York.

Even after my release, I had a financial obligation that would last the rest of my wage-earning life. Theoretically, this was an obligation to cover the balance of any bank losses still outstanding after the government sold my assets. As for what that balance was, the government had not seen fit to share it with me. Indeed, the U.S. Attorney had never—nor has ever, even yet to this day—given an accounting of my assets sold in forfeiture, neither the amounts collected from the sales nor the identity of the purchasers. All I knew was that, going forward, 15% of any income I made—pre-tax—was to be garnished by the federal government.

I did not argue with restitution in principle, but the reality of it turned out to be senseless. Again, theoretically, I was compensating my victims—the banks—for the money I'd borrowed. But the banks had long ago been paid by their insurance companies, so my money was not in fact compensating them for their losses—they had none. Where was it going then? If not to the victims, it was not restitution. It was simply a fine. Which is to say, it was just another way of punishing me beyond my prison term.

To make restitution a little more punishing, the Southern District insisted that it be paid, monthly, with an old-fashioned cashier's check. Why it had to be a cashier's check in the 21st century, when there are many easier ways to make payments, was anyone's guess. Paying by cashier's check required a monthly trip to a bank, during weekday work hours, followed by a long wait in line to process the check, plus a bank fee of ten or fifteen dollars.

I hope I've made it clear by this point that my critique of the criminal justice system is not intended as a personal complaint. I've never denied that I deserved punishment or that my experience, while difficult for me, has been relatively easy compared to that of many people who enter the criminal justice system. Whatever hoops I've been forced to jump through by the government, most felons and former felons face far worse.

That said, I've had a unique opportunity to bear witness from inside the criminal justice system. You can think and talk and write about criminal justice all you want, but until you experience the system firsthand, your understanding will be limited. Before I close this book, then, let me attempt, once more, to highlight some of the pernicious absurdities of what we call the "justice" system. And perhaps offer some advice in how to fix these.

While many measures and programs have been implemented for good reasons, most are so poorly executed that they serve no purpose other than to further punish those who have already been sufficiently and, in some cases, harshly punished. Programs that were initially designed to help prisoners become productive law-abiding citizens—halfway houses, TDAP, supervised release—end up hurting their chances of reintegrating into society. If anything, they guarantee that most men and women coming out of prison will *not* succeed on the outside and will therefore end up back behind bars.

Recidivism rates in this country suggest that is exactly what occurs. Nearly 50% of federal offenders are rearrested within eight years of release. Add in state criminal offenders, and that number rises to an astonishing 80%. A cynic might suggest that this is by design—that the American justice system depends on people continuing to commit, and re-commit, crimes in the same way Apple depends on people continuing to use and upgrade smartphones. It's good for business. Yes, the criminal justice system is government bureaucracy, not a business, but bureaucracies naturally seek growth, just as businesses do. Indeed, the Bureau of Prisons is a perfect example of the kind of government bloat my Republican friends complain about. It's a bureaucratic behemoth that seeks its own perpetuation and expansion, even at the expense of its own purpose and society's best interest.

You don't have to be a cynic to see how dysfunctional the system is. Whatever the original intent behind many of the laws and procedures, the system does not function in the interest of either prisoners, former prisoners, or society at large. There have been recent improvements, such as the First Step Act. But that act is just what it says it is—a first step.

■ ■ ■

Before addressing some of the reforms still needed in the justice system, let's be clear: the justice system is not some abstract concept that applies only to hardened criminals—sooner or later, we all have the potential to fall into its grasp. Anyone sanctimonious enough to think there's a wide, impermeable line between himself and convicts might recall that he has almost certainly broken one of the thousands of local or federal laws on the books. Maybe it was fishing without a license. Maybe it was failing to pay taxes for a nanny, or inhaling an illegal substance in their youth.

He might also consider that the last few U.S. presidents—and many others before them—have committed infractions that could have put them into the criminal justice system. Bill Clinton lied under oath in a federal inquiry. George W. Bush was arrested for a DUI. Barack Obama has admitted he snorted cocaine as a young man. Donald Trump has been indicted on 91 separate charges, including fraudulently and grossly inflating assets (much as I did) to secure loans from banks.

We can debate how serious these crimes were compared to my own or others, but *all* could have put the perpetrator into the criminal justice system, with life-changing consequences. The same could be said for many other Americans. Consider this fact: one in three adults in this country—more than 70 million of us—have a criminal record.

This leads to another truth we need to acknowledge before we can address serious reform: we arrest far too many people in this country. There are presently almost two million people incarcerated in this country. The United States contains close to 5% of world's population, but over 20% of the world's prison population. To incarcerate our fellow citizens, we spend more than $80 billion per year. The true price, of course, is a lot greater than any dollar amount.

Locking up vast numbers of citizens for crimes, big and small, is an absurd solution that benefits only the bureaucracies and private businesses that profit from mass incarceration in America. Unfortunately, as I've suggested earlier, the justice system, including both federal and state prosecutors, as well as the federal Bureau of Prisons and its state-run counterparts, use precisely the wrong metric to calculate their success. Rather than the number of years a prosecutor can add to a sentence or that the BOP can keep men and women behind bars, the measure of success should be the law-abiding productivity of men and women after release from prison. As Nazie has pointed out to me, the critical metric in her industry—healthcare—is not how many people stay sick; it's how many people get better. And so it should be in the justice system.

Keeping this goal in mind, we must address the three areas where the criminal "justice" system fails those who have been accused of a crime, and therefore fails society as a whole. All three could be improved immediately, with no or little cost, were it not for political obstacles and bureaucratic inertia. (My comments here are focused on the federal system, but most apply equally to state systems.)

First, we need to reform the plea system.

As I explained earlier, the system strongly incentivizes those accused of a crime to take a plea deal, even if this means accepting charges that are not fair or even true. Following the Enron and Madoff scandals, Congress imposed federal guideline on judges that severely raised minimum penalties for certain crimes. Under these new guidelines, the sentence for my crime, for instance, rose from 7-10 years to 17-21 years—more than a 100% increase. Judges were under tremendous pressure to follow these rigid and often draconian guidelines and generally did so, even if they disagreed with them. The upshot was that anyone who fought the government on federal charges risked severe penalties if he or she lost.

If you are like 98% of those charged with a federal crime, then, you take the plea deal offered—that is, you agree to the punishment that a prosecutor (not a judge, not a jury) has decided to give you. Technically, you retain a right to self-defense, but a plea deal is essentially a deal you can't refuse. (In my own case, going to trial and losing would have meant a possible 21-year sentence, almost guaranteeing that I'd be incarcerated the rest of my life.) To ensure that accused felons fully appreciate the misery they face if they don't take the deal, they may be sent, as I was, to spend a night or two in some federally-run hellhole like MCC or MDC. All of this is part of an orchestrated and often sadistic ritual of intimidation in which the concept of justice is often forgotten.

Taking sentencing power from jurists and handing it to prosecutors is absurd. For reasons of career advancement and personal gratification, prosecutors have every reason to inflate sentences as much as possible. They are not evaluated by their superiors and colleagues by how "just" they are in dispensing plea deals, but rather by how much punishment they inflict on presumed bad guys—and the more prominent the bad guys, the greater the reward to the prosecutor for putting them away for long periods of time.

Secondly, we need to reform the experience of prison itself.

This begins with the judges who are ultimately responsible for imposing the sentences that prisoners serve. Most judges have no more idea of what prison entails than I did prior to my arrest. Before a judge sends someone to prison for any length of time, he or she should take a day, or even just an afternoon, to go to prison. I don't mean on some official sanitized tour. The judge should spend some time inside to get a true taste of the experience. Indeed, judges should try a few hours in solitary confinement and see what that does to their mental states. And any judge who allows someone to go to a hellhole like MCC or MDC has a moral obligation to spend a night or two there, so he knows exactly what he's signed off on. Frankly, given their plea deal powers, prosecutors should be required to do the same. What they will discover is that they are in many cases subjecting men and women to cruel and unusual punishment.

As I conclude this book, a remarkable and hopeful development has just occurred in the federal prison system: the Justice Department has announced that it will close down MCC—the Metropolitan Correctional Center—until improvements are made at the prison. MCC is where I was held overnight in August of 2010, and where—more famously—Jeffrey Epstein hung himself in August of 2019. Apparently, the decision was made after a deputy attorney general finally toured MCC and concluded that it was every bit as appalling as prisoners have been saying it was for decades. In a statement, the Justice Department affirmed that it was "committed to ensuring that every facility in the federal prison system is not only safe and secure, but also provides people in custody with the resources and programs they need to make a successful return to society after they have served their time." It's a shame it took them until August of 2021 to have this epiphany and make this commitment.

Prison is not meant to be pleasurable, and I'm not suggesting it should be. But it is also not meant to be inhumane. And above all, it *is*—or should be—meant to promote a person's re-entry into society when his or her term ends. Not merely because it is right to bring former felons back into the fold of society, but because it is in society's interest to do so.

One change that would immediately make federal prisons more valuable to society—and more just—would be implementing positive measures to allow prisoners to earn a sentence reduction. As it stands, sentence reductions can only be earned in federal prison by RDAP. I wrote earlier about the boondoggle that RDAP is in practice. There should be positive, pro-active ways to earn time off, such as greater education incentives that would allow prisoners to improve their chances of successfully transitioning to productive and law-abiding lives on the outside. While I was in Texarkana, I taught a GED course to fellow inmates, principally minorities. Given that GED diplomas provide ex-convicts with a realistic path to re-entry, it would make sense to encourage inmates to pursue GED diplomas by giving credits, including sentence reductions, for taking courses. But that does not in fact occur.

Which leads me to the third phase of a convict's life in need of immediate reform: the part that comes *after* prison.

This is when the most senseless and enduring punishment kicks in. Lives are often ruined not by the prison term itself, but by the collateral damage that follows. I've mentioned the hurdles that the justice system itself imposes, many of which seem expressly designed to trip up former prisoners. On top of this are numerous legal hurdles and cultural prejudices—employers who will not hire them, landlords who will not rent to them, banks that will not loan to them, licensing boards will not license them, and educational institutions that will not admit them.

Thus, too often, a prison sentence, even a brief one, becomes effectively a life sentence. This may satisfy our nearly pathological need to punish those who violate our laws, but it does so, as I've explained above, at our own peril: a former felon who cannot successfully reintegrate into life outside is likely to recidivate.

A 2021 op-ed in the *New York Times* by Jamie Dimon, chairman and CEO of JPMorgan Chase & Co, speaks eloquently to this point. Dimon is co-chair of a group called the Second Chance Business Coalition. He gives a compelling argument for lifting some of "financial, legal and logistical roadblocks" that make it difficult for ex-convicts to get jobs. "Nearly half of formerly incarcerated people are unemployed one year after leaving prison," Dimon writes. "That is a moral outrage."

Dimon recommends several important measures that could help address this, including "clean slate" laws that would seal or expunge certain criminal records, as well as actions that his own company and others have taken, such as banning the once universal practice of requiring job applicants to disclose criminal histories.

I fully agree with Mr. Dimon. But I wish he understood that banks are part of the problem. Try getting a bank account or bank loan as a former felon. The current know-your-client (KYC) guidelines of U.S. financial institutions almost guarantee that you will be refused. How is someone supposed to have a job if she can't get a bank account into which she can deposit her salary checks? How will she start a business or buy a home without a loan?

■ ■ ■

If you'd asked me how this story was going to end when I began a draft of this book long ago, on an overcast New Year's Day in Texarkana, I would have been hard-pressed to imagine a happy ending. I was divorced and I was broke. I'd been publicly disgraced and privately devastated. I'd let myself down and let down many who loved and trusted me. While I tried very hard to stay productive and keep my attitude positive, I frankly had no idea what my life would look like when I was finally released.

I often thought back in those days to my Persian grandfather, Mohammed Hassan, who departed his home in Shiraz to commence his long voyage across the Indian Ocean, on the simple but powerful hope that better prospects awaited those who were willing to make the voyage. I thought of my father, who left behind nearly everything he'd built and owned in Hong Kong to board one of his ships and steam to Vladivostok, then head thousands of miles east to the Caspian Sea and, ultimately, to a new home in America.

If history has taught me anything, it is that life is an unpredictable voyage. And so it continues to be. My own life has taken me from the sides of U.S. presidents to the cells of convicted murderers, from fleeing a violent revolution to returning to freedom after a decade in prison. We make choices—some good, some bad—and other choices are made for us by forces outside of our control. Our task is to keep our heads up, learn from our mistakes, stay open to new possibilities, and realize that every challenge, as Hushang Ansary advised me in his letter, is a chance to be reborn.

■ ■ ■

On a Saturday in May of 2021—May Day, as it happened—Nazie and I married. We held the ceremony in the living room of our apartment in New York. Covid had loosened its grip on the city, but not quite enough for a public gathering, so we had a classic Covid wedding. The only people in the room, other than the two of us, were our housekeeper, the officiant who performed the ceremony, and the man we'd hired to videotape it. The kids were all on Zoom, watching from a laptop we'd set up on a coffee table.

In a sense, we were celebrating three weddings that morning, because my youngest daughter, Layla, and Nazie's daughter, Raz, had only recently married. Both joined us on Zoom with their respective husbands, Josh and Chris. Nazie's son, Sahm, was also with us, as were my daughter Yasmine and her husband, Oliver, and my son Kamyar and his fiancée, Maria.

It was one of those perfect spring days that come to New York every now and then, when the air is scrubbed of smog and the whole city seems to gleam in Technicolor. Below us in Central Park, the trees were budding with light green leaves, and to the north the reservoir was fringed by cherry trees in full blossom. A Covid wedding it may have been, but we dressed for the occasion. I put on a jacket and tie, one of the few times I'd done so since my release, and Nazie wore a simple but elegant white dress. In her hands she clutched a bouquet of flowers, a spray of white bell-shaped blossoms. Lily of the Valley, Nazie told me. A flower that has carried many meanings through the ages, but one special meaning above all: the return to happiness.

As the kids watched, we recited our vows, kissed, and shared a champagne toast with everyone on Zoom. It was a simple ceremony and quite brief, but wonderful. My son Kamyar sent us a congratulatory text that summed it up perfectly: "That was the most touching nine and a half minutes ever."

When it was over, we went outside onto Fifth Avenue and strolled to a nearby garden, then over to a French restaurant for lunch. We talked about the path that had brought us here, and the future we would share. Neither of us had any illusions, but we were filled with boundless hope.

Acknowledgements

I set out to write this book on New Year's Day 2012. At that time, I was inmate 62625 054 in FCI Texarkana. Working in longhand on a pad of yellow legal paper, I wrote a minimum of two hours every day, never more than three hours. I had no access to the internet and no access to my files. I wrote entirely from memory. The writing came to me with remarkable ease. It was cathartic.

In order to transcribe my largely illegible handwriting, I hired another inmate to type the manuscript on an old-fashioned manual typewriter. His name was Scott Frear. Before I could complete the manuscript, I was transferred to Otisville Camp. At Otisville, the typing job fell to Tim Lewis. Both Scott and Tim were paid in prison currency—stamps for Scott in Texarkana, mackerel for Tim in Otisville. In both cases, the compensation was made possible by the generosity of my niece, Pamela Steitz. My good friend and college classmate, Jack McLean, took the finished transcript from Otisville and converted it to a Word document. My thanks to both Pamela and Jack for their valuable help.

The manuscript remained untouched until I was released to home confinement in the spring of 2019. I knew that I needed to significantly edit the book in order to prepare it for publication. To begin with, it was far too long. I am indebted to Omid Memarian, who spent countless hours researching editors on my behalf. It was through Omid that I met Jim Rasenberger. Jim by coincidence had attended Landon, the same school that I'd graduated from all those years ago. He was a perfect editor. I am deeply indebted to Jim for the attention to detail and research he provided. He found newspaper stories on my father from the 1920's in Hong Kong which revealed information that I had been unaware of.

Lisa Kloetzke and Firoozeh Firoozmand were invaluable resources in the myriad details necessary to prepare the final version for submission to literary agencies. Larry McMichael was instrumental in assisting in the organizing of Pasha Publishing.

I was exceptionally fortunate that Richard Morris of Janklow & Nesbit took on the project as my agent. There's no better agency in New York and no better agent.

I also wish to thank Bobby Woods, Andrew Golomb, and Marmont Lane Books for their meticulous attention to detail, creativity and commitment to elevate my book in every way possible.

Finally, this book would never have been published had it not been for the love and guidance provided by my wife, Malekeh Nazie. Without her belief in my words, and her faith in me, I may never have found the courage to share my experiences with the world. Her unconditional love and ability to empathize with the emotions captured within these pages have made an immeasurable impact on the final product of this book, and, even more significantly, on my life.

ABOUT THE AUTHOR

Hassan Nemazee was born on January 27, 1950 in Washington D.C., the son of international businessman and philanthropist, Mohammed Nemazee, and Iranian entrepreneur, Fakhri Dehesh Nemazee.

He attended Harvard College, graduating with honors in 1972. When his father passed away that same year, Hassan took charge of the family businesses and philanthropic endeavors, including the renowned Nemazee Hospital, clinics, schools, and waterworks in Shiraz, which were established by his late father.

He moved to Iran, forging joint ventures with many prestigious American and British companies, including American International Group (AIG), Morgan Guaranty Trust, Linbeck Construction and Knight, Frank & Rutley.

In December 1978, the political landscape in Iran took an unexpected turn with the Islamist Revolution. Nemazee was forced to leave the country. The new regime confiscated the Nemazee family's assets, homes, businesses, and charities.

After losing over 90% of his net worth, Nemazee rebuilt his life in the United States. Over the next three decades, his businesses flourished, and he welcomed three children. As an integral member of the New York community, he actively participated in organizations, including the Council on Foreign Relations, the boards of Asia Society, Spence School, RAND Center for Middle East Public Policy, and various Harvard Visiting Committees.

He also founded the first political action committee for Iranian Americans (IAPAC), solidifying his commitment to political involvement.

In 1998, the Clinton White House announced its nomination of Hassan Nemazee as U.S. Ambassador to Argentina.

Hassan became a top supporter and fundraiser for a number of prominent Democrats, including President Bill Clinton, Hillary Clinton, Al Gore, John Kerry, Barack Obama, and Joe Biden. He served as the National Finance Chair for the Democratic Senatorial Campaign Committee (DSCC) from

2004 to 2006, during which time the Democrats regained control of the Senate for the first time in over a decade. Additionally, he served as the National Finance Chair for Hillary Clinton's 2008 presidential campaign and played a significant role in fundraising for Joe Biden.

His life took a turn when the "tech bubble" impacted his diverse range of businesses. Juggling increasing responsibilities in his family, business, political, and philanthropic endeavors, he made choices which ultimately led to his arrest in August, 2009 on charges of bank fraud. The U.S. Attorney's Southern District of New York's office identified Citibank, Bank of America, and HSBC as the victims of his crimes.

In July 2010, at the age of 60, he pleaded guilty to these charges and was sentenced to 12 years in prison—shorter than the 24-year term recommended by the SDNY.

Under the First Step Act, signed by President Trump on December 21, 2018, Hassan Nemazee was released on March 20, 2019, after serving nine years.

Today, Hassan and his wife Nazie Nemazee reside in Miami, Florida. He cherishes the time spent with his three children, their spouses, and his five grandchildren, as well as the loyal friends who stood by his side throughout his journey. Hassan and Nazie are committed to supporting efforts to preserve and protect democracy around the world, to criminal justice reform in America, to promoting political involvement by young members of the Iranian-American community, and to providing medical assistance to mortally ill children.

INDEX

9/11 177-180

Adler, Mike 198
Agah, Mohandess 88
Agassi, Andre 269
Agnew, Spiro 76
Alaei, Faraj 174
Ala, Hossein 26, 36
Alam, Asadollah 41, 62, 72-73
al-Assad, Bashar 209-210
Alavi, Dr. Khalil 72
Albright, Madeline 188
Allied Bank 118
Alloy, Marty 121
American International Group (AIG) 80-83, 172, 213
American Iranian Council (AIC) 172-174
Ameri, Goli 175
Amirahmadi, Hooshang 173-175
Amir-Mokri, Cyrus 175
Amouzegar, Jamshid 62, 92
Angel Falls 127
Angelson, Mark 198
Anglo-Iranian Oil Company 30
Angulo, Gerry 130, 136, 151
Ansary, Bahram 52
Ansary, Cy 69
Ansary, Hushang 40, 52, 59, 61, 67-68, 75, 82, 92, 113, 131, 160, 165, 358, 366
Ardalan, Cyrus 68
Arent Fox 69
Argentina 152, 155-156, vii
Aryan Brotherhood 283-284
Asia Society 194, 241
Atomic Energy Agency 69
Auden, W.H. 10

Ayatollah Khomeini 94-99, 109, 114-118, 137, 295

Bank of America 168, 177, 187, 213, 219-220, 234, 241
Barker, G. Dalynn (Special Agent, FBI) 13, 225-226, 233-234
Behbudistan Nemazee (Nemazee Clinic) 22
Bergen, Candice 78
Berlusconi, Silvio 119
Bernanke, Ben 213
Bernbach, John 261
Bharara, Preet 223-226, 235-239, 250-252, 259
Biden, Beau 179, 198
Biden, Hunter 179, 198
Biden, Jill 198
Biden, Joe 11, 179, 181, 189, 197-201, 207-208, 217, vi, xi
Black Eyed Peas 190
Black Friday 98
Blaylock, Gennario 320-322
Boesky, Ivan 130
Bonyad Iran 31, 65, 70-72, 77, 88
Bowles, Erskine 142
Bowman, Dr. James 215
Bracewell LLP 230, 241
Brag, Anders 248
Brean Murray 213, 217
Brzezinski, Zbigniew 98, 208-210
Buchanan, Pat 169
Bureau of Prisons (BOP) 271, 280-282, 286, 288-290, 294, 297, 304-306, 309-316, 321-325, 328, 333-339, 343, 347, 353-357, 361-362
Burris, Howard 54-58, 78, 114

Bushehr 20
Bush, George W. 124, 168-170, 175, 180, 190-192, 198, 361
Buttenweiser, Peter 145-146

Cage, Nicolas 293
Cahill, Mary Beth 183
CALPERS 131
Capital One 348
Carret 213
Carret, Phillip 194
Carter, Jimmy 92-94, 98, 118, 142, 154, 210
Casino Divonne 48, 136
Castle Harlan 194
Castro, Fidel 29, 142
Caterpillar 135
Central Bank of Argentina 161
Central Bank of Iran 103, 106, 109
Central Intelligence Agency (C.I.A.) 30, 97-98, 133, 167
Chai Nemazee 21
Chanel 194
Chartouni, Fouad 261
Cheney, Dick 190
Chevron 213
Christie, Chris 307
Cisneros, Carlos Enrique 127
Cisneros, Carlos 126-127
Cisneros, Gustavo 126-127
Cisneros, Shahla 61-62, 126-127
Citibank 80, 187, 214, 219-227, 231-234, 250, 281
Citigroup 214
City of the Dead 133
Clark, Wesley 182, 185, 188
Clinton, Bill 11, 51, 78, 137-138, 142-146, 154-156, 159, 166, 170-171, 174, 180-186, 195, 203-208, 217, 247, 257, 262, 361, vii-viii

Clinton Foundation 205
Clinton Global Initiative 205
Clinton, Hillary 11, 159, 180, 194, 197-202, 206-212, 215-218, 237, 255, 267, 292, 314, xiii
Club Fed 304
Coelho, Tony 166-169
Cognitive Behavioral Therapy (CBT) 323
Con Air 293
Cortina d'Ampezzo 201
Corzine, Jon 247
Cotton, Tom 331
Cullman, Edgar 248, 261
Cuomo, Andrew 195
Cuomo, Mario 195

D'Arcy, William 28
Dean, Howard 181-185
Democratic Congressional Campaign Committee (DCCC) 197
Democratic National Committee (DNC) 138-140, 144, 185, 194
Democratic Senatorial Campaign Committee (DSCC) 196-197, 200-204
Deutsch, Levi 308
Development Corporation of Iran (DCI) 75-76
Diagnostic Sciences 130
Diba, Farhad 94, 113
Dimon, Jamie 365-366
Djam, Fereydoun 103, 104
Dobbins, James 154-155, 161
Dodd, Chris 138, 142-143, 162-197
Donilon, Tom 198
Dukakis, Michael 137, 179
Duke, Robin 206

Dulles, Allen 29-30
Durbin, Dick 333
Duvall, Robert 159

Ebtehaj, Abol Hassan 60, 72-73, 80-84, 90-91
Edwards, John 182, 185, 188-189, 197, 201, 206
Effron, Blair 181, 199
Eisenberg, Shaul 97-98
Elganian, Habib 115
Elmendorf, Steve 191
Enron 363
Epstein, Jeffrey 236, 364
Esfandiari, Haleh 293
Exxon 213

Fakhr Iran 36, 39-40, 52, 73-75, 87
Fardoust, Hossein 109
Farmer, Bob 181-182
Farpour, Dr. Ali 47
FCI Cumberland 315-328, 332, 352, xxi
FCI Otisville 288-315, 318, 346, 352, 355-357, xx
FCI Texarkana 13, 17, 260-276, 277, 280, 283-285, 288-289, 296, 301-307, 319, 349, 358, 366, xx
Fellow Inmates
  Ali 296, 298
  Big Mike 319, 320
  Big Red 311
  Eduardo 307
  Ezra 300, 303
  Fat Tony 319-322
  Henry 296-298
  Hicks, Richard 278-279, 289
  Jacob 282-283

  Jaegers, Wayne 274-275, 278, 282-284, 289, xx
  J.P. 14, 17, 272-273, 285-287
  Lonnie 299
  MacNeill, Martin "Doc" 275-278, 289, 303, xx
  Rattler 277-289
  Russell 308-311
  Slice 276-289
  Walt 263-267, 272-274, 284
  Weitzman 346, 357
Fennebresque, Kim 129, 261
Firouz, Eskandar 115
Firouz, Safieh 25
First Capital Asset Management 130, 134, 150-151, 164, 167
First National Bank of Chicago 119
First Step Act 325, 331-337, 350, 361
Forbes, Walter 307-308
Foreign Intelligence Advisory Board (PFIAB) 166
Fowler, Don 139, 142-143
Fox, Henry 69, 79
Foxman, Abraham 160
FTC Oklahoma City 290, 293
Fulbright & Jaworski 120
Fusina, Alex 160

Gajereh 77
General Hasheminejad 90
General Jahanbani 115
General Khosrodad 115
General Minbashian 52, 62
Georgescu, Peter 270
Gephardt, Dick 154, 185
Ghahary, Akbar 174
Ghorban, Morad 174, 327-328
Gingrich, Newt 137, 143-144

Goldman Sachs *176*
Gore, Al *11, 139-144, 147, 152, 166-171, 184-188, 193*
Gorenburg, Mark *185*
Grace, Nancy *276*
Graham, Lindsey *331*
Grassley, Chuck *333*
Great West Life Insurance Company of Canada *130, 148*
Greenberg, Hank *80, 83-84*
Greenberg Traurig *138*
Green, Mark *195*
Grossman, Steven *145*
Gutfruend, John *131*

Harken Energy *124*
Harris, David *160*
Harris, Josh *160*
Harvard *45-51, 60, 63-68, 76, 93, 124, 136, 141, 241, v*
Hassan's Farm *29, 68*
Havaleh system of money transfer *87*
Hayek, Salma *159*
Heinz, Teresa *183, 186, 193*
Helms, Jesse *154, 160-161, 164-165*
Helms, Richard *37, 98*
Hines, Gerald *76*
History of Civilization 88
HN Properties *101*
Hoenlein, Malcolm *160*
Hoffman, Alan *180*
Holbrooke, Richard *156, 160, 188, 194*
Hoveyda, Amir Abbas *103, 115*
HSBC *219-223, 227, 232-234, 250, 281*
Hume, David Douglas *84*
Hume, Sir Alec Douglas *84*

Hutchins, Glen *191*
HydroDive *213, 281*

Iran America International Insurance Company *81-82*
Iran Foundation *31*
Iranian American Political Action Committee (IAPAC) *174-175, 255, 327*
Iranian Revolution *9, 30, 63, 97, 133, 142, 160, 173, 209, 358*
Iranian's Bank Building *78*
Isfahan *26, 44, 94*
Isham, Ralph *169*
Islamic Republic of Iran *116*

Jarrett, Valerie *215*
Johnson, Walter "The Big Train" *29*
Jordan, Jim *182, 183*
JPMorgan Chase & Co *365*
Judge Sidney H. Stein *243, 252-260, 327, 335-336*
Julius Baer *187, 219*

Kashanchi, Shahin *150-151, 222, 297-298*
Kaufman, Ted *198*
Kennedy, John *331*
Kennedy, Ted *188, 191, 208, 251, xv*
Kerry, John *11, 181-195, 198, 202, 208, 211, 215, vi, xvi*
Khalili, Ahmad *52*
King Hussein of Jordan *95*
Kixmiller, David *54-57*
Kleiner Perkins *167*
Klobuchar, Amy *196, 332*
Knight, Peter *139, 147-148, 168-170*

Kopelman, Coco and Arie 194
Kramer, Orin 181, 200
Kushner, Jared 325, 332

Landon School for Boys 37, 45-46, 50, 54, 247, 280
Legal & General 119-122, 129
Lehman Brothers 213
Levy, Daniel 250-253, 259-260, 297-298
Linbeck Construction 77
Linbeck Iran 77, 242
Linbeck, Leo Jr. 76, 102-103, 242
Livanos, Peter 152
Luo, Michael 217

Madoff, Bernie 15, 235, 250, 307, 363
Mahbodi, Manucher 26, 248-249
Mahdavi, Ziba 202, 210, 232, 241
Maroney, Peter 181-182
Malle, Chloe 78
Martin, Kati 156
Masjed Vakil 62
Mathis, Brian 201
McAuliffe, Terry 154-155, 166, 188, 194, 199, 202-203, 207-209, 217, 247
McCain-Feingold Campaign Finance Reform Act 189, 197
McCain, John 189, 213, 218
McCaskill, Claire 196
McConnell, Mitch 313, 333
McGlynn, Raz 367
McGlynn, Sahm 367
Medibuy 167, 176
Mehran, Hassan Ali 52
Menem, Carlos 158-159
Merrill Lynch 213, 219

Metropolitan Correctional Center (MCC) 236, 238, 263, 291, 294-295, 352, 363-364
Metropolitan Detention Center (MDC) 236, 294-297, 300-302, 352, 363-364
M.H. Nemazee & Company 21
Miller, Bob 155
Mondale, Walter 137
Morgan Grenfell 84
Morgan Guaranty Trust of New York 85
Mosaddegh, Mohammad 26-29, 34, 68, 86, 133
Mossad 97
Mukasey, Marc 231, 232-241, 245, 248
Mukasey, Michael 231

Nash, Bob 154, 164
Nassiri, Nematollah 103
National Security Agency 167
Nation's Bank 148-150, 168
Nemazee & Company 22-25
Nemazee, Fakhri Dehesh 26, 34-36, 39-40, 44, 49, 54, 62, 65, 87, 127, 192, iii
Nemazee Hospital 11, 22, 25, 31, 35, 40, 52, 60-64, 72, 215
Nemazee, Kamyar 11, 122-123, 128, 155-157, 223, 248, 280, 288, 315-318, 337-344, 349, 367, xxii
Nemazee, Layla 12, 128, 157, 160, 165, 223, 258, 279, 317, 337-341, 357, 367, xxii
Nemazee, Mehdi 42, 65, 67
Nemazee, Mohammed Hassan 20-29, 34, 38-54, 59-64, 69-72, 88, 107, 112, 125, 192, 246, 257, 366, i-ii

Nemazee, Nazie Eftekhari 255-257, 327-332, 335, 338, 341-359, 362, 367, xxi-xxiii
Nemazee, Sheila 9-10, 79, 88, 91-92, 97, 103-105, 109-110, 113, 117, 122-123, 128-129, 140, 150, 158, 165, 169, 206, 218, 222, 231, 237, 242, 252, 255, 280, 297
Nemazee, Safieh 248
Nemazee, Susie 33-34, 43-45, 60, 62, 70-71, 88, 201, 248
Nemazee, Yasmine 12, 118, 128, 143, 155, 223, 248-249, 317, 355, 367, xxii
New York Finance Committee 182
Niarchos, Stavros 27
Niavaran Palace 93
Nixon White House 76
Noto, Lucio "Lu" 172-173

Obama, Barack 11, 190, 196-197, 200-219, 313, 361, x
O'Connell, Janice 161-165
Old Apple Farm 123, 241, 245
Onassis, Aristotle 27, 214
One West Loop Plaza 118-119, 129
Operation Ajax 29
Organization of Petroleum Exporting Countries (OPEC) 73-74
Oxford, Pat 230-232, 241

Pacino, Al 301
Pahlavi University 40, 72, 88, 329
Parker, Charlie 241
Paterson, David 247
Patricof, Alan 183, 206, 254
Patricof, Susan 206
Paulson, Hank 213
Paul Wilmot Enterprises 124

Peacock, John 50
Peacock Throne 172
Pei, I.M. 101, 118
Pelosi, Nancy 332, xvii
Pershing 220-226, 231, 249
Peterson, Pete 183
Pickering, Tom 172
Plouffe, David 211
Plum, Dr. Fred 59-61
Podesta, John 165
Poonak 88-89, 92, 100, 103-108, 113, 116
Portman, Natalie 301
Portman, Rob 313
Post, Emily 265
Pre-Sentencing Investigation (PSI) 253-255
Pre-Sentencing Report (PSR) 253-256
Preston, Lewis 85
Prince Abdul Reza 95
Prince Ali Reza 89
Prince Mahmoud Reza 78
Prince Patrick Ali 89-92
Prince Reza Pahlavi 172
Princess Pari Sima 95
Princess Shams 54-55, 78, 114
Princess Soraya 91
Program Therapy (PT) 323
Pulling, Tom and Clem 133-134

Qajar 20
Qazvin 116
Qom 94-95
Quasha, Alan 123-124, 136-167, 194, 213, 219
Queen Farah 95, 114, 351
Queen Noor 95
Queen Soraya 35, ii

Rabbi Moshe Margaretten *313, 325, 334*
Rabbi Naftali Schlesinger *306-307*
Ramsar *44*
RAND Corporation *209-210, 241*
Rastakiz *92*
Recidivism *312, 324, 361*
Reid, Harry *196*
Residential Drug Abuse Program (RDAP) *255-256, 316-325, 332, 353-354, 364*
Rex Cinema *97*
Reza Shah Pahlavi *21*
Richardson, Bill *197, 201, 208, 216*
Rikers Island *316*
Robb, Charles Spittal *33*
Robb, Chuck *33*
Rocha, Victor Manuel *159*
Romano, Joe *308*
Romano, Sal *308*
Romano, Vincent *308*
Roosevelt, Teddy *186*
Rosen, Marvin *138, 144*
Roth, Steve *246*

Sabet, Habib *87*
Sadat, Anwar *73*
Salazar, Ken *196*
Salomon Brothers *131*
SAVAK *97, 103, 109, 115*
Schrager, Jerry *132*
Schumer, Chuck *196-197, 203-205, 224, 235, 256*
Scott, Marsha *152-155*
Second Chance Business Coalition *365*

Sentencing Reform and Corrections Act *313*
Sequoia *167*
Sessions, Jeff *331*
Shahestan Pahlavi *77*
Shah of Iran *11, 25, 30, 33-36, 40-41, 53-57, 62-66, 72-78, 87, 92-109, 112-115, 151, 160, 172, 351, i*
Shea, Robert *134*
Shechtman, Paul *242-246, 249-258*
Shell Oil *213*
Shiraz *17, 20, 25, 31, 35, 44, 52, 61-62, 77, 94, 200, 215, 287, 329*
Shiraz University *40*
Shiraz Water Company *72*
Shrum, Bob *182, 186, 189-191*
Shuman, Stan *183*
Singer, Bill *185, 198*
Smoot, Julianna *196*
Solis Doyle, Patti *211*
Solomont, Alan *185*
Sonia Rykiel *124*
Soros, George *124, 200*
Southern District of New York (SDNY) *234-238, 298, 335, 360*
Soviet Union *27-29*
Special Housing Unit (SHU) *286, 29-293, 311, 319-321*
Spinedi, Aghdass *34*
Spinedi, Gerard *34*
Spitzer, Bernard *132*
Spitzer, Eliot *132*
Stalin, Joseph *27*
Stanley Martin *69, 80*
Starr, Ken *300-303*
Steitz, Pamela *248*
Stella, Frank *113*

Stewart, Martha 254
Stillman, Charlie 242
Summers, Larry 161
Suratgar, David 38, 84
Suratgar, Lotfali 38
Susman, Lou 182-185, 188, 191, 203
Swift Boat 190-191

Tabriz 94
Tanavoli, Parviz 88
Tehran 31-33, 36, 39-47, 52-54, 59-60, 68-79, 83, 88, 91, 98-99, 102, 112-118, 246, 293, 329, 344
Tehrany, Syed Jalal eddin 106
Tenet, Rosemary 158
Tester, Jon 196
The National Iranian Oil Company (NIOC) 33
Therapeutic Community (TC) 323
The Silk Road 20
Thurman, Uma 301
Toner, Dennis 198-199, 217
Transitional Drug Abuse Program (TDAP) 353-354, 360
Truman, Harry S. 27
Trump, Donald 130-132, 313-314, 325, 331-335, 361
Trump Organization 132
Tufts 45, 46

Udall, Tom 196

Vagliano, Alec 98, 119
Vahabzadeh, Sohrab 135-136, 162-165
Vance, Cyrus 98, 210
Vilsack, Tom 197, 201

Volker, Paul 125
von Helms, J.C. 50, 76, 93, 100-101, 119-120, 230

Waksal, Sam 253-254
Wallach, Abe 131
Warner, Mark 197
Weatherhead Center for International Affairs 141
Webb, Jim 196
Weiser, Benjamin 335, 350
Weld, Bill 160
Wertheim, Julio 160
Westmacott, Oliver 223
Westmacott, Sir Peter 201, 223
Whitehead, Jamie 188
White House 139-141, 144-145, 152, 155, 158, 166, vi-ix
Whitehouse, Sheldon 196
White Revolution 36
Wilson, Dr. Dennis 59
Wilson, Joe 188
Wisner, Frank 29, 133-134, 148, 172-173
Wolfe, Robert 200

Yarshater, Ehsan 88
Yeager, Jenny 201
Yom Kippur War 73
Young & Rubicam 270

Zahedi, Ardeshir 78

Marmont Lane Books would like to thank Andrew Golomb,
Ellen Baskin, Tom Andre and Bridget Kerley
for their assistance in the making of this book.

MARMONTLANE.COM